A Grand Rapids Sampler

By
Gordon L. Olson

*To Marge,
With Best Wishes
Gordon Olson
1992*

Published by
The Grand Rapids Historical Commission

© Copyright 1992
Grand Rapids Historical Commission
All rights reserved

ISBN 0-9617708-3-X

Library of Congress Catalog Card Number: 92-072735

Designed and printed by
West Michigan Printing, Inc.
840 Ottawa NW
Grand Rapids, Michigan 49503

Edited by
Editorial Consultants
2215 Oak Industrial Drive NE
Grand Rapids, Michigan 49505

Bound by
John H. Dekker & Sons
2941 Clydon SW
Grand Rapids, Michigan 49509

Table of Contents

Acknowledgments

This book is the work of many people, beginning with the Grand Rapids area residents who over the years have produced the thousands of letters, diaries, books and articles, photographs, drawings, paintings, and maps that were examined in the course of making the selections found on these pages. This is, first and foremost, their book.

Three very special people, Aquinas College student interns Steve Laurent, Anne Decker, and Rachael Drenovsky, helped gather the documents and illustrations depicting life in Grand Rapids over the last 200 years. Rachael, Anne, and Steve worked long and hard. The *Sampler* would not have been possible without their help. This is very much their book, too.

Also helping to locate material were staff members at the Grand Rapids Public Library's Michigan and Family History Department. Dr. Richard Harms, Betty Gibout, Martha Bloem, and Randal Jelks always seemed to find just the right item when it was needed, while maintaining a steady flow of encouragement throughout the project. Any reader seeking specific information in the *Sampler* will also want to thank Dick Harms for the excellent index he prepared. Time after time, Bob Viol, archival consultant for the library's Robinson Studio Negative Collection, produced precisely the right photograph. When it was nec-

essary to translate several Spanish-language documents, library staff member Melissa Heckerd stepped forward to help.

Other city employees likewise provided much-needed assistance. City archivist and records manager Bill Cunningham found many early village and city records. Chris Gray from the city planning department made time in his busy schedule to produce several maps for the *Sampler.* Marilyn Merdzinski of the Public Museum of Grand Rapids took time to find images and documents in the museum collection.

Staff members from other institutions also helped. Ken Hafely of the Gerald Ford Presidential Library provided a photograph documenting the moment when Grand Rapids' favorite son became our 38th president. Herb Brinks supplied photographs from the Heritage Collection at Calvin College, June Horowitz found several elusive images in the Temple Emanuel archives, and Peter Jeff at Steelcase, Inc., came up with photographs from Grand Rapids' largest employer. Marc Longstreet from Amway Corporation also provided photographs. By responding quickly, with enthusiasm, all of these people made the *Sampler* their work, too.

Many illustrations, as well as design ideas, came from the Grand Rapids *Press.* Jim Starkey and Nancy Jones made critical design suggestions, and Diane Wheeler spent im-

portant time locating photographs needed to illustrate recent episodes in Grand Rapids history. *Press* photographer T.J. Hamilton took several photographs for the final chapter. A look at *Sampler* footnotes and photo credits will tell readers that this is their book, too.

As each chapter was written, Ellen Arlinsky of Editorial Consultants provided careful editing, eliminating the gremlins of grammar and the saboteurs of syntax that seem forever to hide in any written work. Through her careful reading and steady encouragement, this became Ellen's book, too.

When it came time for design and production, the skilled staffs at West Michigan Printing and Dekker Binding made this book more than just another job. Lynn Gort carefully designed each page to best present the material and story it told, and Sharla Obetts shot and reshot aging historical photographs until we achieved the best possible image. Then the press operators and bindery workers made sure that the final product measured up to the standards set by everyone along the way. This was not just another job, it was their book, too.

In charge of securing financing and overseeing the entire project were the members of the Grand Rapids Historical Commission, whose publications committee, headed by Herb Brinks, carefully read and commented on every chapter. Through the efforts of the commission — and especially its chairpersons during this project, John Logie and Micki Benz — a loan from the Grand Rapids Foundation and a marketing agreement with the Grand Rapids *Press* have ensured that *A Grand Rapids Sampler* will reach the largest possible audience at the lowest possible price. These efforts make this book their contribution to Grand Rapids history.

Every one of the individuals mentioned above, along with others who provided encouragement and support along the way, have contributed to the *Sampler*'s final makeup. To all of them, and to Christine who patiently tolerated a noisy word processor much later in the evening than any marriage compact calls for, I say "Thank you." Each of you can truly claim a part of this book.

As for me, in addition to getting to put my name on the title page, I have had the opportunity of working with a splendid group of people. The *Sampler* belongs to each and every one of them; the pleasure of working with them to put it together was all mine.

Gordon Olson
June 19, 1992

Introduction

A sampler is a varied selection of examples meant to prompt further work. It is a beginning, not an end. By that standard, this is truly a sampler of Grand Rapids history — not the definitive last word.

A Grand Rapids Sampler is an introduction, through photographs and documents, to the people, places, and events that are uniquely Grand Rapids. Each vignette is complete, and each tells of a moment in the life of this community. Together the selections give a sense of the whole, but they are not tied tightly to one another. The pleasure of discovering and understanding these original documents and illustrations, and of finding connections and drawing conclusions, waits only for curious readers to begin the task.

From a distance, Grand Rapids' history looks much like that of any other midwestern city. Originally the site of Native American villages, the banks of the Grand River became the scene at the beginning of the 19th century of a prosperous fur-trading post and the site of Baptist and Catholic missions. A few years later, with the arrival of settlers from New York and New England, Grand Rapids began its evolution from a rural village to an industrial city and on to today's metropolitan urban center. That pattern is not unique. Cities like Milwaukee, Chicago, Cincinnati, Peoria, Minneapolis, and Kalamazoo have followed a similar historical path.

But there have been significant differences as well. Milwaukee's dominant German immigrant group and the Scandinavians of Minneapolis, for example, introduced socialistic political systems and values that would have been alien to Grand Rapids' more conservative Dutch. While Chicago was led by its meatpacking industry, and Minneapolis had its grain elevators and flour mills, Grand Rapids became known as the nation's furniture capital.

Grand Rapids' history is not meant to be viewed from a distance, for it is only when the reader steps closer that distinctive faces, buildings, events, and attitudes can be seen. As a reward for their attention, Grand Rapids' history seekers will find in *Sampler* a fascinating mosaic of heroes and villains, high points and low, and great moments and regrettable incidents that alternately lift the spirit, provoke a chuckle, or give cause for concern.

This is local history — the point where the past becomes real. Some events and themes, like the Civil War and Gerald Ford's ascension to the presidency, have national and international significance. But most of the actors in *A Grand Rapids Sampler* are friends and neighbors, and the locales are down the street or around the corner.

Throughout the book, an effort has been made to include materials that are broadly representative of the major themes in Grand Rapids history. And always, attention has been paid to balance with the inclusion of stories that represent the city's racial and cultural diversity. Business, culture and the arts, recreation, politics, education, military events, government, great achievements, and lighter anecdotes all have a place in providing readers with a full sense of what it has meant over the years to live in Grand Rapids.

There could have been more. Many fascinating stories, like that of local physicians Pearl Kendrick and Grace Eldering who discovered a vaccine for whooping cough, have not been told. Because of space considerations, each chapter was limited to about 20 to 24 individual stories, and the large selection of possibilities had to be pared down. Playing an important role in the selection process was the availability of interesting and appropriate documents. Sometimes, even if a document were available, a story had to be dropped for want of accompanying illustrations.

As you go through the *Sampler*, enjoy what has been presented and reflect on what the book says about Grand Rapids or consider what it means to have participated in the events described on these pages. If you feel strongly about oversights and missing elements, tell the author or the Grand Rapids Historical Commission about your concerns. If you have documents and photographs, share them. That is how this book came into being and, with enough interest, there will be another. For now, read, enjoy, and learn. This is a *Sampler* of your history.

CHAPTER 1

First People

Today's residents are only the most recent people to call the Grand River valley home. The area's moderate climate, rich soil, and ample fresh water have long encouraged wanderers to set down roots.

The first residents, small bands of big game hunters, arrived over 10,000 years ago, following migrating mastodons and mammoths as the last of the glaciers that once covered all of Michigan receded to the north. With warmer, post-glacial weather eventually came more animals and vegetation, and a larger human population that subsisted on small game, edible plants, and the fish that were abundant in the Grand River.

About 2,500 years ago, there emerged on the banks of the Grand an elaborate and complex culture, characterized by the construction of large burial mounds, that flourished for nearly 500 years. Migrating from the Mississippi River valley north through Illinois, the original mound builders established themselves as far north as the modern Grand and Muskegon rivers. Here, each spring, they planted seeds and tended crops of corn, squash, and, possibly, beans. For a part of each year, probably in the early summer after the crops were in the ground, thousands from throughout central and western Michigan gathered at a ceremonial center near the rapids of the Grand

to bury their dead and renew their lifeways for another year.

Although no one knows exactly what caused their demise (it may have been disease, cultural malaise, conquest, or some combination of all three), the mound builders were gone long before European explorers moved into the Grand River valley in the late 17th century. By then, the valley's native inhabitants were the Ottawa, who had been driven west from New York by the Iroquois and came to occupy an area extending from the Grand River north into Canada and from the center of the western half of Michigan's lower peninsula into Wisconsin. To the south of the Ottawa, who served as middlemen in the thriving French fur trade, lived the Potawatomi; to the east of the Ottawa were the Ojibwa.

Throughout the 17th and 18th centuries, as Europeans and then Americans struggled for control of North America, the Ottawa, Ojibwa, and Potawatomi found themselves under constant pressure to ally with one contestant or the other. In little more than two generations between 1760 and 1815, political power shifted from the French to the British to the Americans. The French system of open trade gave way to the more restrictive British licensing system, and, finally, Native American title

to Michigan's vast land area passed into American hands.

By the early years of the 19th century, the transition from Indian country to U.S. territory was complete. The newly independent United States claimed areas once occupied by the different Indian groups. A series of treaties signed in quick succession between 1821 and 1836 extinguished Indian title to virtually all of Michigan and opened the territory to land-hungry settlers. American Fur Company agent Rix Robinson and independent trader Louis Campau opened posts in West Michigan to compete for the remaining furs. Baptist missionary Isaac McCoy and his Roman Catholic counterpart, Fr. Frederic Baraga, established missions at the rapids of the Grand.

For the Indian groups, the final blow came after 1836, when the United States adopted President Andrew Jackson's Indian removal policy, and the government began steps to relocate them on lands far to the west. Although Michigan's native peoples successfully resisted removal, the price they had to pay was nearly all their land. Only a few small reserved areas, generally deemed unsuitable for farming, remained in their hands. On these reservations they remained for the rest of the century, watching the flood of new settlers pour in.

Monuments to a Past Culture

Reports by 19th-century settlers indicate there were once between 30 and 40 burial mounds along the west bank of the Grand River near what is now the heart of Grand Rapids. Although these mounds were leveled to make way for the growing city, another group of 17 mounds south of the current city limits still stands as a monument to the once-thriving mound builders.

From the contents of the mounds, scientists learned that their builders were of medium height and stocky, with long, oval faces and Oriental eyes, and that they were part of a widespread trading network that supplied them with obsidian from the Rocky Mountains, copper from northern Michigan, and large conch shells from the Gulf of Mexico. The mound builders used stone points, knives, and scrapers to hunt animals for food and prepare the skins for clothing and shelter. They wove reeds into mats and baskets, worked wood and pieces of copper into everyday vessels and tools, and carved stone effigy pipes for ceremonial and ritualistic smoking. Their carefully shaped and decorated pottery jars, used for food preparation and storage, offer proof of their dependence on agriculture for a significant part of their subsistence.

It is the burial mounds themselves, however, that provide the best evidence of the complexity of mound-builder culture. A large mound, rising 50 feet above ground level, required a tremendous amount of cooperative labor to gather the nearly 12.5 million pounds of earth used in its construction, and it may have taken as many as 100 people working steadily for over eight months to complete the job.

Early European and American settlers were fascinated by the work of the mound builders and curious about the contents of the giant earthworks. But it was not until 1874 that the first careful excavation was undertaken. Grand Rapids city engineer Wright L. Coffinberry, an amateur archaeologist, explored several of the mounds and reported the results to the American Association for the Advancement of Science at its annual meeting the following year in Detroit. Coffinberry could not date the mounds, but his description of that initial investigation stripped away some of their mystery, and began the era of scientific investigation that continues to inform us of the remarkable architects of those ancient memorials.

Eight groups, containing forty-six mounds in all, were inspected, of which fourteen mounds were explored with great care.

That these mounds are very old seems to be beyond question. Trees are standing upon them as large as some that have been cut on similar soil, which showed two hundred and sixty rings of growth; while by them are lying the remains of larger trees, which must have been giants when those standing were but saplings. And more conclusive evidence of the great antiquity of the mound structures is found in the articles which many of them contain.

About one-third of the mounds examined were clearly places of sepulchre. The use of the others, or the motive which led to their construction, can only be conjectured. They may have been monumental or commemorative, or erected as observatories, the latter being considered the least probable. They were simply empty but structural piles of earth, mingled confusedly with those of the burial class, and not distinguishable from them by any external signs. Where there were no human remains there were no other relics, while in no case were skeletons exhumed without finding something else of interest, and often several different kinds, such as stone, bone and copper implements, pottery, drinking vessels, and other articles.

Copper articles found appear as if they had been wrapped in coarse woven cloths, and in several instances, where the earth has been carefully cleared from bone, spears, flint implements, or even the common fragments of quartz pebbles, impressions of fabrics were clearly visible, such as might be made by slack-twisted threads of coarse, loosely woven cloth. Shells were found, shaped apparently for carrying or storing water, in one case having holes near the edges, as if to hang by a cord or thong. Fragments of coarse pottery had markings as if shaped and baked or dried in a basket of rushes or coarse grass.

▲ Albert Baxter, *History of the City of Grand Rapids*, pp. 15-16.

◄ Wright L. Coffinberry, city engineer and amateur archaeologist. [Grand Rapids Public Library (hereafter cited GRPL), Photo Collection]

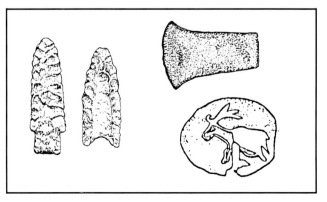

Left to right: Projectile points, a ► copper axe, and turtle shell with carved decorations from the Norton Mounds. [GRPL, *Grand River Valley Review* Collection]

This map shows mounds ▶
once located along the west
bank of the Grand River.

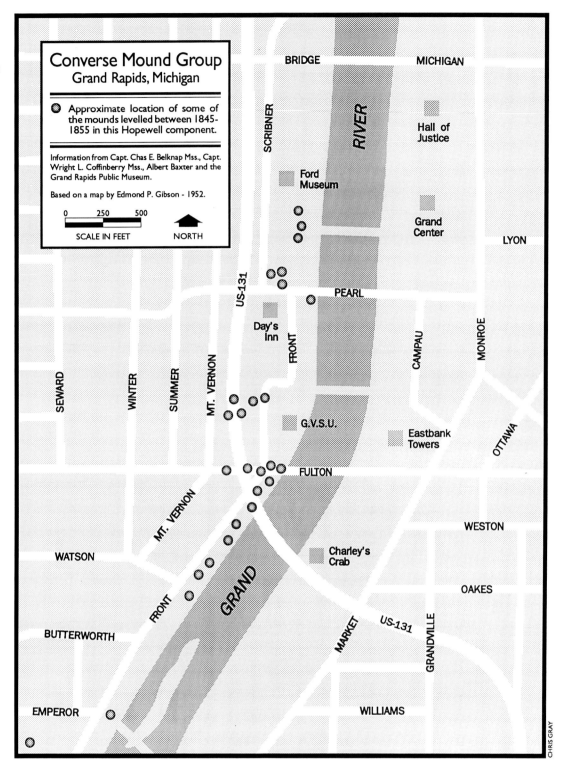

Converse Mound Group
Grand Rapids, Michigan

⊗ Approximate location of some of
the mounds levelled between 1845-
1855 in this Hopewell component.

Information from Capt. Chas E. Belknap Mss., Capt.
Wright L. Coffinberry Mss., Albert Baxter and the
Grand Rapids Public Museum.

Based on a map by Edmond P. Gibson - 1952.

```
0        250        500
```
SCALE IN FEET   NORTH

Platform pipes, and deco- ▶
rated and undecorated clay
pottery found in mound excavations. [GRPL, *Grand
River Valley Review* Collection]

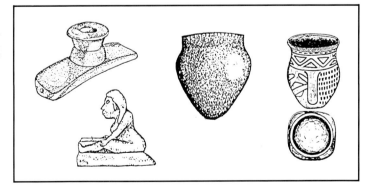

Collecting the Remnants of the Past

Not everyone who lived in Grand Rapids at the time had Coffinberry's scientific curiosity about the mounds, or appreciated their historical significance. By the time of his excavations, workmen had already leveled several of the giant earthworks and used the soil to fill in nearby low-lying areas. Available records indicate that several mounds were destroyed to provide fill dirt for street improvements. Unearthed during the process were pottery vases, clay pipes, copper tools, animal teeth and bones, and two large silver nuggets. Many of these artifacts were sold to Yale University's Peabody Museum.

During the 1850s, young Charles Belknap worked as a water boy for the labor crews building streets and laying sewer and water pipes on the city's west side, and took home many of the artifacts found beneath the mounds. Later a well-known community leader, Belknap authored a long-running column of historical reminiscences in the Grand Rapids *Press,* and wrote a book titled *Grand Rapids Yesterdays.* In the following excerpt from *Yesterdays,* Belknap describes the leveling of mounds on the west bank of the Grand near the present site of Grand Valley State University's downtown campus.

When there was no longer use for the Mission land on the west side, it was sold by the government to eastern parties who platted it for residential and commercial purposes, with no regard for its scenic beauty.

It was a project of cutting down or filling up, and so the Indian mounds, with their historic contents, were carried away to fill the low places.

There was no regret over this leveling of the mounds. Even the men who gathered the curios reaped considerable financial benefit from their sales to museums.

Early missionaries and traders said the Indians of their day had no knowledge of the origin of these mounds. They only knew they were the work of men and had great veneration for them.

On the mission land along the river south of what is now Bridgest. stood many of these mounds, which were leveled in the grading of streets in the fifties. For several summers I was water boy for the men who did this grading and had ample opportunity to gather the flint arrowheads and other implements that were unearthed in nearly every burial mound along with the bones of the vanished race.

There were three very ancient mounds at the present corner of Allen and Court streets. In one of them was a stacked mass two feet in diameter and twenty inches high of jet black flints and arrowheads of the finest workmanship. No flint of this kind was found in any other mound. Below the original surface of the ground was found a strata of human remains and with these bones were earthen vases, pieces of clay pottery, bears' teeth with holes drilled for stringing as ornaments and many stone smoking pipes of fine design.

In digging a sewer trench a few years later two nuggets of pure silver weighing thirteen pounds and one flake of copper weighing fourteen pounds, were found. These, with a great accumulation of other curiosities, were sent to the Peabody Museum in Massachusetts and the Smithsonian Institute in Washington.

Alfred Preusser, the jeweler, bought from me quite a bit of silver ornament that I had collected, which he melted to use in his shop work, neither of us realizing its historic value at the time. By the time of the Civil war I had accumulated so many relics from the mounds that the attic of our home was full of skulls with grinning teeth, arrowheads, bits of pottery, smoking pipes of clay, and stone implements.

▲ Charles E. Belknap, *The Yesterdays of Grand Rapids,* pp. 42-43.

▲ Charles E. Belknap carried water to city workmen and collected artifacts they found beneath the mounds. [GRPL, Photo Collection]

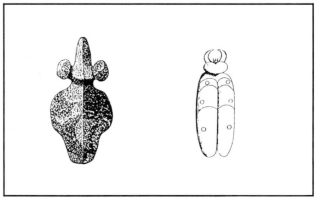

Left to right: Carved stone ▶ and carved deer antler, in the shape of insects, found in west-side mounds. [Albert Baxter, *History of the City of Grand Rapids,* p. 17]

Wawatam's White Brother

By the time Europeans arrived in the Grand River valley, the mound builders had been gone for centuries, and the Ottawa occupied much of West Michigan. Although the Ottawa had no written language of their own, the diaries, letters, and memoirs written by fur traders and missionaries provide descriptions of their rituals, recreation, clothing and tools, and daily and seasonal activities.

One of the more interesting of these accounts was written by Alexander Henry, an English trader at Fort Michilimackinac. Like all other French forts in the New World, Michilimackinac had come under British control in 1760 following the British victory over the French and their Indian allies in the French and Indian War. Triumphant in the struggle for a North American empire, the British treated their defeated Indian foes badly, arousing widespread resentment among the tribes.

In June 1763, Ottawa warrior groups organized by Chief Pontiac captured several British forts in Michigan. Michilimackinac fell when warriors used a lacrosse game as a ruse to enter the fort and capture its British garrison. Alexander Henry was among the captives taken. Some time before the attack, however, Henry had been adopted by an Ottawa named Wawatam, who now stepped forward and secured his release.

For the next year, Henry lived as a member of Wawatam's family, traveling south to wintering grounds along the Muskegon River, and participating in all family activities. In 1764, after the British quelled the Ottawa attacks, Henry left his adopted family and once again entered the fur trade. In 1809, slowed by old age, he moved to Montreal where he ran a fur wholesale business until his death in 1824 at the age of 95. While in Montreal he wrote a detailed account of the year spent with Wawatam's family.

◄ Alexander Henry was saved by his friend Wawatam when Ottawa and Ojibwa warriors captured Fort Michilimackinac. [Raymond McCoy, *The Massacre of Old Fort Mackinac*, p. 64]

The season for making maple sugar was now at hand and...certain parts of the maple woods having been chosen...a house twenty feet long and fourteen broad was begun in the morning, and before night made fit for the comfortable reception of eight persons and their baggage. It was open at top, had a door at each end, and a fireplace in the middle running the whole length.

The next day was employed in gathering the bark of white birch trees with which to make vessels to catch the wine or sap. The trees were now cut or tapped, and spouts or ducts introduced into the wound. The bark vessels were placed under the ducts; and as they filled, the liquor was taken out in buckets and conveyed into reservoirs or vats of moose skin, each vat containing a hundred gallons. From these we supplied the boilers, of which we had twelve of, from twelve to twenty gallons each, with fires constantly under them day and night. While the women collected the sap, boiled it, and completed the sugar, the men were not less busy in cutting wood, making fires, and in hunting and fishing in part of our supply of food.

On the twenty-fifth of April our labor ended, and we returned to the fort, carrying with us as we found by the scales, sixteen hundred-weight of sugar...sugar was our principal food during the whole month of April.

In the course of the month of January I happened to observe that the trunk of a very large pine tree was much torn by the claws of a bear, made both in going up and down. On further examination I saw that there was a large opening in the upper part near which the smaller branches were broken. From these marks and from the additional circumstance that there were no tracks on the snow there was reason to believe that a bear lay concealed in the tree.

On returning to the lodge I communicated my discovery; and it was agreed that all the family should go together in the morning

Each spring, Ottawa ► and Ojibwa families gathered to make maple sugar. [Henry Rowe Schoolcraft, *History of Indian Tribes of the United States*, pt. 2, p. 59]

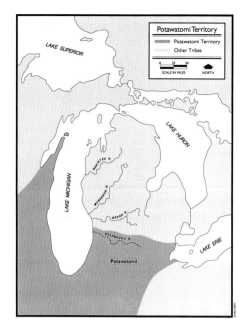

▲ In 1820, the Potawatomi occupied portions of southern Michigan, northern Indiana and Illinois, and eastern Wisconsin.

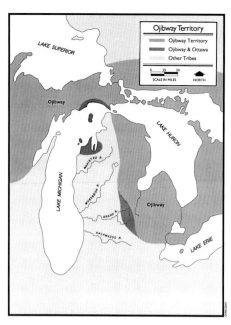

▲ Michigan Ojibwa lived in an area from Lake Huron on the east to the Upper Peninsula on the west.

▲ The Ottawa occupied western Michigan from below the Grand River to the Straits of Mackinac.

to assist in cutting down the tree, the girth of which was not less than three fathoms. The women at first opposed the undertaking because our axes, being only of a pound and a half weight, were not well adapted to so heavy a labor; but the hope of finding a large bear and obtaining from its fat a great quantity of oil, an article at the time much wanted, at length prevailed.

Accordingly in the morning we surrounded the tree, both men and women, as many at a time as could conveniently work at it; and here we toiled like beaver till the sun went down. This day's work carried us about half way through the trunk; and the next morning we renewed the attack, continuing it till about two o'clock in the afternoon, when the tree fell to the ground. For a few minutes everything remained quiet, and I feared that all our expectations were disappointed; but as I advanced to the opening there came out, to the great satisfaction of all our party, a bear of extraordinary size, which, before she had proceeded many yards, I shot.

The bear being dead, all my assistants approached, and all, but more particularly my old mother (as I was wont to call her), took her head in their hands, stroking and kissing it several times; begging a thousand pardons for taking away her life: calling her their relation and grandmother; and requesting her not to lay the fault upon them, since it was truly an Englishman that had put her to death.

As soon as we reached the lodge the bear's head was adorned with all the trinkets in the possession of the family, such as silver arm bands and wrist bands, and belts or wampum; and then laid upon a scaffold, set up for its reception within the lodge. Near the nose was placed a large quantity of tobacco.

The next morning no sooner appeared than preparations were made for a feast to honor the dead bear's spirit. The lodge was cleaned and swept; and the head of the bear lifted up, and a new shroud blanket, which had never been used before, spread under it. The pipes were now lit; and Wawatam blew tobacco smoke into the nostrils of the bear, telling me to do the same, and thus appease the anger of the bear on account of my having killed her....

At length the feast being ready, Wawatam commenced a speech [deploring] the necessity under which men labored thus to destroy their friends. He represented, however, that the misfortune was unavoidable, since without doing so, they could by no means subsist. The speech ended, we all ate heartily of the bear's flesh; and even the head itself, after remaining three days on the scaffold, was put into the kettle.

▲ During winter months, Ottawa families subsisted by hunting, and spearing fish through the ice. [Henry Rowe Schoolcraft, *History of Indian Tribes of the United States,* pt. 2, p. 53]

◀ Alexander Henry, *Travels and Adventures in the Years 1760-1776,* pp. 69-70, 138-41.

The "Feast of the Dead"

As with other cultures, the Grand River Ottawa conducted particular rituals and ceremonies at specific times during the year. Each spring, for example, they gathered for a "Feast of the Dead" to honor those who had died during the past year. Present on one such occasion was Gurdon S. Hubbard, an employee of John Jacob Astor's American Fur Company. Later, he recorded his observations in his autobiography.

▲ After her husband's death, an Ojibwa widow would carry a bundle of his clothing during a mourning period. [Thomas L. McKenney, *The History of the Indian Tribes of North America,* p. 61]

We did not desire to reach the mouth of Grand River (Grand Haven) before the May full moon, for annually at that time the Indians assembled to fast and feast their dead, the ceremonies occupying eight or ten days.

The "Feast of the Dead" had commenced, and many Indians had already arrived, and for five or six days we were witnesses to their strange yet solemn ceremonies.

A noted burying ground was selected and the ground around the graves thoroughly cleaned, they being put in the best of order. Many of the graves were marked by small poles, to which were attached pieces of white cloth. These preparations having been completed, all except the young children blackened their faces with charcoal and fasted for two whole days, eating literally nothing during that time. Though many of them had no relatives buried there, all joined in the fast and ceremonies in memory of their dead who were buried elsewhere and the sounds of mourning and lamentation were heard around the graves and in the wigwams.

At the close of the two days' fast they washed their faces, put on their decorations, and commenced feasting and visiting from one wigwam to another. They now placed wooden dishes at the head of each grave, which were kept daily supplied with food, and were protected from the dogs, wolves, and other animals, by sticks driven into the ground around and inclosing them. The feasting lasted several days, and the ceremonies were concluded by their celebrated game of ball, which is intensely interesting, even the dogs becoming excited and adding to the commotion by mixing with the players and barking and racing around the grounds.

▲ Gurdon S. Hubbard, *Autobiography,* pp. 66-67.

◀ Often, Ottawa and Ojibwa dead were placed on platforms. [Thomas L. McKenney, *Sketches of a Tour of the Lakes,* facing p. 108]

Taking Michigan by Treaty

Like the mound builders before them, the Ottawa found the area around the rapids of the Grand River to be an ideal gathering place. European fur traders' accounts report villages above and below the rapids in the late 18th century. Here, the Ottawa lived for several relatively quiet decades until American settlers began moving into Michigan after the War of 1812.

With travel difficulties eased by the opening of the Erie Canal in 1825, increasing numbers of settlers arrived in the Upper Great Lakes. The federal government, which regarded Indian groups as foreign powers, was pressed to extinguish Indian claims to the land. The result, shown on this map, was a series of treaties, begun in 1795 and completed in 1842, that opened nearly all of Michigan's 57,900 square miles to settlement. When the treaty making was complete, Indians owned only 32 square miles in the state.

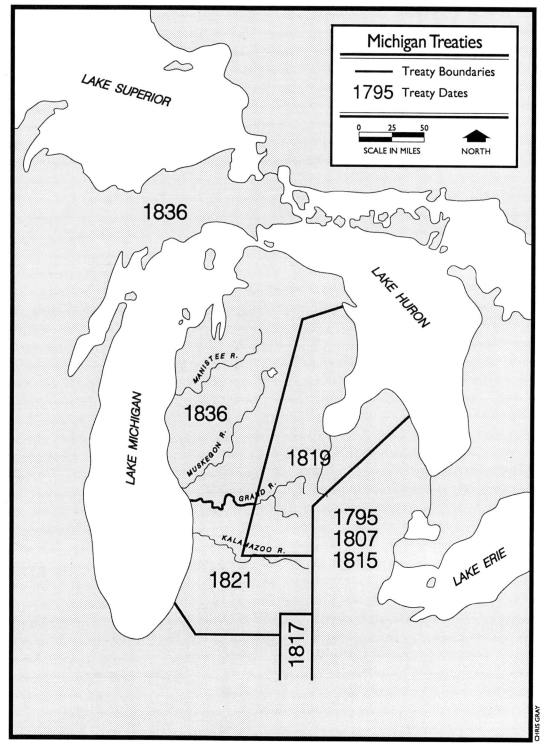

Treaties between Michigan ► Indians and the United States opened the state for settlement.

Michigan Treaties

— Treaty Boundaries
1795 Treaty Dates

0   25   50
SCALE IN MILES   NORTH

CHRIS GRAY

All Land South of the Grand River

The government used a variety of tactics to induce the Indians to part with their land. Officials manipulated one tribal faction against another, employed influential half-breed traders, and liberally dispensed liquor. In exchange for their land cessions, Indians received annual cash payments, hunting and fishing rights, small land parcels, craftsmen to help them adjust to a new lifestyle, and, in some cases, even college education opportunities for their children.

Treaties were generally made in response to pressure from settlers who wanted to move onto Indian land. When demand was sufficient, a call went out to Indian leaders, notifying them to meet at a specific time and place. In more than one instance, Indians responded with stalling tactics such as requests to delay the meeting or change the meeting place. On other occasions, they sent only young men without power to negotiate. Even when they were successful, however, these tac-tics merely postponed the inevitable.

The first treaty to affect the Ottawa of West Michigan was negotiated in Chicago in 1821. Designed to open all land in southwestern Michigan south of the Grand River for settlement, its main provisions defined the terms of payment and specified the rights retained by the Ottawa.

TREATY WITH THE OTTAWA, ETC., 1821

Articles of a treaty made and concluded at Chicago, in the state of Illinois, between Lewis Cass and Solomon Sibley, Commissioners of the United States, and the Ottawa, Chippewa, and Potawatamie, Nations of Indians.

Art. 4 In consideration of the cession aforesaid, the United States engage to pay to the Ottawa nation, one thousand dollars in specie annually forever, and also to appropriate annually, for the term of ten years the sum of fifteen hundred dollars, to be expended as the President may direct, in the support of a Blacksmith, of a Teacher, and of a person to instruct the Ottawas in agriculture and in the purchase of cattle and farming utensils. And the United States also engage to pay to the Potawatamie nation five thousand dollars in specie, annually, for the term of twenty years, and also to appropriate annually, for the term of fifteen years, the sum of one thousand dollars, to be expended as the President may direct, in the support of a Blacksmith and a Teacher. And one mile square shall be selected, under the direction of the President, on the north side of the Grand River, [currently site of A-Nab-Awen Park and the Gerald R. Ford Museum] and one mile square on the south side of the St. Joseph, and within the Indian lands not ceded, upon which the blacksmiths and teachers employed for the said tribes, respectively, shall reside.

Art. 5 The stipulation contained in the treaty of Greenville, relative to the right of the Indians to hunt upon the land ceded while it continues the property of the United States, shall apply to this treaty.

Art. 6 The United States shall have the privilege of making and using a road through the Indian country, from Detroit and Fort Wayne, respectively, to Chicago.

◄ Charles V. Kappler, ed., *Indian Affairs Laws and Treaties,* Vol. 1, pp. 138-40.

▼ Treaty making was conducted at councils of Indian and U.S. government leaders. [Thomas L. McKenney, *Sketches of a Tour of the Lakes,* facing p. 380]

Enter Isaac McCoy

Most of the treaties made provisions for the United States government to supply farmers, blacksmiths, carpenters, and teachers to instruct the Indians in the settlers' ways. Quite often, the government contracted with missionary organizations who, for an agreed-upon fee — paid from the treaty annuity — would provide the craftsmen and teachers at the same time that they built a mission and began their quest for converts.

After the Treaty of 1821 was ratified, the government arranged for the Baptist Board of Foreign Missions for the United States to provide the stipulated services. Ap-

pointed to lead the West Michigan missionary contingent was Isaac McCoy.

Nearly 40 years old when he received his assignment, McCoy had previously been sent to minister to the Potawatomi of northern Indiana. There, he had seen enough of the impact of white frontier culture upon the Indians' way of life to conclude that the Great Lakes tribes would be rendered destitute unless they were moved far away. His subsequent experience in Michigan, at Carey Mission near St. Joseph and Thomas Mission at Grand Rapids, confirmed those early impressions and made him an ardent proponent

of Andrew Jackson's plan to remove all Indians to Oklahoma Territory.

Concerned about the Ottawa's welfare, he and his family endured great discomfort as they labored to meet their obligations. McCoy, who developed an interest in the Ottawa way of life, recorded their customs and beliefs in his journals, and later published a book describing his experiences. Included in his *History of Baptist Indian Missions* are descriptions of his first visit to the two Ottawa villages at the rapids of the Grand River, and his subsequent efforts to establish a mission there.

◄ Isaac McCoy established a Baptist mission on the west bank of the Grand River in November 1824. [Kansas State Historical Society]

◄ Leonard Slater took over as Baptist missionary in 1827 and remained until 1836. [GRPL, Photo Collection]

On the 27th, we encamped at Gun Lake, and on the following day had an interview with Naoqua Keshuck, an Ottawa chief, who was encamped, with his family and some others, on the opposite side of the lake. He said he had long desired to see me, and had sent the messenger to ascertain the cause of my delaying to visit them. He urged me to make a settlement at his village, at the rapids of Grand River, declaring that he and some others desired to adopt the habits of civilized life, and would be glad to avail themselves of our assistance. He was anxious for the establishment of a school for the benefit of the youth, and wished also to hear preaching.

While I informed him what we proposed to do for them, I was deeply affected with the fears he manifested that we, as he said other white men had often done, would deceive them. He desired me to commit to writing my proposals, which I did.

We decamped on the following day, November 29th, and proceeded towards the rapids of Grand river. At twelve o'clock we were joined by Noonday, alias Naoqua Keshuck. That night I was violently attacked with dysentery, occasioned by the mode of living necessary on my journey. I usually carried medicines with me, but at this time happening to have none, the skill of both Noonday and myself was put in requisition in seeking vegetable

remedies in the forest. I spent a night of great distress. With some abatement of pain I became able to sit on my horse the following day, but continued much indisposed during the remainder of the tour.

Two days later we reached Grand river, which it was necessary we should cross. Noonday had two canoes hid in the brush, smaller than I had ever before seen. He brought one on his shoulder, and placing it in the river, directed me to lie down in it, as in a sitting posture there would be danger of capsizing. When I was thus adjusted, he said he believed he could get me across, as I did not appear to be so heavy as a deer he had once taken over in the same canoe. I spent the night in camp. As far as indisposition admitted, and assisted by the chief, I made examinations on horseback, for the purpose of selecting a site for our missionary station. Having marked out a place...on the 2d of December...I set out for home.

On the 10th of March, 1825, Mr. Polke, with the blacksmith, an Indian apprentice to the blacksmith's business, and a labourer, set out in a pirogue for our station on Grand river. On the way he availed himself of the assistance of our Ottawa friend, Gosa. He found a majority of the Ottawas well disposed towards the mission, and the prospects of its usefulness very pleasing. At the

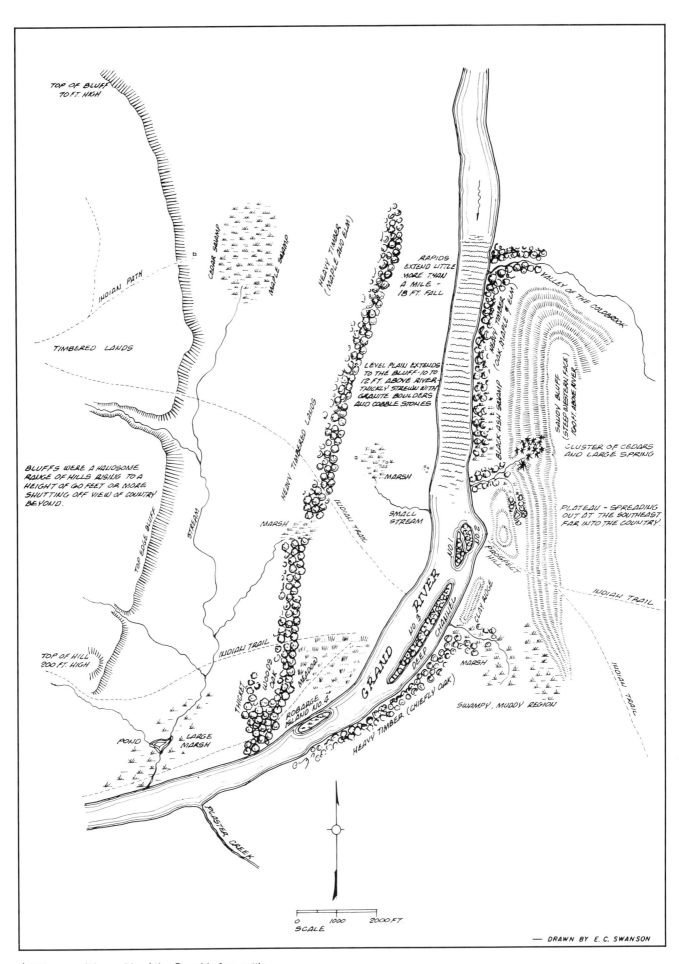

TOP OF BLUFF
70 FT. HIGH

INDIAN PATH

CEDAR SWAMP

MAPLE SWAMP

TIMBERED LANDS

HEAVY TIMBER (MAPLE AND ELM)

RAPIDS EXTEND LITTLE MORE THAN A MILE - 18 FT. FALL

VALLEY OF THE COLDBROOK

BLACK ASH SWAMP (OAK, MAPLE & ELM)

HEAVY TIMBER

LEVEL PLAIN EXTENDS TO THE BLUFF - 10 TO 12 FT. ABOVE RIVER - THICKLY STREWN WITH GRANITE BOULDERS AND COBBLE STONES

SANDY BLUFF (STEEP WESTERN FACE) 100 FT. ABOVE RIVER

CLUSTER OF CEDARS AND LARGE SPRING

BLUFFS WERE A HANDSOME RANGE OF HILLS RISING TO A HEIGHT OF 60 FEET OR MORE SHUTTING OFF VIEW OF COUNTRY BEYOND.

HEAVY TIMBERED LANDS

MARSH

INDIAN TRAIL

SMALL STREAM

PLATEAU - SPREADING OUT AT THE SOUTHEAST FAR INTO THE COUNTRY.

TOP EDGE BLUFF

STREAM

MARSH

NO. 1

NO. 2

PROSPECT HILL

INDIAN TRAIL

GRAND RIVER

NO. 3

CLAY RIDGE

DEEP CHANNEL

MARSH

INDIAN TRAIL

TOP OF HILL 200 FT. HIGH

INDIAN TRAIL

THICKET

WOODS OAK

MEADOW

ROBARGE ISLAND NO. 4

SWAMPY, MUDDY REGION

POND

LARGE MARSH

HEAVY TIMBER (CHIEFLY OAK)

PLASTER CREEK

SCALE
0   1000   2000 FT.

— DRAWN BY E. C. SWANSON

▲ This map of the rapids of the Grand before settlement was drawn from original survey records made in
1831 and 1837. In later years, the islands were eliminated
when the east channel was filled in. The river bank now
runs along what was once the islands' western edge;
today's Grand Center stands just above islands No. 1
and 2. [GRPL, Map Collection]

same time, some malicious persons had resolved on breaking up the establishment.... These men had brought whiskey on the ground, to aid in making disturbance. All, however, appeared friendly towards Mr. Polke, except one....

...Many Indians near our house were in a state of intoxication. The blacksmith, our apprentice, and Gosa, were on the margin of the river, while I was standing on the river bank, near our door, looking at some canoes of fishermen in the river, when more noise than usual occurred in an Indian camp near. At this instant the fishermen in the canoes, who could perceive what was going on in the camp, hallooed lustily to us on the bank. I could not understand them; but Gosa, who understood them, rushed up the river bank towards me. On turning my eyes towards the camp, I discovered an Indian running towards me with a gun in his hand.... The Indian apprentice boy came to Gosa's assistance, and they disarmed the wicked man, who was taken away by some of the people of his camp.

Settlements of white people were at this time rapidly multiplying near us, attended with ruinous effects upon the Indians.

...In August, intoxication prevailed to such an extent on Grand river, that our young men employed there as smith and labourers requested leave to abandon the station. An attempt had been made on the life of our friend Gosa, and on one occasion he and his family took refuge in the house with our young men, where the whole party remained watching all night.

I delivered to the Indians ploughs, yokes, chains, and other farming utensils, and also some mechanics' tools, all which had been forwarded to our charge by the Government. The articles, as too often happens in such cases, were not of good quality. By such delinquencies the confidence of the Indians is impaired, and the obstacles to the success of missionary labours are increased. Advice was given them in regard to places for improvements, and the most eligible modes; and they seemed to do well. Hands were now set to work to erect permanent log buildings, such as the operations of the mission called for.

To hear these people entreating that a school should be furnished them, to find them actually improving farms, and to observe them listening attentively to religious instruction, could not but make a deep impression on my mind.

Had these Indians been permanently located in a place in which it was possible to avoid the effects, to a ruinous extent, of the proximity of white settlements, our prospects in relation to them would have been fair, and our satisfaction great....

By the 20th of May [1827], we had made some improvement in our buildings; had fenced over fifteen acres of land, ten or eleven acres of which we had planted in corn, potatoes, and other vegetables.

Our religious meetings were better attended at this place than at Carey [mission on the St. Joseph River near Niles]. It was common for neighbouring Indians to walk three quarters of a mile to attend family prayers, both morning and evening. It was most interesting to see them at morning prayers, because they were under the necessity of rising very early, which was contrary to their ordinary habits.

Noonday had said that he designed to put a boy, for whom he was guardian (having no children of his own) in our family. He delayed doing so four or five days longer than we had expected. The boy was frequently at our house, and we wondered why the brief ceremony of saying, "here he is, take him," should be delayed. These queries were all answered on the following Sunday, when Noonday and his boy appeared at our house very early. "I wish," said he, "to speak to you. I have brought hither my son, for the purpose of placing him in the mission family."

◄ Isaac McCoy, *History of Baptist Indian Missions,* pp. 249-307.

▲ The Rev. John Booth made this drawing of Grand Rapids in 1831. In the right foreground is Louis Campau's trading post, across the river is the Baptist mission. [GRPL, Photo Collection]

Trapped Between Two Worlds

For those Indians who embraced McCoy's teachings, an entirely different world awaited. In addition to receiving instruction in Christianity, a few young Indian scholars were sent to eastern schools for further training.

Although there were benefits for all who mastered the missionaries' teachings, there were also disadvantages. Often, after several years in the East, returning students found themselves no longer comfortable in either camp. That was the case with Adoniram Judson and George Boardman (their Indian names are not known), two young Potawatomis from the St. Joseph area who were sent by McCoy to Madison University at Hamilton, New York, to prepare themselves for "superior usefulness among their own countrymen." Upon completing their education, they returned to their people with high expectations, but their hopes were quickly dashed.

In 1838, while in Grand Rapids for one of the treaty annuity payments, Judson told his story to a writer who later published the following account in the New York *Christian Union*. It is a tragic tale of a man who understood two worlds and was accepted in neither.

▲ An artist's depiction of Adoniram Judson. [Darius Cook, *Six Months Among the Indians*, p. 10]

I went home among my own people full of purpose and sanguine expectation. They should have schools. They should have churches. They should learn mechanics and farming, and have crops and stock and books, and all the blessings of civilization. Our work was before us. We were young and strong and patient. What should hinder? So we thought. But everything did hinder. Our people did not want such things. They turned from us with contempt and derision. Our civilized clothing was an unceasing object of their ridicule. Our names, which they made ridiculous by their pronunciation, were a sign that we had renounced our parents and our people. We were neither Indians nor white men. We were not wanted by either. Having no Indian virtues or accomplishments, we were useless in the woods; and the whites did not need us, for they were our superiors. Even the young girls, when we approached them, openly showed their contempt. At last we could no longer stand the scorn and ridicule which overwhelmed us. We gave it up in despair. Our own people fairly drove us away from them as useless and disagreeable members of their society. We left them, completely cowed and disheartened, and returned to the settlements. Hearing that a teacher was wanted for an academy at Gull Prairie, I presented my credentials of character and scholarship to the trustees, and was appointed Principal. Life now opened very brightly before me. I had a good school, loved teaching, loved my pupils, was active in religious meetings, taught the choir and singing school, and every house was open to my visits. The whole community seemed to love me, and I was happy. Especially was I fond of a bright and beautiful young lady, one of my best pupils. We went together everywhere; to church, to singing school, evening parties and social visits. Everywhere she went with me, and seemed proud of my devotion. After a few months I proposed to marry her, and was referred to my warm friends, her parents. And this is what they said to me: "What! you, an Indian, presume to address our daughter! Our daughter marry an Indian! You are crazy. She might as well marry a Negro. You will never be anything but an Indian for all your education. Remember this, and never presume again with your attentions. We are your friends, and if you will consider it, you will see that it must be as we state it." All that night I did consider it. Crushed to the earth in my humiliation, bruised and half stunned by the cruel scorn which accompanied my rejection, I saw clearly that it could never be different. I was an Indian, and could never be anything but an Indian, God help me! So the next day I resigned my position, dismissed my pupils, gave away my broadcloth suit, boots, and beaver, put on moccasins, leggins and blanket, and took to the bush, where I shall thus live and die among my own people. This was three years ago, and for the future I can only be an Indian, as God has made me.

▲ Albert Baxter, *History of the City of Grand Rapids*, pp. 35-36.

Competing for Souls

Americans and Europeans were crowding in on the Ottawa from all sides. In 1833 a Catholic missionary, Fr. Frederic Baraga, arrived in Grand Rapids. Welcomed by the Catholic fur trader Louis Campau, who had been in the area since 1826, Baraga immediately set to work constructing a set of buildings on the west side of the river, south of the present Pearl Street bridge.

Born in 1797 to a prosperous family in Slovenia (in what is present-day Yugoslavia), Baraga forsook his privileged background and dedicated himself to a life of service to the Indians of North America. Crossing the Atlantic in 1831, he went first to Cincinnati, and then to Michilimackinac, before taking up residence along the Grand River in 1833.

Like Isaac McCoy, Baraga was fascinated by the culture of those whose souls he came to save, and by the time he moved to the Grand River, he had already published a dictionary and grammar of the Ottawa language. Although Baraga's first months in Grand Rapids were difficult, with perseverance and timely help, he soon established St. Mary's Mission, where he remained for two years before heading north to take up new challenges, leaving the mission in the hands of his successor, Fr. Andreas Viszoczky. Baraga's account of the founding of St. Mary's Mission, like the writings of Isaac McCoy, portrays conditions early missionaries encountered as they struggled to spread their gospel.

Most Reverend Central Director of the Leopoldine Foundation!

The establishment of the new mission on Grand-River, in this unfavorable season of the year, goes ahead only because this year we have an exceptionally mild winter; there was very little snow, and for 3 weeks there has been no more, and we have only some few particularly cold days. My carpenter, (I have now only one,) works constantly on the mission building. Since this mission is only in its beginning, and for that reason still insignificant, therefore for the time being I am having only one building erected, 50 feet long, 30 feet wide and 12 feet high, one half of which will be fitted as a chapel and the other half will be divided into a pair of small school and living rooms. Therefore I have under one roof *all* the buildings belonging to the mission. I could not manage it more economically, and yet this single, mediocre and entirely wooden building will cost over $800 dollars before it is entirely finished.

...Now we are in the so-called sugar time. Not a single Indian is now here in the village; all are in the forest, in their sugar huts. They spend the winter there in order to hunt the many deer, bears and other smaller animals, whose pelts are sold at a good price to the fur traders; and at the same time they also make their sugar there. There are Indians in these regions, who in a single winter slay and catch in their traps so many wild animals that their pelts are worth over 200 dollars, for which then they buy clothing and household utensils for themselves and their families; however, since the fur traders here so shamefully defraud the poor Indians, they nevertheless always receive little for their many pelts.

...For some time people are again talking very strongly that it is the plan of our government to remove all the Indians from the *civilized* states and territories of this republic, and to assign to them a district on the other side of the Mississippi for their own common abode. Now if this happens, then also my poor Indians will have to wander. However I console them with the assurance that I shall never abandon them, even if they should be driven into the most inhospitable regions. Now that I have, with much effort, learned so fairly well this extremely difficult language of the Indians, and still daily make progress in it, therefore I am inclined to devote the remaining days of my life to the missions of the Indians and to follow them to wherever they may be banished.

Frederic Baraga, m.p.,
Missionary.
Mission of St. Mary
on Grand River,
March 7, 1834

▲ Albert Hyda Papers, Clarke Historical Library, Central Michigan University.

▲ Fr. Frederic Baraga brought the Catholic religion to the Grand River in 1833. [P. Chrysostomus Verwust, *Life and Labors of Rt. Rev. Frederic Baraga*, facing title page]

A License to Trade

In mid-November 1826, Isaac McCoy and his fellow Baptists noted the arrival of fur trader Louis Campau and two assistants who wintered among the Ottawa. By the time Campau brought his bride, Sophie, to join them the next summer, the traders had constructed two cabins, one for dwelling and one for trading, and a small blacksmith shop on the east bank of the Grand River where the Grand Center now stands.

Born in Detroit in 1791 and raised in that city, Campau was descended from a French-Canadian family that traced its roots to Etienne Campau, a Frenchman who came to Montreal in the mid-1600s. After joining the Americans in their fight against the British in the War of 1812, Campau went to work for his uncle Joseph, trading with Indians in the Saginaw valley. There he became so well known that Territorial Governor Lewis Cass turned to him for help in making a treaty with the Saginaw Ojibwa. When Campau concluded he had not received adequate payment for his services, he used free liquor to stir up an Indian mob to harass the governor for the money.

This and similar incidents established a reputation for shrewd dealings and (in the minds of some observers, at least) illegal practices that followed Campau for the remainder of his life.

In 1825, Campau resolved to move west to the rapids of the Grand River and establish a permanent home. The terms of his trading license, issued in 1822, demonstrate the government's desire to control his more objectionable practices.

Instructions to Louis Campau, this day licensed to trade with the Indian nation at—

1. Your trade will be confined to the place to which you are licensed.

2. Your transactions with the Indians will be confined to fair and friendly trade.

3. You will attend no Councils held by the Indians, nor send them any talk or speech, accompanied by wampum.

4. You are forbidden to take any spirituous liquors of any kind into the Indian country; or to give, sell or dispose of any to the Indians.

5. Should any person attempt to trade in the Indian country without a license; or should any licensed traders carry any spirituous liquors into the Indian country; or give, sell or dispose of any to the Indians, the Indians are authorized to seize and take to their own use the goods of such traders; and the owner shall have no claim on the Indians or the United States for the same.

6. Should you learn that there is any person in the Indian country, trading without a license, you will immediately report the name of such person, and the place where he is trading, to some Indian agent.

7. The substance of the 5th regulation you will communicate to the Indians.

8. You will take all proper occasions to inculcate upon the Indians the necessity of peace; and to state to them that it is the wish of their Great Father, the president, to live in harmony with them; and that they must shut their ears to any wild stories there may be in circulation.

Given under my hand, at the city of Detroit, this 15th day of November, 1822.
William Woodbridge, Secretary, and at present vested with the powers of Superintendent of Indian Affairs therein.

▲ Albert Baxter, *History of the City of Grand Rapids*, p. 48.

▲ Louis Campau posed for this daguerreotype in the late 1840s. The restoration was made by Celene Idema. [GRPL, Photo Collection]

Annuity Days

Negotiating a treaty was one thing; fair apportionment of the money and goods called for was quite another.

"Annuity Days," as the annual distribution of treaty payments and goods was called, drew huge crowds of Indians, traders, and observers. At a time when currency was scarce and all manner of business conducted by barter, annuity payments made in gold coins gave a dramatic boost to the local economy. Knowing the occasion meant a bonanza for local merchants, scores of towns and cities aggressively competed to be the location for "annuity days." All too often, these gatherings became uncontrolled scenes of larceny and debauchery during which the payments found their way into the hands of traders and merchants without the Indians so much as touching the money before it passed from their control.

For several years, Grand Rapids was the site of the annual payments prescribed by the 1821 and 1836 treaties. If the following two documents are any indication, the situation was no better here than at other locations. John M. Gordon, a Maryland speculator on a trip west, was present in 1836 and recorded his observation of the process. The second document, a letter to fur trader Rix Robinson written ten years later by Acting Superintendent for Michigan Indian Affairs William Almy Richmond, suggests that little had changed in the intervening decade.

At our return to the meeting house we found most of the Indians assembled and the distribution of good[s] begun. Mr. Slater acted as crier, holding in his hands a list he called each one by name in his turn and handed him his share tied up in a blanket. It contained broad cloth, calico, cotton, thread, needles, yarn, soap, fish hooks, cooking utensils, such as one bell metal boiler, teapot, tin pans, and a few tools and agricultural implements, a coarse shot gun to the men & a $10 rifle to the Chiefs. The savages were arranged around the house in family groups, some reclining on the Ground, some leaning motionless against the fence, others were seated on benches. The children of the Chiefs were distinguished by more silver rings & bracelets & a better style of dress than the lower class. The majority present presented a miserable and squalid appearance, with few clothes except a blanket and in some cases without mockasins. I noticed one old woman who had nothing on but a small thin blanket worn to shreds & patches. Some of the girls, however, were very pretty. All had delicate & well formed feet, which their tight trousers and ornamented buskins shewed off to much advantage. Of the Chiefs there were some noble looking men.

...The Indians generally appeared to be much amused with the ceremony of distribution and often shouted with laughter.

...The Chiefs received $500 and $250 according to rank, as of the first or second degree. The men and women from $2.50 to $50 according to the number of persons in their families....In a few days...most of those who are now paid a few silver dollars will have spent or been cheated out of all in a drunken debouch which always follows a payment and from which they have been kept only by the joint resolution of the town to sell no liquors until the payment is over. Every thing they now receive, will then be bartered at the tipling shops for drink, and in another week, they will be stripped of their lands and the price of them....the overwhelming tide of emigration is fast gaining on them and passing over their heads & the rigours of a few more winters upon constitutions shattered by drunkenness will leave but few miserable survivors victims & a living reproach to the gross injustice, and revolting, mercenary, swindling treatment of the Genrl. Govrt.

▲ John M. Gordon, "Michigan Journal, 1836," *Michigan History*, Vol. 43, December 1959, pp. 459-71.

▼ A group of Ottawa and Ojibwa in Traverse City in 1910 for an annuity payment. [GRPL, Grand Rapids Inter-tribal Council Collection]

Office Supt. Indian Affairs
Detroit October 29, 1846
Hon. Rix Robinson
Sir
We intend starting for G. River on Monday next and shall make the payment to the Indians as early as can be accomplished after our arrival.

Will you have the Indians notified, and suggest to the citizens and traders at the Rapids the propriety of making some arrangement to prevent the sale of whiskey to the Indians.

It will become my duty to make the payment at some other point hereafter unless the practice is abandoned — and I should regret exceedingly the necessity for so doing.

I am yours with respect
Wm. A. Richmond
Actg. Supt. Ind. Affairs

◄ Indian agent William Almy Richmond wrote this letter to Rix Robinson in 1846, asking him to maintain order during annuity days. [Letters sent by the Michigan Superintendent of Indian Affairs, 1845-1851; vol. 4, roll no. 1-40, p. 46]

Rix Robinson operated ► the American Fur Company post at the Thornapple and Grand rivers from 1821 to 1837. [GRPL, Photo Collection]

Petitioning the "Great Father"

Although some Ottawa managed to buy land and establish homes in the Grand River valley, most left during the 1850s for reservations further north. Thereafter, the annuity payments were made in Traverse City, and the number of Ottawa seen in Grand Rapids was limited to occasional visitors, and to those few who still owned property in the area.

Moving north did not protect the Ottawa from threats of removal to territory west of the Mississippi River. The federal government's removal policy, introduced by President Andrew Jackson in the 1830s and endorsed by missionary Isaac McCoy, propounded the idea that Indians would be better off if they were completely separated from direct contact with Americans. For McCoy, this belief was based on the altruistic notion that the Indians' culture would be destroyed if they remained in the East. For others, the "removal" policy was a convenient device to secure Indian land.

To resist removal to the alien prairies of the West, the Ottawa and other Michigan Indians relied on their own negotiating skills, friends who encouraged their determination to remain, and politicians who understood the annuity payments were an important state asset. The following petition, presented to President James Polk in 1844, is an eloquent statement of the Ottawa's desire to remain on the land that had been theirs eight years earlier.

To the President of the United States of America, this petition of his children, the Ot-ta-was and Chip-pe-was of Michigan, respectfully showeth:

Father —

...We, therefore, the Ot-ta-was, who before petitioned, and we, the Chippewas, who now join with them in the prayer; do earnestly express you our Great Father to present our wishes to our Brethren the Senators and Representatives of the United States. We are comparatively few in number and with our ameliorated habits can subsist, with proper industry, upon a small portion of the National domain. Many of us have built houses in imitation of the white men, and are engaged in the cultivation of the soil. We are allied also by the rite of marriage and by consanguinity, to many of the citizens of this state.

The country we occupy from the severity of its climate is not well adapted to the advanced culture of the white men, whilst it is all-sufficient for our moderate wants and will afford us the means of livelihood.

We desire earnestly to become good citizens and to live in friendship with our Brethren and White Men: to die on the soil where we have always lived, and to leave it as an inheritance to our children.

We entreat you then, our Father, to make these our wishes known to our Brethren in Congress, and to join your influence in our humble efforts to accomplish them.

And that the Great Spirit may smile upon you, our Father, and our native land, your children will ever pray.

▲ "Letters Received by the Office of Indian Affairs, 1824-81, Michigan Superintendency, 1842-1851," vol. 234, roll no. 425, pp. 595-96.

▲ Like "The Light," an Assiniboine painted by George Catlin, Michigan Indian leaders often adopted new styles of dress after visiting Washington. [Smithsonian Institution]

◄ Indian delegations often posed for photographers while visiting Washington, D.C. [*Frank Leslie's Illustrated Newspaper*, September 10, 1881, p. 24]

"Relieved of Their Possessions"

In 1854 the last of the Grand River Indians boarded a steamer at Grandville and headed north to land set aside for them in Oceana County. In little more than a single generation, they had witnessed the arrival of missionaries, fur traders, and then permanent settlers. Most of their land had been opened to settlement in return for payments that later courts would rule to have been grossly inadequate. Twentieth-century judges have ordered new, additional payments for land taken in the 19th century. The courts have also reasserted the Indians' right to hunt and fish on unsold lands, and

ruled that they are entitled to free college tuition. But Michigan's Native American citizens still grapple with the economic and social problems that are directly related to the manner in which their ancestors' lives were disrupted 150 years ago.

Late in his life, Louis Campau looked back on the changes he had seen and remarked, "A few white men arrived, and there was a little trouble. A few more white men arrived, and there was more trouble. Then a lot came, and the Indians became bad, and times grew worse. Finally, the Indians were relieved of their possessions."

Like the Indians he lamented, Campau ended up with few possessions. At one time the owner of much of today's downtown, he was left virtually penniless at the end of his life by a series of financial reverses. Sophie Campau died in 1869, and Louis followed two years later, 45 years after he had first come to the area. By then, few of the city's residents could imagine, much less remember, a time when commerce in the Grand River valley was controlled by the simple instructions that Campau had received nearly half a century earlier from Michigan's territorial secretary.

◄ Many Grand River valley Ottawa were removed to remote portions of Oceana County during the 1850s. [GRPL, Native American Photo Collection]

▲ Louis and Sophie Campau saw most Ottawa Indians removed from Grand Rapids, and their villages replaced by a city of 16,500 people. [GRPL, George E. Fitch Collection]

◄ Many West Michigan Ottawa were reduced to lives of desperate poverty by the end of the 19th century. [GRPL, Native American Photo Collection]

CHAPTER 2

A Village on the Grand

In 17 short years, between 1833 and 1850, Grand Rapids grew from a trading post, Indian villages, and mission buildings on the banks of the Grand River to a frontier city with a population of over 2,500. Accounting for the rapid growth was a series of developments that drew increasing numbers of settlers from New York and New England into the area.

Most important of these developments was the extinguishment of Indian title to Michigan's lower peninsula by 1836; although Indian groups continued to live in their traditional village locations, the land was available for claim and purchase by settlers and speculators as soon as surveyors laid out range and township lines. By 1825, ten years after the project began, most of the southern third of the Lower Peninsula was surveyed. Fifteen years later, the work was virtually complete, and within another decade the Upper Peninsula was fully surveyed as well.

With Indian claims settled and southern land surveys completed, the sale of public lands began. In the decade following the first public auction held in Detroit in 1818, a lowering of the minimum bid per acre from $2 to $1.25 slowly heated up land sales. Most of these sales were in the southeastern corner of

the territory; not until 1831 was a land office opened in White Pigeon to serve western Michigan.

Settlers might have moved more quickly into Michigan if adverse reports about the land quality and health conditions had not pervaded the East. After a review by federal surveyors in 1815, Surveyor-General of the United States Edward Tiffin reported to President James Madison that Michigan consisted largely of swamps, lakes, and poor sandy soil, and that not more than one acre in a hundred, or perhaps a thousand, could be cultivated.

Compounding the negative impact of Tiffin's report were rumors and untruthful accounts of widespread disease and death among soldiers serving in Michigan. Potential travelers were warned about Michigan's unhealthy conditions in a rhyme:

Don't go to Michigan,
  that land of ills;
The word means ague, fever,
  and chills.

▲ R. Carlyle Buley, *The Old Northwest: Pioneer Period, 1815-1840,* Vol. I, p. 242.

Michigan's territorial governor, Lewis Cass, took several steps to counter the unfavorable publicity. After reading Tiffin's report, he insisted that a second review of the land be undertaken, and later, he led an expedition around the territory that was designed to promote interest in its resources and potential for settlement. Downplaying any difficulties, Cass filed reports concluding that the Indians were peaceable and the land promising.

Even if public perception of Michigan had been more favorable, it is unlikely that settlement would have proceeded any faster. No roads entered the territory from Ohio, and until the introduction of larger sailing vessels, travel on the Great Lakes was dangerous, unreliable, and uncomfortable. That all began to change in 1818 when the 330-ton *Walk-in-the-Water* inaugurated steam navigation on the Upper Great Lakes. By the late 1820s, numerous steamships and larger sailing vessels lowered transportation costs and improved traveling conditions.

One more piece of the transportation puzzle fell into place in 1825 with completion of the Erie Canal across upstate New York. Now, travelers could make their way in slow, but reasonably comfortable and moderately priced, canal boats from the Hudson River to Lake

Erie, and there board lake vessels for Detroit or the Straits of Mackinac. Although still not cheap, the cost of the journey was now within reach of many more potential settlers. Steerage rates for the entire trip ranged from $20 to $30; cabin passengers could expect to pay twice as much or more.

Land transport within Michigan Territory was also improved. Federal funds helped build a road between Toledo and Detroit that was completed in 1819 and improved a few years later. Roads to the interior were started in the 1820s, and a short stretch from Detroit to Pontiac was completed by 1822. A military road from Fort Detroit to Fort Dearborn (Chicago) was laid out in the late 1820s, and by 1835 regular stagecoach service connected the two growing outposts. A second highway, called the Territorial Road, was laid out from Ypsilanti to St. Joseph in 1830, and opened to travel in 1834. Farthest north and last to be completed was a road running west from Detroit to Grand Rapids. Although initial surveying was finished in 1832, the road remained only a trail for several years thereafter.

Once the rumors about disease and unhealthy conditions were put to rest, improved travel conditions together with rising land prices in the East drew a floodtide of settlers to Michigan. From 1830 to the time of its statehood in 1837, Michigan was the most popular destination of westering Americans. The "Emigrants Song," first published in a Detroit paper in 1831, captured the feelings of many of those who ventured west.

Come all ye Yankee farmers,
    Who'd like to change your lot
Who've spunk enough to travel
    Beyond your native spot
And leave behind the village
    Where Pa and Ma do stay,
Come follow me and settle
    In Michigania.

What country ever growed up
    So great in little time,
Just poppin from the nurs'ry
    Right into like its prime;
When Uncle Sam did wean her.
    'Twas but the other day,
And now she's quite a lady,
    This Michigania.

Then come ye Yankee farmers,
    Who've mettle hearts like me,
And elbow-grease in plenty,
    To bow the forest tree;
Come take a "quarter Section,"
    And I'll be proud you'll say,
This country takes the rag off,
    This Michigania.

▲ Willis F. Dunbar, *Michigan: A History of the Wolverine State*, p. 193.

The "Michigan Caravan"

Among those who heeded the call to Michigan was Samuel Dexter, a promoter from Herkimer County, in east central New York along the Mohawk River. Dexter came west in the fall of 1832 and selected a quarter section (160 acres) of land where Ionia is now located, and another 320 acres in a two-mile strip along what later became Grand Rapids' Division Avenue between Wealthy and Leonard streets. Having made his selections and entered his claims, Dexter returned to Herkimer County. Working throughout the winter, he put together a party of 63 emigrants who were ready to head west by the time warm spring breezes melted the snow and ice.

Six families and five single men set out for Michigan from Herkimer County in 1833. Besides Dexter and his family there were the families of Erasmus Yeomans, Oliver Arnold, Joel Guild, Edward Guild, and Darius Winsor; the single men were Dr. William B. Lincoln, Patrick M. Fox, Winsor Dexter, Warner Dexter, and Abram Decker.

Samuel Dexter's daughter, Prudence, was a member of the group, and years later she recorded her recollection of the first leg of the journey in the *Michigan Pioneer and Historical Collections*.

▲ Samuel Dexter led the first settlers to Grand Rapids in 1833. [Franklin Everett, *Memorials of the Grand River Valley*, p. 19B]

We started from Frankfort village, Herkimer county, New York, April 22, 1833, with three families, Mr. Yeoman's, Oliver Arnold's, and Samuel Dexter's — using their own horses to draw the boat, which was named "Walk-in-the-Water," [after the earlier, larger, steam-powered vessel], but some one wrote on the side of the boat with chalk, "Michigan Caravan." At Utica, Joel Guild and his brother Edward and families embarked with us. We traveled by day and at night had to go ashore to sleep at hotels. At Syracuse, Mr. Darius Winsor and family joined the party. The boat was a motley sight, as the dock was piled with wagons taken to pieces and bound on, and every conceivable thing that could be taken to use in such a country where there was nothing to be bought. From Buffalo to Detroit we came by steamer *Superior*. Here we procured oxen and cows and cooked provisions and started on our journey through the wilderness. On leaving Detroit the party consisted of sixty-three people, and on the first day but seven miles were made.

▲ Prudence Tower, "The Journey of Ionia's First Settlers," *Michigan Pioneer and Historical Collections*, Vol. 28, 1900, p. 145.

▼ The *Walk-in-the-Water* was the first steamboat on the Upper Great Lakes. [Dossin Great Lakes Museum]

▼ Travel by water from the East to Michigan was made possible by the completion of the Erie Canal across New York State in 1825. [New York Historical Society, New York City]

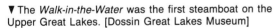

Aunt Hattie's Story

Once the Dexter party left Detroit, travel became much more difficult, as Joel Guild, his wife, Abby, and their six daughters and one son were soon to discover. Twenty-year-old Harriet, the oldest Guild daughter, was expected to carry an adult's share of the burden and stoically endure the hardships encountered as the group made its way across Michigan. Years later, in 1889, Harriet (or Aunt Hattie as she was known throughout the community) related her memories of the journey. In the following account, she describes the arduous overland trip across Michigan, the death of Samuel Dexter's young son, and her father's decision to continue on from Ionia and take up Louis Campau's invitation to buy land from him and settle in Grand Rapids.

We (Joel and Edward Guild, and their families), started from Paris, Oneida county, N.Y., taking goods and teams. At the Erie Canal we went aboard a boat purchased by Samuel Dexter for the party. In all there were sixty-three of the company. We had our horses to draw the boat, and the boys to drive. At Buffalo the boat was sold, and we shipped our goods and took passage on the steamer *Superior* for Detroit, where we selected only such goods as we could carry overland, and left the rest to be sent around to the mouth of Grand River. We stopped in Detroit two or three days, buying oxen and cows, and laying in supplies. Every family had a wagon. From there we went to Pontiac, where we staid two nights in a tavern. The third day we went about ten miles and camped near a tavern, where the women and children found shelter, and the rest slept in tents. The next day we left the roads and went into the wilderness, with no guide except a compass and a knowledge of the general direction to be taken. Each family had a tent; the six tents were pitched together as one long tent, and every night twenty-three beds were made upon the ground. At Pontiac Mrs. Dexter's youngest child, a boy, became sick with scarlet fever, and seemed to grow worse every day. But we could not stop, for our progress was slow and our supplies running short.... It was raining when we reached the Looking-glass River, and that night the little boy was so sick that his mother and Mrs. Yeomans, whose babe was but four weeks old when we started, and myself, sat up all night, holding umbrellas over the two little ones, and nursing them....

Our provisions were nearly gone, and we could not stop, but about noon Mrs. Dexter called a halt, noticing a change in the boy. Dr. Lincoln gave him some medicine, but in a few minutes the little sufferer was dead. We could not tarry, but went sadly on carrying his body, and camped early: when my mother furnished a small trunk that had been used for carrying food and dishes, which served for a coffin, and by Muskrat Creek, as the sun was going down, the little one was buried. A large elm by the grave was marked, and logs were put over the mound and fastened there, to protect it from wolves that were then plenty in that vicinity. The only service over the little grave was a prayer by Mr. Dexter. The mother seemed broken-hearted, and we all were grieved, but could not tarry there.

We had reached the point where we had to use meal that father bought at Pontiac for the horses, letting the latter pick their living as best they could from grass and twigs by the way. Each family had cows — in all fifteen or twenty. We made log-heap fires, filled a large brass kettle with water, placed it over the fire, stirred in meal and made hasty-pudding, which, with milk from the cows, was our only food. After reaching the timber land, we girls had to rise very early and get breakfast for the young men, who would then start ahead to cut out the road, and only came in when it was time to camp at night. At the end of sixteen days we reached Grand River at Lyons, where father and his family made a brief stop, while the rest proceeded at once to Ionia.

In a few days father and Mr. Dexter started from Ionia, on horseback, by way of the Rapids of Grand River, for the land office at White Pigeon. On reaching the Rapids they met Uncle Louis Campau, who wanted them to settle here, the lands having come into market the year before. He had taken some land, and was platting it into lots; he did not "talk Yankee" very well, he said, and he wanted a settlement of Yankees here. So father went and

▲ Thompson's Tavern near Dearborn resembled the tavern where the Dexter party stopped for two days. [William Nowlin, *The Bark Covered House*, p. 43]

◄ Hattie Guild (front right) posed with three of her sisters for this photograph sometime in the 1850s. [GRPL, Photo Collection]

took up the forty that is now the "Kendall addition," and also took up some pine land a little southeast of here. When he came back from the land office, he bought, for $25, a village lot of Mr. Campau. Uncle Louis, and some of his French help, went to Ionia for us with bateaux. All of our family came down. We reached the Rapids and landed...on the east side by the foot of Huron street [site of today's Civic Auditorium], near where the Butterworth & Lowe iron works are. Two log houses and a shop were there. All about were woods, mostly. We were received with a warm welcome by that good woman, Mrs. Louis Campau, who did her utmost to make us comfortable. This was Sunday, June 23, 1833 — the day that I was twenty years old. We stayed there a few days; then removed to Mr. Campau's fur-packing house and store, where we lived till about the first of September, when we removed into the new house that my father built.

▲ Albert Baxter, *History of the City of Grand Rapids*, pp. 54-55.

▲ "Aunt Hattie" Guild Burton was a much-honored pioneer. [GRPL, Photo Collection]

"Perfectly Contented and Doing Tolerably Well"

The lot Joel Guild selected for his house was on the east side of today's Monroe Mall, at its junction with Pearl Street, where the McKay Tower now stands. On that site, using lumber from the Indian sawmill operated at the Baptist mission across the river, he constructed the first frame house in the village — a "story-and-a-half" structure, about 16 feet wide by 26 feet long. Less than 200 feet away, on the river bank, were the buildings of Louis Campau's trading post, where the Guilds lived while building their house, and from which they secured basic provisions. Six months after moving into their new home, Joel and Abby Guild wrote a letter to Abby's brother, Jesse Vaughn, and his family in New York, urging them to come to Grand Rapids.

Grand Rapids, December the 23rd, 1833.

To: Jesse Vaughn, Sarah Vaughn:

Most Respected Brother and Sister: The land here in this country generally appears to be of the first quality. Our water is good as I ever saw in any country, and a plenty of it. People are flocking in from all parts. The country is settling very fast with respectable inhabitants.

After looking about for a home, I thought best to move about fifty miles down Grand River to a place called Grand River Falls. I landed here on the thirteenth day of June — no one here then that could speak English excepting a French trader by the name of Campau. I bought 120 acres of first rate land near this place, and since I bought I have had the satisfaction of going with the Commissioners and sticking the stake for the Court House in our county within twenty-five rods of my land.

There is now a village laid out here and recorded, and the lots are selling fast, from twenty-five to two hundred dollars each. I own two village lots. I bought the first lots that were sold, and have built a framed house, the first that was ever built within one hundred miles of this place, and I am under the necessity of keeping tavern, as my house was built first. I moved into it the last day of August, and from that time to this my house has been full by day and by night. Some of the time we have had twenty in the family. Our women have a plenty to do, are able and willing to work. Abby says [I] must write to you that she baked nine barrels of flour by the side of a white oak log after we came here before we moved into our house. Our girls have as much sewing as they can do. We are all perfectly contented, and I think we are doing tolerably well.

Our river is eighty-five rods [a rod is 16.5 feet] wide at this place, and the greatest water privilege there is in the Territory; here is twenty-five feet fall [actually, about 16 feet] in one mile of the river at this place. We expect mills built here another season. I have a full set of mill irons stored in my cellar for that purpose. We have plenty of provisions here, although they come as yet by water from Detroit. Here is plenty of fish and plenty of game, and the greatest country for honey that I ever saw.

Joel Guild
Abby Guild

Joel Guild urged others to ► follow him to Grand Rapids. [Albert Baxter, *History of the City of Grand Rapids*, p. 58]

◄ Albert Baxter, *History of the City of Grand Rapids*, p. 57.

▼ The Guild family cabin, on the site of today's McKay Tower, was the first residence on the east bank of the Grand River. [Albert Baxter, *History of the City of Grand Rapids*, p. 56]

Establishing a Community

As new settlers arrived, the need for local government became increasingly apparent. Although Kent County (named for James Kent, a New York jurist) had been set off and named in 1831, the machinery for its government was not organized until March 24, 1836; until then, the area was treated as part of Kalamazoo County.

In the meantime, the families living along the Grand River and in the surrounding vicinities took matters into their own hands. Gathering at Joel Guild's house on April 4, 1834, they established the township of Kent (later renamed Grand Rapids), which encompassed all the area in Kent County south and east of the Grand River. Although there were more offices to fill than there were potential officeholders, the citizens of the newly created township were determined to establish a full-fledged government. By the time the voting was over, the following men had been named to township office, some to serve in more than one position.

Town Clerk	Eliphalet H. Turner
Supervisor	Rix Robinson
Assessors	Joel Guild, Barney Burton
Collector	Ira Jones
Poormaster	Luther Lincoln
Constables	Myron Roys, Ira Jones
Overseer of Highways	Jonathan F. Chubb
Fence Viewers	Luther Lincoln, Jonathan F. Chubb, Gideon Gordon, Barney Burton
Justice of the Peace	Leonard Slater

▲ Town clerk Eliphalet Turner came to Grand Rapids in 1833. [GRPL, Photo Collection]

▲ Fence viewer and assessor Barney Burton also came to Grand Rapids in 1833. [Albert Baxter, *History of the City of Grand Rapids*, p. 61]

▲ Kent County was named for prominent New York jurist James Kent. [Alonzo Chappell, *National Portrait Gallery of Prominent Americans*, vol. II, facing p. 39]

Speculation Fever

Myron Hinsdill and his family came to Michigan from Hinesburg, Vermont, in 1833. After three years in Gull Prairie, Hinsdill purchased a partially built hotel from his cousin, Hiram Hinsdill, and moved his wife, Emily, and their children to Grand Rapids. While waiting for the hotel, on the northeast corner of Ionia and Monroe, to be completed, the family made its home in a new barn building erected on the property.

Decades later, Hinsdill's daughter, Marion, by then the much-respected wife of Judge Solomon Withey, recalled her first days in Gull Prairie and Grand Rapids at a meeting of the Michigan Pioneer and Historical Society. Her account tells of the bustle of activity as increasing numbers of people crowded into western Michigan. Land speculators bought and sold land at a furious pace, and newcomers arrived almost every day, drawn by the nearly irresistible magnet of cheap land and the promise of opportunity.

Our evenings [in Gull Prairie] were enlivened by visits from our neighbors, who often came several miles for that purpose. Hickory nuts were our usual refreshments, of which the woods yielded an abundance. My father often read aloud for our entertainment. I have a vivid remembrance of his reading Cooper's "Leather Stocking."

That summer of '36 [in Grand Rapids] seems to my recollection a long one. The arrival of so many strangers, the rapid changes, the hurry of people to get some place to live before the cold weather, the funny ways people did live, the feverish excitement of speculation, crowding so many events into the space of a few months, seems now like so many years. To recall the state of things, I extract from a letter of my father's to a brother-in-law, dated April 23, 1836. "I have applied for fine lots of pine land up Grand River, but there is such a press of business at the Land Office, one cannot know under six or eight days whether he can get it or not, and if two men ask for the same land, the same day, they must agree which shall have it, as it is set up at auction. There has been four or five hundred people at Bronson [Kalamazoo] for a week past, all waiting to get land, if I get the pine land it will cost about $2.25 per acre, and a great bargain at that."

▲ Albert Baxter, *History of the City of Grand Rapids*, p. 85.

▲ This cabin in the woods exemplifies the kind of homes built by many easterners who caught "Michigan Fever." [William Nowlin, *The Bark Covered House*, p. 31]

The White Pigeon land office ▶ bustled with activity. [Michigan Bell Telephone Company]

School Days

Across the street from Hinsdill's Hotel (later renamed the National Hotel) stood a hastily constructed building intended to be a barn, but pressed into duty as a school building during the hectic summer of 1836. The following winter, rooms in the National Hotel were converted into classrooms — a lower room for girls and one on the upper level for boys. A school district had been created in 1835, and by 1837, organizational matters had proceeded to the point where a permanent full-time teacher was hired, ending the ad hoc arrangements of the previous year. In 1839, the village's first school house, a wood frame building, was constructed on the north side of Fulton Street, opposite Jefferson Avenue. The new building must have been an impressive change for Marion Hinsdill, who described her first classes in the barn for a meeting of the Pioneer Society of the State of Michigan.

That summer [1836] was mostly a holiday to us children. We gathered flowers everywhere, strawberries on what was Prospect Hill, leading altogether a Bohemian life. We had a school for a time, Miss [Sophia] Page, afterward Mrs. Judge Bacon of Monroe, at the importunity of several families who had young children, acting as teacher. It held its sessions in a new barn a little to the southeast across the street from the present Morton House. Being built of boards set up endwise, with a floor of boards laid down without matching, no school committee was vexed with the matter of its ventilation.

▲ Marion Withey, "Personal Recollections and Incidents of the Early Days of Richland and Grand Rapids," *Michigan Pioneer and Historical Collections,* Vol. V, 1884, p. 436.

▲ The National Hotel had part of its upper floor used for classrooms. [GRPL, George E. Fitch Collection]

John Ball's Travels

Among those who responded to the calls to head west was a young adventurer from New York named John Ball. Already a seasoned traveler, Ball had followed the Overland Trail to Oregon in 1832 with Nathaniel Wyeth, as part of an ill-fated effort to establish a trading company in Oregon. During the winter of 1833, the Dartmouth-educated Ball, an experienced teacher, conducted the Oregon Territory's first organized school classes. Today, he is honored by the Oregon Historical Society for his teaching, for planting the region's first farm crops, and for publishing a descriptive geological and geographical account of his journey in Silliman's *Journal of Science.* Leaving Oregon Territory in 1834, Ball took passage on a ship that stopped at the Sandwich Islands (Hawaii) before rounding Cape Horn. Finally returning

to his Lansingburg, New York, home by year's end, he learned he had been given up for lost by many of his family and friends.

After practicing law for two years in nearby Troy, New York, Ball in 1836 once again succumbed to wanderlust. This time the inducement was an offer from New York investors to act as their agent, and invest their funds in Michigan land. Arriving in Grand Rapids in November 1836, Ball had found the place he would call home until his death at age 90 in 1884.

A systematic diarist during his early years, Ball used his daily jottings as the basis for later writings about Grand Rapids. After his death, Ball's daughters compiled his diaries and other notes into an *Autobiography* that remains one of the better accounts of early Grand Rapids. The following excerpts from

Ball's writings reveal him to be an accurate, sometimes witty, and always insightful commentator.

▲ John Ball traveled to Oregon Territory, Hawaii, and around the tip of South America before settling in Grand Rapids. [Oregon Historical Society]

Having resided some years at Troy and Lansingburg, N.Y., in that year of speculation, 1836, I entered into a contract with Dr. T. C. Brinsmaid, Dr. F. B. Leonard, Mr. J. E. Whipple, and a Mr. Webster, of those places, to go west, and invest for them, on speculation, so much money as they would supply for I had none. The talk was, some sixty or eighty thousand dollars; but, from the change of times, it ended at about ten thousand. I was to operate in any of the western (not slave) States, buy and sell in my own name, and receive for my services one-fourth of the profits. I made up my mind that the Grand River district was the promised land, or at least the most promising one for my operations. So I purchased a horse, and mounting him, I started out through mud which I found so deep that I was unable to trot him until I got to Ypsilanti.

When I left Troy, at the urgent request of my friends I purchased a pair of pistols, and put them in my trunk. I left them in my trunk in Detroit, not wishing the trouble of carrying them, though I had considerable gold in my saddlebags. Everybody then carried money, and traveled on highways and by-ways; stopped by dozens in the same log cabins, and slept in the same common garret; thrusting their saddlebags and packages loosely under their beds, and perhaps leaving them there for days, though heavy with specie — for then only specie bought Government lands. Still there were no robberies heard of. Nevertheless, it must be confessed, in bargaining, people did not always show themselves saints without guile.

Mr. Anderson, and myself, mounted our horses, and put out to look for pine lands down in Ottawa, and came the first day to Grand Rapids. This was my first visit. We put up at the Eagle Tavern, then the only one in the place, and kept by Wm. H. Godfroy. It was then November, the nights cold, the house not plastered, the house full — two in a bed. When the lights were out, I heard from all quarters bitter complaints about bed fellows, that they pulled the clothes off; not just understanding that, the coverings being narrow Indian blankets, if a man covered himself he uncovered his neighbor. I rather enjoyed the complaining.

▲ Albert Baxter, *History of the City of Grand Rapids,* pp. 70-71.

We went on to Grandville the next morning before breakfast. And when we got there we found no tavern, but a Mr. Charles Oaks said he could put up and feed and keep our horses, but had no feed for us, not even a breakfast. Still after some urging as to our hungry condition, his wife, a half-breed lady, gave us some coffee and a quite good though not very bountiful breakfast. But as for anything in the way of food for us to take into the woods they protested that they or their few neighbors had nothing. But they said a Mr. Ketchum, who was building a sawmill down a mile below on the Rush Creek, could supply us. So we left our horses to be cared for and went on down to where the mill was building, and there found a Mr. Nathan Boynton, keeping house for the workmen, but Mrs. Boynton had no cooked provisions, not even bread, and then seeing no better way we stopped until she could bake us an unleavened loaf, which we took with some raw beef, and packed for our woods' supplies. This made it late in the morning to start out.

...This was the first of encamping out in Michigan, being November 4th, 1836. We stopped for the night, not among pines, but in the regular hardwood beech and maple, and on a small creek, which we saw by our map was a branch of what is now called the Black River falling into the Lake at Holland.

So we built us a fire and broiled some of our steak, took supper, wrapped ourselves in the blankets we had packed along for the purpose, and slept as well as the tramping deer and howling wolves would let us, they being probably attracted by our fire. In the morning, though we had not found the pine land where we expected, we concluded to look some farther, and did find a small tract.... We came into a dense forest of pines, and, to learn its extent we turned west on the section line and finding the timber of the finest quality, it enticed us on in the same direction till night overtook us. When without supper, to leave the morsel we had left for a breakfast, we wrapped around us our blankets and laid down for sleep, making the protecting root of a pine tree our pillows.... [We] soundly slept until morning, when awakening we found ourselves covered with an inch or two of snow. After eating our scant supply we were so desirous of seeing the extent of pine that we traveled in different directions for some time, till admonished by our failing strength that it was time to leave

▲ John Ball built this two-story home for himself in 1838. [Albert Baxter, *History of the City of Grand Rapids,* p. 72]

the woods to get some food.

Supposing that there was some kind of road from Grandville to Grand Haven on that side of the river, we put out in that direction to find it. And did find an Indian trail but no other road, and following that it brought us to the river where we found some Indians. We offered them the silver dollars to take us up to Grandville in their canoes. They declined the offer saying, as we understood by signs, that they were doing hunting. So we pushed on over broken ground, as we could pick our way, up and near the river till night again overtook us in the forest. And our last match lighting our fire we laid us down to sleep. But before sleep came we heard a cow-bell, an indication that a house was near, but in the darkness we did not seek the same and slept it out.

The next morning...we made our way out to Grandville in rather a dilapidated condition, having been three or rather the third day on the one day's allowance. I had before been longer without food, but was then traveling on horseback, not as now on foot.

This time the Grandville folks readily gave us a breakfast, after taking which, and settling our bills, mounted our horses for Grand Rapids and next day to [the] Ionia [land office.] We felt that we had found a valuable prize.... So in a few days after we started out again to re-look the same, and this time...we furnished ourselves with a tent and an ample supply of food. Though the weather was very bad, rain and snow, we made a thorough exploration of the lands, finding some 2,500 acres of good pine almost in a body, on a part of which there was also some good white oak. One oak tree was seven feet in diameter with a clear body of seventy feet high and a fine spreading top, the largest tree I ever saw in Michigan.

◀ Kate Ball, Flora Ball Hopkins, Lucy Ball, eds., *Autobiography of John Ball,* pp. 140-43.

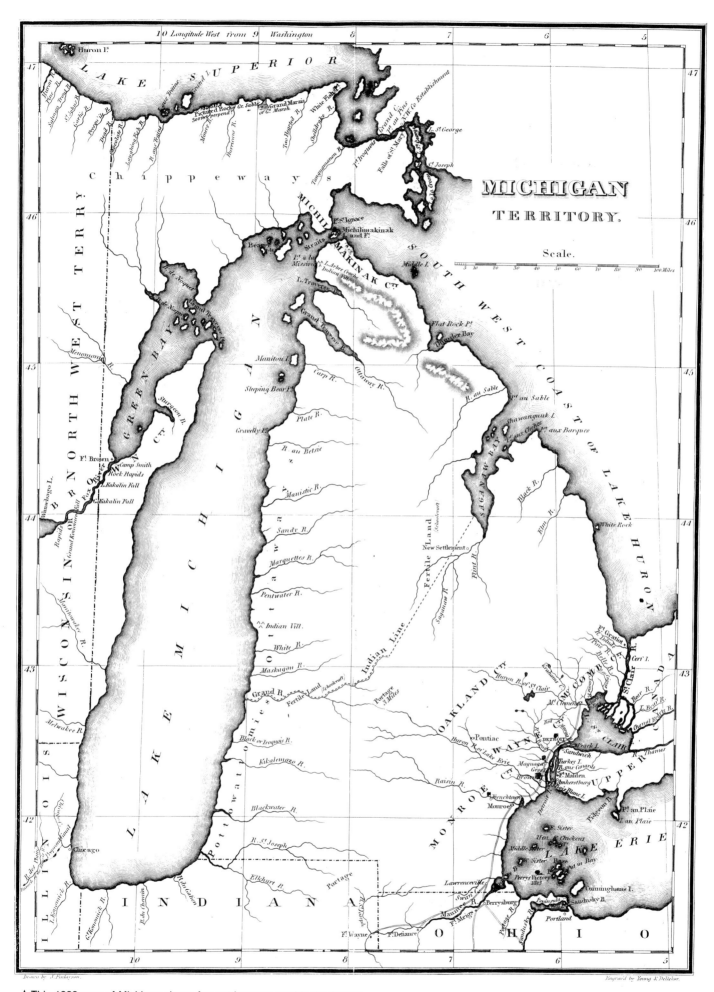

▲ This 1822 map of Michigan shows few settlements outside the Detroit area.
[GRPL, Map Collection]

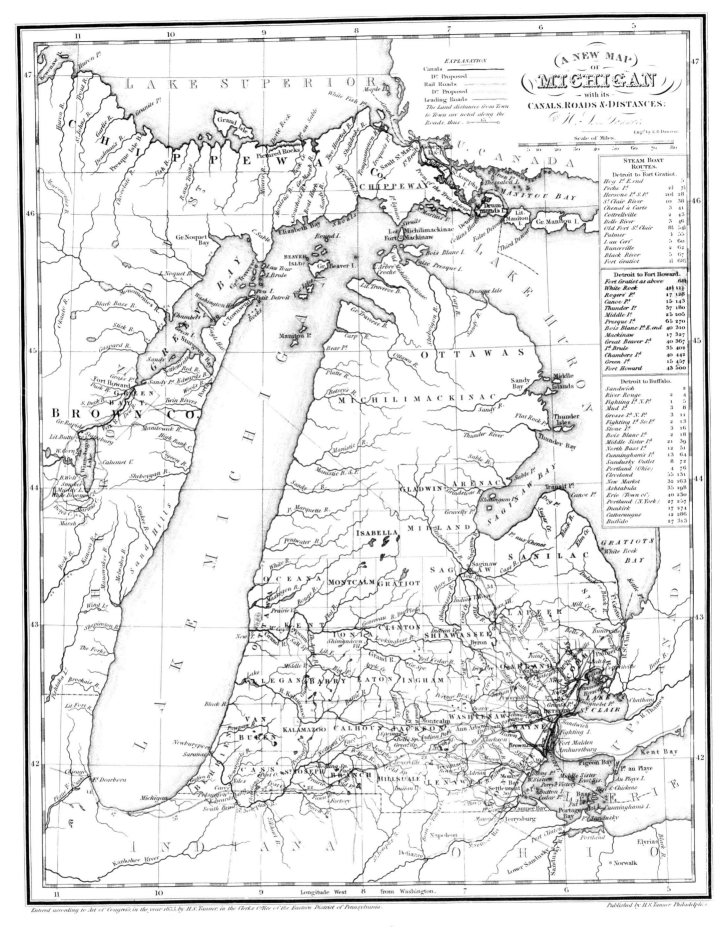

▲ Eleven years later, the southern portion of the territory had been surveyed and numerous villages established. [GRPL, Map Collection]

If a Building Could Speak

If only the law office of 19th-century attorney Charles P. Calkins could speak! The small Greek Revival-style building that today stands at the intersection of State Street and Jefferson Avenue, next to the Public Museum of Grand Rapids, is the only surviving structure from the community's early years. In its more than 150-year history, the three-room structure has borne silent witness to the transformation of Grand Rapids from a 19th-century village of a few hundred souls to a modern city of nearly 200,000 preparing for the 21st century.

Charles P. Calkins arrived in Grand Rapids at about the same time as John Ball. The 33-year-old bachelor had heard of the bustling village at the rapids of the Grand River, and with his recently granted Michigan attorney's license in hand, he was eager to set up his practice and establish a permanent home.

Originally from Hinesburg, Vermont, Calkins no doubt knew the Hinsdill family, and it may have been correspondence with them that brought him to Grand Rapids. In any event, Calkins married Hiram Hinsdill's daughter, Mary Ann, in June 1839. He and his bride moved into the home that was situated just next door to his law office on Lot 1, Section X of the Campau Plat (at the northeast corner of Monroe and Ottawa). Built in 1836, while the property was owned by one Junius Hatch, the home and office were subsequently sold to Edward Macy for $1,800 in 1837 and were valued at $2,000 when Calkins purchased them in 1839. Calkins and John T. Holmes, who became his partner in 1843, occupied the office until 1847 when the partnership was dissolved. Calkins stayed on until 1849, when he and Mary Ann moved their family of five children into a larger home and he relocated his practice in the nearby Faneuil Hall building.

After renting out his old office for a few years, Calkins sold the lot and the building in 1853. By that time the village had become a city and the property was needed for a larger structure. Instead of being torn down, the law office was moved to a location on Ionia north of Coldbrook and made into a residence.

Except for an occasional newspaper article, the building reposed on Ionia in relative obscurity for more than a century. Then, in the 1960s, local historians initiated a preservation effort that culminated in the purchase of the historic structure in 1969 by local businessman Jack R. Stiles and his wife, Mary. The building was given to the city, and set in Lincoln Park adjacent to the Public Museum. Carefully restored and furnished by the museum staff with financial support from several community organizations, the Calkins Law Office was dedicated as part of the city's Bicentennial observance on July 4, 1976.

▲ Charles P. Calkins arrived in Grand Rapids in 1836 and established a legal practice. [GRPL, Photo Collection]

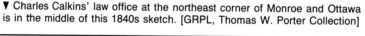

▼ Charles Calkins' law office at the northeast corner of Monroe and Ottawa is in the middle of this 1840s sketch. [GRPL, Thomas W. Porter Collection]

▲ The Calkins law office was restored by the Grand Rapids Public Museum. [Albert Baxter, *History of the City of Grand Rapids,* p. 762; Grand Rapids Public Museum (hereafter cited as GRPM)]

◄ Inside the restored Calkins Law Office are authentic furniture, law books, and business papers. [GRPM]

The Lyon-Campau Feud

One of the signs of the rising value of Michigan land in the early 1830s was an intense competition between land speculators Louis Campau and Lucius Lyon to lay out a village and sell lots at the rapids of the Grand River. In September 1831, Campau acquired, for $90, a total of 72 acres, generally bounded by the Grand River and Division Avenue, and by Fulton and Michigan streets, in what would eventually become the heart of the modern city. Later, Lyon and his associates, calling themselves the "Proprietors of Kent," acquired and platted the land immediately north of Campau's tract. Thus was the groundwork laid for a confrontation that would have ramifications for city residents ever after.

As the story goes, Campau laid out the principal street in his plat — Monroe — along an Indian trail that ran diagonally from the river and led to his trading post. Lyon, on the other hand, was a surveyor, and laid out the proposed Village of Kent in a generally accepted grid format with streets running according to compass directions.

Between the two plats and their conflicting street systems was a strip of 16 lots owned by Campau. Determined to thwart Lyon's plans to connect the competing developments, Campau would not permit a street to be cut through his land barrier. Eventually, however, Lyon secured a portion of lot no. 2 and, with a slight jog because the two streets did not meet squarely, cut his Canal Street through to Campau's Monroe Avenue. When Campau prevailed in denying his competitor any further access, Lyon responded by platting a string of lots, numbered 38 through 56, in a continuous row on the north side of Campau's lots. And for every two streets in Campau's tract, Lyon laid out three.

The result of all this maneuvering, shown clearly on the map below prepared by John Almy in 1836, was a downtown layout that took years to unravel and is complicated to this day by streets that join at odd angles or not at all.

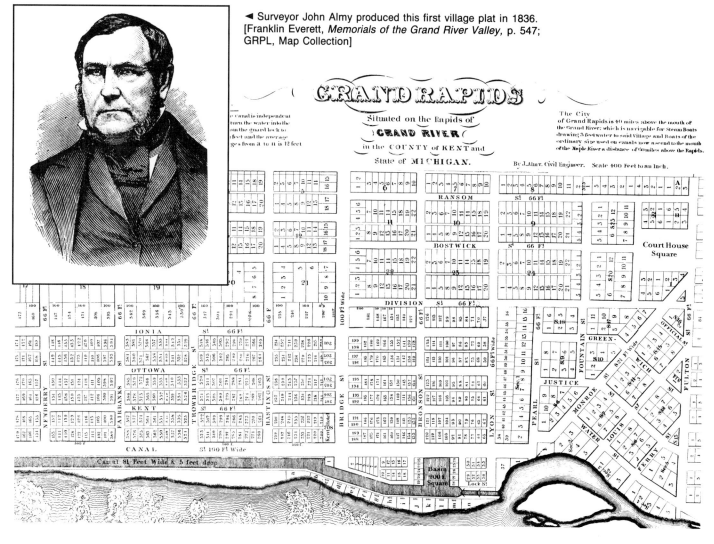

◄ Surveyor John Almy produced this first village plat in 1836. [Franklin Everett, *Memorials of the Grand River Valley*, p. 547; GRPL, Map Collection]

Creating the Village of Grand Rapids

On April 5, 1838, an act of the Michigan legislature created the Village of Grand Rapids, embracing both Campau's and Lyon's tracts. Beginning with the Grand River on the west, the general village boundaries (using modern markers) were Fulton Street on the south, Hastings Street (north of Michigan) to the north, and Prospect on the east.

The original village charter called for the popular election of a board of seven trustees who, in turn, were to elect a village president. The voters within the chartered limits of the Village of Grand Rapids convened at the Kent County Courthouse on Monday, May 1, 1838, for the purpose of choosing seven trustees. Louis Campau, William A. Richmond, Richard Godfroy, Henry C. Smith, Charles J. Walker, George Coggeshall, and James Watson were elected, and at their first meeting, the new trustees designated Henry C. Smith the village's first president.

Vested in the trustees were the power to purchase, hold, sell, and convey real estate for village purposes, and "all such powers of control and management over streets, fire and police and municipal affairs as are usually exercised by similar corporations," including the ability to levy and collect necessary taxes. The original minute book kept by the village clerk now resides in the Grand Rapids City Archives and Records Center. A perusal of its initial entries tells a great deal about the problems facing the newly elected trustees and the interests of those they represented.

Article 15th

That if in any private family having the small pox or any contagious disease, and shall not give notice to the village council within twenty-four hours, they shall be subject to a fine of ten dollars; and every tavern keeper, if the small pox shall come into his house, shall take down his sign, or cover the same with a white cloth, or he or they shall forfeit and pay for every such offense the sum of fifty dollars, to be recovered.

Article 17th

No Grocer or any other person or persons (licensed tavern keepers excepted) shall be allowed to sell or vend intoxicating liquors by the small quantity, within the village limits, and any person who shall be guilty of the offence, shall be liable to a fine of twenty-five dollars, for each and every offence, the same to be recovered by an action of debt, in the name of and for the use of the corporation.

Monday 4 June 1838
On Motion

Resolved that the Street Commissioners be authorized and are hereby registered to make such ditches as may be necessary to drain the marsh in the region of Fountain, Greenwich, Division and Lyon Streets.

Monday, 25 June 1838
On Motion

Resolved that Louis Campau, Myron Hinsdill, Wm. G. Henry, and Alanson Harris, be permitted to sink a well in the center of Greenwich Street immediately adjoining the North East side of Monroe Street, provided that a pump shall be inserted in it, and so protected by platform, so that the public suffer no inconvenience, and that the pump be kept in good order.

It shall be the duty of the Marshal between the first day of August and the first day of September of each year, to make out a list of the owners of dogs and bitches, together with the number that each person owns, and to collect the tax upon such dogs and bitches in accordance with the ordinance, and in case of refusal to pay such tax, the same shall be collected in an action of debt for the use of the corporation, of the owners.

After this ordinance shall have taken effect it shall be the duty of the owner or owners of every dog or bitch to have a strap of leather or other substance put around the neck of said dog or dogs and bitch or bitches with the owner or owners name plainly inscribed thereon.

▲ *Minutes of the Village of Grand Rapids,* Grand Rapids City Archives and Records Center.

▲ Charles J. Walker (top) and William Almy Richmond (below) were two of Grand Rapids' first elected trustees. [Albert Baxter, *History of the City of Grand Rapids,* facing p. 382; Franklin Everett, *Memorials of the Grand River Valley,* p. 57B]

The "Rochester of Michigan"

One mark of an up-and-coming 19th-century community was the presence of a newspaper to dispense news from the outside world and provide a forum for local commentators and advertisers. And as copies made their way to other locales, hometown papers also served to extol their community's virtues to anyone considering resettling. How Grand Rapids acquired its first newspaper is a classic story of promotion and determination, with a little melodrama thrown in for good measure.

Having decided their community was large enough to support a newspaper, local investors purchased the printing press and other appurtenances of the Niagara Falls *Journal* and arranged to have them shipped to Grand Rapids aboard the aptly named steamer *Don Quixote.* When the *Don Quixote* was wrecked off Thunder Bay Island, all of the printing equipment was salvaged, transferred to a second sailing vessel, and delivered to the mouth of the Grand River at Grand Haven in the early winter of 1836.

Purchased from the original investors by George W. Pattison, the printing apparatus was transported up the frozen river by dog teams, but not without further incident. Outside Grandville the sled bearing the press broke through the ice and sank to the river bottom. No damage was done, however, and the press was soon fished out and brought on to Grand Rapids.

On April 18, 1837, the first issue of the *Grand River Times* was printed and distributed to an expectant gathering of prominent citizens. Most pleased was Louis Campau who had paid $1,000 for a subscription of 500 copies a year. In acknowledgement of his support, Campau was given the first copy, printed on silk-satin cloth, as a memento of the event. Linen-cloth copies were also presented to other major subscribers. One linen-cloth issue is now in the collection of the Public Museum of Grand Rapids.

Evident in the paper's very first editorial, written by George Pattison, is the pride he and his fellow citizens took in their hometown and their desire to promote the virtues of the "Rochester of Michigan" far and wide.

◄ George W. Pattison brought the first newspaper to Grand Rapids in 1837. [GRPL, Photo Collection]

◄ Pattison's Washington printing press survived a dunking in the Grand River. [Albert Baxter, *History of the City of Grand Rapids,* p. 275]

Who would have believed, to have visited this place two years since, when it was only inhabited by a few families, most of whom were of French origin, a people so eminent for exploring the wilds and meandering rivers, that this place would now contain its twelve hundred inhabitants?

The river upon which this town is situated is one of the most important and delightful to be found in the country — not important alone for its clear, silver-like water winding its way through a romantic valley of some hundred miles, but for its width and depth, its susceptibility for steam navigation, and the immense hydraulic power afforded at this point.

Several steamboats are now preparing to commence regular trips from Lyons, at the mouth of the Maple River, to this place, a distance of sixty miles; and from this to Grand Haven, a distance of thirty-five or forty miles; thence to Milwaukee and Chicago.

Thus the village of Grand Rapids, with a navigable stream — a water power of twenty-five feet fall — an abundance of crude building materials — stone of excellent quality — pine, oak and other timber in immense quantities within its vicinity, can but flourish — can but be the Rochester of Michigan! The basement story of an extensive mill, one hundred and sixty by forty feet, is now completed; a part of the extensive machinery is soon to be put in operation. There are now several dry goods and grocery stores — some three or four public houses — one large church erected, and soon to be finished in good style, upon the expense of a single individual [Louis Campau], who commenced business a few years ago by a small traffic with the Indians. Such is the encouragement to western pioneers! The village plat is upon an irregular plain, some eight to a hundred rods, to rising bluffs, from the base and sides of which some of the most pure, crystal-like fountains of water burst out in boiling springs, pouring forth streams that murmur over their pebbly bottoms, at once a delight to the eye, and an invaluable luxury to the thirsty palate.

It is from this point, too, that you can see in the distance the evergreen tops of the lofty pine, waving in majesty above the sturdy oak, the beech and maple, presenting to the eye a wild, undulating plain, with its thousand charms. Such are the location, the beauties and advantages of this youthful town. The citizens are of the most intelligent, enterprising and industrious character. Their buildings are large, tasty and handsomely furnished — the

GRAND RIVER TIMES.

GRAND RIVER TIMES,
Printed and published every Saturday Morning at the Rapids of Grand River, Kent County, Michigan.
BY GEORGE W. PATTISON,
EDITOR AND PROPRIETOR.

TERMS—Two dollars and fifty cents per annum in advance, three dollars at the end of six months, or four dollars at the end of the year. Subscribers paying within thirty days from the time of subscribing will be considered in advance.

VILLAGE Subscribers, having their papers left at their door, will be charged fifty cents in addition with the above prices.

ADVERTISING—For twelve lines or less, three insertions, One Dollar; and twenty-five cents for every additional insertion. Longer advertisements charged in proportion. A liberal discount made to those who advertise by the year.

No paper discontinued until all arrearages are paid, unless at the option of the publisher.

FANCY, JOB, AND BOOK PRINTING, done with neatness and dispatch at this office.

GRAND RIVER TIMES.

BY GEORGE W. PATTISON.   "WESTWARD THE STAR OF EMPIRE TAKES ITS WAY."   EDITOR AND PROPRIETOR.

VOLUME I.   GRAND RAPIDS, TUESDAY, APRIL 18, 1837.   NUMBER 1.

POETRY.

For The Grand River Times.
FAREWELL.

Farewell to the land of my birth,
Sweet home of my father's shrine.
I'm destined to wander the earth,
And never more gaze upon thee.

The son of my youth now I've met,
As brightness o'ercast with a cloud,
Hopes' laurels are withered and wet,
And trampled upon by the crowd.

Ye friends whom I love now adieu,
May blessings your footsteps attend,
Yes, wherever I own my hope for a
I hold by the name of a friend.

Fond land of my fathers farewell!
Tho' when they roll swift from the door,
Where I wander, alas! who can tell
I go, but return never more.   D. S.

GENIUS OF NIAGARA.

BY REV. J. C. LORD.

Proud Demon of the waters! Thou
Around whose stern and stormy brow
Circles the Rainbow's varied gem,
The Vapor Spirit's diadem;
While rushing headlong at thy feet,
The everlasting Thunders meet!

Thron'd on the mists, around thy form
Is dashing an eternal storm
...

MISCELLANY.

From the New York Mirror.
THE NOVICE, OR THE CONVENT DEMON.

BY JESSE HONE.

The convent of Frauenlob was one of the most deliciously situated in the countries of the Rhine; and its domain was so rich that it was for several centuries the object of contention between two...

---

clatter of mallet and chisel — the clink of hammers — the many newly raised and recently covered frames — and the few skeleton boats upon the wharves of the river, speak loudly for the enterprise of the place! Mechanics of all kinds find abundance of employ, and reap a rich reward for their labor. Village property advances in value, and the prospect of wealth is alike flattering to all! What the result of such advantages and prospects will be, time alone must determine.

. . . This will soon be a bright star in the constellation of western villages.

▲ The inaugural edition of Grand Rapids' first newspaper, the *Grand River Times,* was published on April 18, 1837. [GRPL, Newspaper Collection]

◄ *Grand River Times,* April 18, 1837, p. 2.

◄ John W. Pierce (left) operated a book store (below) from 1836 to 1844 at the site of today's Vandenberg Plaza. [Franklin Everett, *Memorials of the Grand River Valley,* p. 51B; Albert Baxter, *History of the City of Grand Rapids,* p. 762]

The Boom Goes Bust

For a time, it seemed that the national boom in public land sales that was powering Grand Rapids' growth would go on forever. Then, as quickly as it seemed to have begun, it was over.

What triggered the inflationary spiral was President Andrew Jackson's decision in 1832 to withdraw government funds from the Bank of the United States and deposit them in selected state banks — called "pet" banks by Jackson's enemies. But removing the fiscal restraints that the national bank had exerted on the economy brought about a tenfold increase in the value of government lands being offered

for sale and ushered in a period of wild speculation.

In 1836, with credit vastly overextended, hard currency in short supply, and most of the payments for public land being made in the form of unsecured notes issued by local banks of questionable stability, Jackson acted to curb the runaway inflation by issuing the "specie circular." Requiring federal agents to "receive in payment of the public lands nothing except what is directed by the existing laws: gold and silver, and in the proper cases, Virginia land scrip," the circular greatly reduced the funds available to buy western land. The result was

the Panic of 1837 — a sharp depression accompanied by a steep decline in public land sales and the collapse of many small western banks.

Included among the victims of the "specie circular" were many in Grand Rapids who had invested heavily and incurred large debts in anticipation of increasingly inflated prices. One such man was soon-to-be-married Jefferson Morrison who had run up a remarkable debt for a lot and a house. Writing in 1878, author and teacher Franklin Everett recalled Morrison's plight, and that of others who shared his speculative zeal.

In 1836, Jefferson Morrison, having been successful in business, having been elected Judge of Probate, and, more than all, being about to get married — built him a house. He ever afterwards, with tears of humble penitence, called it "Morrison's Folly." Everything was high, but he must have a fine house; so a house he built; finished it in style, and seriously embarrassed himself by so doing; run himself in debt $5,000. This house was near the junction of Monroe and Ottawa streets, where now stands a block of stores. To show the change in the fancy value of real estate: he sold that house to Mr. Campau for $6,000, and took his pay in lots at $1,500 each; and which, in the crash that followed, he could hardly sell for $150. This same house, as good as new, was afterwards bought by Capt. Gunnison for $700. Time did not work a greater change in the valuation of that property, than it did in the other real estate.

◄ Franklin Everett, *Memorials of the Grand River Valley*, p. 11.

▲ This fine house was "Jefferson Morrison's Folly." [GRPL, Thomas W. Porter Collection]

Jefferson Morrison had ► a successful business career as a land speculator and storekeeper and was also Kent County's first probate judge. [GRPL, Photo Collection]

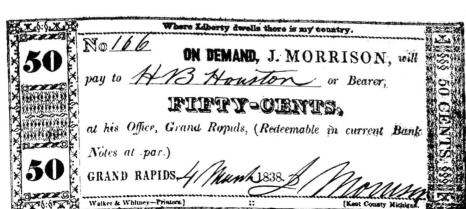

◄ At the depths of the depression that began in 1837, Jefferson Morrison issued his own currency. [Albert Baxter, *History of the City of Grand Rapids*, p. 671]

An Early Flood

▲ Lovell Moore and his family were stranded on the West Side during the flood of 1838. [GRPL, James Keeney Collection]

Frank Little was another observer of Grand Rapids' early development. He and his family stopped for a time in Grand Rapids in March 1838, but even though they had ties to Grand Rapids through Lovell Moore, they soon moved on to Kalamazoo. However, Frank Little returned to live in Grand Rapids on two subsequent occasions, and later, when Albert Baxter was compiling his *History of the City of Grand Rapids,* Little offered the following recollection of an early flood that left the steamboat *Stevens T. Mason* [named for the state's first governor] high and dry, several hundred feet from the river channel it normally traversed.

Our family — father, mother, sister, a younger brother and myself — were residents of Grand Rapids in the summer of 1838. My first personal acquaintance with the place dates from the first of March, 1838. I was then an inexperienced lad of fourteen and a half years. I was impressed with the magnitude and grandeur of the river, particularly the falls or rapids. The village swarmed with Indians who were spearing sturgeon in the river. We arrived just as a notable ice gorge — memorable in history, that commenced at the lower island and backing up rapidly, had submerged the whole town seemingly, save the elevation known as Prospect Hill — had broken through and the flood of waters subsided. All that portion then known as Kent was literally jammed and crammed full of immense icebergs. Judge Almy's house on the river bank, a short distance above the present site of Sweet's Hotel [today's Amway Grand Plaza], was nearly all under water.

My uncle, Lovell Moore, and family then occupied the Mission house on the west side, and it was a number of days before we could safely cross the river to visit them. Mr. [Alanson] Cramton took us over in a canoe, although the mountains of ice made it very difficult to get access to the channel.

The *Stevens T. Mason,* a steamboat that had been running on the river the previous summer, was jammed from its moorings by the ice and flood and driven inland up the valley of a small creek to a point well toward Dr. Platt's early residence, corner of Fulton and Division streets. The waters subsiding left the boat stranded high and dry, a long distance from the river. Capt. Short, and his son-in-law Jennings, in the spring of 1838, spent a number of weeks getting the boat back again into the river, a work that I viewed with much boyish interest and curiosity, at short intervals, until it was accomplished.

▲ Albert Baxter, *History of the City of Grand Rapids,* pp. 89-90.

Newspaper ads show steamboat ▶ passenger and freight service and other goods and services available at Grand Rapids in the 1840s. [*Grand River Eagle,* May 7, 1845, p. 3]

Lucius Lyon — Tireless Promoter

Despite the economic distress of the times, Grand Rapids entrepreneurs strove mightily to turn dreams into realities. One of those men was Lucius Lyon. Originally a government surveyor who came to Grand Rapids in 1831, Lyon saw great promise in the area and decided to stay, casting his lot with the Proprietors of Kent and speculating in downtown property.

Not long after settling in Grand Rapids, Lyon was appointed to serve as a territorial delegate to Congress and was later a delegate to the Michigan constitutional convention. When Michigan became a state, the legislature named him to the U.S. Senate. Election to the House of Representatives followed, and in 1846, when his two-year term was up, he was appointed surveyor-general for Michigan, Ohio, and Indiana, a position he still held at the time of his death.

In 1840, Lyon embarked on a project to extract salt — a necessary product in those days for preserving and seasoning food — from salt-water beneath the Grand River. Needing money for his well drilling, as well as customers for his salt and buyers for his town lots, Lyon seldom missed an opportunity to promote the Grand Rapids area. His letters to family and friends in the East were unstinting in their praise of the West Michigan business climate, and optimism about his own ventures, particularly the ill-fated salt well, persisted to the last.

Lucius Lyon never struck it rich.

Even though he secured significant state support, he finally gave up on the salt well, after three years' work and losses of more than $20,000 — a sum equivalent to 20 times that amount in modern dollars. The drillers struck plenty of brine, but costs were high, the water's saline content was low, and the walls of the well were unstable.

In 1851, two decades after he arrived in Grand Rapids, Lucius Lyon died at the age of 51 without ever realizing the riches he fervently believed the West offered to an ambitious young man. In terms of his contributions to community and country, however, he was a great success.

To Lucretia Lyon, May 5, 1838.

Grand Rapids [is] the county seat of Kent county, on the Grand river, about 50 miles below Lyons. The first house was built there about four years ago, and it now contains a population of about 1,200 persons, or is about one-third as large as Burlington [Vermont] and within ten years it will unquestionably be larger than Burlington ever can be. I am one of the principal proprietors of the town.... The society is very good and is daily improving. A branch of the University of State has lately been located there with a department in it for the education of young ladies in the higher branches.... There is a society of Roman Catholics there and a church erected for them, but that only makes an Episcopal church more desirable.

Yours ever,
Lucius Lyon

[Lyon was engaging in hyperbole or wishful thinking when he spoke of a university. There was no such institution in Grand Rapids, nor would there be a state college or university in the city for another 125 years.]

To James Gordon Bennet, Aug. 20, 1842.

In the last number of your paper received here I see you advise the poor immigrants who are returning to Europe because they can get no work in New York to go to the west.... This is excellent advice both to those who have money and to those who have none; because all can get plenty of work here and fair wages which will enable them in a short time to purchase small farms whether they have money when they arrive here or not. Many of the most prosperous and independent farmers of this country came here less than six years ago without a dollar in their pockets and now they have land, cattle, horses, sheep and hogs in abundance, and some of them, by the labor of themselves and family alone produce from 500 to 2,000 bushels of wheat for sale every year, and hardly any one less than 400 bushels, besides a large quantity of other grains. It would do your heart good to see the prosperity of these industrious immigrants who came here penniless and are now on the road to wealth.

To C.H. Carroll, Jan. 7, 1840.

I believe that good salt water may be obtained by boring deep enough, at almost any point on Grand river, as well as at the salt springs; and if you will send on to me or to Judge Almy one-half the necessary money I will furnish the other half immediately and we will try the experiment and see if salt cannot be procured and manufactured at this place. It will not cost over $4,000 or $5,000 to sink a well on the rapids to the depth of 700 feet.

◄ "Letters of Lucius Lyon," *Michigan Pioneer and Historical Collections*, Vol. 27, 1897, pp. 454, 557, 529.

▲ Lucius Lyon dreamed of a large salt works when he began drilling his well in 1840. [*Harper's New Monthly Magazine*, September, 1857, p. 446]

▲ From 1831 until his death 20 years later, Lucius Lyon was a tireless promoter of Grand Rapids and West Michigan. [GRPL, Photo Collection]

To Asa Lyon, Vermont, May 12, 1841.

Truman H. Lyon removed last month to Grand Rapids where he now keeps the public house called the Exchange.... My men began the well in January, 1840, and have now got down to the depth of 550 feet, or within 50 feet of the level of the ocean. They have been working night and day and have drilled the whole distance through lime rock, sandstone, plaster or gypsum and clay slate. They will probably go to the depth of 700 feet before they stop, though they have got salt water now stronger than I expected to obtain when I began, and so strong that if it should prove to be sufficiently abundant salt can be manufactured from it with a good profit. From present appearances it is probable that salt enough will be manufactured on the Grand River within five or six years, or as soon as the requisite number of wells can be sunk, to supply all the people living around Lake Michigan, whether in this State, Indiana, Illinois or the Territory of Wisconsin, say about 350,000 persons, who, if they consume an average of half a bushel each will require and in fact do now require 175,000 bushels annually.

To Douglas Houghton [State Surveyor], Sept. 12, 1842.

We are now down to the State salt well 770 feet and are striking more water, but the strength of this water we do not know.... Since the last water was struck, the gas rising up out of the gum has been far more abundant than before. The bubbles come up now for an hour together sometimes, as big as peas and even as large as bird's eggs, when before, you recollect, they were not larger than a pin head.

To Douglas Houghton, June 11, 1843.

The State salt well is now the depth of 870 feet, which is 32 feet deeper than it was on March 31. To cover my actual expenses incurred in sinking this last 32 feet I must receive in awards the price of $26 per foot; the next 30 feet will probably cost about $32 per foot if we meet with no accidents. Everything is in good order and works well now, but the depth of the well is so great that our pumps are very slow.

To Douglas Houghton, July 30, 1843.

The State salt well has become hopelessly obstructed. The only way to remedy it would be to begin back at the top of the rock and rim it out large enough to put in a sheath tube down to and below where the well crumbles and caves in.

▲ "Letters of Lucius Lyon," *Michigan Pioneer and Historical Collections,* vol. 27, 1897, pp. 542-43, 557-58, 561.

▲ Salt water from brine wells was evaporated in wicker baskets to produce salt. [*Harper's New Monthly Magazine,* September, 1857, p. 448]

When currency was scarce, ▶ merchants like Lucius Lyon resorted to barter to keep their businesses afloat. [GRPL, Restricted Materials Collection]

Come to Grand Rapids

When Lucius Lyon turned away from his entrepreneurial adventures to resume his career as a surveyor, others continued the work of promoting Grand Rapids. In 1845, a group of local businessmen headed by John Almy and E.B. Bostwick produced a promotional pamphlet for distribution in the East. A copy of the pamphlet has survived in the collection of the Public Museum of Grand Rapids. Although claiming to promote the entire state, it is clear the small book's primary purpose was to direct attention to West Michigan.

There are fifteen stores, three flour mills, two saw mills, two furnaces and machine shops, two pail factories, two tanneries, one woolen factory, one sash factory, salt works, plaster mill, two hatters, three shoe shops, three tailors, one tin and coppersmith, one saddler, several blacksmiths, three public houses, two printing offices, four churches, one incorporated academy, and four physicians.

One important fact for the consideration of the emigrant, is that lumber on Grand River can be obtained at five dollars per 1000 feet. About fifteen million feet of lumber was manufactured on Grand River for export trade during the last season, and sent to Milwaukee and Chicago.

From Grand Rapids to the City of New York, there is an uninterrupted water communication, and merchandise was shipped from New York to the mouth of Grand River at sixty-five cents per 100 lbs., during the past season.

The water power at this place is created by taking the water out at the head of the Rapids and running a canal parallel with the bank of the river, at a sufficient distance from the river to place building, between it and the river.

The canal is 80 feet wide, and five feet deep, making a water power of greater magnitude than any other in the State. Grand Rapids must soon be a large manufacturing town.

We call the attention of persons about to seek new homes in the West, to the facts set forth in this communication, and caution them against interested persons who may wish to direct them elsewhere.

J. ALMY,
E.B. BOSTWICK

▲ *Emigrant's Handbook,* 1845, Grand Rapids Public Museum, pp. 1-4.

▲ Dr. Charles Shepard (above) built this stone home and office (below) on Ottawa Avenue in 1843. [Franklin Everett, *Memorials of the Grand River Valley,* p. 63B; George E. Fitch, *Old Grand Rapids,* p. 20]

▲ The National Hotel (above) was built in 1835 and the Eagle Hotel (left) opened in 1834. [GRPL, Thomas W. Porter Collection and George E. Fitch Collection]

A Story-and-a-Half Village

By the late 1840s, Grand Rapids, like the rest of the nation, was pulling itself out of the depression. In place of the speculative fever that had gripped the entire Midwest ten years earlier, people were now engaged in steady, if unspectacular, business ventures. The real estate boom had ended — lot prices came nowhere near those of the previous decade, and sales were much slower — but the worst was past, and confidence slowly returned.

In 1846, Professor Franklin Everett arrived in the village to take up his post as principal of the Grand Rapids Academy. A careful observer with a fine facility for recall, Everett later recorded his impressions of Grand Rapids as it was in the years nearing the century's mid-point. Those recollections were published in 1874 as *Memorials of the Grand River Valley*, the first formal history of the region.

We will now look at Grand Rapids as it appeared in 1846; then, as now, the chief town in the Grand River Valley.

It was emphatically "a story and a-half village," with a population of 1,500, mostly on about fifty acres of land. Taking the region enclosed by Fulton street on the south, Division street on the east, Bridge street on the north, and the river on the west, we have all that had the appearance of a village. The buildings, with very few exceptions, were of wood; the residences and a good part of the business places, a story and a-half high. The buildings, whether for residences or business, were simple structures, for use and not display. The exceptional buildings were five stone stores and two brick ones on Monroe street, two stone blocks or double stores up Canal street, near Bronson; two stone stores at the foot of Monroe street, where now is "Campau Place." To these we may add the wing of the Rathbun House, the residence of Mr. Turner on the west side of the river; and the Almy House, on Bronson street. There were, besides, seven small brick or stone houses.

The churches were the Congregational, the Methodist, the Episcopal, and the Dutch Reformed. The Congregational was the only one that had the air of a church. It stood at the head of Monroe street, between that and Fulton street. It was a pretty, modest structure, in good architectural proportions. The Episcopal church stood at the corner of Division and Bronson streets. It was a mere temporary concern, until the society could afford to build. It afterward did service for the Baptists in the same way. The Methodist church was a better building, but still of modest size. It stood where their present building stands. The Dutch Reformed church was an unfinished stone building, afterward sold for business purposes.

The Catholics had no church edifice. They had a house which was fitted up for a chapel at the corner of Monroe and Ottawa streets. In 1849 they built a stone church on the adjoining lot.

The Baptists had an organization, but no place of worship. They held their meetings in the temporary court house on the common.

The streets were none of them graded, and there were sidewalks only on Division, Monroe and Canal streets; those, with the exception of a part of Monroe street, simply a track the width of two planks.

As regards the appearance of the village and its surroundings, there was a primitive air to the whole. Enterprise had been checked, and had not recovered from the shock. Capital was woefully lacking. The streets of the village were simply horrible. West of Division street and north of Fountain street, was a fine musical frog-pond, and between that and Canal street was the beautiful "Prospect Hill."

Trade was a round-about concern. The mercantile interest was represented by about a dozen general merchants, one drug store, two hardware stores, and eight or ten groceries. The stocks of goods were small — from $3,000 to $5,000 — generally bought and sold on credit. Two or three combined lumbering with their mercantile business. Others did business as they could; getting some cash; trusting extensively, especially those who were carrying on such business as required the employment of help. As most of the business men had little capital, they were obliged to make arrangements with the merchants to give orders on their stores, themselves to pay when they got their returns. Of course, to do business in this way, goods must be sold at a high figure. "One per cent," was the ruling profit; that is, one cent profit for one cent investment.

▲Franklin Everett, *Memorials of the Grand River Valley*, pp. 377-81.

◄ William Haldane was one of several furniture makers doing business in Grand Rapids during the 1840s. [*Grand Rapids Weekly Enquirer*, July 11, 1845, p. 3]

Franklin Everett ►
became Grand Rapids'
resident scholar following
his arrival in 1846.
[GRPL, Photo Collection]

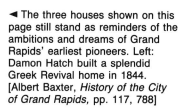

◄ The three houses shown on this page still stand as reminders of the ambitions and dreams of Grand Rapids' earliest pioneers. Left: Damon Hatch built a splendid Greek Revival home in 1844. [Albert Baxter, *History of the City of Grand Rapids,* pp. 117, 788]

▼ Abram Pike's home, built facing Fulton Street in 1845, later became the Grand Rapids Art Gallery. [Franklin Everett, *Memorials of the Grand River Valley,* p. 53B; Albert Baxter, *History of the City of Grand Rapids,* p. 764.]

Truman Lyon built his Grand ► River limestone home next door to Abram Pike's house. [Franklin Everett, *Memorials of the Grand River Valley,* p. 39B; Albert Baxter, *History of the City of Grand Rapids,* p. 765]

◄ Four houses constructed in the late 1830s and 1840s. Clockwise from left: E. Anderson residence, 1846, G.W. Daniel house, 1846; E.H. Turner house, 1846; John Almy house, 1839; [Albert Baxter, *History of the City of Grand Rapids,* pp. 764-65]

◄ Several churches also went up before 1850. St. Andrew's Catholic Church was built in 1849 on the southeast corner of Monroe and Ottawa Avenues. [GRPL, Thomas W. Porter Collection]

▲ Three houses from the 1830s. Top to bottom: Charles Mason house, 1838; "Tanner" Taylor house, 1839; William Haldane residence, 1837. [Albert Baxter, *History of the City of Grand Rapids,* p. 763]

▼ St. Mark's Episcopal Church first occupied a wood frame structure (below left) at the northwest corner of Crescent and Division, before moving into its current quarters (right) at Pearl and Division in 1848. [GRPL, George E. Fitch Collection]

Even Our Hogs Are Civilized

The residents of Grand Rapids found many ways to assure themselves that West Michigan was on its way to an exalted place in the nation. None perhaps was more amusing than Franklin Everett's contention that the civility of an area could be measured by the quality of its hogs. By that standard, the Grand River valley in 1850 had left behind the dark ages of despair and was now poised to enter a new period of development characterized by refinement and culture.

▲ Top: An uncivilized hog. Bottom: A civilized West Michigan hog, proof positive the area was well on its way to taking its place among the more highly developed portions of the planet.

Mr. McKelvy, who more properly belongs to Lyons, brought the first "civilized hogs" into the Grand River Valley. Those, who have seen the old-fashioned, yellow, long-nosed greyhound hogs of Michigan, will appreciate this act of McKelvy. Those, who in former times ate "Western pork," know well the difference between a civilized and a savage hog. The hog, unrefined by culture, is a savage beast; lean as a wolf; one-third nose; a sinister, gaunt, long-eared nuisance. Cultivated, he is the noble Suffolk, with his sleek sides stuffed with juicy pork; or the beautiful Chester, whose mild eyes and glossy sides seem smilingly to say, "eat me." What cannot culture do? 'Tis as useful in man as in the hog. Under culture, the old brutal swine, a byword for slovenly brutishness, is disappearing; yes, has disappeared. When will culture cause to disappear the brutish, superstitious, even unhogly human swine? Alas, it is to be feared that "careful selection" and the knife will never exterminate the old kind, as in America they have done with the hog.

▲ Franklin Everett, *Memorials of the Grand River Valley*, p. 114.

CHAPTER 3

Growing Closer to the Rest of the World

The middle decades of the 19th century ushered in an era of rapid population growth and economic expansion that saw the southern half of Michigan's lower peninsula cleared and cultivated, and the beginnings of timber and mining industries further north. By 1860, railroads connected the western side of the state with Detroit, Jackson, and points east, and newly strung telegraph lines and improved postal service established quicker, closer connections with the eastern seaboard.

Michigan's population growth kept pace with the rest of the nation. By mid-century the national total stood at 23 million, while the state claimed itself home to 400,000. Ten years later, on the eve of the Civil War, the figures stood at 750,000 for the state and 31.5 million for the country.

By 1860, Michigan's residents came from three distinct groups: About 35 percent had been born in Michigan, 45 percent had come west from other states, and 20 percent had immigrated from foreign countries, mostly in northern and western Europe. Those who chose to move to Michigan were attracted by the same opportunities that had appealed to the first generation of settlers: inexpensive, fertile land, and abundant timber and mineral re-

sources. Also among the new residents were businessmen seeking a chance for profitable investments, and professionals — lawyers, doctors, and teachers — who saw promise, not wilderness, written on the maps of Michigan.

Agriculture was the backbone of the state's economy, but by 1860 the small factories operating in several cities foretold Michigan's future industrial might. One key to Michigan's progress was the advent of cross-state railroads that lessened the state's dependence on its rivers and Great Lakes waterways. Although enthusiastic crowds greeting their arrival heralded the coming dominance of railroads, steamboats were still the major cargo and passenger carriers until after the Civil War, and transportation costs kept most people tied throughout their lives to the communities of their birth. Detroit, with a population of 45,000 by 1860, was the focal point of transportation and communication lines, and the site of much of the state's nascent industry. Smaller cities, although linked economically to the state's leading urban area, still reflected their surrounding rural environment. Numbering 8,000 by 1860, Grand Rapids residents had rail and telegraph connections that enabled them to communicate with

all parts of the country and travel to the eastern seaboard in two days. Agriculture and rural interests still dominated the area, but the scent of change was in the air.

> *Although Michigan had come a long way out of the wilderness by 1860, vast areas of the state were still covered by unbroken forests and isolated hamlets.... In spite of improved transportation, the world beyond still seemed strange and remote for many Michiganians. But it was coming closer.*

▲ Willis F. Dunbar and George S. May, *Michigan: A History of the Wolverine State*, p. 328.

Joining the Ranks of Michigan Cities

Grand Rapids' population stood at 2,686 by 1850, and officials chaffed under the restrictions of their village charter. So that they might reorganize as a city, they sought a new charter from the state legislature that would expand village boundaries and allow officials to exercise broader taxation, governing, and legal authority. Their petition defined the proposed city as encompassing sections 19 and 30 of Grand Rapids Township and sections 24 and 25 of Walker Township. Under the proposed charter, all vestiges of township and village government would be replaced by a city government consisting of five wards, governed by a Common Council made up of a mayor and five aldermen.

Compared to the relatively limited authority held by the village trustees, the powers delegated to the newly created Common Council demonstrated Grand Rapids' growing autonomy and influence in West Michigan. Enacted by the Michigan legislature on April 2, 1850, the new Grand Rapids city charter prescribed the procedure for general elections, established a mayor's court to enforce the charter and council ordinances, and set forth the duties and powers of the Common Council, which included responsibility for public safety and health, regulatory control over the sale of liquors and spirits, and authority for public works construction. To finance its efforts, the council had the power to collect poll taxes and property taxes. These and other provisions are spelled out in the following excerpts from the original city charter.

Sec. 14. The common council shall have full power and authority to organize, maintain and regulate the police of the city; to pass all by-laws and ordinances for that purpose, and relative to the duties and powers and fees of the marshal as marshal, and as collector and street commissioner, city surveyor, solicitor, treasurer, clerk and constables or other officers of said city, except as is hereinafter provided; relative to the time and manner of working upon the streets, lanes and alleys of said city; relative to the manner of grading, railing, planking and paving all side walks in said city, and to setting posts and shade trees in all streets, lanes and alleys in said city; relative to the manner of assessing, levying and collecting all highway and other taxes in said city, except as hereinafter provided. And the said common council shall have power to make by-laws and ordinances relative to all nuisances within the limits of said city, and for the abatement of the same, and for the punishment by fine or otherwise of all persons occasioning the same; relative to the cleaning of chimneys and protecting said city from fires; relative to the manner of warning meetings of the freemen of said city; relative to the city watch; relative to the public lights of lamps of said city; relative to the keeping and sale of gunpowder in said city; relative to the restraining of swine, cattle, horses and other description of animals from running at large in the streets, lanes or alleys, and other public places in the city; to regulate and establish one or more pounds for

▲ Market Street south from Monroe in 1857. The entire area was later raised to the level of Monroe. [GRPL, George E. Fitch Collection]

said city; relative to billiard and other tables kept for hire, gain or reward in said city; and also full power and authority to make all such by-laws and ordinances as may be deemed by the common council expedient or necessary for preventing and suppressing all disorderly houses and houses of ill-fame; and also to prohibit the exercise of any unwholesome or dangerous avocation in said city; for the preservation of the salubrity of the waters of the Grand River or other streams within the limits of the said city; relative to the opening of sluices and building all wharves; relative to the filling up all low grounds or lots, covered or partially covered with water; relative to the embankment of the margin of said river within said limits.

◀ *Acts of the Legislature of Michigan*, 1850, pp. 264-67.

◀ Billiard halls were subject to Common Council regulation. [Clarence P. Harnung, *Handbook of Early American Advertising Art*, p. 38]

The Lure of Gold

As the village of Grand Rapids looked forward to becoming the City of Grand Rapids, gold fever struck the community, and some of its most ambitious young men were thinking of leaving for the newly discovered California gold fields. In January 1848, James W. Marshall had discovered a gold nugget in the millrace of John A. Sutter's mill, and when President James K. Polk announced the discovery in December of the same year, the race to California was on. Grand Rapids men, eager for quick riches, gathered to discuss the latest information from California. Most were content simply to talk about going west, but for some the lure was too great, and they hit the California trail.

Among the California-bound was a 12-man group headed by Canton Smith and Edmund Bostwick, both of whom had come to Grand Rapids in 1837. After a short stint working at the Eagle Hotel, Smith had owned and operated the National Hotel since 1840. Bostwick, who had developed "Bostwick's Addition" on the village's eastern border, had the soul of an adventurer. Before the California expedition, he had co-authored a pamphlet urging easterners to migrate to West Michigan, and in 1846 he had joined an exploring party heading north to search for copper in Lake Superior country.

Perhaps it was Bostwick's exploring experience that persuaded Grand Rapids *Eagle* editor A.B. Turner to engage him as a western correspondent and agree to publish his letters chronicling the trip to California. Bostwick's reports came to an abrupt end with his sudden death on the western plains, but those printed in the *Eagle* exemplify both the spirit of hope and the awful hardships that were a part of the westering experience.

▲ Canton Smith (above) and Edmund Bostwick led a group of gold-seekers bound for California. Bostwick died on the journey, but Smith later returned. [GRPL, Photo Collection]

Steamer J.S. McLean,
Missouri River,
May 29, 1850

Mr. Editor, Dear Sir: We left St. Louis on Friday the 24th last, (on board of the above named steamer) at 6 o'clock in the afternoon, and at 8 o'clock made the mouth of the great Missouri river. In passing up I saw many most beautiful and some most magnificent scenes.

●

Just after passing Jefferson, while we were at dinner we were all thrown into pi, (as editors say) by the boat striking a snag and upsetting the table dishes and all. Fortunately I was on the upper side and saw my plate, which was well filled with good things slide into the bosom of my vis-a-vis, a fat Dutchman, who struggled manfully to repel his unbidden guest.

Such a laughable scene you never beheld — a hundred and fifty persons all panic struck and rushing towards the door, stumbling over prostrated chairs, and wading through puddings, pies, tarts and jellies all of which lay in beautiful confusion in the "wreck of matter and the crush of crockery." In many places the river is extensively wide and shallow, and by the quantity of old logs appearing in it, you would think it a stagnant pool, if floating masses of wood were not passing at a rapid rate. It is the most turbid stream you ever beheld, and it is really revolting to think of drinking the water, until it has passed through a filter, though the natives and those who are naturalized get it down and say they like it. It is just about the consistency of good soup and should be taken with a spoon having rather too much material in it to swallow with ease....

It is generally a prairie country though immediately on the river it is heavy timbered. We are the last of the California adventurers, and it is said that at least 80,000 have gone forward.

Yours, Very truly,
E. B. Bostwick.
St. Joseph, May 29.

Camp No. 1, May 31
Dear Editor: Left St. Joseph and came six miles along the Missouri river.... Good camping and fine food for the horses.

Camp No. 4, June 3.
Passed during the day, three graves. A board at the head of one of the graves, stated that J.C. Albert, of Hancock county, Ill., died 27th of May, 1850, aged 29 years. Saw during the day two dead mules, one dead horse and three dead oxen; made about 27 miles.

Note.—The grave of J.C. Albert stands by the roadside, on a beautiful elevation of prairie land, near a clear stream of water. His name, age and death, were cut in handsome letters on a board standing at the head of his grave, and ten or fifteen large elk horns, were laid over it. The imagination can scarcely conceive a more beautiful spot, a more glowing landscape than was here stretched out to view but did he, poor fellow, admire it?

◄ *Grand Rapids Eagle,* June 17, 1850, p. 2.

Camp No. 5, June 4.

Came 20 miles over a broad and beautiful prairie; saw seven dead horses and two dead oxen; passed two new graves; one a child three months old, and the other a man 35 years old; the latter was killed accidentally with a gun; camped on a small stream of good water.

Note.—After camping, up came a wagon from the West with a man and two women, and a man in company on horseback. They had all been as far West as Fort Kearney, 200 miles ahead, and were turning back. The women were rather good looking, and were complaining that they were going back. They said their husbands were too chicken-hearted to go further.

●

Camp No. 10, June 9.

This was rather a gloomy day; passed 17 graves 13 of which were new and the other four bore records of last year, saw four dead oxen and two dead horses; met about 200 Indians mostly on horseback.—It was a hunting or a war party, there being no squaws and children with them. They were quite friendly, and one of them took me in his arms and embraced me, and then begged some tobacco. Passed one large Oregon train with a numerous herd of cattle; saw one California company numbering 16 or 18, most all of whom were sick—they had buried four of their company [on the] 5th, we saw their graves a few miles back. The company had moved but five or six miles from the graves of their friends, and were still resting.—They were a woe-begone looking set.

●

Camp No. 13, June 12.

This day reach Fort Kearney on the Platte river, where we shall rest a day or two....

We are all in good health, have not been obliged to stop one hour for sickness or accident, our horses doing well; and we hope to be able to make a good report at the end of our journey....

It is really a melancholy sight to pass the fresh mound of the last resting place of so many of the human family, remote from home and friends. Their graves mostly occupy little eminences, and can be seen some time before you reach them; they look desolate enough, not being shaded by any thing except the clouds of heaven.

▲ *Grand Rapids Eagle,* July 29, 1850, p. 2.

Death of E. B. Bostwick.

A gloomy shadow spread over our city on Tuesday morning last. The painful intelligence of the death of E. B. Bostwick, came to us by letters from Canton Smith and Henry Cook, members of company of which he was the head. He was attacked with cholera on the 16th June, three days after the date of his last letter to us; from which, however, he partially recovered, and about the 20th was taken with hiccoughs which continued up to the time of his death, the 25th.

The loss of Mr. Bostwick is deeply and univerally regretted in this community. He came here at an early day, and expended a large fortune with a liberal hand in advancing the interests of the Grand River Valley. Public spirited and generous to a fault, as a financier, but to the credit of his heart as a man; foremost in every plan having for its object the prosperity of this section; affable and pleasant in his social intercourse, kind and obliging as a friend, he won and retained the warmest esteem of his fellow citizens.

◄ *Grand Rapids Eagle,* September 19, 1850, p. 2.

◄ The Bostwick-Smith party encountered many other gold-rush parties on their journey west. [J.S. Holliday, *The World Rushed In,* p. 151]

10,000 Chairs for Chicago

Most West Michigan residents avoided the risks of the trip to California and confined their contact with the gold fields to newspaper accounts and irregular letters home from adventurers like Smith and Bostwick. Marriages, births, and deaths, rather than gold discoveries, were the guideposts in their lives, and events at home more than kept them busy. There were school districts to organize and new schools to build, church congregations to gather whenever a sufficient number of believers could be found, and shops and factories to open and close in response to changing community needs.

Unlike the earliest cabinetmakers in Grand Rapids, who fashioned their wares by hand, entrepreneurs Ebenezer M. Ball and William T. Powers were probably the first to open a furniture factory and produce their goods on an assembly line. Ball had come to the city in 1845 at the suggestion of his uncle, John Ball, after a dismal career as a schoolmaster in Indiana. Seeking some kind of business opportunity, he offered his services to Powers, a distant relative who operated a small furniture-making shop.

Four years later, with the money Powers had managed to save, supplemented by a loan from Ball's father in New Hampshire, the two men formed a partnership and took steps to fulfill their dreams of a larger operation with greater profits. Each year, as part of his loan agreement, Ball reported to his father on events in Grand Rapids and the condition of the Powers and Ball venture.

The first letter, written in November 1849, is full of optimism, although Ball's experience as a teacher did not prepare him for all the work associated with the enterprise. At first the partners managed a small profit, but bad luck in the form of a major flood, and a temporary dissolution of the partnership from 1855 to 1857, kept them from the great prosperity they envisioned.

Powers and Ball continued their business association until after the Civil War, when Powers sold all his furniture and lumber holdings, and devoted his energy to constructing the West Side Water Canal and later the Powers Opera House. In 1885 he purchased the Michigan Iron Works, and three years later, he helped organize an electric lighting company that made Grand Rapids the first city in the state to be lit by electricity. William T. Powers died on June 17, 1909.

Ebenezer Morris Ball remained in the hardware and furniture retail business. He lived in Grand Rapids until his death in 1891 at the age of 74.

November 29, 1849

Dear Parents

William Powers has been selling more than the usual quantity of furniture this fall which had reduced his stock quite low. What he had on hand at the time of the inventory amounted to about $350 at retail price. The stock of lumber on hand, and tools and machinery employed in the business were priced at about $400, making in all $750 which you can see is considerable less than he estimated it at the time we first talked of going into partnership, which is all the better for me. He also allowed me to share the profits of a lot of lumber he had collected to send over the lake, on which we got about $108 of all expenses.

After I had been with him about a week he went over the lake with his lumber leaving me drove to death with business, half a dozen men to look after and no experience in the business which has made it very hard, but I got along much better than I anticipated.

June 25, 1850

Dear Parents

We have been so much troubled for want of a water power and good shop that we have thought best to buy a water power and lot and have contacted for one which is one of the best on the Canal and are to pay one thousand and fifty dollars, one third on receiving a deed which will probably be in about a year, one third in about two years and the remainder in three years. We shall try and get a shop up this fall. It is running in debt more than we wished but we could rent no good shop and were compelled to secure a water power or do business to a great disadvantage. We have pretty strong competition and shall have to make strong exertions and manage economically to carry through what we have undertaken but I think it can be done if we have no very bad luck.

March 22, 1852

Dear Parents

The lower part of the town has been so under water that people have had to leave their houses and seek higher ground. The water breaking over the banks of the canal and sweeping through the streets like a mill tail. It has been an anxious week with us. I assure you there being great danger of losing not only our logs and lumber but the water power, but we are coming out a great deal better than the most sanguine anticipated. We have lost no lumber of any amount and not many logs. The bank of the canal next to the river is still whole and although the water has washed the inside bank badly yet it can be

▼ Powers and Ball advertised a full line of household furniture. [*Grand Rapids Enquirer*, August 3, 1853, p. 2]

POWERS & BALL,

Manufacturers & Dealers in Furniture, Wholesale and Retail, Foot of Monroe street.

BUREAUS, Bedsteads, Tables, Stands, Chairs, Sofas, Ottomans, Rockers, Cribs, Cradles, Looking-glasses and Furniture of every description ; also, Hair, Cotton and Straw Mattrasses, Coffins, &c., &c., constantly on hand or made to order on short notice.   [1y604]

soon repaired and we think in about a week we shall be running again. You may form some idea of the flood when I tell you that it rose 17 feet from low water mark and as you know the country is quite level, it covered an immense surface. We had heavy lumber contracts and probably more at stake than any one else. The cause of the flood was the large body of snow being carried off by a warm and heavy rain.

March 8, 1857
Dear Parents
When we get all the machinery put up that we intend to [we] shall be able to supply not only this market, but furnish considerable for the market over the lake. We have just completed our machinery for making Winsor [sic] (or wooden) chairs which works finely, so that we can almost, as it were, throw in whole trees in the

hopper and grind our chairs ready for use. We have contracted to furnish one firm in Chicago with 10,000 the coming season. Our home trade has been very dull this winter and rather hard times for money, but we have got along so far very well. We have plenty to do and a chance to enlarge it indefinitely if we find the means. We have some lumber contracts to fill at Chicago and Milwaukee and shall ship a cargo to Albany during the coming season if we have good luck. So you see we have a nice little summers work before us to manufacture furniture for this market, collect together and ship over the lake about 150 thousand feet of lumber and about the same quantity east, beside the 10,000 chairs for Chicago market.

▲ E.M. Ball Collection, Grand Rapids Public Museum.

▲ William T. Powers often managed to secure more business than his partner, Ebenezer Ball, wanted. [GRPL, Photo Collection]

Steaming Down the Grand

Although Grand Rapids had started out as an isolated frontier outpost, by the mid-1850s it was served by several steamboats daily. Trips on Grand River steamboats between the rapids and the mouth of the river at Grand Haven were leisurely daylong cruises. Pas-

sengers boarded in the morning and prepared themselves for a series of stops as the boat made its way down river. The travelers were a varied lot, and the slow pace provided ample time to talk with friends and make new acquaintances.

The following account tells of a

day 11-year-old Charles Belknap spent aboard a Grand River steamboat as it traveled downstream to Grand Haven in 1857.

One spring morning in 1857, drifting away from the pier at the yellow warehouse, the steamer *Olive Branch* set forth to the Haven with a cargo of package freight, a top deck loaded with passengers, and Capt. Robert Collins, Pilot Tom Robbins and Cook Jim Dailey, with a full crew of husky Irishmen. We were soon winding between banks heavily wooded and bordered with wild fruit trees in full bloom — plum, cherry, crab and thornapple — all festooned with wild grape vines.

At the dock of Hovey's plaster mills a hundred barrels of land plaster were taken aboard. Then angling across the river we were against the bank at Grandville.... Here we left

package freight and took aboard a few passengers.

At Haire's landing we gathered up a lot of maple sugar in tubs and a pile of slabwood for the boilers.

At the mouth of Sand Creek, where there had once been an Indian village, we added a couple going to the Haven to be married. Coming down from the upper road they crossed the creek on a tree footbridge and the young lady had taken a tumble and had to swim out.

They built a fire to dry out as well as to signal the boat. Once aboard the women passengers fitted the young woman out in dry clothing and the couple were seated at the captain's table for the noon meal. The bride-to-be was

game all right. She had come west to teach the Sand Creek school, but the first month she found a better job and the log shack's pupils had a vacation.

At the Blendon hills two families of Hollanders all wearing wooden shoes, were met by a man with a yoke of cattle. Their goods were piled high on his cart and the boat tooted a goodby as they trailed away into the forest.

At Eastmanville Mr. Eastman came aboard with a party of ladies and gentlemen. The ladies were carrying many things made by the Indian women of the vicinity, beaded belts and beaded money bags; some had traveling bags of smoke-tanned buckskin ornamented with native dyes and woven designs of porcupine quills. The freight taken here consisted of many packs of ax helves [handles] shaved out of white hickory.

The long dining table was crowded at the evening meal. Capt. Collins toasted the bride-to-be who was garbed in the best that several "carpet sacks" afforded.

At the landing at Bass river Mr. Eastman took charge of the dining cabin and with song and story the *Olive Branch* rounded Battle point, paddling past great river bottom meadows of cattail and wild rice, from which flocks of wild duck came swirling overhead.

There were many inviting channels and waterways and the pilot needed to be well informed.

As we neared the Haven the sun in the golden west disclosed smoking mill stacks, forests of ship masts and drifting sand dunes. Beyond was a great sea of white caps. This was the end of a "perfect day."

▲ Charles E. Belknap, *The Yester-days of Grand Rapids,* pp. 56-58.

▲ The *J.F. Porter* was built in 1852. [GRPL, Godfrey Anderson Collection]

The *Daniel Ball* and the *L.G.* ► *Mason* were two of five steamboats put in service on the Grand River between 1860 and 1870. [*Grand Rapids City Directory,* 1865, p. 140]

The Hummingbird *Blows Up*

Those "perfect days" along the Grand River were all too often marred by equipment failures and accidents. One long-remembered episode was the time the steam boiler on the *Hummingbird* exploded. C.C. Comstock was on board that day and described the experience in his memoirs.

After coming to Grand Rapids, in Aug. 1854, I took a boat for Grand Haven and Chicago. On my return Sept. 2nd, I was on a small steamboat above Grandville, about 7 miles below the City, when the boiler exploded. The Wheelman had moved the weight so as to hold down the safety valve and secure a greater pressure of steam, far beyond what was intended to be carried. The wheel house was all blown away and the wheelman was thrown several hundreds of feet; his clothes were all blown off, except his boots, and it required an hour or more to find his body. I had been sitting for some hours, leaning against the wheel house, and left it not more than a quarter of an hour before the explosion. I had gone down upon the lower deck, and was sitting on the guard rail, nearest the boiler, in conversation with Damon Hatch and Thomas Greenly, both of G.R. We were all blown into the river. The water was about ten feet deep. I went to the bottom, came up and swam as I never had before, and reached up to get hold of the boat. I lacked about two inches of securing a hold. I went to the bottom again, and thinking that my only chance was to come up and swim to the front of the boat, and get hold of a strip of wood there, which I did, and drew myself out of the water. A man on the back of the boat had helped Hatch out of the water. I had on a new hat which I never saw again. My hair down to my scalp was filled with cinders, dirt and ashes, but I was not injured. The boat belonged to and was run by Daniel Ball. I went back to the boat the next day, and found it upon a sand bar, stripped of its machinery and all that was worth taking away. The boat was never repaired, and I saw what remained of it 15 or more yrs, after, out upon the marsh near Grand Haven.

▲ Charles C. Comstock, "Early Experiences and Personal Recollections," Grand Rapids Public Library, p. 8.

▲ Charles C. Comstock (top) and Damon Hatch (below) were on board when the *Hummingbird*'s boiler blew up. [GRPL, Russell Family Collection; GRPL, Photo Collection]

◄ Like this artist's depiction of another steamboat disaster, the *Hummingbird*'s explosion sent passengers and cargo flying in all directions. [Lucius Beebe, and Charles Clegg, *The American West*, p. 36]

"A Few Hours' Distance From Everywhere"

It is difficult to overemphasize the two dramatic changes that occurred in Grand Rapids in 1858. On July 10, the first railroad came to town, followed on September 14 by the telegraph. News that had taken days to reach West Michigan now arrived in hours, if not minutes. Residents who wished to journey east could catch one of two daily trains and be in New York two or three days later, rather than the nearly two weeks the journey had previously taken. No wonder the *Grand Rapids Enquirer and Herald* wrote on July 10, 1858,

> Hurrah! Hurrah!! Hurrah!!
> They are coming. The first
> "Grand Entree" into this city,

since the spring of 1836 [when the first steamboat arrived] will take place at 4 o'clock this afternoon.

In anticipation of the momentous event, Grand Rapids Mayor Gilbert M. McCray called a citizens' meeting on July 8 and proposed that a celebration be organized to mark the occasion. After some discussion, a committee was appointed to "ascertain the best method upon which to celebrate the event." While the committee was deliberating, *Grand Rapids Daily Eagle* editor Aaron B. Turner took matters into his own hands, proposing an impromptu greeting for the first train to reach the city.

On July 12, Turner's newspaper reported the train's arrival. His rival, the *Grand Rapids Enquirer and Herald,* published the railroad's first daily timetable. Modern readers will be interested to note the $4.75 fare from Grand Rapids to Detroit.

Less fanfare accompanied the completion of the telegraph line that connected Grand Rapids and Detroit. Wire had been stretched from pole to pole following the train route, so that station masters could keep track of trains headed in each direction and prevent collisions. When the last wire was strung, mayors of Michigan's first and second cities, conscious of the importance of the moment, exchanged congratulatory messages over the wire.

Prepare to Shout!

We now have it from undoubted authority that the passenger train of the Detroit and Milwaukee Railway will make her first run through, from Detroit to the depot in this city, tomorrow—arriving at about four o-clock!

We propose that our citizens resolve themselves into a committee of the whole; and with bands of music, and the big guns of the artillery companies, be on the ground to greet the arrival with demonstrations of joy.

We should be glad to see all our military, fire and other companies, out on this occasion. Why not?

When the iron horse snorts his passage through the Coldbrook bluff, let us greet him with guns, music, and the exultant shouts of thousands of our people!

Citizens! What say ye?

▲ *Grand Rapids Daily Eagle,* July 9, 1858, p. 3.

◄ German traveler Franz Holzlhubber captured on canvas in 1857 the first Detroit, Grand Haven, and Milwaukee train. [State Historical Society of Wisconsin]

With this day commences a new era in the city of Grand Rapids. We are now connected by railway with all the great cities of the east and west, and bound by railroad ties to nearly all the Atlantic States. This morning, for the first time, have the people of the Valley City had the privilege of leaving their home by another public conveyance than that of our river steamers and the old-fashioned stage coaches. We are now but a few hours' distance from everywhere. Let us shout over the triumph.

▲ *Grand Rapids Daily Eagle,* July 12, 1858, p. 3.

The Detroit, Grand Haven, ► and Milwaukee depot is in the center of this photo taken from Belknap Hill in 1865. [GRPL, George E. Fitch Collection]

◄ Grand Rapids was served by two daily passenger trains in 1858. [*Grand Rapids Enquirer and Herald*, July 13, 1858, p. 2]

Telegraphs Exchanged by Detroit and Grand Rapids Mayors

Grand Rapids, September 14, 1858.
To the Honorable, the Mayor of the City of Detroit:

The Valley City shakes hands with the city of Detroit, and, while nations rejoice at the successful laying of the Atlantic Telegraph, we may be permitted to congratulate each other that distant parts are joined together by that mysterious agent which makes all nations one and mankind a brotherhood. Peace and prosperity to the city of Detroit, and may her noble-hearted citizens ever enjoy the blessings of civil and religious liberty.

G.M. McCray,
Mayor of the City of Grand Rapids

Detroit, September 14, 1858.
To the Honorable, the Mayor of the City of Grand Rapids:

The city of Detroit heartily responds to the friendly sentiment of the Valley City, and rejoices with her that science and art are combining to diffuse the blessings of civil and religious liberty throughout the world, and are by the railroads and telegraph bringing us into closer union with our sister cities, identifying our interests and cementing our friendships.

John Patton,
Mayor of the City of Detroit.

▲ Albert Baxter, *History of the City of Grand Rapids*, pp. 123-24.

◄ Mayor G.M. McCray sent Grand Rapids' first telegram. [GRPL, Photo Collection]

Simeon Baldwin and the Bear

Although their city numbered more than 5,000, and they had direct transportation and communication links with other parts of the nation, Grand Rapids residents were occasionally reminded that not far beyond their back doors was a natural environment unchanged from that of earlier decades.

Simeon Baldwin ran a brickyard in a wooded, scrub oak area on the eastern edge of the city where Lake Drive and Fulton Street now meet. There, while preparing clay for his kiln one day, he had the uneasy feeling that someone was standing behind him and quietly surveying his work. Turning slowly, he found himself face to face with a big black bear — but let Charles Belknap tell the story.

[The bear] gave a sort of salute, raising on his hind legs and making the high sign with his paws, saying "woof," which translated meant "howdy." He only wanted to be a good neighbor, but Baldwin misunderstood "the bear who walked like a man" and he cast the shovel away and made fast time to his cabin.

The wild brother of the woods thought no doubt that was the white man's invitation to dinner and ran a close second, saying "woof, woof" at every jump. If it had been a longer distance he would have been in the lead at the cabin door. All the time there was running through the brickmaker's mind the then popular song, "Johnnie, get your gun, get your gun." The gun was hanging near the door, loaded with buckshot for blue racers that abounded in that vicinity and sometimes played tag with the boys when they went to drive the cows home in the evening. The first shot finished the bear and nearly kicked Baldwin into the next lot.

The following day the bear skin was hanging outside a store on Monroe-st. The meat, dressed, weighed three hundred and twenty-four pounds and found a ready sale.

Bear meat is not unlike pork and dad brought home a roast, but somehow I could not eat it. I felt sorry for the brother of the woods who in a spirit of friendliness had lost out and became a party to a skin game.

The bear's fat was made into oil. Mixed with alcohol and scented with bergamot it was quite a popular hair dressing for men of early days.

I never did take kindly to hair oil, for mother made us wear night caps if we oiled our heads and only girls wore night caps.

◄ Charles E. Belknap, *The Yesterdays of Grand Rapids*, pp. 121-22.

◄ Simeon Baldwin killed a bear at today's Lake Drive and Fulton Street in 1854. [GRPL, Oversized Photo Collection]

Fire Hoses and Firewater

City leaders were hard pressed to provide the police and fire protection demanded by the growing population and expanding economy. More people meant more lawbreakers, and even though the city prided itself on the lawfulness of its citizens, in 1856 downtown merchants along Monroe Avenue found it necessary to hire Henry Baker as a night watchman to patrol Monroe between Ottawa and Lyon streets. Later, the Common Council appointed constables and watchmen for each of the city's five wards, but Grand Rapids did not have a full-time police force until 1871.

The fire department was established in much the same way. During the 1850s the city relied on volunteers to battle the blazes that often broke out in the wooden shops and homes. A single blaze could wipe out a large area in short order, and businessmen were only too willing to support several volunteer fire companies.

Competition among the fire companies was popular entertainment, and each group took great pride in its uniforms and fire-fighting apparatus. Early historians report that on some occasions, volunteers were known to race home when they

heard an alarm and quickly change into their bright red shirts, heavy leather hats, and highly polished belts before heading off to battle the fire. Although they trained regularly, and often affected the marching and drills of military companies, volunteer firemen did not always maintain their discipline after they arrived at a blaze. Fights sometimes broke out between competing companies, and on one occasion, the city lost several downtown business places because the firemen did not attend to their work. Charles Belknap, a youth at the time, later described the episode.

One afternoon in 1857, I occupied a reserved seat on the top of a house on Monroe street along with some forty odd boys and girls and saw twenty-five business places destroyed by fire. The fire started in a drug store on Monroe between Waterloo and Ottawa streets.

There were three fire companies at that time and Number One and Number Two were in the crater, while Number Three was working to save surrounding property. It looked from my position as if all the people of the town were helping; throwing glass and china from upper windows and lugging feather beds down stairways.

From one of the stores many large boxes of dry paints were carried into the street. Every store kept whisky in those days: none of them drinking water. As a result the male population, thirsty and hard pressed by the flames, got a little dizzy and began tumbling into paint boxes. Yellows and greens and purple began to blend with the blue and gray of smoke and ashes. If any of you have a desire to know how funny a man can really look, fill his inside with fire water and his outside with the colors of the rainbow.

Were it not that the wind-driven fire brands threatened the entire town it would have been the most successful carnival the people ever put on the street.

From a doctor's office some fellows salvaged a pickling cask. It tipped into the gutter and scattered the contents and an Indian with a scalping knife could not have stampeded a crowd more quickly.

Number One and Number Two fire companies became badly demoralized by evening. Overcome by spirits and crusted with color they disappeared from the scene of conflagration. Number Three saved the town by working until daylight next morning, the women keeping them going by carrying coffee and sandwiches. The following Sunday every church in town was given a sermon on temperance.

As a reward of merit to Number Three company for keeping sober, the women of the town expressed their appreciation by the gift of a beautiful satin banner, which is now among the treasures of the Kent Scientific Museum.

▲ Charles E. Belknap, *The Yesterdays of Grand Rapids*, pp. 176-77.

▲ Monroe Avenue, south of Campau Square as it looked in the 1850s. [GRPL, George E. Fitch Collection]

▲ In 1860, the men of the West Side Volunteer Fire Company posed at the same location with their hose and pumping machine. [GRPL, George E. Fitch Collection]

The Old Stone Schoolhouse

Along with police and fire protection, there was a growing demand for improved public education. Citizens paid for the construction of a large stone schoolhouse on the corner of Ransom and Lyon in 1848, and there the children learned the basics of "readin', writin', and 'rithmetic." Probably because it was home for him and his friends several hours each day, young Harlan Colby had especially vivid memories of the school. Like other city schools, it was ungraded, with pupils grouped not by their age, but by the level of their learning. Colby's recollection is a fine review of mid-19th-century public education in Grand Rapids.

Although Grand Rapids is of such recent origin, yet its founders have neglected no effort to secure to their children the blessings arising from a good education. The greater part of the city limits is divided into two school districts, the one lying on the east side and the other on the west side of the river.

The Union School on the east side of the river is situated on the summit of one of the noble hills which environ the city, and commands an extensive view of the delightful plains and hillsides forming the Grand River Valley. Its dimensions are 64 feet by 44 feet, three stories in height, and surmounted by a cupola from which may be had a most delightful view of the city and surrounding country. This cupola also contains a bell which chimes most disagreeably upon the ear of the schoolboys as

"With satchel and shining face,
He creeps like a snail,
unwillingly to school."

In all its interior arrangements and divisions, excepting its desks which are an instrument of barbarism yet most excruciating to the luckless scholar who is obliged to be pinned down to them all day, it is well adapted to the purpose for which it is designed. There are three large study rooms, six smaller recitation rooms, and two rooms the one used as a dressing room by the girls and the other as a library and apparatus room. The City Library comprising about 450 volumes and the mineralogical cabinet of the Grand Rapids Lyceum of Natural History, now in process of being collected, are kept here.

The "Faculty" consists of eight female and two male teachers. The school is divided into three departments, in the first of which are taught the Alphabet, Reading, Arithmetical tables, and Primary Geography. In the second department, Spelling, Reading, Writing, mental and written Arithmetic, and Geography. In the Third Department are taught all branches commonly taught in Union Schools.

In summing up the character of the school, we may say that its buildings are substantial, its divisions good, its internal fixtures decidedly bad, and its teachings such as might be vastly improved did not a perverted public taste prevent a more strict and energetic government.

The school on the west side of the river is in a very flourishing condition under Mr. Milton S. Littlefield, formerly of Syracuse, New York assisted by misses Hyde and Chubb. It numbers about 100 pupils with a list constantly growing. The old hovel now occupied by this school might be supplanted during the coming summer, by a neat brick building, 40 by 70 feet, and two stories in height. "A consummation most devoutly to be wished." We can but wish them Godspeed.

◄ Harlan P. Colby Collection, Grand Rapids Public Library.

◄ Left: This school building was built of river limestone in 1849 at the southeast corner of Ransom and Lyon. The building also housed the natural history collection of the Kent Scientific Institute (below). [GRPL, George E. Fitch Collection; GRPL, Stereo Card Collection]

A Tragedy Averted

Of course, youngsters did not spend all of their time in school, and for Charles Belknap and his childhood friends there were many games and activities to fill their days. Summer meant fishing and swimming in the Grand River, exploring the bluffs and wooded areas outside the city, and passing the hours playing made-up games. Winter brought skating, sliding, snowball fights, and cold-weather games. Belknap's favorite pastime was skating, and he loved to join his friends out on the ice of the Grand River. Grand Rapids parents undoubtedly warned their children to avoid thin ice and open water, but as the following story makes all too clear, children having a good time were as oblivious to danger then as they are today.

Of all the winter sports skating was the most popular and there developed many expert men and women skaters. Most of the skates were home made. Factory made skates were just finding their way into the hardware stores and were distinctly American in style; short at the foot and blunt in taper, which was all right on clear, hard ice.

When the Hollanders began coming over they brought their skates, long in front and gradual taper. They were an innovation and looked odd, as did the people who wore them.

Our American girls wore long skirts and trim shoes while the Holland girls dressed in short corduroy skirts, heavy wool stockings and stout shoes that supported the ankle. When one of these girls went down, which was not often, she made a dent in the ice, but it was a modest tumble, while the home girl cut capers and blushed.

One winter day...a party of Holland girls came down an open space like a whirlwind and going into the air one by one in their short skirts they cleared the glade and landed safely on this island of temptation.

The challenge was too much for the American boys and several crossed successfully and were soon linked arm in arm with the rosy cheeked, sensibly dressed Netherland girls. A dark haired American girl saw her beau cutting "pigeon wings" and doing the "long roll" with a pretty blonde and she tried the jump. When she left the ice her short skate caught in the long skirt and she plunged head first into the water with such force that she came up under the ice on the farther side.

In about a minute the crowd was frantic; all except a twelve-year-old boy — a "water rat" — they called him, who pushed his way through the crowd and followed the girl under the ice, where she could be plainly seen floating and being carried along by the current. Men yelled and women fainted or fell upon their knees sobbing.

Those who could see said the boy had caught her hand and with his feet braced on the bottom was struggling for a place in the open.

It was a Holland girl lying on her face at the channel's edge who caught the boy's hand and pulled them out. Men brought planks and bridged the glade and the unconscious girl was wrapped in blankets and rushed to her home.

The boy refused to be helped out but waded to the shore side of the glade and climbing up to the roadway he hiked for the blacksmith shop. Here he was stripped and wrapped in a horse blanket while his clothes were drying. He was sitting on the forge by the fire surrounded by an admiring crowd when a big hearted Irish woman came in with a stew-pan of hot soup, saying, "There is nothing like hot soup to drive the cold out of his insides."

▲ Ice skating, and sledding were popular 19th century winter activities for Grand Rapids youngsters. [*Harpers Weekly*, February 17, 1877]

◄ Charles E. Belknap, *The Yesterdays of Grand Rapids*, pp. 90-92.

◄ To the consternation of other users, tobogganers often took over city streets after a winter snow. [*Century Magazine*]

Let's Party!

While their children enjoyed playing outside in the winter, adults preferred indoor entertainment. To fend off the "blahs" during the long gray winter months, they organized holiday parties, musical concerts, masquerades, and fancy dress balls. The following newspaper accounts of some of those events clearly show a healthy sense of community spirit.

▲ Top: Herman Strassberg and W.H. Barnhart (below) were popular Grand Rapids musicians. [GRPL, James Keeney Collection]

We are informed by Mr. Barnhart, the popular and talented leader of the Valley City Band, that the company are preparing for a Grand concert, to take place on or about the 26th of which further notice will be given hereafter.

During the past few weeks, Mr. Barnhart has been engaged in training a full orchestra for the occasion, to play in connection with the band; and he has added to his repertoire a large number of new and beautiful pieces. But perhaps the most brilliant gem of the evening will be a new march, from his own pen, dedicated to the Military of this city.... From our own knowledge, backed by the opinions of many of our best musical critics, we predict the largest audience and the most perfect musical furor at the coming concert, ever witnessed in this city. Secure your tickets early, gentlemen, as there will be a grand rush to hear the new March of the Valley City.[1]

Fancy Dress Ball —
St. Cupids Levee!

Prof. Strasburg — the indefatigable — has conceived a brilliant idea, and is making preparations to reduce it to practice, thus:—On Feb. 13th, St. Cupid's eve., a Grand Fancy Dress Ball will be held at Collins' Hall, where the very best of music, &c. [etc.], will be provided; and, at precisely twelve o'clock—midnight—every guest present will receive a Valentine, sentimental, comic, or satirical, as the case may be. The dance will continue until 4 o'clock in the morning.[2]

Fancy Dress Ball.

The fancy-dress ball of Prof. Strasburg's classes, at Collins' Hall, Friday evening, passed off very pleasantly, and to the great satisfaction of the participants. The number of fancy costumes was quite large, and dictated by good taste, while the characters assumed were admirably acted.

Though not one of the gay throng there assembled, we "happened in" a little after the hour of twelve — at which time many of the masqueraders had laid aside their unique costumes, and assumed those of ordinary use — and noticed especially the representations of a Quakeress, Highland Maid, several Flower Girls, Daughters of the Regiment, Shepardesses, Maid of the Mist, Star Spangled Banner, Night, and old man and old woman, dressed in old style, a negro and negress, Highland Chief, Clown, Dutchman, Yankee, Don, &c., &c., many of which created much mirth. It was the party of the season, and we hope to see many more in years to come.[3]

The Concert of the Misses Coles, on Thursday evening, was not as well attended as it deserved. The singing was very fine, and the selection of pieces good. The fact is, we are slightly overdoing the business of amusements this winter. Balls, Concerts, Exhibitions, Donation parties, sociables, sleigh-rides, lectures, etc., &c., &c., ad libitum, have followed each other so rapidly and constantly, that the public have grown indifferent, and will only turn out to witness some extra novelty. The Cole Family have been requested to repeat their concert; whether they will do so or not, remains to be seen. If they do, it would be policy, we think, to delay the repetition for some weeks, until the rush of amusements is somewhat over; and meanwhile, a concert at Grandville or Grand Haven, or both, would pay.[4]

▲ [1]*Grand Rapids Enquirer,* August 3, 1856, p. 3. [2]*Grand Rapids Enquirer,* January 27, 1857, p. 3. [3]*Grand Rapids Enquirer,* February 15, 1857, p. 3. [4]*Grand Rapids Enquirer,* February 14, 1857, p. 3.

▲ Collins Hall, erected on Canal (now Monroe) in 1855, was the first four-story brick building in Grand Rapids. [Albert Baxter, *History of the City of Grand Rapids,* p. 767]

Full Cellars for Long Winters

In addition to the community parties, old timers fondly recalled family and neighborhood gatherings, and the many delights that graced local tables, especially during the Christmas holiday season. Charles Belknap wrote about "The Pioneers' Winter Food" with his usual humor and gusto.

> ### Roast 'Possum
>
> To roast a 'possum, first catch the 'possum. Dress it and soak in salt and water from 6 to 12 hours, then parboil in salt water for ½ to ¾ hour; if an old animal it requires longer boiling and roasting than a young one. Prepare a dressing the same as for a turkey or chicken, of which oysters may form an ingredient, as the dressing should be rich and savory; stuff, sew up and place in the baking-pan, the same as a turkey, with a little water. Place in the oven for 15 or 20 minutes; in the meantime partially boil some sweet potatoes; remove the pan from the oven, pour off the liquor in a dish in which it can be kept hot, and layer the sweet potatoes closely round the 'possum in the pan; cut some slices of bacon and lay them across the 'possum and on the potatoes; use the liquor that was turned off for 2 or 3 bastings, basting both the 'possum and the sweet potatoes, until it is all returned to the pan. Let bake for an hour or more, according to the age and size of the 'possum.

▲ Roast possum would hardly please modern palates. [Larry and Priscilla Massie, *Walnut Pickles and Watermelon Cake,* pp. 194-95]

Southern Michigan offered an abundance of game and wild fruit to the man who sought a home within its boundaries... and the cellar of our first home comes to mind more clearly than the parlor....

This cellar had a dirt floor and riverstone walls. Along one side were the potato and apple bins; on the other the port, beef, pickle and sauerkraut barrels and a bin for turnips, carrots and beets. Mother's spiced wild pigeons were a specialty and every fall father made an outing with others to Battle point down the river and put up barrels of black bass in salt. It was possible to get a twenty-five pound kit of salt whitefish at [Grand] Haven for two dollars. When it was time for Thanksgiving turkey we went over toward the John Ball Park country and shot one. And if we got two, mother made us give one to the minister.

This was long before the time of glass fruit jars or before one could buy canned stuff of any kind, but all during the summer we gathered the wild fruits, blackberries for jam, wild plums and verily the apple of temptation must have been the wild crabapple stewed down in maple syrup. During autumn days the kitchen was the drying place for pumpkins. A spokeshave was used to pare the rind, then they were sliced in rings and hung on a pole to dry. When well dried they were stored in the attic and rings were brought forth about once a week to be stewed for sauce or pies.

Apples, and peaches, when we could get them, were pared, quartered, strung on twine and hung to dry over the kitchen stove, where they made a fine place for flies to roost. Housewives who were finicky covered the stuff with netting.

Ham and shoulders — beef and venison — were dried in the old smokehouse. Then the cellar had its barrel of soft soap, kept well covered because for some reason or other it seemed always to be a trap for the family cat; and also its barrels of vinegar and cider. Beside them stood smaller kegs of wild grape juice and elderberry wine.

Nearly every family had its own chickens and the price of eggs did not go up every time the sun went behind a cloud; it also had a cow and had a pig.

Along about Christmas time jars of fresh lard, sausage and mincemeat were added to the cellar stock. Mince pies were made a dozen at a time and set out to freeze. Mother liked a bit of apple brandy added for flavor, but always had a temperance one or two laid by for the emergency of a guest who had signed "the pledge."

In spite of all the preparation a hard winter often found the provisions running low. Donation parties were given to help the poor, the sick or the needy. Charity was an individual not an institutional affair and it all came "out of the cellar."

◄ Charles E. Belknap, *The Yesterdays of Grand Rapids,* pp. 26-27.

◄ Left: Beginning in 1855, the Kent County Agricultural Society held fairs in the Madison Square area for nearly 100 years. Below: Wild game was an important part of 19th-century diets. [GRPL, George E. Fitch Collection, James R. Hooper Collection]

The "Great Crash" of 1857

Economic difficulties befell Grand Rapids and the rest of the nation in 1857. After a half-dozen years of unbroken prosperity, investor expectations were high. Even the widening sectional split over slavery and conflicting Northern and Southern cultures and economic systems did not stifle Wall Street's optimism. But investors failed to heed warnings about bank weaknesses, speculation, and over-expansion, and were caught short when the market began to tumble in August. Falling stock prices brought about bank failures, and when the market crashed in mid-October, the nation plunged into an economic panic.

Although far from the New York center of the storm, Grand Rapids was not spared. Prices and property values plummeted, and borrowers fell behind or defaulted on loan payments. In the following excerpt, C.C. Comstock, who had invested in several businesses, describes the difficulties that assailed the local economy and bedeviled him after the crash.

In the Fall of 1857 Enoch and Samuel [Winchester] became embarrassed. I had endorsed some of their paper which they were unable to pay and they had got about to the end of the rope. On Sept. 15th with the advice of Judge Withey, their own and my attorney, I bought out their property and business, with the expectation that Enoch would remain with me in charge of the Factory. Fifteen days after this purchase, Oct. 1st came the noted crash of 1857. Money all left the country.... During the three or four yrs. which followed property, especially unimproved real estate was not of any value. Much was sold for taxes and never redeemed by former owners. I was determined to pay 100 cents for every dollar I owed. I had a good faculty to dicker and sold my goods during the years of 1858-59-60 & 61 for anything and everything my men needed.... The dark days from Oct. 1st, 1857 to early in 1862 were beyond any description I can give. I arose at day-break, my wife would fry a few griddle cakes for my breakfast. I would eat alone and start for the Factory, came home for my dinner and seldom left my office before ten in the evening....

Things did look very dark indeed; but my will and energy put forth their full force and in the Fall of 1861, though severely embarrassed I nearly doubled my Factory and machinery, for I had concluded that I must have both in order to make any money in the furniture trade, and that I must sell more than I could sell at Grand Rapids.... In the Spring of 1862 business improved and I had my Factory in condition to manufacture about double it had ever been able to do before. A. B. Pullman, of sleeping car fame, helped set up the machinery at $1.25 per day; but he left me and went to Chicago. I had a wareroom at Peoria Ill., sold in Chicago and also started salesrooms in Milwaukee, and began to make money.

Elias Matter was and had been with me for three or more yrs. and as soon as he could see that I was making money, he wanted an interest in the business; but although he was a good man, he had no money to put in, and I declined to take him as a partner. He left me Oct. 1st and went into partnership with Julius Berkey. The Widdecomb Boys not in the Army, were also at work for me, and in 1863 the old gentleman Widdecomb, sold his stock in the furniture trade to me, and also came into my employ. He was an excellent workman but not a successful business man. The boys all worked for me more or less before they engaged in manufacturing for themselves.

▲ Shortly after placing this ad, Enoch and Samuel Winchester sold their business to C.C. Comstock. [*Grand Rapids Daily Eagle*, July 22, 1857, p. 3]

◄ Charles C. Comstock, "Early Experiences and Personal Recollections," Grand Rapids Public Library, pp. 9-11.

▼ These men from C.C. Comstock's sash, window, and door Company were kept working after the crash of 1857. [GRPL, Photo Collection]

Grand Rapids Prepares for the Civil War

The economic recovery that began in 1862 came at an awful price: four years of civil war that left no family untouched. Brothers, fathers, and sons volunteered to serve in Union and Confederate armies, and more than a few families found members on both sides of the conflict. Initially envisioning a short, one-sided confrontation that the larger, better-equipped, and better-financed Union army would easily win, the protagonists realized all too soon they were engaged in a protracted, deadly affair.

President Lincoln's first call for troops received an enthusiastic response in Grand Rapids. For some time young men had been training in militia groups, and at a war meeting on the night of April 15, 1861, many of the companies volunteered for army duty. By April 20, local militia officers had organized the Third Michigan Infantry, and a training ground named Cantonment Anderson was set up on the edge of the city, south of present-day Hall Street and east of Division Avenue.

Nearly everyone in Grand Rapids was caught up in the war excitement. While young men trained at Cantonment Anderson, older men raised money for arms and equipment. Area women organized an aid society to prepare bedding and bandages, sew shirts and caps, and even bake cakes and cookies for the training camp.

Rebecca Richmond, daughter of early settler William Richmond, devoted long hours to the war effort, and kept a detailed journal recording events on the home front. Her description captures the patriotic enthusiasm of the war's early days, as well as the romantic innocence that lasted until the fighting claimed its first casualties.

◄ Rebecca Richmond and other young women sewed and baked for the men of the Third Michigan Infantry. [GRPL, Mary Richmond Kendall Collection]

◄ Col. Daniel McConnell commanded the Third Michigan Infantry. [GRPL, Photo Collection]

[1]Grand Rapids Chronicle, January 17, 1923, p. 2; [2]Grand Rapids Chronicle, January 24, 1923, p. 2.

Tuesday, April 23 - This afternoon... I attended a meeting of the ladies of our city at Mills and Clancy's hall, convoked in order to concert measures for providing a stand of colors for the Third regiment, Michigan volunteers, to be encamped here shortly.

Thursday, April 25. - Attended the meeting of the Soldiers' Aid society this afternoon at Mills' hall. A large number of ladies were present, most of whom brought contributions of material for "housewives" [simple sewing and mending kits] and bandages. Committees upon both these articles were appointed. These occupied opposite quarters of the room and prepared work for applicants.[1]

Friday, April 26, 1861 - Pleasant. We are now to have daily meetings at the hall from 2 to 5 o'clock in the afternoon. The attendance is good and much work is accomplished.

June 3. - This afternoon took place at Cantonment Anderson the ceremony of presenting to the noble Third by the ladies of Grand Rapids the havelocks, housewives, testaments and stand of colors which we have been so long engaged in preparing for them.

At 4 o'clock this afternoon the procession formed in front of Mills & Clancy's hall in the following order:

Brass band, carriage containing six young ladies who were to present the flag; carriages containing 20 young girls bearing the testaments and housewives; the Glee Club consisting of six gentlemen; the chaplain and family, then carriages of interested citizens.

Those appointed to present the flag were Miss Charlotte Cuming, Hannah Hovey, Mary Jewett, Alabama Moore, Cubley and Rebecca Richmond, representing the various religious denominations which have engaged in the work of assisting our troops by meeting at Mills & Clancy's hall. We all wore blue dresses with sashes of red and white confined on the right shoulder by a small star. On each of our blue parasols we had a cluster of thirteen small silk stars.

The other 20 girls, among whom was sister Mary, wore Zouave jackets and brown jockey hats trimmed with red, white and blue.

The brass band opened the exercises with a national air, the Glee club followed with "Our Glorious Union Forever," and Col. McReynolds then delivered the address in behalf of the ladies presenting the flag. Col. McConnell responded, in behalf of the regiment in an affecting and patriotic manner. The Glee club then sang "The Star Spangled Banner," the 26 joining in the chorus. Rev. Dr. Cuming closed with an appropriate prayer and benediction.

Col. McConnell then transferred the banner to the flag company of the regiment, which received it with evident pride and thankfulness.[2]

At the word of command ten officers stepped forward and each escorted to his company a couple of Zouave girls furnished with two baskets, one containing testaments and the other housewives, which they proceeded to distribute, one of each to every man in the company not already supplied. The captain of each company received in addition a handsome bouquet of flowers. One was also presented to Col. McConnell by the six young ladies aforesaid.

Cheers for Ladies

At the conclusion of the distribution, the soldiers gave three cheers for the ladies of Grand Rapids, three for the flag and three for Col. McReynolds. Then they marched to the parade ground, followed by "the 26," who were assigned the honorable and complimentary positions of reviewers of the troops. Dress parade being over, we returned to the city, fatigued but pleased and satisfied.[1]

Tuesday, June 11. The Third regiment received marching orders today. They are to leave here on Thursday and go direct to Washington.

The official summons to appear at Washington was read to the troops, and orders given in regard to packing and other duties incident to departure.

Glad News for Soldiers

When the men were disbanded they seemed perfectly wild with excitement, congratulating one another in the most hearty manner, cheering and singing. Many of them immediately brought forth from the barracks their bundles containing their worldly effects, and proceeded joyfully to packing their knapsacks.

Thursday, June 13 - One of the saddest days in the record of Grand Rapids. Our pet regiment, the Third, has departed at last and left many, many sorrowing hearts behind.

They started from Cantonment Anderson at about 8 o'clock, accompanied by a vast procession of carriages. Their march through the city to the depot was a continual ovation. The Star Spangled Banner floated over them from almost every building along the route, handkerchiefs waved from thousands of fair hands, and young girls showered the troops with bouquets.[2]

▲ [1]*Grand Rapids Chronicle,* January 31, 1923, p. 3; [2]*Grand Rapids Chronicle,* February 7, 1923, p. 6.

▲ The Rev. Francis H. Cuming of St. Mark's Episcopal Church was chaplain for the Third Michigan Infantry. [GRPL, Photo Collection]

▲ Silas Perkins (standing) and Theodore Lampert of Grand Rapids (right), with two unidentified comrades in the Twenty-Fifth Michigan Infantry. [GRPL, Photo Collection]

Too young for service ► when war broke out, John Mann, Joseph Herkner, Thomas Mitchell, and Charles F. Kendall joined the Grand Rapids Greys, a youth's militia group. A few months later they joined the regular army. [GRPL, Photo Collection]

▲ Many Grand Rapids men joined the First Michigan Mechanics and Engineers, shown here at Chattanooga, Tennessee, in the winter of 1863-64. [GRPL, Photo Collection]

Into the Thick of the Battle

One month after leaving Grand Rapids, the Third Michigan Infantry Regiment saw action at Blackburn's Ford, Virginia, one of the preliminary skirmishes leading up to the famous Battle of First Bull Run or Manassas. Four days later the Third Michigan covered the retreat of the Union Army from Bull Run. Accusations flew in several directions in the wake of the disastrous defeat; more than one regiment was accused of fleeing the battlefield in disarray, and many officers were blamed for incompetence or cowardice. No such criticism was leveled at the Third Michigan, whose men had performed well. In a letter written home shortly after the fighting ceased and published on August 17, 1861, in the Grand Rapids *Weekly Enquirer*, Captain Byron Pierce of Company K described the Grand Rapids regiments' first battle experience.

We left Camp Blair on Tuesday, the 15th at 3 P.M. We traveled 12 miles and went into camp at Vienna, reaching there at 10 o'clock P.M., very much fatigued, when we threw ourselves on the ground with our oil-cloths under us and blankets over us. We did not take our tents with us, and therefore we had the high canopy of heaven for our tents. I think I never enjoyed a sounder and sweeter sleep than I did that night. We were up at sunrise and off for the seat of war, and this day traveled about ten miles, stopping on the other side of Fairfax Court House, where we found several batteries that had been deserted that morning by the enemy. This night there were about 15,000 troops all in the camp. We were alarmed in the night by our pickets being driven in. The next morning we took up the line of march in the direction of the enemy, our Brigade taking the lead with a portion of Sherman's Battery in advance. About 12 o'clock we heard the booming of cannon which warned us that we were in close proximity to the enemy and they had made preparations to receive us. Our skirmishers had ran upon a masked battery, and, as it proved, their forces far outnumbered ours. We could not see them as they were in the woods. We therefore made preparations to drive them from their hiding place. Our skirmishers were in the woods when we arrived in sight, and such vollies of musketry I never heard before. We at once went to their relief, and made preparations to charge upon the woods. We were in an open field, and stood for a length of time under a direct fire from their guns. As we were about ready to charge the 12th regiment of New York, instead of charging, broke and ran; upon this we were ordered to retreat, which we did in good order. Too much cannot be said in praise of our regiment, for to a man they stood up in the ranks all the time with bullets whistling all around them. We marched back about two miles that night and went into camp the next morning we started again for Bull-Run; this day we kept quiet in hopes of drawing out the enemy. Nothing of importance occurred today with the exception of exchanging shots with the pickets. At night we lay upon our arms in the line of battle, and were called out several times in the night by the arc of musketry, but no fighting yet. The next day was but a repetition of the task. The next was Sunday, the day of the great battle, which happened about three miles above us. We were kept in this position in order to engage the enemy and keep them from out-flanking the main army. We opened our batteries in the morning, but could get no reply. Getting tired of them, Capt. Judd's Company were sent to reconnoiter the woods. When we got within a short distance of them they opened upon us such a furious fire that we were obliged to fall back into a ravine. This convinced us that they were not dead yet. At five o'clock we were ordered to fall back on Centreville, where upon our arrival everything was in confusion; the main army had been defeated and were retreating in broken order, some stopped at Centreville, while others rushed on to Washington. At ten o'clock we had orders to retire back to Fairfax, and our brigade was to cover the retreat, which we did, and our Regiment was the last, and Company K, of course, the very last. So you see we had the honor, if you would think it so, of covering the retreat of the Grand Army, although we do not get the credit of it through the press, we made a forced march 86 miles without stopping for food or rest, and arrived at Arlington in a drenching rain at 10 o'clock A.M.; and such a tired lot of soldiers I never saw before. We made out to get shelter for the night, and the next morning had our tents brought over from Camp Blair. Now we are here on a beautiful location, where I trust we may remain until the men get recruited, although we are expecting to be called out every moment.

◄ Grand Rapids *Weekly Enquirer*, August 17, 1861, p. 1.

▲ The Third Michigan paraded through Detroit on its way to Washington, DC. [Detroit Public Library, Burton Historical Collection]

▲ Within days of their arrival in the east the men of the Third were engaged in the Battle of Bull Run. [Rossiter Johnson, *Campfires and Battlefields*, p. 30]

"I Want to See You and the Children So Bad..."

There were many more battle experiences to come. The "Old Third," as it came to be known, was a stalwart and dependable unit which saw service at Fair Oaks, Second Bull Run, Chancellorsville, Gettysburg, the New York draft riots, and Cold Harbor, before its troops were mustered out in Detroit, in June 1864, three years after being called into action. When the regiment was reorganized many of the veterans re-enlisted and served out the war.

Other Michigan units with large contingents of men from the western side of the state acquitted themselves with equal distinction. By war's end Kent County had sent 4,214 men into battle, and left at least 548 of them dead on the battlefields. Countless others returned bearing the scars of war.

Although not so visible, the scars of war also left their mark on those who remained behind. David and Mary Noble had a small farm near Sparta, and when the 44-year-old

Noble enlisted in the First Michigan Engineers and Mechanics on September 17, 1861, his wife was left to care for farm and family. Excerpts from his letters to her demonstrate the great difficulties she faced, and show that the family's suffering had begun long before news arrived that David had died of disease on June 22, 1862, in Tuscumbia, Alabama.

January 15th 1862
Respected wife:

I will try and write you a few lines to let you no that I am well and I hope that these lines will find you the same. I received your letter of the 29th of December and was glad to hear from you but I was sorry to hear about the children was all sick. It makes me feel bad to think that I can't cum home to help you take care of them. I hope they will not be sick long. I hope the next letter I get from you to hear they are all well. I no that you will take good care of them. Don't let them take cold.

I have not dun a days work since I left home. I want to get to work. The men is geting discoradged. They all want to get to work and to get our pay. The pay is what we need but I don't no when we will get it. I hope we will get it before long. Today is the day they told us that we should get our pay but it did not cum yet.

under take to take property to sel you can prevent them taking or seling property for debt as long as I am in the service of the United States.

I want to se you and the children so bad that I hardly no how to content my self. I ges you will think by the lookes of my writing that I am crasey. Wel I am not but I want to se my family once more and will before long. This from your affectionate husband.

David Noble

▲ Dorothy Keister Collection, Grand Rapids Public Library.

▲ Recruiters offered cash bounties to entice men to enlist. [GRPL, Henry McConnell Collection]

January the 25th, 1862
Respected wife I will write a few lines today to let you no that I am still ok but not very well. I have had diaea [diarrhea] and if I don't get better of it before long I shal cum home if I have to desert. I stil think I will be home by the first of March. I shan't expect to get my pay until that time. I will send you a few lines from my capitan. I want you to go to the Supervisor with it and tel him you want him to help you to get sum money to pay your taxes and I will pay it back when I cum home. I want you to take care of these lines from my capitan and if any one should

Soldiers built crude ► cabins to keep warm and dry in winter. [GRPL, Photo Collection]

"The Rebellion Is Crushed...Glory to God"

The war slogged on until April 9, 1865, when Robert E. Lee surrendered the tattered remnants of his Confederate army of Northern Virginia at Appomattox Courthouse, Virginia. The surrender of other Confederate forces quickly followed.

Grattan Township farmer-turned-soldier Chester Slayton was with the Twenty-fifth Michigan Volunteer Infantry under General William Tecumseh Sherman outside Raleigh, North Carolina, when he learned the war was over. His letter home to his wife, Sarah, written over the course of several days at war's end, captures the nation's changing moods in early April 1865 — from joy that the fighting was finally over, to sorrow at the news of President Abraham Lincoln's assassination, to somber concern for the nation's future.

My Dear Wife:

It has been a little over a week since I wrote to you last, telling you that you might not hear from me again in some time, yet there has so much transpired since then, and so successful has been our campaign, that we now have the privalege of again writing with the fair prospects of soon meeting once more. How happy the thought. *The rebellion is crushed the war is ended.* Glory to God.

Wednesday the 12th. we got started early, and was plodding wearily along, when about eight o'clock, a man came back on horseback with his horse on the full run, and swinging his hat, and said that Gen. Lee had surrendered his whole army to Gen Grant! How I wish you could have been there then to see & hear the boys. An instants pause than there arose such a yell and cheer as you never heard. The boys threw up their hats, caps, guns, coats, knapsacks, haversacks, and their government property in general. They jumped, shouted and danced; cheered and hollered, and shouted again, till they were all hoarse. The column now moved on with light hearts, and apparently light loads....

Thus this cruel war of four years duration ends. How happy the thought; how pleasant the idea; how bright the prospect. Soon we are to be relieved from this weary and dangerous strife and go to join those we love at home. I can hardly express my thoughts or the pleasure I feel that the war has so suddenly and so successfully been brought to a close. Yet during our rejoicing, we hear this afternoon the sad intelligence that President Lincoln is dead, and not only dead but that he died by the hand of an assassin. Was shot dead in the theatre. We have heard no particulars yet, but probably you have. What is going to become of our nation, if such is the case? Will Andy Johnson prove true to the high post to which he has been elected by loyal men? I hope he will; yet I cannot but wish that we had a good northern man there. How sad the thought that Lincoln has struggled so long through a bloody & cruel war and just as peace is about to crown his efforts, he is killed....

I remain yours as ever,
Chester M. Slayton

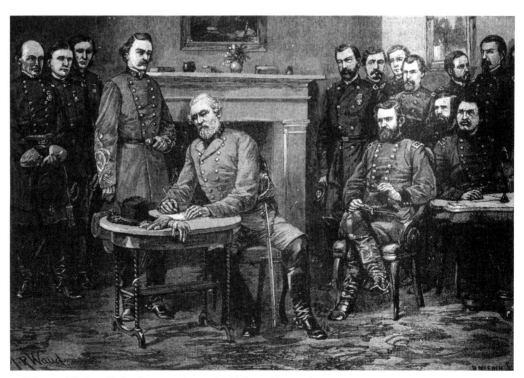

▲ *Grand River Times,* November, 1880, pp. 4-5.

▲ Following Abraham Lincoln's assassination, Grand Rapids Mayor C.C. Comstock delared a day of mourning. [GRPL, Restricted Materials Collection]

▲ General Robert E. Lee's surrender at the McLean House, Appomattox, Virginia, brought the Civil War to an end. [Rossiter Johnson, *Campfires and Battlefields,* p. 447]

One of the Finest Celebrations Ever

Once the war had ended, soldiers began returning home almost immediately. On May 23, Grant's Army of the Potomac passed in a last review in Washington, D.C., before companies began heading for their respective home states. On all fronts regiments were mustered out and sent home as quickly as possible.

Returning soldiers began arriving in Grand Rapids in June, and by the end of the month, hundreds of veterans were back with their families, preparing to resume their interrupted lives. Independence Day was full of special meaning that year, and planners worked hard to produce an appropriate celebration.

By all accounts, they succeeded. The Fourth of July of 1865 was an event long remembered by area residents. While the celebration marked the close of four years of war, it also left those in attendance with a sense of hope and optimism for the future.

◄ Judge Solomon Withey presided over gala Fourth of July festivities in 1865. [GRPL, Photo Collection]

The anniversary of our National freedom—the glorious "Fourth"— was celebrated in this city yesterday in a manner worthy of an intelligent people and creditable to the patriotism and liberality of freemen. Notwithstanding the early morning was welcomed with rain, and dark, foreboding clouds covered the horizon, the day was a delightful one, cooled by a gentle breeze throughout, while there was no dust and the scorching rays of a mid-summer's sun were obscured by floating clouds.

There were a large number of people here, as many probably as ever gathered in our city on any one occasion and there would undoubtedly have been many thousands more had it not been for the unpromising state of the weather in the early part of the day. As it was the streets, particularly Canal and Monroe, were perfectly lined on either side, from Bridge to Fulton street, with a surging mass of men, women

and children throughout the day and evening.

The day was ushered in and welcomed by the firing of cannon and the ringing of bells, at sunrise. At about ten o'clock a procession was formed, on Canal street, under the direction of Chief Marshal Maj. M. D. Birge....

The procession was led by the Grand Rapids Brass Band, F. Sylvester, leader, followed by numerous carriages containing Mayor Foster, Members of the Common Council, Orator, Reader and Chaplains; United States civil and military officers; aged and invalid officers and soldiers of the War of 1812, Mexican War, and the War for the Suppression of the rebellion; choir members of the "Old Third," and other regiments, on foot carrying at the head of those gallant war worn veterans the battle flags of the immortal Third; Engine No. 1, drawn by four horses, and followed by the members of that company in uniform; the steam fire engine,

"*David Caswell*," drawn by four horses and manned by the members of Niagara Fire Company No. 2; Fire Engine No. 3, in uniform. The fire department under the management of Chief Engineer J. M. Cook, and some thirty or forty wagons and carriages, filled with men, women and children.

His Honor, Judge S. L. Withey presided and opened the exercises with some well chosen remarks.

The Declaration of Independence was most admirably read by Byron D. Ball, Esq. Indeed, it was the opinion of nearly all present that the reading was the best we ever heard in this city on the Fourth of July.

The oration was considered by the majority of those who heard it as the best ever delivered on such an occasion in this city. It was, certainly, the most eloquent address we have listened to in a long time. The orator, Robert M. Hatfield, is a graceful, easy, gentlemanly speaker, possessing rare powers over an audience, and a master of language.

▼ Boys with firecrackers kept everyone stepping lively on the Fourth of July. [*Harpers Weekly*, July 4, 1857]

The soldiers dinner was the most extensive and sumptuous repast ever gotten up in our city, and the crowning feat of the occasion. It was given on the Pearl Street Bridge [which had] an evergreen cross over the passage way, on which was woven in letters of living green "In God is our trust," and on the arch of the bridge, "Welcome Soldiers - Michigan my Michigan." On the west end of the bridge was inscribed, in like manner, "Soldiers Welcome." A table, with seats on either side, straight as an arrow, was set through the entire length of the bridge, covered with sweet white linen and laden with choice edibles, all the substantials and luxuries that human ingenuity could invent— roast pigs, turkeys, chickens, beef, hot and cold, hot potatoes and other vegetables; pies, puddings, in great variety, jellies, various kinds of sauce, currants, berries, ice cream, &c.

The table was made sweet and attractive by numerous bouquets and mammoth vases of fragrant flowers. In the center of the table was an arch over a beautiful vase of flowers on which was written in flower letters, "Soldiers Welcome Home." About eight hundred people were seated at the first table, over five hundred of

▲ The steam fire engine *David Caswell* was a big attraction in the afternoon parade. [Albert Baxter, *History of the City of Grand Rapids,* p. 183]

whom were soldiers. Added to this number, were many soldiers, wives, all who could be found and induced to take seats. Dinners were given to some fifteen hundred people....

A national salute was fired at sun-set, and the display of fireworks, on Crescent Place, in the evening, was very fine and decidedly satisfactory to the

people, a large number of whom witnessed the exhibition. And with this display closed one of the finest and most important celebrations of our National Anniversary that has ever taken place in the Valley City.

▲ *Grand Rapids Daily Eagle,* July 5, 1865, p. 1.

▲ The Pearl Street bridge was set with food tables from end to end on July 4, 1865. [GRPL, George E. Fitch Collection]

New Year's Day, 1866

On January 1, 1866, for the first time in five years, New Year's Day dawned without stories of new horrors from the battlefront. Reunited families fervently hoped that the bright skies over Grand Rapids and the cheerful mood of its residents were omens for the coming postwar period. For the most part, as they made their customary holiday calls on friends and neighbors, exuberant celebrants heeded community leaders' pleas to abstain from wine and liquor, and the day passed without incident. Franklin Everett, longtime Grand Rapids resident, teacher, and historian, described the mood of the day and captured the citizenry's joy that the war was finally over, and the Union had been preserved.

A Happy New Year.

Yesterday was all that could have been desired for the inauguration of the New Year. An almost cloudless sky canopied the earth, and while the side walks were in tolerably fair order for pedestrians, there was snow enough on some streets to give the sleighs and cutters full swing; while others were obliged to wheel in the line. Many of the turnouts were gorgeous, particularly the six mule team, and the parties seemed as happy as the wish, that hung, for every friend and acquaintance, on their tongues end.

The calling commenced early, and held to a late hour, and it was the general report that more persons were astir, on that day, than heretofore on similar occasions. The ladies, owing somewhat to the fine weather and absence of mud, lent more to their benevolent happy hearts, were in excellent mood, and beautifully arrayed in bibs and tuckers, and tucks and bibbers. Some of the callers were quite hilarious, but the big load, the old load, the load that always calls on New Year, were very well behaved gentlemen, quite sedate; a waggish fellow among them insisted that they were the temperance load, as every man had set his face against wine and the "rosy god" during the day. The tables as a general rule were properly set out, especially the "Yankee table" with pork and beans, mush and milk, pumpkin pies and cider, and wines were not entirely discarded, to the extent that some had anticipated. Enjoyment was the main law, and each caller permitted to contribute his share. May the year just dawned be the emulator of the past, in crowning our spirits with new and mightier victories, until the whole people shall rally under its banners, "crossing their palms as brother men," and freemen, and swearing by the sacred past of our country, that this Union shall be American, and "must and shall be preserved."

◄ *Grand Rapids Daily Eagle,* January 2, 1866, p. 1.

◄ As it did for these celebrants later in the century, New Year's Day 1866 found the community out in a festive mood. [GRPL, Ada Glass Plate Negative Collection]

CHAPTER 4

Industry Takes Command

Grand Rapids grew to industrial maturity after the Civil War. The resources of its lumbering and gypsum-mining enterprises, the talents of its many skilled craftsmen, the ingenuity of its entrepreneurs, and the thousands of jobs created by a burgeoning furniture industry helped transform the city by the end of the 19th century into a regional manufacturing center, best known as the site of the nation's largest concentration of home-furniture producers.

Veterans returning to West Michigan after the war were impatient to pick up the pieces of their interrupted lives. Farmers were eager to trade battlefields for cornfields; shopkeepers wanted to hear the orders of customers, not generals; and laborers, tired of destruction, wanted to build things again. The returning veterans filled the city and surrounding area with a spirit of optimism unseen in many years, and within a short time their energy, coupled with new technologies, helped change what was manufactured in local factories, and the way people did business in Grand Rapids.

Perched on the northern edge of a developing manufacturing belt that stretched west from Massachusetts and Maryland to Wisconsin, Illinois, and southern Michigan, Grand Rapids was linked by railroad and telegraph to larger cities throughout the region, giving its manufacturers an opportunity to exploit distant urban markets. Local industrialists saw a diverse array of their products — carpet sweepers, farm wagons, sticky fly paper, and cigars among them — successfully competing in markets throughout the United States.

By taking advantage of improved shipping and communications, as well as technological innovations that speeded manufacturing and lowered costs, one group of entrepreneurs used aggressive marketing and sales tactics to make Grand Rapids' name synonymous with the furniture industry. By 1876 Grand Rapids' furniture companies were capable of producing furniture equal in style and quality to any in the country, a fact they proved in open competition at the national exposition held in Philadelphia to celebrate the centennial of the Declaration of Independence.

Economic growth of the type generated in the last half of the 19th century does not come easily. For every company that succeeded, many others failed. No individual or group of individuals can claim singular credit for Grand Rapids' economic transition. Laborers, innovators and inventors, owners and investors all played a role. The costs were often steep, but most Grand Rapids citizens seemed willing to commit themselves to progress.

The Great Timber Harvest

It was timber that had attracted many of Grand Rapids' earlier settlers, and it was to timber that many citizens turned for jobs and revenue after the close of the Civil War. Within five years of Lee's surrender, 50 million board feet of logs were being "run" down the Grand River by nimble lumberjacks who worked in grueling and primitive conditions. Wearing bright flannel shirts, dark wool pants, and spiked boots to keep their balance as they moved from log to log in the stream, the "jacks" earned $1 to $3 per day, plus meals, to cut the logs in the forest and guide them downriver, with pike poles, peaveys, and cant hooks, to the booming company holding areas just above the rapids.

Like cattle, the logs were all stamped with the brands of their owners so they could be sorted at the log booms and sent to sawmills in Grand Rapids and Grand Haven. Despite being well marked, not all the logs made it to their rightful owners. Often, as the following newspaper story attests, unscrupulous mill operators "hogged" the logs and cut them into boards before anyone could detect their felony. However, timber was so plentiful at first that "hogging" was more of a nuisance than a threat to the lumbermen's livelihood, and quite likely the practice was so widespread that the gains and losses tended to even out. At any rate, according to businessman and lumberman C.C. Comstock, no one got rich stealing another man's logs.

It was said to be disloyal to the people on Rogue river to take any business away from them. Much bitter feeling was engendered and it formed a basis for some lawlessness on the part of the Rogue river mill men. This lawless conduct consisted chiefly in "hogging" logs in transit and cutting them up into lumber. "Hogging" was the polite term for what would now be called stealing.

This sentiment against sawing the logs anywhere except at the nearest points possible to where they were cut, grew as time went on, and in later years, when lumber mills were built below Grand Rapids at Nortonville, Mill Point (now known as Spring Lake), Ferrysburg and Grand Haven the people of Grand Rapids made many futile demonstrations against permitting the logs to go past this point. "Hogging" was carried on to quite a degree among the Grand Rapids mills and to indicate how lightly the crime of stealing logs was held in those days this story is told.

It was the custom of one of the Grand Rapids mill owners to be about the plant a good portion of each day and watch the operations of the workmen and machinery. The log mark was the mark of W.T. Powers. On at least one occasion he noticed a fine log with the O mark on it go on the carriage in his mill.

"Hold on," said he to the head sawyer, "that is not our log."

"Oh, yes it is," was the laughing reply. "Don't you see the mark? O, that stands for ours," and the log was cut up without further remark.

In commenting on log and timber thieving in the early days C.C. Comstock said the other day that it is a remarkable fact that not one of that numerous class has prospered. "I think I knew all of the thieves in this part of the country," said Mr. Comstock. "It was an important part of our business to know and keep track of all of them. I have continued to watch their several careers up to the present time and it is safe to say that there is not an old timber thief living today who is not a poor man."

▲ Unidentified clipping, Scrapbook Collection, Grand Rapids Public Library.

▲ Teamsters and their horses were an integral part of lumbering in the Michigan woods. [GRPL, Black History Exhibit Collection]

▲ "Wanigans," or floating cook shacks, were a happy sight to the lumberjacks. [GRPL, Photo Collection]

GRAND RAPIDS LOGMARKS

Surface	End	Company
0-0-0	3L	A.B. Long & Son
0 0 0	JD	D.C. Little & Son
	Q̃	I.L. Quimby
	🐕	'' ''
V	Ⓓ	Goodsell & Carson
111 111	U (OxBow)	'' ''
1	PJ	'' ''
V	Ⓐ	John McGee
⊢⊣	KOR	George L. Knight
ΔΔ	Ⓗ	L. H. Withey & Co.
	H.S	R.B. Smith & P.R. Howe
1X	C▢	Hicks Brothers
1X	MC	'' ''
1X	M	'' ''
	O	J & J Bigole & Co., Muir, Mich.
	8	'' ''
AH	⌊	'' ''
1X	✳	Horace Roatch, Muir, Mich.
	U	'' ''
	Ⴟ	'' ''
⟨▭⟩	エ	'' ''
111111	1	C.C. Comstock, Michigan Barrel Co.
	CR	E. Putnam

◄ Some of the logmarks used on the Grand River. [GRPL, Grand Rapids Booming Company Collection]

Log "rollaways" ► were built on banks and rolled into rivers. [GRPL, Photo Collection]

◄ Grand Rapids lumber mills, like Reuben Wheeler's, were the destination of most log drives. [GRPL, Godfrey Anderson Collection]

▲ Stationary "donkey" steam engines pulled logs to sawmills (top), where they were cut into stacks of lumber (above). [GRPL, Photo Collection]

◄ Riding the logs downriver was the best-paying, but most dangerous, lumberjack work. [GRPL, Photo Collection]

The Rivermen Come to Town

The arrival of the lumberjacks always caused a stir in Grand Rapids. After a long winter in the woods cutting down trees, and several weeks spent herding their logs to the booming companies, the rivermen were ready to party.

Novelist Stewart Edward White was the son of a lumberman and knew the lore of the woods. He had gone with his father to the winter camps and seen firsthand the log drives and carousing that accompanied each drive's end. In his novel, *The Riverman*, he describes an area called "Hell's Half-Mile," in the fictional town of Redding, a pseudonym for his hometown of Grand Rapids.

White's tale features a youthful protagonist, Johnny Orde, leading his work gang of rivermen for a night on the town after winning a race to drive his logs to the "Redding" mills.

"Well, boys, ready for trouble?" he greeted them. "Come on."

They set out up the long reach of Water Street, their steel caulks biting deep into the pitted board-walks.

For nearly a mile the street was flanked solely by lumberyards, small mills, and factories. Then came a strip of unimproved land, followed immediately by the wooden, ramshackle structures of Hell's Half-Mile.

In the old days every town of any size had its Hell's Half-Mile, or the equivalent. Saginaw boasted of its Catacombs; Muskegon, Alpena, Port Huron, Ludington, had their "Pens," "White Rows," "River Streets," "Kilyubbin," and so forth. They supported row upon row of saloons, alike stuffy and squalid; gambling hells of all sorts; refreshment "parlours," where drinks were served by dozens of "pretty waiter-girls," and huge dance-halls.

The proprietors of these places were a bold and unscrupulous lot. In their everyday business they had to deal with the most

▲ "Hell's Half-Mile" saloons were no place for the faint-hearted. [*Early American Book of Illustrators and Wood Engravers, 1670-1870*, Vol. 2, p. 224]

dangerous rough-and-tumble fighters this country has ever known; with men bubbling over with the joy of life, ready for quarrel if quarrel also spelled fun, drinking deep, and heavy-handed and fearless in their cups. But each of these rivermen had two or three hundred dollars to "blow" as soon as possible. The pickings were good. Men got rich very quickly at this business. And there existed this great advantage in favour of the divekeeper; nobody cared what happened to a riverman. You could pound him over the head with a lead pipe, or drug his drink, or choke him to insensibility, or rob him and throw him out into the street, or even draw him tidily through a trap-door into the river flowing conveniently beneath. Nobody bothered — unless, of course, the affair was so bungled as to become public. The police knew enough to stay away when the drive hit town. They would have been annihilated if they had not. The only fly in the divekeeper's ointment was that the riverman would fight back.

As yet the season was too early for much joy along Hell's Half-Mile. Orde's little crew, and the forty or fifty men of the drive that had preceded him, constituted the rank and file at the moment in town. A little later, when all the drives on the river should be in, and those of its tributaries, and the men still lingering at the woods camps, at least five hundred woods-weary men would be turned loose. Then Hell's Half-Mile would awaken in earnest from its hibernation. The lights would blaze from day to day. From its opened windows would blare the music, the cries of men and women, the shuffle of feet, the noise of fighting, the shrieks of wild laughter, curses deep and frank and unashamed, songs broken and interrupted. Crews of

men, arms locked, would surge up and down the narrow sidewalks, their little felt hats cocked to one side, their heads back, their fearless eyes challenging the devil and all his works — and getting the challenge accepted. Girls would flit across the lit windows like shadows before flames, or stand in the doorways hailing the men jovially by name. And every few moments, above the roar of this wild inferno, would sound the sudden crash and the dull blows of combat. Only, never was heard the bark of the pistol. The fighting was fierce, and it included kicking with the sharp steel boot-caulks, biting and gouging; but it barred knives and firearms. And when Hell's Half-Mile was thus in full eruption, the citizens of Redding stayed away from Water Street after dark. "Drive's in," said they, and had business elsewhere. And the next group of rivermen, hurrying toward the fun, broke into an eager dog-trot. "Taking the old town apart to-night," they told each other. "Let's get in the game."

▲ Stewart Edward White, *The Riverman*, pp. 60-62.

▲ Riverman Fred Utley with his peavey. [GRPL, James R. Hooper Collection]

◄ Stewart Edward White. [GRPL, Photo Collection]

The Great Log Jam of '83

The vagaries of nature presented a far greater threat to lumbermen than did lumber "hogs" or barroom brawls. Forest fires and floods could destroy many more logs than "hoggers" could steal, and at no time was that point more forcefully made than in the wake of the "big rain" that began on July 22, 1883. So much rain fell that day that an estimated 80 million board feet of logs broke free of their Grand Rapids Booming Company boom and jammed against the Detroit and Milwaukee (now Grand Trunk) Railroad bridge above Ann Street. For the next few days, the logs pressed against the bridge, threatening to break away and rush uncontrolled all the way to Grand Haven, while mere mortals contemplated the jam and wondered how they might take it apart before further damage was done.

West Michigan poet Asa Harding Stoddard, of Cooper Township in Kalamazoo County, was so impressed by the storm and flooding river that he was moved to commit the tale to verse. While his effort was clearly not up to the standards of the great poets of the age, Stoddard's "The Big Rain" certainly captures the impact of that long-ago summer storm. Newspaper accounts and photographs of the resulting log jam provide modern readers with a vivid account of the events that followed.

The last episode in the story was played out in Grand Haven. There, the "big boom" above the city was put to a severe test as the freed logs struggled to reach Lake Michigan. Reinforced by courageous pile drivers who constantly drove new pointed timbers into the river bed, the boom held. What some called the greatest log jam in the nation's history was over.

In addition to the excitement it generated, the log jam should be remembered for two other reasons. First, a primary cause of the jam and the flood was the heavy lumbering that had been done along the banks of the Grand River and its tributaries. With only a few trees left standing, spring thaws and heavy summer rains sent their waters rushing into the streams. A few years earlier, more of the water would have soaked into soil held firmly in place by tree roots and smaller vegetation. Until a second growth of foliage and better dams once again held soil and water in place, the threat of future flooding would remain a reality for Grand Rapids and other river cities. Also significant is the fact that logging in the Grand River valley never again reached the volume it had enjoyed before 1883. Some lumbermen rebuilt the destroyed log booms, but others sensed a change was coming and went out of business. There were several more big years in the 1880s, but by the last decade of the century, logging was on the wane. The good trees were gone and even the less desirable timber had been cut. The Great Log Jam of 1883 was at once the most spectacular moment and the beginning of the end for logging on the Grand River.

▼ A portion of the Detroit and Milwaukee Railroad bridge was carried downstream by the 1883 log jam. [GRPL, Photo Collection]

Shortly after 7 o'clock a long, heavy G.R. & I. freight train passed over to the westward, and two or three minutes later a handcar passed. Four mechanics, said an eye witness, were standing near the center of the bridge, and near them were Mr. [Ichabod H.] Quimby and Mr. Burr Wartrous, foreman of the booming company. The men were about to take orders in regard to additional bracing to be put in at one of the piers when an ominous crack that went right to our bones was heard. It appeared to come from right under where the men were standing. The bridge swayed perceptibly and moved several inches to the south. Wartrous and the men rushed for the west end of the bridge and Mr. Quimby pulled out like a whirlwind for the east shore. It did not take him many seconds to reach land. The logs hardly appeared to move, but the middle bent of the bridge was carried steadily down stream. It seemed ten minutes, but I suppose it was not more than one, when the south side of the girder slipped off the pier timbers and the bent rested on its side on the log jam held by the boom. It groaned and trembled, and then sank almost out of sight. We wondered for an instant if it might dam the break, when to our utter surprise, that mass of 100 tons of iron with 25 tons of rails added was lifted more than half out of the water by the buoyancy of the logs. The water boiled up furiously on all sides of it as it was borne down stream 100 feet or more, heaving heavily up and down all the time, until finally it rolled over to the right and sank to the bottom, while the

logs that had buoyed it sprang clear out of the water.

Following the broken spans of the bridge came the great mass of logs like a monster demon mad and bent on destruction. The logs groaned and pitched and tumbled in every conceivable shape in the mad chase through the breach. Wherever the water was visible, at points here and there, it seethed and boiled and foamed like the whirlpool at Niagara. Logs were time and again thrown clear out of the water as they got out of the jam. The jam seemed to move in a solid mass, and as soon as it passed the bridge it spread out, occupying three times the surface space it did passing through.

As soon as Mr. Quimby reached land he yelled to the chair factory office to have word telephoned down town. He was afraid, as he said afterward, that the telephone might not work, or that the operators would get excited and make some mistake; so he rushed down the bank to Canal street, got into a buggy and drove as for his life down Canal street. . . .

As he plied the whip to the horses sometimes on the seat and sometimes on his knees in the box of the buggy his stentorian voice was raised in a way that made the warning heard away beyond the hill top, as well as on the west side. "Fog Horn" Bradley's thunder was like the "wee small voice" compared to his. . . .

▲ *Grand Rapids Daily Democrat,* July 27, 1883, p. 1.

▲ Logs blocked by the D & M bridge broke loose (top) and roared under the Pearl Street bridge (middle) for over two hours. [GRPL, Photo Collection] The "big rain" forced many people to flee in rowboats (below). [GRPL, Godfrey Anderson Collection]

THE BIG RAIN

-----and now I have a word to add
About the weather we have had.

It's rained by night and rained by day,
Enough to almost spoil our hay
And keep our cornfields in a state
Too wet for us to cultivate.
The weeds and grass are rank and green
But corn is sorry to be seen.

The little creek across our farm
That seldom thinks of doing harm,
Followed the fashion of the day,
Got on a swell and bore away
Fences and bridges in its course.
No dam(ning) could withstand its force,
At least I thought would do no good
to dam(n) a creek in such a flood.

If once the water rose so high
That we must either swim or die,
We had one boat, 't would carry four,
With some supplies, but nothing more,
And in our family were five
That we proposed to keep alive.
There were myself and my good wife
Anxious of course to cling to life,
My son, his wife, and the hired man
(A faithful boy; they call him Dan),
We could not think of leaving him
And thought perhaps he could not swim.

'Twas very plain that we had need
Of one more boat; we had indeed,
And went to work that very day
And made a boat without delay.
'Twas made upon the stone boat plan
But large enough to carry Dan.

Of course we needed some supplies;
We had no cakes or chicken pies
To take with us on sudden call
Such as you take to granger hall;
But Wife had got a loaf of bread,
She sometimes has one loaf ahead,
And so we seemed provided now
If we could only take a cow.
But in our boat it would not do
It would sink the craft and all the crew.
But we could tie one to the boat
And she might either swim or float.

And now we thought our way was clear
And we had little more to fear,
For should the rising water come
And drive us out of house and home,
We'd take our boats you understand
And paddle for the nearest land.
But I am happy now to say
The clouds at last have cleared away.
We think our prospects all together
Are brightening with the brighter weather.
And I sincerely hope with you
In every sense the same is true.
Long may you live, and long possess
Peace, plenty, health and happiness.
May your dear children every day
Your care and kindness well repay.

▲ Asa Harding Stoddard memorialized the "Big Rain" with this poem. [GRPL, Stoddard-Close Collection]

Way Down in the Mines

Lumbering was not Grand Rapids' only industry. While some men labored in the forests and on the river, others were at work below the ground mining gypsum. The industry, still in operation today, got its start in 1838 when state geologist Douglas Houghton published the first account of the local gypsum deposits. Three years later, Daniel Ball and Warren Granger built a simple plaster mill and began grinding plaster.

Following the Civil War the original Ball and Granger mill had been forgotten, and four separate gypsum works operated at full capacity to meet the demand for plaster. Two quarries on the east side of the Grand River provided an estimated 25,000 tons of plaster per year from deposits that were a mere 10 to 12 feet below the surface, while mines on the west side of the river ran into hillsides and down to much greater depths. The Grand Rapids *Daily Eagle's* 1869 description of mines and milling operations provides a look at the nascent years of Grand Rapids' longest-running local industry.

The West Side of Grand River.

The first plaster discoveries on the west side of Grand River were made by Mr. R.E. Butterworth, an English gentleman of culture and enterprise, now proprietor of one of the principal machine shops and foundries in Grand Rapids. He purchased 162 acres of land, now owned by the Grand Rapids Plaster company, in 1842. His knowledge of geology led him to think that his land contained plaster rock, and he made repeated borings to ascertain the fact. In 1849 he discovered plaster near the present site of the Eagle Mills, and erected a plaster mill in 1852. In 1856 he sold to Hovey & Co. for $35,000.

Eagle Mills.

Hovey & Co. bought their property in 1856, and built their mill during the summer of 1857. The first year they mined about 2,000 tons. The business steadily increased until 1860, when the Grand Rapids Plaster Company was organized and the firm of Hovey & Co. merged in that. The amount of plaster quarried and sold by them prior to 1800 was about 98,000 tons, for 1869 the total will be about 18,000 tons. They have now increased their facilities, so that they can manufacture 60,000 barrels of calcined plaster annually, and can grind 200 tons of land plaster [lime] in 20 hours, and have the power to double their capacity if they choose. They have just completed and put in running order a new engine of 200 horse power, and have facilities for loading from 40 to 50 cars per day. They have also recently put in one of the Illinois Pneumatic Gas Company's machines for lighting their quarry and mill. The quarry is under a low bluff and is widely known as the great plaster cave, being about five acres in extent and covered with from 20 to 75 feet of earth and rock. The [gypsum] stratum is about 12 feet in thickness. The Lake Shore & Michigan Southern Railroad (Kalamazoo Division) runs through their mill yard, connecting with other railroads leading into the city.

Emmet Mills.

These mills are owned and worked by Taylor & McReynolds, who own about 40 acres of plaster land which will work out about 35,000 tons per acre. They bought the property two years ago, and have mined for the past two years an average of 8,000 tons per year. Their works have been trebled in extent during the year 1860, and can manufacture 250 tons of ground plaster in 22 hours, and 20,000 tons of stucco per year. Their location is on the Grand River, near the city limits and on the line of the Lake shore and Michigan Southern Railroad (Kalamazoo Division) and they quarry under the hill the same as the Eagle Mills. The product of this mill for 1869 will be about 8,000 tons.

The East Side of Grand River

There are two plaster quarries on the east side of Grand River, one owned by Geo. H. White & Co. and the other by F. Godfrey & Bro.

Geo. H. White & Co. now own the 80 acres on which the first mill was built, and land adjoining to the amount of 425 acres in all, of which about 300 acres is underlaid with plaster. The stratum now quarried is 12 feet in thickness, and is overlaid with from 12 to 16 feet of earth, and in places by a stratum of partially decomposed plaster, known as the "seven foot course." The following is the estimated product of these works from 1852 to the present time:

From 1842 - 1850 500 tons yearly.
" 1850 - 1860 2,000 " "
" 1860 - 1864 3,000 " "
" 1864 - 1869 8,000 " "
During the year 1869 12,000 " "

They have a water mill with one run of stone capable of grinding two tons per hour and a steam mill with two run of stone that grind four tons per hour, and storage for 4,000 tons of ground plaster. Their capital is sufficient to supply all the present or future

▼ Plaster mine workers gathered for this photograph in 1928, many years after the first mines were opened. [GRPL, Photo Collection]

demands of the trade. The works are located a half a mile south of the city limits, on the Grand Rapids & Indiana Railroad, having easy access to all other railroads, leading to the city, and also to Grand River. The plaster works of F. Godfrey and Brother furnishes 35,000 tons per acre. F. Godfrey discovered plaster at this point in 1859, and works were erected in 1860, the product for that year being about 1,000 tons. From this amount the yearly product has steadily increased until 1869, in which year they have quarried 12,000 tons. They have one water mill and a steam mill, each with two run of stone, and can grind in the two mills 80 tons of plaster in ten hours, or 160 tons in 20 hours.

◄*Grand Rapids Daily Eagle,* December 18, 1869, p. 1.

▲ The Grand Rapids Plaster Mill was a maze of buildings by 1888. [GRPL, *Grand Rapids Illustrated* Collection]

Hear That Lonesome Whistle Blow

Both the gypsum and lumber industries benefited from the expansion of railroad services to Grand Rapids. For ten years after the first train pulled into town from Detroit, residents dreamed of the day when the Grand Rapids and In-diana Railroad would be completed and a second line would enter the city, this one from the south, to provide a connection with major east-west lines between Chicago and New York. However, the Civil War and then a series of financial reverses conspired to prevent completion of the second road. Finally, on September 12, 1868, after several corporate restructurings and construction delays, an excited populace greeted the first passenger train on Grand Rapids' second railroad.

◄ The Grand Rapids and Indiana depot at Ionia south of Fulton was completed in September 1870. [GRPL, Stereo Card Collection]

◄ Next door was an office building that served the entire line, which ran from Fort Wayne to Petoskey. [GRPL, James R. Hooper Collection]

On Saturday evening, September 12th, a locomotive with a train of cars crossed Grand River, in this city, on the bridge of the Grand Rapids and Indiana Railroad; and this event may be properly termed an epoch from which is to be dated an important era in the history of Grand Rapids.

It is well known that this road has been in operation since the first of January last, from Cedar Springs to this city, terminating at Bridge street, on the west side of the river. . . .

Several days past the work of laying the track around the curve from West Division street to and across the bridge has attracted much attention on the part of our citizens; and when, on Saturday afternoon, the fact became known that the train, on its arrival from Cedar Springs would pass over the bridge, there was a lively and enthusiastic interest manifested by the friends of the road, a large number congregating around the busy tracklayers who were then extending the track from the east end of the bridge on Ferry street. As the time approached for the arrival of the train, the crowd moved to the depot on the West side, for the purpose of riding over the bridge. Several platform cars loaded with ties and iron, stood on the track south of Bridge street, to be pushed over by the train. A portion of the crowd mounted these cars, while others waited for the arrival of the coming train, preferring to ride on the locomotive. The train came in "on time;" Conductor Blaisdell shouted "all aboard," and the train, with its cheering load of passengers, moved on over the new and untried bridge. While passing over the bridge a *feu de joi* came up from a cannon planted on the hill below, and many roofs and windows were occupied by those who witnessed the cheering spectacle.

When the train stopped, at the crossing of Justice St., loud cheers were given for the Grand Rapids and Indiana Railroad, its directors, contractors and operators.

▲ *Grand Rapids Daily Eagle,* September 14, 1868, p. 1

Riding on the Plank

Railroads were relatively fast and smooth, and more and more people turned to them for travel. However, they served only a limited area, and stagecoaches still ran daily between Grand Rapids and neighboring cities, bumping their way over dirt and gravel roads augmented by planks in low-lying spots. A.H. Stoddard "rode the plank" as a youngster and, later, with his poetry, captured the jolting rhythm of the ride.

RIDING ON THE PLANK.

Did you ever, friend or stranger
Let me ask you free and frank.
Brave the peril, dare the danger,
Of a journey on the Plank?

Ever see the wild commotion.
Hear the clatter, din and clank,
Feel the quick electric motion,
Caused by riding on the Plank?

Horses balking, drivers lashing,
Wishing all plank roads in — blank —
And their owners with them flashing,
So it goes upon the Plank.

Wagons creaking, groaning, crashing,
Wrecks bestrewing either bank,
Jarring, jolting, jamming, dashing,
This is riding on the Plank.

Crocks and baskets rolling, smashing,
Helpless owners looking blank,
Eggs and butter mixing, mashing,
Cannot help it on the Plank.

Hats and bonnets strangely rocking,
Leave no space between them blank;
Kisses stolen, oh! what shocking
Things do happen, on the Plank.

Fathers swearing, children squalling,
Angry mothers try to spank;
Seats upset and they go on sprawling
In the wagon on the Plank.

Tipping over, mercy on us!
Broken ribs, or shattered shank,
These afflictions come upon us,
Come from riding on the Plank.

Here, if you can save the pieces,
Lucky stars you well may thank,
Though your doctor bill increases,
'Tis for riding on the Plank.

Ye, with torpid livers sickened,
Cold and languid, lean and lank,
Needing life-blood warmed and quickened,
Try a journey on the Plank.

Ye, half dead with indigestion,
Stomachs cold as Greenland's bank,
This will cure without a question,
Take one ride upon the Plank.

▲ Stagecoaches provided regular service on the Kalamazoo road to Grand Rapids. [GRPL, Photo Collection]

▲ Wide, thick, wooden planks carried wagons and buggies over swampy low-lying areas. [GRPL, Photo Collection]

◀ A.H. Stoddard, *Miscellaneous Poems*, pp. 8-10.

The Not-So-Grand River

With the city's growth came changes in the natural landscape. Most obvious were those occurring along the banks of the Grand River, where steamboat landings, factories, and garbage dumping conspired to create a drab urban riverscape that stood in stark contrast to miles of relatively untouched rural river scenery.

Cadette Everett Fitch, the daughter of Professor Franklin Everett, was an avid reader of adventure and travel books. In 1889, after reading the description of a rowboat trip down England's Thames River, she immediately decided that, with her teenage children, Louise and George, she would make a similar trip down the Grand River from Grand Rapids to Grand Haven. Along the way the trio encountered Grand Rapids' urban pollution as well as peaceful rural stretches little changed by either industry or riverboat travel. Like Elizabeth Robins Pennell, her inspiration for the rowboat adventure, Cadette Fitch kept a journal of her voyage, complete with detailed drawings.

Fitch's account begins at the boat landing in Grand Rapids where she and her children selected a small rowboat for the trip.

The outlook was unpromising. Every boat was leaky, not one in perfect condition. Some, on being turned over, would show cracks, below water line, wide enough through which to inspect a landscape. The larger boats were positively dangerous; and the owner seemed to think it doubtful if any were fit for so long a journey. . . .

To give up so much anticipated pleasure, was out of the question, so the smallest boat was, at last selected, and although it was shabby and somewhat damp and slimy, it was considered better than to terminate the trip at this early stage. . . .

The frail boat was loaded, and the happy crew pushed off. . . .

The channel was, as usual, covered with a green odoriferous scum, mixed with oil from the gas works, and was uninviting to ride through, but this was an unpleasantness of short duration, and a few minutes served to leave it behind.

Then came the sense of relief and calm enjoyment of the clear, dignified, moving current of the river.

Willows, Elms, Maples and other trees, and shrubs, line the banks in rich profusion, and when once accustomed to the motion of the boat, and more confident that it was not going over, if reasonable quiet was maintained, all enjoyed, to the utmost, the delicious panorama.

The plaster bed, with its tall white chimney, and quaint buildings, with surrounding verdure was soon in sight, and the reflections in the water, were especially charming, and it was hard to pass without some feeble attempt to make a sketch, but it was late, and the sun was warm, so it was decided to take an overland route to the same locality, in the near future. . . .

The steamer *Barrett* passed us, dragging a scow loaded with lumber, and bushel baskets. One

◄ Cadette Everett Fitch sketched this scene as she and her children selected a leaky rowboat for their trip down the Grand River. [GRPL, Cadette Everett Fitch Collection]

of the men, in the pilot house, paid the young lady of our party the compliment of grabbing a hat from the head of the man standing by him, and waving it . . . .

We reached Grandville at five o'clock, left part of our baggage at the nearest house, after having turned the boat over, and then walked to the hotel, half a mile away . . . .

At eight in the morning we were on our way again. The river and woods were more lovely than ever, and we sang and chattered as merrily as the robins and thrushes from their hiding places in the green foliage . . . .

At different times we gathered Asters, Cardinals, and Goldenrod, and also landed where we were told to inspect the Silver Springs. The water here seems wonderfully pure and sparkling, and the dark rich woods, behind the spring form a fitting setting for the crystal fountain . . . .

At half past six we reached Lamont and thought some of pushing on to Eastmanville but it was getting dark and vapor was rising. George went up the hill to a store to get a lock and chain for the boat, and the merchant advised us to remain there as the hotel at Eastmanville could not be recommended. Lamont had no establishment of the kind, but an old lady, Mrs. Rice, sometimes opened her house to transients . . . .

The evening was spent in listening to old reminiscences, accounts of the struggles of early settlers and of their dances, and good times generally. This lady's home was a favorite resort. We had good beds, and a fair breakfast, biscuit, apple sauce, coffee.

Lamont is built upon hills, and is very picturesque, owing, partly, to its numerous houses, mills and barns that are not only deserted, but in a ruined condition. The piers of an old bridge stand, as sentinels, in the river, and will probably remain many a year longer before falling, as no one chooses to help time in his destructive work. It was hard to leave this locality as there were many fine points for sketching; we remained until eleven o'clock, and the sun was very warm.

We found Eastmanville like Lamont a place of only three or four hundred inhabitants. Enterprising citizens have left, one by one, and those who remain have no hope that the old time prosperity will return . . . .

On, on we go, sometimes singing, or reading aloud, and always noting and speaking of every new object of interest. The glowing sun, in its fiery gorgeous setting; peculiar trees, of many kinds, and fluffy willows; tall waving rice grass, much higher than our heads, among which flock myriads of birds, looking from a distance, like mosquitos; patches of lily pads; long stretches of piles, which extend for miles to hold secure the logs of our enterprising lumbermen.

We pass under the swing bridge after leaving Spring Lake, and feast our eyes upon the white sand hills in the distance. We notice several ruined boats, great hulks that are mere skeletons; having bravely done their work, their worn out frames are left, exposed to wind and sun and are interesting only to the antiquarian. New boats are being built not far away, one of which is beautiful and symmetrical in its proportions; a yacht of some jaunty sort.

A heavy mist like a cloud hangs, like a veil, over the lowland, at our right, as we approach Grand Haven, and at the dock we see the grand steamer *Milwaukee* and our little *Barrett*, which looks like a pigmy in such aristocratic company. All are loading up for the next trip, and we pass them and draw up to the landing . . . .

We expressed much regret that the river was only 40 miles long from our starting point and would have gladly continued a trip which had been so full of rich enjoyment. We can easily see why Gypsies loathe the confinement of houses. Their long accustomed wanderings in the fresh air, and freedom from all the conventionalities of life, totally unfit them for what we call higher civilization.

◄ Cadette Everett Fitch Collection, Grand Rapids Public Library.

▲ The Fitch family: Cadette, children Louise and George, and husband George Clay Fitch. [GRPL, George E. Fitch Collection]

◄ Lamont was the second-night stopping place for the Fitch party. [GRPL, Cadette Everett Fitch Collection]

Clang, Clang, Clang Goes the Trolley

Gradually, rail travel came to dominate 19th-century public transportation. Between cities railroads supplanted steamboats and stagecoaches, and within cities horse-drawn trolleys were replaced by cable cars and electric streetcars. New advances in travel technology were always greeted enthusiastically, and a large crowd turned out to witness the inauguration of Grand Rapids' first cable-car system.

From a powerhouse at the top of Lyon Street hill, a "wire rope" cable ran beneath a slot in the street centered between narrow iron rails. On these tracks ran "grip" cars, each with a clutch on its underside that clamped onto the cable; the moving cable pulled the cars noiselessly along their route.

Stopping was usually a simple matter of releasing the clamp and applying a brake to the car's wheels. Occasionally, however, strands would break loose from the cable and become entangled with the clamp so that the car would not stop. In these instances, the car man would clang away on his bell, warning carriages and pedestrians to clear the way until the cable could be stopped.

Fortunately, no such mishap marred the car's maiden run on April 16, 1888, and onlookers were treated to their first view of a smoothly functioning system that promised to make light work of the long, hard trip up Lyon Street hill.

Despite the excitement they generated, Grand Rapids cable cars were destined for a short life. In 1890, the company switched to electric streetcars. Although the streetcars were critically acclaimed by riders from the beginning, financial success came more slowly. Because of the expense involved in laying track and building adequate powerhouses, it took several years and a large capital investment before the electric railway company managed to turn a profit.

Nearly everybody on the hill had been called out by the unusual sound of the cable as it hummed away out of sight under the surface of the street, and many were the attempts to see the mysterious hummer. No one, however, succeeded except the ubiquitous small boy who was willing to sacrifice his dignity and put his eye down to the crack. . . .

The crowd, gradually thickened; men, women and children stopped at the Ionia, Ottawa and Lyon street crossings, peered anxiously down through the narrow slot into the dark conduit in the endeavor to get a glimpse at the cable which was to drag the heavy cars up the Lyon street hill (eight feet rise to the hundred); they could see nothing, however, and had to content themselves with the music of the hum. "Is the grip car really coming down this afternoon?" was a question asked over and over again; but no one seemed to know, though the impression grew, that it certainly would. Between three and four o'clock the people began to thicken perceptibly all along Lyon street from the post office building to the river, and by 4 o'clock the sidewalks and the street were quite black with the crowds, all gazing earnestly up Lyon street hill. Still no cable car, but the streets grew blacker with people; an unusual number of policemen put in an appearance along the cable track; Supt. I.C. Smith was seen spurring his horse about the various crossings, and then the crowd knew for sure they'd see the first grip car if they only waited.

At 4:27 precisely by the tower clock the long-looked for grip hove in sight on Lyon street hill at about Lafayette street. "There she comes," shouted a voice, a chorus of voices echoed the words; all faces were turned hillwards, the noise of voices settled to a low murmur, and everybody watched the car as it steadily moved down the hill with no visible propelling power, stopping at various street crossings along the way. When the grip car bell rang for the Canal street crossing the Tower clock marked 4:33, and when the grip stopped at the river terminus it was 4:34, the car having been just seven minutes making the run from Lafayette street to the river bank. Not until the car stopped at the foot of Lyon street did most of the people remove their steady gaze from it. Then they all seemed to take a long breath.

At 4:36 the car started back up the hill, and a still larger crowd watched its returning course, and as it steadily climbed the steep grade remarks like these were the order: "That beats horse or mule power;" "The cable road's the thing;" "I tell you, that cable road will increase the value of property on the hill fully half a million dollars at the least calculation;"

◄ Newspaper sketch of one of Grand Rapids' new cable cars. [GRPL, Harry Lincoln Creswell Scrapbook]

"Just see how she walks up that grade;" "Oh, it's a big thing for the town, I tell you," etc. At just 4:43 the returning car disappeared behind the hill having made the return from the river bank terminus to Lafayette street, in seven minutes, exactly the same time in which it made the downward trip between the same points.

But citizens on the hill who do not keep a carriage may rejoice. No longer will it be necessary for them to stick their toes in or walk backwards in order to ascend the icy incline in winter or to toil upwards in the wilting heats of summer; for the cable road is now an accomplished fact.

▲ Harry Lincoln Creswell Scrapbook, Grand Rapids Public Library.

◄ Horse-drawn trolleys, like this car used in a 1920s parade, served Grand Rapids from 1865 until the early 1890s. [GRPL, Morris Collection]

Horse trolleys and ► cable cars could travel in either direction without having to turn around. [GRPL, Photo Collection]

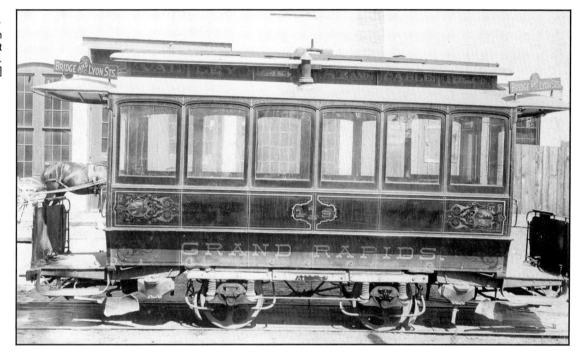

◄ Introduced in 1891, electric streetcars quickly replaced trolleys and cable cars. [GRPL, Photo Collection]

A Clash in the Dark of Night

In another part of its plan to build a single, citywide transportation network, the Street Railway Company of Grand Rapids bought up several existing horse-trolley and steam-powered car lines, and laid new track to extend streetcar service to all parts of the city.

In 1888, the company set about building a new line to run along Eastern Avenue (then known as East Street) between Sherman Street and the newly built car barns on Cherry Street. Company officials planned to operate the line on a full seven-day schedule, with two steam-powered "dummy" engines pulling open "summer" cars.

Area residents however, did not want the noisy, and in their minds potentially dangerous, cars passing through their neighborhood. Nor did parishioners of the Eastern Avenue Christian Reformed Church welcome the possibility that services would be interrupted by raucous Sunday revelers on their way to and from the gin mills and dance halls at Reeds Lake. Court petitions seeking to stop the company were unavailing, so when company workmen tried to install tracks in front of the church late one night, protesting citizens took matters into their own hands, tearing up the tracks as quickly as they were laid. Their vigilante tactics only stalled construction for a time; the new line was eventually put into service.

Last evening as soon as it was known that Judge Montgomery had decided the East St. injunction suit in favor of the Street Railway Company, the officers immediately called in every available man in the employ of the company, and about 9 o'clock commenced laying the track for the dummy road on the east line of East St., from Sherman St. to Buckeye St., one block south of Cherry St. As the work progressed the citizens of that part of the city and township gathered around the men at work and used all kinds of threats to make them quit work, but it was of no avail. It was then announced that the company would not be permitted to lay its rails in front of the Holland church, on East St., and then the crowd congregated, and as fast as the men would lay down the ties and spike the rails, they would be carried away by the citizens. Trackmaster Campbell soon put a stop to the racket by spiking the rails as fast as they were laid down, and sometimes the men would be spiking a rail at one end while fifteen or twenty men and women would have hold of the other end trying to carry it away. Finding that this scheme did not work they commenced to shower the men with stones and clubs, and for a short time things were very interesting, no one was seriously hurt, however, except one man in the attacking party, and he was struck on the head with a stone by one of his own crowd.

When a *Telegram Herald* reporter visited the seat of war at 2 o'clock this morning the cruel war was over and everything was quiet. The track was being laid at a lively rate northward to Wealthy Ave. so that when the paper is read this morning the track will no doubt be laid from the Sherman St. barn to Buckeye St. and a dummy will be steamed up and passed over the track.

The work was done under the direction of trackmaster Donald Campbell, who had forty-five men at work all night.

As the track is laid and a train passed over the road this will, in all probability, put an end to all further law suits, unless the property owners on East St. sue the company for private damages.

▲ *Grand Rapids Telegram-Herald*, May 10, 1888, p. 3.

▲ The Eastern Avenue Christian Reformed Church was the center of the anti-streetcar protest. [Calvin College Heritage Collection]

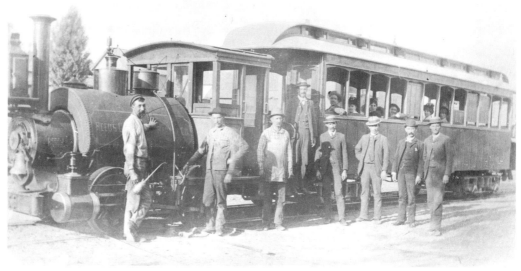

▲ Streetcars pulled by a "dummy" steam engine were a disruption for Sunday worshipers. [GRPL, Godfrey Anderson Collection]

Special Delivery

Along with transportation changes came communication improvements. Nearly isolated in their earliest days, the pioneer citizens of Grand Rapids had looked forward to the arrival of riverboats and stagecoaches, and rushed to see what new mail they carried. After the Civil War, local residents grew accustomed to the regular, daily arrival of mail on the trains, and the even more speedy arrival of news over telegraph lines. But with each improvement, impatient citizens called for still better service, including daily home delivery. They got their wish on September 1, 1873, when regular home mail delivery was instituted to over 3,000 homes. With the usual amount of boasting about Grand Rapids' steady march toward the front ranks among modern cities, local newspapers proudly hailed the inauguration of the new mail delivery service.

We are fast gathering about us the institutions and characteristics of a large city, such as Grand Rapids is destined to be within fewer years than most of us, probably, are aware. With our water works, noble school buildings, churches raising their towers and spires above us, numerous new business blocks of the grandest appearance, extension of horse railroads and manufactories, splendid new opera house in erection, and another first-class hotel coming next — with these and other rapidly increasing elements of metropolitan prosperity, today comes the postal delivery, in addition to all the rest. For among the multiplying benefits conferred, under a beneficent Administration, upon all communities of sufficient number throughout the broad land, is this of having our letters left at our houses and places of business, instead of having to go to the post-office for them.

By the force of habit, the great mass of our people will continue, for some time, going to the post office, and especially a large class who make daily visits there at certain hours of general congregation, not so much to post or get letters, or to transact postal business, as to see who else is there, or meet acquaintances and gossip, as if it were a sort of public social exchange. This was always a nuisance to all who wanted to do their post-office business and then get about their other business as speedily as possible, besides being improper for other and obvious reasons. If the establishment of the postal delivery and the posting of letters in boxes distributed throughout the city shall have the effect of breaking up this practice, it will be so much extra good, besides the manifold conveniences and expedition of the postal service among our citizens.

In compliance with the request of Postmaster Turner the carriers have been at work for the past two or three weeks in getting posted in regard to their routes, and they expect to be able to deliver 3,000 letters on Monday. For their accommodation a distributing table twenty-three feet in length has been placed in the office, which is furnished with pigeon holes for letters. For the present there will be only three deliveries per day. The first, at 8 a.m., will be confined to the business portion of the city, and will embrace all late night mails and the early morning mails from Detroit and Chicago. The second is at 11:30. This will be a general delivery, extending to all parts of the city. The carriers will leave the office promptly on time, and attend first to the wants of business men. The third and last delivery takes place at 5:30 p.m. This one has been made thus late in order to distribute the large eastern mail which comes via the Michigan Central, arriving soon after 5 o'clock. The average number of letters received by this mail is 2,000, and it speaks well for the promptness of the office to state that the carriers will commence operation twenty minutes after its arrival. This delivery extends to every business man in the city, but does not take in the outskirts, there being only one suburban delivery per day. During their rounds the carriers will collect mail as well as distribute; at least they will as soon as the boxes arrive. Owing to an unaccountable delay they have not yet arrived, but are expected at any moment. We are informed that they can be put in place in one day. These collections will be made so as to connect with all outgoing mails, and an extra one will be made at 6:30 p.m. to connect with the evening trains. As soon as the present force become well accustomed to their duties, the number of carriers will be increased, and four daily deliveries made; but at present the department thinks it best to only make three and make them correctly, instead of more with a liability to mistakes.

◄ *Grand Rapids Daily Eagle,* September 1, 1873, p. 1.

▼ Below left: Grand Rapids' mail carriers, photographed shortly after daily delivery began. [GRPL, James R. Hooper Collection].
The new Post Office and Federal Building, (right) on the corner of Pearl and Division, was opened in September 1879. [GRPL, Stereo Card Collection]

"Hello, Leitelt, This Is Apted"

No one thought to write down what was said during Grand Rapids' first telephone call. But it is known that the call took place on October 30, 1877, between the downtown office of the Grand Rapids Plaster Company, and the gypsum mine three miles away. On one end of the line was company manager William S. Hovey, on the other was his assistant, Alfred Apted.

Grand Rapids had gotten into the telephone business early because J.W. Converse, president of the plaster company, was a friend of Alexander Graham Bell, who had given him two primitive, wooden, telephone receivers. Back in Grand Rapids, a wire was strung between the company office and the mine, and preparations were made for the first call.

Among those invited to witness the historic moment was city alderman Adolph Leitelt who refused to believe voices could be transmitted by wire. Leitelt may have observed Grand Rapids' first telephone conversation with skepticism, but others saw great potential and set to work capitalizing on the new invention. Within two years of the first call, a central station had been established with nearly 100 subscribers, and by 1883, limited long-distance service was available to Muskegon, Big Rapids, Grand Haven, and Ionia. In 1884 the telephone company began offering 24-hour service.

▲ William Hovey (top) and Adolph Leitelt participated in Grand Rapids' first telephone call. [GRPL, Photo Collection]

The possibilities of the telephone were just coming to light — a few believed but nearly every one scoffed and ridiculed the idea of talking by wire.

William Hovey and his able assistant, Mr. Apted, were heads of the Grand Rapids Plaster Co. Mr. Hovey's office on Monroe Ave. and Mr. Apted's at the mills three miles away were the first places connected by wire. This was an experiment and was made largely with a view of securing quick fire service.

I was eagerly watching the venture. One day Mr. Hovey sent his buggy for me and on the way picked up Mr. [Adolph] Leitelt. We entered the office to find several other men there. Mr. Hovey said to the alderman: "Apted at the mills wishes to talk with you." He placed the receiver to Mr. Leitelt's ear and told him to speak up loud. Leitelt's voice was in proportion to his body and when he spoke everything in the office vibrated. Mr. Apted replied with a joke that caused a roar of laughter.

Mr. Leitelt dropped the receiver, going out into the hallway. It was empty, so he explored the coatroom and every place where a man might be concealed, all the time getting more impatient until at last he turned on Hovey with a roar that was far from a song of peace and returned to his own office in full belief that he was being made the victim of farce.

▲ Charles E. Belknap, *The Yesterdays of Grand Rapids*, p. 35.

◄ These simple instruments were used for the city's first telephone call. [GRPL, Photo Collection]

▲ Grand Rapids' first telephone directory, published in 1879, easily fit on a single page. [GRPL, Unprocessed Collection]

Turning on the Lights

Not long after Grand Rapidians had begun to string telephone lines around the city, the advent of electric lighting introduced a second set of wires in the downtown area. Gas lamps had lit downtown city streets and well-to-do homes since 1857, but it was not until July 24, 1880, that electric lights, operating on power generated by the Grand Rapids Electric Light and Power Company, made their appearance.

▲ Electrical appliance dealers sprang up quickly after the introduction of electricity to the city. [*Grand Rapids and Kent County Directory,* 1886-87, p. 53]

The Electric Light.

Grand Rapids has the electric light as a permanent feature. As expected Saturday afternoon, Sweet's Hotel, the Great Wardrobe, Spring & Co.'s, A. Preusser, the Arcade, the Star Clothing House and the Wolverine Furniture Factory were lighted with sixteen of Brush's electric lights, put in by the Grand Rapids Electric Light and Power Company. The light was a grand success, strong, steady, white and uniform. It called thousands of people on the streets and into places lighted by it, and was admired and enjoyed by all. Some complained that it was too bright and made their eyes ache, dazzled them; but such had looked directly at the light. When they become more accustomed to the light they will not think of gazing at the lanterns any more than they now do at the sun.

The dyno-generator which furnishes the electricity is the Brush patent, and is located in the Wolverine company's factory, where it is propelled by water power. It will furnish eighteen lanterns. It was driven at 820 revolutions to the minute Saturday night. Probably it will not run quite so fast, as a rule.

If more lights are to be used, and there probably will be, as several persons are talking of getting them, another generator will be put in. The price charged for the use of these lights — like telephones, they are not sold — is $120 per annum. The Brush light is probably the best in use.

▲ *Grand Rapids Daily Eagle,* July 26, 1880, p. 3.

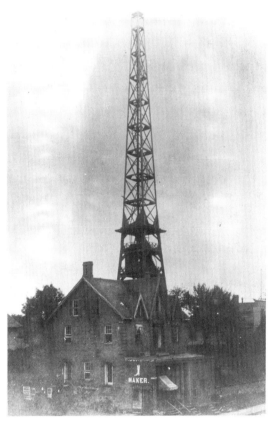

▲ Carbon arc lights atop tall towers supplied the city with its initial electrical street lighting. [GRPL, George E. Fitch Collection]

◄ Sweet's Hotel was one of the city's earliest electrically lighted buildings. [GRPL, George E. Fitch Collection]

The Furniture City

Before the Civil War, furniture manufacturing in Grand Rapids was confined to a few shops and small factories. Taking root in the postwar decades, however, the industry grew to a point where it employed an estimated one-third of all city laborers. By 1890, the nation's largest furniture companies were located in Grand Rapids, and the city ranked third, behind only New England and Chicago, in the amount of furniture its factories produced.

Industry leaders invented new equipment, streamlined manufacturing processes, created retailing networks, and devised innovative marketing schemes using the latest photographic and printing technology. Among the industry's enterprising young men was William A. Berkey, who started his company in the months just before the outbreak of the Civil War and watched it prosper in the postwar decades. In 1890, when his original factory building, near the corner of today's Michigan Street and Monroe Avenue, was about to be torn down, Berkey recalled the beginnings of Berkey and Gay, one of the best-known names in Grand Rapids furniture manufacturing history.

As the 19th century drew to a close, Grand Rapids had a reputation for furniture design and manufacturing that attracted buyers from across the United States. Local manufacturers had won awards and acclaim from all corners and built up a vast marketing system that included two major shows in Grand Rapids each year. As orders multiplied, the furniture makers built and expanded their factories with astonishing speed. So great was the expansion that there was virtually no resemblance between the earliest factories, remembered by William Berkey below, and the thriving industry that was described by the *Weekly Democrat* at the end of the century.

▲ Julius (top) and William Berkey (below) were Grand Rapids furniture industry pioneers. [GRPL, Photo Collection]

Today twenty workmen are engaged in dismantling the old Berkey furniture factory that has stood for more than thirty years upon the East side canal, about 200 feet north of Bridge street....

The structure was erected by Wm. A. Berkey in 1859 for a sash and door factory and the pioneer furniture manufacturer said of it this morning:

I bought the lot upon which the building stands in 1859 for $2,000 and the corner lots where the Clarendon hotel now is for $1,500. Everybody laughed at me at the time for purchasing those corner lots; they said they would never be of any more value and that I would lose in my investment.... When I began to do business in that old shop I was so poor that it took me about three years to get all the floors laid. I put down a patch of floor, about 40x50 feet, and did business in this section of the building for a long time. I manufactured sash, doors, etc., here using water power for the little machinery operated.

Later on I began making furniture in a small way, manufacturing the cheaper grades of bedsteads, wash stands, etc., and disposing of the goods in the white [unfinished]. The building has been filled with the most inflammable of material during its existence; all kinds of lights have been used in it, and yet it had never been on fire but once that I can remember. The fire originated through carelessness. One of the employees took some scorched wood and dumped it into the wooden box flue we used to put the shavings into. The wood set fire to the dust and shavings caught in the cracks of the conveyor and it was at once ablaze. William Solomon, now deceased, came along and discovered the fire; he took off his overcoat, soaked it in the canal and readily put out the flames.

▲ *Grand Rapids Evening Leader*, February 4, 1890, p. 1.

▲ George Gay joined the Berkey brothers to form what became the giant Berkey and Gay company. [GRPL, Photo Collection]

Nelson Matter Furniture Company won a Centennial certificate (above) for this elaborate bedroom suite. [GRPL, *Nelson Matter Furniture Catalogs*, ca. 1880; *Furniture Manufacturer and Artisan*, December 1932, p. 13]

◄ Carefully handcrafted finishes were a hallmark of Grand Rapids' best furniture. [GRPL, Furniture Manufacturers Association Collection]

This city has become the recognized furniture center of the United States. When the seasons open buyers come here from all parts of the country to see the fresh styles and to place orders, and not only do the buyers come, but also the most accomplished salesmen of the leading manufacturers in other cities, whose object is to intercept the trade that would otherwise pass them by. Already this season about one hundred and fifty buyers have been in town.... Forty outside manufacturing firms have temporary headquarters here....

There are two seasons in the furniture business, the spring opening in January and the fall in July, and twice a year the manufacturers make complete and sweeping changes in their goods. Furniture which in the spring may be considered elegant, in the fall is put in the background and something entirely different takes its place.... In the regular line of many of the manufacturers there are from 150 to 200 different places. Every six months the designs and patterns of the whole lot are completely altered. The designer is the most important man about the establishment and draws the highest salary, and earns every cent he gets.... One designer in this city is said to receive an annual salary of $7,000, and several get $5,000 or more.

The furniture manufactured here is almost exclusively for the bedroom, dining room, hall and library; one concern turns out parlor goods, another produces rattan chairs and another makes lounges, but all the others devote their entire energies to manufacturing the kinds of furniture named.

The most popular material for the medium priced goods, and even the very best, is quarter sawed oak. Mahogany, of course will always reign as a cabinet wood, and its popularity will never grow less with those who can stand the expense, but it is oak that has captured the hearts of the masses, and oak is today the king

of all the woods.... Cherry is also used, walnut, once so popular and fashionable, has gone completely out of style, bird's eye and curly maple are very handsome for light colored goods and are being used to a limited extent, and birch, finished in the natural color is pretty, popular and cheap....

There are so many finishes now that the manufacturers are cautious in making up their stocks for fear that some particular style may be left on their hands. It is the custom to manufacture the goods in the white and then finish them in such styles and quantities as the trade may desire....

Cheap furniture is made chiefly of ash or maple, and, considering the price, is remarkably good. Suites that are sold to the trade today for $12.50 each, at a profit to the manufacturers, would have cost 10 years ago twice or three times as much. It is only by having all the latest improved and time saving tools and machinery that this result can be attained. No unnecessary time is lost in handling materials or manipulating parts. The lumber is unloaded from the cars into the dry kilns, thence without extra handling is shoved into the machine room on trucks, and then passes through the factory without a hitch or delay, until at last it lands in the shipping room complete and ready for immediate

use. It is the same with the factories where the higher grades of furniture are made; the materials are handled with as little delay and friction as possible, and the progress of the lumber is rapid and steady toward the shipping room....

After the rush of buyers the traveling men start out with their photograph albums to visit the dealers who failed to show up at the opening. They travel "light" and get to all parts of the country, and until the middle of June the orders will continue pouring in from all directions. The designers have already commenced their labors for next season, and next July will be prepared to show a complete line of goods, new in design and finish, and the buyers will again be here to place their orders for the fall season.

◄ Grand Rapids Weekly Democrat, February 13, 1890, p. 4.

▼ George (left) and William Widdicomb were founders with their brothers John and Harry, of Widdicomb Brothers Furniture Co. [GRPL, Photo Collection; Oversized Photo Collection]

◄ The Widdicomb brothers and T.F. Richards operated this factory in 1870. [GRPL, Furniture Manufacturers Association Collection]

Picture This

One of the innovations Grand Rapids manufacturers brought to the furniture industry was catalogs of photographs to display their wares. Initially, new pieces were photographed for albums that traveling salesmen could use to show all the latest product lines without the nuisance of carrying scale models or sample pieces. Later, when printing technology improved, elaborate catalogs with reprinted photographs and color drawings were distributed throughout the nation.

◀ Photographer James Bayne started a Grand Rapids company specializing in photographing furniture. [*Grand Rapids Furniture Record*, October 1900, p. 166]

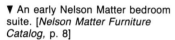

▼ An early Nelson Matter bedroom suite. [*Nelson Matter Furniture Catalog*, p. 8]

◀ Clockwise from above: Early furniture photos from a Phoenix Company catalog. [GRPL, *Phoenix Furniture Company Catalog*, 1876, pp. 44, 32, 60]

Danger in the Factories

The price for the furniture industry's growth was paid with more than one currency. For some the investment was personal financial risk and endless hours of office work. For others, the cost was counted in dangerous working conditions where one careless movement could mean permanent injury — or death.

Whether contending with unguarded, high-speed, power equipment, hazardous paint and finishing chemicals, or cold, poorly lit, unventilated buildings, furniture workmen were at risk. Regulation of working conditions was minimal, and insurance benefits for the injured or their families were virtually nonexistent.

Injury and death were the workman's constant companion. Graphic newspaper descriptions of factory accidents were commonplace, but even by standards of the past century, the following account of three men who fell into a boiling water tub in the floor of a veneer works must have caused more than one reader to shudder.

"My God, boys, Jack's fell in the hole," was a cry that greeted the employees at the Grand Rapids Veneer Works a few moments before 6 o'clock Thursday evening as Andrew Killen dashed open the rear outside door and rushed inside. The full meaning of his words can only be realized when it is known that the hole he referred to is a large vat of boiling water used for soaking logs before cutting the veneer. It was in this same vat that Thomas Shields lost his life only a week ago, and the spot has since been regarded with horror by his former associates. Superintendent George Kingsnorth was standing near and together with several men started for the outside. Killen waited only long enough to say the words and with Kingsnorth rushed toward the vat, from which the steam was rising in such quantity as to make it difficult to see more than a foot ahead. A moment more and there was a loud splash, followed by screams of agony, and the men then realized that there were three men instead of one in the boiling water.

To reach the side of the hole took but a moment, and ready hands assisted the victims from their horrible positions. Killen was removed first and his injuries were not serious as he had been in but a moment and then only up to his knees. When Kingsnorth was raised and carried inside the shop, his groans were heartrending. "I'm done for, boys," said he with perfect consciousness, which he never lost.

"Jack" Gipson, the man who first fell in, must have been in the water fully five minutes before his comrades succeeded in getting him out. He was perfectly conscious, but shut his teeth tightly and allowed not a moan to escape. He was placed upon a panel and carried to his home, 41 Scribner street. As the bearers were turning into the yard, he said faintly, "hurry up boys, I am losing strength fast. . . ."

He called for his wife, an aged woman who was nearly heartbroken with grief. Gipson addressed but a few words of parting farewell and fell back to the pillows exhausted. From this he failed rapidly and at 8:45 the attendants passed out the word that he was dying. His wife tottered to his bedside and with frantic efforts tried in vain to get another word from her husband. He was unconscious and in a few moments ceased to breathe.

In the meantime the other two victims, Superintendent George Kingsnorth and Andrew Killen were conveyed to the residence of the former, 276 Turner street. Mr. Kingsnorth was placed upon a bed down stairs while Killen was carried upstairs and his wife notified. When she arrived, and in fact before it, the house was filled with sadness. The friends of the man upstairs surrounded his bedside and did everything possible for his relief. Opiates were administered and he was soon in a state of unconsciousness, not realizing his pain. His injuries were not serious as the burn extended only to his knees and he will recover. He resides with his wife and two children at 693 Coit avenue.

Much more sad was the scene downstairs where Mr. Kingsnorth was receiving the best medical assistance which could be had, four physicians being in attendance. His injuries were severe as he was scalded from his chest down. As with Gibson, his limbs and delicate portions of his body were completely parboiled and flesh almost falling off. . . .

George H. Kingsnorth, died at 5 o'clock yesterday morning at his residence, 276 Turner street. The blow was indeed a sad one to the family, by whom he was greatly beloved, for he was a kind and affectionate father and good husband. . . .

The factory where the sad catastrophe occurred was closed down soon after it happened and will not be started again until after the funeral of Mr. Kingsnorth. Among the employees and managers a general feeling of gloom prevails and the bereaved families have their deepest sympathy. "This blow is indeed a heavy one to me," said Manager Thwing last evening. "I get the blame or censure of the general public toward the company, and not only that but from the fact that George Kingsnorth was my personal friend. He was also my right bower at the factory. I see the jury says the place is dangerous but I don't consider it so, that is any more so than a railroad or buzz saw. However, we will improve and make the place more safe by all possible means that genius can suggest. The officials of the company always take care of any man injured in their employ, and we will do so in this case. Thus far I have stood all the expense myself personally."

◀ *Grand Rapids Weekly Democrat,* January 30, 1890, p. 3.

▼ With uncovered belts and open saws, furniture factories were the scene of many accidents. [GRPL, Widdicomb Furniture Company Collection]

A Factory Roll Call

With more than 4,600 workers in their employ, the Grand Rapids furniture makers accounted for an estimated four out of every ten manufacturing jobs in Grand Rapids. But while the furniture companies were far and away the city's largest employer, they were not alone. The following list, produced in 1888 by the Grand Rapids Association of Trade, indicates the many other factories, large and small — making everything from animal traps to washing machines — that contributed to the city's economy.

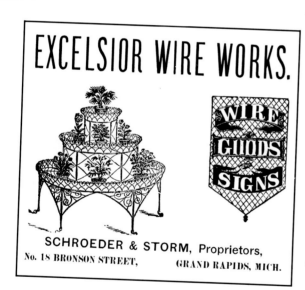

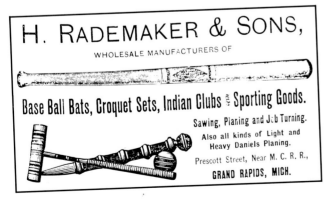

▲ These city directory advertisements illustrate the diversity of Grand Rapids manufacturers. [*Grand Rapids City Directories*, 1888, p. 118; 1885-86, p. 53; 1890, p. 109]

ALPHABETICAL LIST OF PRESENT FACTORIES

No. of Factories		Capital Employed	Product for 1887	Employees
1	Animal Traps	$ 2,000	$ 5,000	3
1	Asbestine Stone	3,000	20,000	12
1	Asphaltum Stone	5,000	35,000	15
1	Agricultural Implements	50,000	200,000	29
1	Awnings and Tents	4,000	11,000	5
2	Baking Pwdr, Spices, etc.	23,500	143,000	22
3	Blank Books	20,000	47,000	52
2	Burial Caskets	78,000	125,000	66
1	Brush	100,000	100,000	115
3	Bent Wood	35,000	60,000	34
2	Boat	3,500	14,000	9
5	Brick and Tile	155,000	805,000	167
7	Breweries	400,000	600,000	130
6	Bottling (Soda, Beer, etc.)	40,000	118,000	32
4	Broom	8,300	33,050	34
2	Belting	65,000	230,000	44
1	Base Ball Bats	20,000	40,000	30
12	Barrel and Keg	372,000	510,000	286
2	Brass Foundries	8,000	30,000	28
1	Bed Slat Fastener	1,000	3,500	4
2	Boot and Shoe	350,000	685,000	193
17	Boiler and Machinery	481,000	706,000	503
1	Basket	2,000	6,000	11
3	Coffee Extract	2,000	9,000	6
1	Curtain Pole	28,000	40,000	41
1	Car Shops	200,000	425,000	325
2	Cracker	145,000	185,000	45
14	Carriage and Wagon	482,500	787,500	425
4	Cornice (Metallic)	21,000	80,000	36
5	Clothing	100,000	200,000	138
1	Clothes Wringer	7,000	25,000	15
1	Cider and Vinegar	5,000	25,000	9
29	Cigar	205,000	376,000	136
12	Carpet Weaving	5,000	26,000	36
1	Carpet Sweeper	150,000	300,000	211
9	Confectioneries	125,000	432,000	175
1	Door Plates	1,000	3,000	3
1	Electrotype	10,000	20,000	5
2	Edge Tools	11,000	16,000	17
2	Electric Motors	50,000	75,000	7
4	Excelsior	57,000	110,000	58
1	Embalming Fluid	20,000	40,000	7
3	Engravers, etc.	15,000	37,000	28
2	Electric Light	250,000	250,000	35
2	File	4,000	7,000	8
1	Fishing Rod	10,000	15,000	15
3	Flavoring Extracts	45,000	145,000	23
6	Flour Mills	565,000	1,360,000	77
3	Furniture Wood Trimmings	150,000	110,000	81
1	Fire Grate	60,000	175,000	54
1	Faucet	2,500	6,000	3
1	Fly Paper	2,000	5,000	6
1	Furniture Clamp	2,500	5,000	4
28	Furniture	3,723,000	5,941,000	4,662

ALPHABETICAL LIST OF PRESENT FACTORIES

No. of Factories		Capital Employed	Product for 1887	Employees
1	Glue	25,000	25,000	10
1	Gas	250,000	130,000	30
5	Granite and Marble	40,000	110,000	45
1	Glove	1,000	2,500	6
1	Hand screw	2,000	8,000	8
8	Harness	26,000	78,000	39
1	Hat	1,000	5,000	4
1	Hoop Skirt	2,000	10,000	11
1	Ink	1,000	2,500	4
1	Knitting	15,000	25,000	39
1	Ladder	600	2,000	2
37	Lumber and Planing	3,861,000	4,586,000	684
1	Middling Purifier	25,000	50,000	23
2	Mattresses	17,000	75,000	36
2	Pickle	7,500	21,000	10
3	Packing Boxes	39,000	143,000	60
2	Paper Box	7,000	15,000	38
1	Piano	85,000	125,000	101
1	Portable House	5,000	20,000	9
1	Portable Letter Press	15,000	15,000	8
5	Patent Medicines	16,000	31,000	19
3	Potteries	6,000	18,000	14
5	Plaster Mills	750,000	200,000	127
1	Pump	25,000	6,500	4
1	Pot Ash	2,000	8,000	4
1	Refrigerator	75,000	100,000	81
3	Shirt	7,000	41,000	36
3	Stamp Stencil	6,000	26,000	7
6	Sash, Doors and Blinds	145,000	215,000	131
2	Show Cases	4,500	17,500	16
3	Saw	10,000	20,000	23
3	Soap	35,000	63,000	17
1	Spoon Hook	5,000	15,000	6
1	Tab and Pail	250,000	350,000	263
2	Trunk	13,500	49,500	19
1	Truss	2,000	5,000	5
3	Tanneries	415,000	1,030,000	316
5	Upholstering	49,000	161,000	54
1	Veneer	30,000	35,000	30
4	Wall Coating Compound	200,000	250,000	78
2	Well and Cistern Brick	2,000	7,500	9
1	Wire Nail	4,500	8,250	5
3	Willow and Rattan Ware	9,500	30,000	34
1	Wire Works	3,000	8,000	5
2	Wooden Shoe	1,500	4,000	5
1	Wheelbarrow	17,000	25,000	79
1	Wood Mantel	2,000	4,500	4
4	Wood Bank & Store Furn.	11,000	75,000	35
13	Woodenware (all kinds)	20,000	50,000	40
2	Wood Carving	2,000	5,000	5
1	Washing Machine	3,000	5,000	6
	Total	$15,216,400	$24,048,800	11,150

▲ *Grand Rapids As It Is*, pp. 20-21.

▲ *Grand Rapids City Directories*, 1890, p. 1156; 1888, p. 118.

▲ The Michigan Brewery was one of seven breweries in Grand Rapids in the 19th century. [Robert Baker, *The City of Grand Rapids*, p. 150]

The Globe and Valley City flour ▶ mills were a dominant feature along the west side of the Grand River. [Robert Baker, *The City of Grand Rapids*, p. 143]

"More Wagons"

Among midwestern farmers, "Harrison" was another familiar Grand Rapids name. William Harrison had moved his farm wagon business to Grand Rapids from Kalamazoo in 1856, and built a factory on Front Street. Unable to secure government contracts during the Civil War, he struggled to make ends meet, but recovered quickly once hostilities ceased. Soon Harrison wagons were following the agricultural frontier west to the prairie states and beyond.

At its peak, the Harrison wagon works, moved from its original Front Street site, sprawled over approximately 100 acres on Grand Rapids' far northwest side. Forming a community known as "Harrisonville," the site was complete with several factory buildings as well as houses built by the owner so that his workers could live close by. Charles Belknap, himself a wagon maker, knew Harrison well, and recalled his old competitor in a Grand Rapids *Press* column.

Mr. Harrison's motto was "More wagons." His every effort was to produce more wagons than any other factory in the world. Only the Studebaker factory at South Bend turned out a greater number. Soon after the Civil war the government backed the South Bend company in order that the great west might have transportation. Mr. Harrison had no backing other than the local bankers could give with long term farmers' notes as security. At one time Mr. Harrison had in his office an apple barrel full of notes tied in alphabetical bundles.

But the factory under competent management spread from the old stone fort to many branches, sawmills, smith shops, vast lumber yards. The manufacture of wagons became a leading industry of the north; other factories sprung up and competition was fierce, but still more wagons was the Harrison slogan, backed up with the bulldog persistency. For years long trails of wagons were a common sight on Monroe and Canal streets, the Harrison name going to every part of the universe.

In later years Mr. Harrison lived on the crest of West Bridge St. hill, his great plant was moved to the north end of the west side and he drove between home and factory in an open buckboard wagon. He was very simple in his taste. His lunch at noon often consisted of bread with a thick-cut steak toasted on the end of an iron rod over the coals of the battery boilers, the grimy stokers and greasy engineers sitting about with their full dinner pails, enjoyed their noon-day meal no more than did the "old man."

He never spent an idle day and at one time was very well-to-do, but unfortunate investments in oak forests that turned out to be huckleberry marshes depleted his resources and he departed this life just about the time a black frost in the guise of a gasoline smudge from the newly-invented automobile settled upon the wagon industry.

◄ *Grand Rapids Press,* October 10, 1922, p. 6.

Harrison wagons ► were well known to midwestern farmers. [*Grand Rapids City Directory,* 1886-87, p. 45]

Harrison Wagon Works

Cor. G. R. & I. R. R. and North St., Grand Rapids, Mich.

Awarded First Premiums at numerous County and State Fairs in the Eastern, Western and Middle States. Established 1850. Awarded Diplomas and Premiums at several fairs held on the Pacific Slope and in California.

THE BEST IS ALWAYS CHEAPEST.

The Cheapest because it is the Best. The General Favorite with all who use them.

(Ha! How easy it is to draw a Harrison Wagon. My Rabbits don't mind it.)

The HARRISON WAGON is Famous for its Stylish Appearance, Perfect Proportions, Excellent Construction, Strength of Material, Lightness of Running.

WM. HARRISON, Prop'r, GRAND RAPIDS, MICH.

▼ Harrison's Wagon Works, ca. 1890. [Albert Baxter, *History of the City of Grand Rapids,* p. 453]

▲ William Harrison. [Albert Baxter, *History of the City of Grand Rapids,* p. 454]

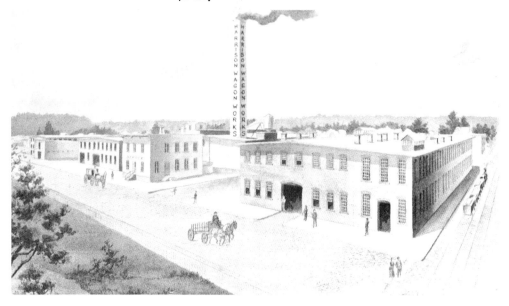

The Bissells' Better Idea

One of the larger manufacturing companies in Grand Rapids was the Bissell Carpet Sweeper Company, founded by husband and wife Melville R. and Anna Sutherland Bissell. The Bissells started out operating a china store, but both were entrepreneurs, and when Melville's tinkering produced a functioning mechanical sweeper, they devoted their energy to making and selling the relatively inexpensive labor-saving device.

The Bissells worked as a team, and when Melville died in 1889 at the age of 45, Anna took over the company and ran it until the 1920s. With enlightened management practices and astute economic decisions, she built up a successful international business. Shortly before her death, Anna Bissell's children produced the small, hand-lettered book honoring her achievements from which the following excerpts are taken.

In 1990, Anna Sutherland Bissell was inducted into the Michigan Women's Hall of Fame.

▲ Anna Sutherland Bissell. [GRPL, James R. Hooper Collection]

Bissell sweepers became ▲ an essential tool in American homes. [GRPL, Photo Collection]

▲ A carpet sweeper float by Bissell (above), reminded Grand Rapids residents of the company's products. [GRPL, James R. Hooper Collection]

The Bissell factory ► was for many years a familiar landmark along the Grand River. [GRPL, James R. Hooper Collection]

There is an epic quality in a life which has almost spanned this past century. Mrs. Melville R. Bissell of Grand Rapids personifies the enormous changes and possibilities of this kaleidoscopic hundred years. Since bravely setting out to teach school in an ox-cart with wooden wheels, she has lived to become a business executive keeping pace with the complexities of modern industrialism, a respected and beloved philanthropist in her own city, and a true matriarch in her family.

Melville Bissell, always of an inventive and ingenious turn of mind, began to experiment with a mechanical sweeper. He soon found ways to improve it and to contrive new devices. This fascinated his wife, who could not fail to be interested in a machine designed to lighten the monotonous burden of household drudgery.

The first Bissell sweeper was manufactured in an upper room of the china store, and as soon as patents were obtained, in 1876, Mr. Bissell began to produce them under his name. The first model was crude and noisy but it worked. It made housekeeping and storekeeping easier and solved the dust cloud problem. The sweepers were not all manufactured under one roof at first; but were assembled from parts made round about the town.

Mrs. Bissell helped to organize the onerous details of making and assembling and seeing that orders were delivered. She and Mr. Bissell had to do most of the selling, and they went from town to town and from city to city demonstrating the usefulness and value of their carpet sweepers. When the Bissell Carpet Sweeper Company was established in 1883, orders began to pour in. The sweeper was well and honestly built, and a standard of good workmanship was set at the beginning that has been maintained ever since.

In 1889, . . . Melville Bissell, never very strong, died and left her desolate. With a young family and a young industry to support she put aside her grief with great philosophy and courage and stepped behind her husband's empty desk and into the presidency of the Bissell Carpet Sweeper Company.

For the next thirty years Anna Bissell devoted her energies to building up an amazingly successful and stable business. Two things helped her. The first was the Bissell policy of establishing workmen's compensation insurance and a pension system when few other companies did so. Their workmen were and are proud of the factory and its traditions, and there has never been a strike. Second, Mrs. Bissell's remarkable gift of inspiring loyalty in anyone who comes in contact with her. She unified her factory, friends and family by her personality. She was implicitly fair, kind and reasonable; and there was a soothing kind of balance about her.

▲ *A Tribute to Anna Sutherland Bissell by Her Children,* Grand Rapids Public Library.

Sticking to Business

Of all Grand Rapids' 19th-century entrepreneurs, Otto and William Thum had perhaps the most interesting story and unusual product. Using a secret formula they originally developed in their father's drugstore during a summer vacation from college, their Tanglefoot Company produced sticky fly paper for consumers around the world.

Flies were a constant threat to public health during warm months. Early efforts to produce a sticky paper that would attract the insects and hold them fast were only partially successful. Too often, the paper dried out or the poisonous chemicals left permanent stains. Then, the Thum boys put their heads together and developed a non-staining, permanently sticky paper that could be pulled out from a small roll as it was needed. Before long, the Tanglefoot name was an international household word.

Coming home from Russia recently for a summer vacation [former Grand Rapids resident] S. Beach Conger, Associated Press representative at St. Petersburg, talked in regard to the Grand Rapids products that go abroad.

"Do you know," he exclaimed, "that Grand Rapids is better known in Europe as the home of Tanglefoot than as the producer of fine furniture? Grand Rapids furniture is found in an occasional home of wealth, but Tanglefoot is found everywhere. The name is this city's best commercial asset."

The same might be said by the traveler from South Africa, from Japan, from Australia, from China, from Italy, from Persia, from India, from Hawaii, from the Philippines, from Morocco, from Egypt and from almost any civilized land on the face of the globe. "The world is our market" is a slogan of the fly paper manufacturers of Grand Rapids and the slogan is absolutely true to fact.

A quarter of a century ago Otto Thum of the O. & W. Thum company, the pioneer sticky fly paper makers, was an ordinary well to do druggist. Flies were a pest in those days as they are now and their unwelcome presence and attentions bothered Mr. Thum to such an extent that he set about finding a method of catching them. Possibly he imitated nature and followed the method of the plant which captures insects by means of a sticky fluid it exudes, or possibly he hit upon the idea in some other way, but at any rate he produced a fly paper which caught and held flies when once they alighted upon it. Moreover it attracted flies to it.

Other druggists and persons had experimented with similar papers before that time, but their preparations were all of a temporary character, and quickly dried up. Mr. Thum evolved a preparation that did not dry up and Tanglefoot was the result. It was placed on the market in Mr. Thum's own store and Grand Rapids, which is generally quick to recognize and appreciate a good thing, speedily began to buy it in rapidly increasing quantities.

Before long the drug store fly paper department had to be made a separate institution. Then it grew into a factory. Now the O. & W. Thum company occupies a large plant that furnishes employment to nearly two hundred persons about half of whom are girls. And the business grew even faster than the manufacturing end. Tanglefoot became known outside of Grand Rapids and then outside of Michigan and finally outside of the United States.

The Thums having made a wonderful discovery "stuck" to their secret with the persistency of the stickiness they manufacture. They had to employ help to assist them in the manufacture of the paper but they did not reveal their formulas to their employees. To this day the secret has been kept.

Certain rooms of the Thum factory are forbidden ground to all save the officials of the plant and those who are directly employed there. And the employees who work in these rooms see only one part of the process. They do not know what is going on in the other secret departments.

Tanglefoot gained a firm footing in South Africa in an odd manner and as a result of the Boer war. The British volunteers, when they reached the Transvaal wastes were greatly tormented by flies. They wrote home to their relatives to send them relief. Their relatives sent Tanglefoot. This furnished the desired relief and was hailed with open joy.

So enthusiastically did the soldiers write home about the comfort given them by the sticky fly paper from far away Grand Rapids that the London newspapers commented on the fact in their headlines.

The London Times even ran a Tanglefoot cartoon. It showed the British soldiers surrounded by Tanglefoot, with Boers caught on the paper and struggling to get free. Underneath the cartoon was the suggestion that the British army use Tanglefoot in catching and disabling the Boers.

The Thum company has warehouses in St. Petersburg, Russia; Genoa, Italy; Hamburg, Germany; London, England; Laube, Trieste and Odessa, Russia.

▲*Grand Rapids Press*, August 18, 1910, p. 21.

Brothers Hugo (top) and Ferdinand ▶ joined Otto and William Thum in the management of the Tanglefoot Company. [GRPL, Photo Collection]

▲ Workers in the packing room (top) were not permitted to know what went on in other parts of the Tanglefoot factory. [GRPL, Robinson Collection]

CHAPTER 5

The City
Comes of Age

A s with other American cities, industrialization in Grand Rapids was closely intertwined with immigration. Tens of thousands of the nation's more than 13.4 million immigrants made their way to Grand Rapids between 1860 and 1900. Speaking only their native language, possessing little money and few skills, these newest Americans found housing where they could and took whatever jobs were available. Their presence assured entrepreneurs of an almost limitless supply of cheap labor, and they provided constantly expanding markets for manufactured goods. Large numbers of Dutch, German, Polish, and other northern European immigrants swelled Grand Rapids' population, bringing with them great hopes for a better life in a new land.

City leaders, meanwhile, faced the challenge of providing services to an increasingly diverse population that was doubling each decade, from slightly more than 10,000 at the end of the Civil War to nearly 90,000 by 1900. For government agencies, schools, and social service organizations, this meant a constant struggle to keep up with demands for better police and fire protection, sewer and water service, transportation facilities, health care, education, and cultural and recreation activities.

Immigrant Voices

In the late 19th century, Grand Rapids was very much a city of immigrants. Census records show that by the mid-1880s, one-third of the city's population had been born in another country.

Once they arrived in Grand Rapids, the new immigrants became workers in factories where a third of the work force spoke little or no English, and their children attended schools filled to overflowing with youngsters seeking to master the fundamentals of "reading, writing, and 'rithmetic." As the flood of new-comers continued to increase, church groups and social service organizations were strained to the limit to help them adjust to their new surroundings.

Most immigrants took steps to become American citizens shortly after setting foot in the United States. The process of naturalization took five years and concluded with a short test and an appearance in circuit court where the new Americans renounced their old country, swore allegiance to the United States, and received their citizenship papers.

Too often, latter-day historians look upon immigrants only as numbers, or large masses of humanity, without remembering that these were often tired, frightened people, who had left family and friends half a world away to find their dream in the United States. But each immigrant family that came to the United States represents a distinct story. Although many tales have been lost with the passage of generations, surviving letters and memoirs speak for the multitudes.

▲ Naturalization papers were every immigrant's dream [GRPL, Unprocessed Collection]

Although his family lost all their belongings at sea during the crossing to America, Evert Wonnink maintained a positive outlook. Upon arriving in West Michigan, the Wonninks received help with lodging and employment, and within six months he wrote to friends in the Netherlands about the splendid opportunities he found waiting.

On Sunday morning at about 4:30 we left Rotterdam and passed alongside Delftshaven, Schiedam, Vlaardingen, and Hellevoet-sluis.... We lost sight of the Dutch coast finally at 10:00.... Truly an important moment.... We sailed nicely until about ten in the evening when suddenly we stopped. The whistles and alarms sounded. We moved slowly forward until suddenly a great shock came which awakened everyone. The water came pouring into the ship....

Everyone climbed on deck to look for help. The sailors were busy trying to make all possibilities of salvation ready. A French boat, named the *Frankland*, came directly alongside of us, but the fog was so thick that it was difficult to tie up with each other. Soon the *Frankland* was ready to take the people from our ship on board. Our ship was sinking so quickly that the passengers stood in water up to their knees and their arms, but God kept the water below their lips. Everyone was brought over to the other boat—no one remained. But one German woman fell into the water between the boats. Immediately her husband jumped into the water, and because he could swim, they both returned safely to the ship.

We thought we were safe, and for the moment that was true. But then the sailors from the new boat sounded the alarm....

◄ A German immigrants' exercise club, ca. 1880. [GRPL, Photo Collection]

Our second boat had sprung a leak from its collision with our first boat, but it was not so great as to cause it to sink quickly. Fortunately, and again because of God's goodness, another boat came sailing from behind us and took us in tow. Then we were truly beyond danger....

America is good land for a laborer who wants to improve his lot by honorable labor with his hands. That has been written time and again, and it is the truth. Even so, it is not right to urge people to come. In some cases it appeared that those who came were not following God's will—and many come here and find it totally unpleasant. As for us, from the first moment that we settled here, we found it as good as in Holland.

Our work is the same as before and we are clearly blessed. Our city grows from year to year; this summer at least 600 new buildings will rise. If you were here on Sunday, everything would be quiet. All the shops, taverns, and inns are closed all day. The only exception is the Pharmacy. If a saloon keeper should dare to open his saloon on Sunday and is caught by the police, he is tossed in jail. If it is only the first time, he must pay a fine of $30. That is law and order. Now it is summer here— good. This spring we had heavy rain and now warm sunshine. The crops grow more quickly here than by you—and in favorable weather people are often surprised by that. There are plans about here to build another Holland church, because our church, built only two years ago, is already too small to contain the worshipers.

▲ Herbert J. Brinks, ed., *Write Back Soon: Letters From Immigrants in America*, pp. 15-16, 53-54.

IMMIGRANTS TO GRAND RAPIDS, 1850-1900			
Year	Population Category	Grand Rapids	% of Total
1850	Total	2,686	100
	Foreign Born	600	22
	Holland	189	7
1860	Total	8,085	100
	Foreign Born	2,000	25
	Holland	867	10
1870	Total	16,507	100
	Foreign Born	5,725	35
	Holland	2,944	18
1880	Total	32,016	100
	Foreign Born	10,000	31
	Holland	7,110	22
1890	Total	60,278	100
	Foreign Born	19,404	32
	Holland	8,275	14
	Germany	3,140	5
	Canada	2,968	5
	Ireland	1,227	2
1900	Total	87,565	100
	Foreign Born	23,917	27
	Holland	11,137	13
	Canada	3,487	4
	Germany	3,253	4
	Poland	1,670	2

▲ Grand Rapids' immigrant population based on U.S. Census data. [*U.S. Census Bureau Decennial Population Statistics, Michigan Schedule, 1850-1900.* Washington, D.C., U.S. Government Printing Office.]

Polish immigrant Jan Jasciensky successfully weathered the long ocean crossing and sought employment in Grand Rapids. But finding work was not easy, prices were high, and he missed his family.

Dear nephew I'll write you a few lines about America. What a good life we have, meat or sausage, bread, coffee or tea with various sweets and which you too will enjoy. Of them I am somewhat fed up.

Dear nephew I speak of my goodness, it would be better had they sent me to the army since I would not be so sullen as I am in this country for one cannot understand them even though one has work, and you cannot understand or get work so it is with us Poles.

Oh unhappy America why did you bring me this grief. Yes, dear nephew if I were alone and had no debts I could live freely and well, but I have debts and would work but I have no work. Good bye.

Dear nephew I wrote to adam and that he should in my name tell you how things are here. He wrote that he sent a letter. I now send you another letter for your kindness. I your loving uncle wish you the best and wish that you not come to America for there is nothing for which to come. The newspaper reports that some 2000 come weekly; that life is growing dearer and wages less.... I only live on bread and meat, coffee or tea, bought some sauerkraut for half dollar.

▲ A young Dutch boy's funeral photographed for his family in the Netherlands. [Calvin College Heritage Collection]

Members of the ► Slusarsky family, late 19th-century immigrants from Poland. [GRPL, Photo Collection]

◄ *Listy Emigrant Ow Z Brazylii I Stanow Zjednoczonych, 1890-1891,* pp. 277-99.

FOREIGN BORN POPULATION OF KENT COUNTY, 1900	
Asia	11
Australia	2
Austria	147
Belgium	29
Bohemia	80
Canada (Eng.)	4,775
Canada (Fr.)	244
China	10
Denmark	419
England	1,579
Finland	44
France	86
Germany	4,151
Greece	5
Holland	13,366
Hungary	14
Ireland	1,726
Italy	90
Norway	127
Poland	1,772
Russia	71
Scotland	335
Sweden	1,350
Switzerland	214
Wales	31
West Indies	9
Other Countries	52
Born at Sea	18
Total	30,757

▲ By 1900, U.S. Census data showed Kent County's foreign born came from many countries.

The American Spirit of Liberty

In addition to economic opportunities, immigrants were drawn to America by the prospects of a more tolerant spirit, a greater chance to participate in the democratic process, and the absence of the kinds of class and ethnic conflicts that often prevailed in the lands of their birth. The more open society of the United States led to cooperation among groups who had kept their distance from one another in Europe.

In Grand Rapids, people of many nationalities joined together in labor organizations, sent their children to neighborhood public schools, and sometimes shared the same house of worship. In the following letter, Isaac M. Wise, founder of the Reform Jewish movement in the United States, assures Moses May of Grand Rapids, president of the newly built Temple Emanuel, that, in keeping with the "American Spirit of Liberty," it is entirely proper to rent the facility to a non-Jewish group (the Protestant Swedenborgians) for religious services.

Cincinnati, February 20, 1885
Mr. Moses May Pres.
Congregation Emanuel
In reply to yours of the 17th inst. permit me to say, that it has been done, as you perhaps know, in various congregations in our country, that the house of worship was opened to Christian sects, on condition that no symbols be erected and no conflict in time be constituted. The opinions outside of those congregations differ on the subject, in the whole, however, it is considered due to the American spirit of Liberty to be as liberal as possible. In Jewish law no provision is made for such cases, simply because none ever happened. The Swedenborgians are no Trinitarians, as much as I know. There are what is called Liberal Christians, and I would not object to let them have your place of worship, when you do not need it, if the congregation is benefited by it, and it causes no ill feelings among your members. It is certainly beneficial that we show a liberal spirit.

Yours Respectfully
Isaac M. Wise

▲ Temple Emanuel Archives, Grand Rapids.

Temple Emanuel, built in ▶ 1882. [Albert Baxter, *History of the City of Grand Rapids*, p. 301]

▼ Below left to right: David Amberg, Jacob Wolfe, Sidney Hart, Isaac Levi, and Moses May were among Temple Emanuel's founders. [Temple Emanuel Archives]

Breaking Down the Color Line

The "American Spirit of Liberty" did not extend to all citizens. African-Americans who came to Grand Rapids often found themselves barred from the American dream for no other reason than the color of their skin. Progress in breaking down the color line has come slowly, but because courageous citizens would not let this barrier to equality stand unchallenged, change has occurred.

In 1897, Hattie Beverly entered the Grand Rapids Public Schools' teacher-training program. Even though she successfully completed all the required course work and a classroom internship, she had trouble securing a teaching assignment because of her color. Fortunately for Grand Rapids, responsible heads prevailed and irresponsible bigotry did not deny local students the benefit of an outstanding young teacher.

Miss Hattie Beverly for the past year has been one of the students of the Wealthy avenue training school, which was established and is maintained by the school board for the purpose of drilling the graduates of the Grand Rapids high school for the duties of a teacher in the public schools of the city. Miss Beverly has been an apt pupil and according to the practice of the school, has been frequently sent out to take the place of sick or absent teachers in other buildings. With the end of the present semester, Miss Beverly will have finished the period of probation and will be ready to accept a position as one of the teaching force of the city. However, there now appears to be some opposition to her appointment. The reason lies in the fact that she is unfortunate in color. Quite a number of the board are opposed to the idea of placing a colored woman in such a responsible position over white children. They say that such a course is sure to give rise to objections on the part of some of the parents of the children under such instruction. The remarkable feature of the opposition to the measure lies in the fact that the members maintain considerable reticence on the subject, it being exceedingly difficult to get them to express an opinion one way or the other.

F.J. Bolithe of the Ninth ward was seen, however, and he expressed himself freely upon the subject. He said: "I am in favor of employing Miss Beverly. She has shown herself to be a young lady of ambition and push to get as far as she has, and I can see no justifiable reason why she should be turned down. She certainly should not be discriminated against because of her color, a matter over which she has absolutely no control. If it was contrary to the established policy of the board to employ colored teachers she should never have been permitted to enter the training school, where her education has been an expense to the city. In fact, when a student is permitted to enter the training school that establishes a tacit understanding that if her work is satisfactory she will be accepted as a member of the regular force of teachers when her term of probation is over.

"It is in my opinion now too late to refuse her a position and such an action would be a positive injustice."

▲ Unidentified newspaper clipping, Hattie Beverly Biography File, Grand Rapids Public Library.

▲ Hattie Beverly, Grand Rapids' first African-American teacher. [GRPL, Black History Exhibit Collection]

Call the Fire Department

Grand Rapids' remarkable growth in the post-Civil War 19th century placed an enormous strain on government and the services it provided, and no group was under greater pressure than the city's fire fighters. The wooden homes, factories, and retail establishments of the time were little more than tinderboxes, and a blaze that began in one building burned quickly, often spreading to neighboring structures before volunteer fire fighters and their untrained, elected marshals could reach the scene.

At four o'clock on Sunday afternoon, July 13, 1873, a devastating fire swept through a large portion of the city, north of Michigan Street, threatening Grand Rapids with the same mass destruction that the great Chicago fire had caused two years earlier. By the time the first volunteer fire company arrived at the scene, the fire, which started Bridge Street House hotel and its barn, was raging out of control. Hours passed before it could be contained by the fire fighters, bucket brigades, and a fortuitous evening rain. No lives were lost, but the blaze destroyed nearly 100 buildings in a 15-acre area that had been home earlier in the day to 130 families.

From accounts of the 1873 fire it is easy to understand the citizen fears that led to successful efforts to expand the number of paid, full-time fire fighters employed by the city, and to place them under a professional administration.

▼ The fire of 1873 did extensive damage in the area north of East Bridge Street (now Michigan) between Canal (now Monroe) and Ionia avenues before it was brought under control. [GRPL, Godfrey Anderson Collection]

Yesterday afternoon, Sunday, the 13th, was oppressively sultry. A hot wind blew from the west to southwest in changeable gusts, at times dying down to a whisper, affording but little relief. Many people had driven out to the lake or elsewhere to seek shade and free air. The streets of the city were unusually silent, even for the Sabbath.... A spirit of general sleepiness seemed to pervade the city, when, at a quarter past four o'clock, the tapping of the fire bell on the Kent street engine house startled all ears.

A thick black smoke rolling up from the Bridge Street house, visible from nearly every part of the city, gave assurance that fire was doing its best with some highly inflammable substance. It was just the time for a general turnout, and that was what immediately took place. The streets, to the remotest parts of the city, were at once alive with people hurrying to the suddenly attractive center, while the engines, hose carts and hook and ladder wagon went thundering along, as readily as if the whole fire department had been expecting the call....

Within half an hour an immense host of spectators— seemingly the entire population of the city, and certainly a large majority of it—was thronging all avenues of near approach to the fire, as close to it as the intense heat would permit, and swarming along the crest of the bluff, witnessing the most tremendous conflagration that has ever raged in Grand Rapids....

The hostler of the stable of the Bridge Street house reports that he saw two men, whom he did not know, passing out at a rear door of the stable, one of whom had a cigar in his mouth. Very soon after a pile of straw and manure, thrown out from and lying partially against the southwest corner of the stable was seen to be afire. It was very dry, as was the stable and all its contents, of course, and in an incredibly short time the whole structure was wrapped in solid fire and smoke, which a heavy and wavering wind from the southwest was hurling on both sides and driving forward....

In fifteen minutes from the striking of the alarm, the vast throngs of people crowding on all sides of the fire, except in its swiftly advancing path, were fully impressed with a sense of the tremendous destruction impending. It was plainly apparent to all that no possible means of managing it could be brought to bear, to avert the greatest destruction ever yet experienced by fire in this city, in the number of buildings involved. And so it proved....

Grand Rapids' city mills, (flouring mills) were now ablaze all through the two upper stories, bringing the fire to face Canal street, with a heat so insufferable that only by turning the nozzles upon themselves, and by occasionally leaping into the canal, could the firemen there stationed endure it....

The wind seemed to steadily strengthen by the ruin it fed upon, and by this time had shifted from a little south of west to about one southwest, and had increased to an absolute gale. The descriptions of the Chicago and Peshtigo fires were strikingly brought to mind. Masses of blaze were continually hurled through the air horizontally above the houses without any apparent substance accompanying them. Sheets of blaze seemed to settle down from the firmament and begin devouring the roofs of houses half a block to leeward of the nearest one burning in the principal mass, leaving several not yet ignited between, but for a short time only. Massive tree tops suddenly dried to a crisp, singed, then blazed up with one flash and nothing but a smoking trunk and limbs were left. Streams of blaze ran swiftly along the plank sidewalks, devouring them suddenly. Out-houses, fences and shrubbery melted away at a touch of the fiery breath. These and other fearful and singular operations of the fiery element were watched with intense excitement by thousands....

The time of greatest alarm, when the conflagration rode on the high tide of triumphant power, and it looked as if it would level everything as far as to Coldbrook, began three quarters of an hour after the fire broke out, lasting from five o'clock to half-past—one long, dreadful half hour. During this time more than a hundred families, mostly poor people, and principally Germans and Hollanders, were distractedly hauling their household effects out of doors and pitching them out of windows, with the usual pro-

portion of ruinous excitement, often working, by breakage or otherwise, the demolition of the property they strove to save. It was a hard sight to look at poor men and women red in the face, reeking with sweat, exerting themselves to desperation, overloading themselves and rushing frantically with their furniture, bedding, trunks, babes and cradles, to places of apparent safety, and on returning with another load finding they must carry them still further away....

If lives had been lost it would have been sadder; but there were none, not with standing a prevalent report to that effect last night....

By a quarter past six o'clock, or to speak with more certainty, by half past six, the final limits of the conflagration became plainly marked out, and sense of blessed relief came over the entire community.

The engines remained at work, playing on the most threatening ruins still blazing, and guarding weak points, till sometime after the heavy rain began falling, which was about half past ten o'clock.

◄ The area in the center of this picture looking south from Lookout Hill, was totally burned in the fire. [GRPL, Godfrey Anderson Collection]

◄ Using the long narrow building at the right of this photo, and in the photo above, as a reference point, the magnitude of the fire damage becomes clear. [GRPL, Godfrey Anderson Collection]

◄ *Grand Rapids Daily Eagle,* July 14, 1873, p. 1.

◄ After the fire, the burned area was rebuilt with brick buildings. Once again, the narrow building at the right edge of the photo serves as a reference point to the earlier images shown above. [GRPL, Godfrey Anderson Collection]

The Pride of Grand Rapids

Like the fire department, the Grand Rapids police force also grew at a rapid rate in the latter stages of the 19th century. Once protected by just a few elected constables, citizens now demanded a full-fledged, well-equipped police force to preserve order and keep them from harm. In 1871, the city was served by a police chief and eight patrolmen; two decades later, a 70-man force included 51 patrolmen who worked around the clock, bringing safety to the city's streets.

▲ Grand Rapids policemen were regular marchers in turn-of-the-century parades. [GRPL, Photo Collection]

The life of the patrolman of the local police force is not one continuous round of merriment, neither is it entirely composed of shadows. When stern duty compels them to walk the streets for eight consecutive hours, they are required by "section eight" to wear sober faces, walk erect, with clothes and shoes neatly brushed. They move like clock work from one signal box to the other, report to headquarters every few minutes from each end of the beats, besides watching and making a note of everything which falls under their observation....

Nor is this all. The patrolman not only has a continued strain regarding his duty and moral conduct upon him, but he must have an eye upon several seemingly ironclad rules, to take care that none of them are infringed. His weapons, such as a revolver, baton, "billy," etc, must be in good working order and absolutely clean. As for personal appearance, the officer's linen, collar and cuff, must be free from dirt, his hair in a presentable shape and the "grass" kept mowed down on his face. He cannot smoke while on duty or in a public place while off duty. Neither is he permitted to use liquor outside of his own house and even then it must be taken with great moderation....

The force numbers 70 men in all, including regular patrolmen, reserve men, court officers, wagon attendants, detectives and specials. The work of the regulars is divided into three parts. First there is the day squad, who go on duty at 8 o'clock a.m., and remain until 4 p.m. Strange as it may seem only nine men are required to preserve the peace on regular beats in the day. Next comes the "dog" watches. The regular "dog" goes on from 4 to 8 a.m. and from 4 to 8 p.m., besides which there is a "long dog" for the distant precincts from 4 to 12 p.m.

The pay of the men varies. For the first year of service a patrolman is paid at the rate of $1.60 per day; for the second, $1.91; third, $2.05, which is the limit. Next comes the sergeant who draws $2.30 for the first year, $2.50 for the second and $2.75 for the third. The lieutenant is paid at the rate of $2.90 a day or $1,058.50 per year. The captain receives $3 per day or $1,095 per year, while the superintendent is paid $1,800 per year....

The popular tradition relative to the Irish policeman seems to be a misfit on the local force at least, for the list of patrolmen comprises men of all nationalities and the number of Irish is the smallest of all. Out of the 70 men there are six native born Irishmen and three who were born in this country of Irish parents. There are Hollanders, Germans, etc., but the great majority of the men are straight out Americans.

▲ *Grand Rapids Weekly Democrat,* February 13, 1890, p. 6.

▼ Police patrol wagons hauled in miscreants from all corners of the city. [GRPL, James R. Hooper Collection]

A Mighty Deluge

When Grand Rapids' population was smaller, municipal officials had been content to let private companies, under contract to the city, provide water and sewage services to city residents. Gradually, however, in an effort to maintain uniform cost and quality for all residents, these services were taken over by government.

Clean, potable water was particularly important to the health of the community. By the 1870s it was clear to the Common Council that a city water works must be built. In 1874, proceeds of a $260,000 bond issue underwrote a four-acre reservoir on the bluff at the head of Livingston and Mason streets and 12 miles of pipe. A dozen years later, city water service came to the West Side through a 16-inch pipe laid in a trench on the bed of the Grand River by a team of workmen.

In the fall of 1880, after a heavy rain, a portion of the reservoir eroded and water sluiced down to Ottawa Avenue. After extensive repairs, the Board of Public Works issued a detailed report in 1889 declaring that since the repairs, "the reservoir has never leaked." Eleven more years took their toll, however, and on the morning of July 2, 1900, the reservoir walls broke, spilling a cascade of water to Coldbrook Creek, ruining portions of Newberry, Coit, Clancy and Bradford streets along the way, and sending frightened citizens scurrying for higher ground. No deaths or serious injuries occurred, but several houses were completely destroyed and property damage exceeded $100,000.

After reconstruction, the reservoir stored about six million gallons of water for emergencies and night supplies to low-pressure areas. Reconstructed again in 1938 as a public works project, the reservoir still serves that function today.

The city reservoir burst early this morning and caused a flood unparalleled in its destructiveness in the history of Grand Rapids. The loss to property is estimated at more than $100,000. A strip more than three blocks long and nearly two blocks wide was swept by a swift, mighty deluge, and scarcely a piece of property in its limits escaped costly damage. Houses and barns were swept away by the rush of waters, and some were smashed into kindling wood. Streets were torn up to a depth of forty feet, and water mains that lay deep below the surface were left exposed and some were broken.

With a little rivulet of water scarcely six inches wide the avalanche of water started on its mad course toward the northeast. Gradually it enlarged until it had bored a hole three feet across in the solid cement that forms the basin of the reservoir. When the waves lashed their way through, the pieces of cement two feet thick commenced to give, and in a moment with a great roar that was heard all over the hill, the water poured out in a flood. The stream was thirty feet wide and more than ten feet deep. Everything was swept before it. . . .

A little newsboy saw the first stream and notified everyone in the street into which the water had started. To him is due the credit entirely for arousing scores from their sleep to escape before their houses were washed away by the flood. He is Burt Botsford . . . , and he carries one of the morning papers. . . .

There is a general disposition in the neighborhood to sharply criticize the pumping station authorities for the alleged failure to closely watch the reservoir. It is said that Superintendent John VanAmberg, who was released when the positions of superintendent of the water works and lighting plant were consolidated for the sake of economy, was in the habit of examining the reservoir every twenty-four hours. . . .

The board of public works met in special session at 9:30 this morning, with all members present except Charles A. Phelps, who was out of the city. Mayor [George] Perry was intercepted as he was about to take the train for the Democratic convention at Kansas City, and he returned to the city hall. Upon learning of the extent of the catastrophe he gave up his trip and declared that he would stay here. . . .

There is a serious legal phase to the situation, relative to the liability of the city, and the board will have another session with City Attorney Salsbury over this feature of it. It is said that a number of lawyers were busy on the ground this morning writing the claims of those who suffered damage. One man was so eager for settlement with the city that he had his claim all ready.

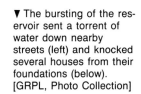

◄ *Grand Rapids Press,* July 2, 1900, p. 1.

▼ The bursting of the reservoir sent a torrent of water down nearby streets (left) and knocked several houses from their foundations (below).
[GRPL, Photo Collection]

Caring for the Sick

As America's post-Civil War urban population grew, cities became home to increasing numbers of immigrant industrial workers. Often living in densely populated tenements and multifamily houses in ethnic enclaves, and working in factories that used fast-moving and dangerous machines, immigrants were vulnerable to illness and injury. With little more than subsistence incomes, many were unable to afford medical care. Municipal governments, and charitable, social, religious, fraternal, and ethnic organizations responded to their need by establishing hospitals.

Grand Rapids' experience mirrored that of cities throughout the nation. The Union Benevolent Association, which was founded in 1846, raised money for indigent families, and as Grand Rapids' population and health-care needs increased, opened the city's first rest home and hospital (which eventually became Blodgett Memorial Hospital) in 1875. Following closely on its heels was St. Mark's Home and Hospital (later Butterworth Hospital) in 1877. The third Grand Rapids medical institution of the time, St. Mary's Hospital, got its start in 1893 when Mrs. Mary McNamara donated her home to the Catholic Sisters of Mercy.

The seventh annual report of St. Mark's House and Hospital varies little so far as concerns figures, from that of the previous year! There have been admitted into the home during the time 168 persons, of this number 147 have been dismissed, leaving the present number of inmates 21. The deaths that have occurred during the year have been 4; births 1; number of permanent inmates 15; sixteen children have been received and cared for, good homes having been provided in such cases as needed.

Of those who

paid in whole or part for board there have been	39
Chargeable to the city	29
" " county	33
" " St. Mark's Church	6
" " Newaygo K.K. Co.	1
" " G. R. & I Co.	1
" " Masonic Fraternity	2
" " Cigar Makers Union	1
" " I. O. O. F. [Oddfellows]	1
" " Charity	32
Self Supporting	21
Meals and lodgings given at the Home	30

▲ Emily Deming Collection, Grand Rapids Public Library.

▲ This large UBA hospital was built in 1885. [GRPL, Grand Rapids Illustrated Collection]

▲ St. Marks Home and Hospital, ca. 1880. [GRPL, James R. Hooper Collection]

▲ St. Mary's Hospital opened in 1893. [GRPL, Photo Collection]

Angels of Mercy

Associated with these hospitals were nursing schools that offered young women a two-year hospital training course that focused on practical experience more than classroom sessions. At the same time that they prepared the women for careers in health care, these nursing schools assured hospitals of inexpensive help. Dr. G.K. Johnson's commencement speech to the eighth graduating class of the Butterworth Hospital Training School for Nurses addressed the new nursing professionals from the perspective of a male doctor's attitudes toward women at the time. Acknowledging their role in the changing health-care industry, Johnson echoed the widely held assumption that women had a special aptitude for nursing, and that the satisfaction derived from caring for the sick should be their greatest compensation.

When the world was young the occupations of men and women were few and simple. Hunting and fishing were the first thought. Later men watched their flocks by night and thus learned to commune with the stars that spangled the heavens above them.

But as population increased, as human faculties unfolded more and more, new wants and new views of life sprang up, and then, as a consequence, there came new industries and new occupations. . . .

During the past twenty or thirty years this process of expansion and of evolution has been very marked. New employments and new industries have sprung up with unwonted rapidity. One result is that women have found new avocations, new avenues of activity and of usefulness. They typewrite, they practice the photographic art, they gather news for the press, they become proficient as accountants, they ply the telephone, and they send the lightning current, freighted with important messages, to every city and country on the globe.

But last, though not least, the instructed nurse has come upon the stage and challenges our attention. Hers is one of the new callings, a new profession. What are we to think of her and of her claims?

First, let it be remembered that woman has by nature special aptitudes for the care of the sick. In all ages this has been shown. As daughter, she had given tender and sympathic care to invalid mother and father. As wife, whether in hovel or in palace, her ministry to the sick husband has been a boon and a glory. As mother, who can tell the depths of her tenderness, or the tirelessness of her watching?

▲Lulu Cudney Collection, Grand Rapids Public Library.

▲First graduating classes of nurses from the UBA Hospital (top) and Butterworth Hospital. [GRPL, Photo Collection]

The Grand Rapids Medical College

The training of 19th-century physicians was not rigorously controlled, and since no accreditation was required, there were numerous medical colleges throughout the country. Grand Rapids Medical College was organized in 1897 by a faculty of local physicians. During its brief existence, the college offered both a three-year medical course and a similar course in veterinary medicine. Later, a short farrier (horseshoeing) and hoof care course was also added. Before its closing in 1906, the college produced 108 medical graduates and an unrecorded number of veterinarians and farriers.

VETERINARY DEPARTMENT.
While it is the intention of the management that the Grand Rapids Veterinary College shall continue to be a high grade school in every sense of the term, still, after mature deliberation and consideration, it has been decided best to make the requirements for graduation two sessions of six months each. The reasons for so doing must be apparent to all. The country is suffering from one of the greatest industrial depressions known to history, and because of that fact many an ambitious young man, anxious to obtain a veterinary education, finds himself quite unable to raise sufficient funds to carry him through a college course extending over three or four years. This being true, it would certainly seem like inviting disaster to establish a college on a three or four year basis.... After eliminating a great deal of what might be called technical rubbish, it will be found quite possible to give any young man of ordinary intelligence an excellent veterinary education in two six months sessions.

FARRIER'S DEPARTMENT
A Department of Scientific Horse-Shoeing has been established in connection with this college whereby a thorough knowledge of the preparation of the hoof and the fitting of the shoe can be obtained.

In order to afford an opportunity for persons to attend who are busily engaged in their professions during the day, it has been decided to conduct this department as a night school. Both practical and theoretical work will be given and on completing the course and passing a satisfactory examination a diploma conferring the degree of M.F. will be awarded.

Fees for this course are . . $25.00
Graduating fee . . . . $ 5.00
Department of Scientific Horse shoeing begins January 4, 1898 and continues to the end of the term.

Grand Rapids Medical ► College building, [GRPL, Morris Photo Collection]

Grand Rapids Medical ► College's science lab. [GRPL, *Grand Rapids Medical College Prospectus, 1905-06*, p. 24]

Grand Rapids Medical ► College's associated veterinary hospital. [GRPL, *Grand Rapids Medical College Prospectus, 1897-98*, p. 27]

◄ *Grand Rapids Medical College Prospectus for Session of 1897-98*, Grand Rapids Public Library.

Dr. McDonald, the "Specialist"

Not all providers of medical care adhered to accepted treatment standards. With no universal certification, it was easy for practitioners of all persuasions to hang out their shingles and solicit patients. Listed in the city directories of the time were spiritualists, advocates of water cures and fresh air cures, and those who claimed to have developed life-prolonging dietary supplements. One such practitioner was Dr. Donald McDonald, who dispensed "Mental, Magnetic, and Absent" treatment from his office on East Fulton Street. The following prescription, sent to Mrs. Mary Skinner, speaks for itself.

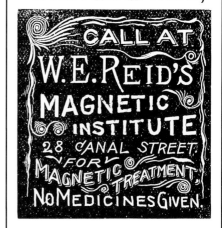

Business and Test Medium, Editor of Banner of Life
Office 28 Canal - Residence 440 Jefferson Avenue

Mrs. Mary Ann Skinner
Middleville, Michigan

You will receive Mental, Magnetic and Absent treatment, from this office:
on *Monday, Wednesday, Friday, Saturday, Sunday* from *7:30 PM to 8 PM*

Special Directions.

1. Be alone if possible and seat yourself in a comfortable chair with back toward the light, or turn the light low—

2. Fold your hands quietly in front of you—Close your eyes, but do not go to sleep.

3. Enter the room with a feeling of love for every one—If you have hated anyone in the past you must not hate them now. At the threshold of this silent chamber you must bury every suspicious, jealous, vicious or revengeful feeling.

4. Think of yourself as a spirit, that you are from God, that you are a part of God, that you are a deathless life; that you can no more be diseased than God Himself and that Health and Strength and Happiness is your birthright.

5. During treatment I want you to be in a condition to receive thought—Think of health with its smile and song—Think of love, what it does for the heart, the soul and the life; and as you think of these things draw them into your being and believe and fully affirm that they are yours.

6. Deny away every sick, weak, evil and sinful thought.

7. Reject from your mind all thoughts of fear. Do not be afraid of sickness and death—Allow nothing to worry you.

8. Hold up in your mind the picture of a person in perfect health. See yourself in perfect health; will that you have good health. Think of health and life and God and that you are a part of God, and that you cannot be sick and suffer and die.

9. During treatment take several deep and slow breaths, breathe deep and slow—Open your soul to the Divine Breath.

10. Make yourself quiet and passive to receive my thought. I will project upon your mind the thought of perfect health, strength, harmony and happiness. I will project the thought of freedom from disease and pain. My thought will electrify and magnetize your mind with health and strength; but you must have faith and believe that God will crown my efforts in your behalf with success.

11. During treatment, I want you to repeat over slowly once or twice the twenty-third psalm, (XXIII Psalm).

12. During treatment, think only the good, feel only the good, trust and realize only the good, and open yourself fully to God who is the infinite source of all health, all strength, all peace and harmony, all joy and happiness.

Yours kindly
Dr. Donald McDonald,
The Specialist,
Grand Rapids, Mich.

▲ Donald McDonald Manuscript, Grand Rapids Public Library.

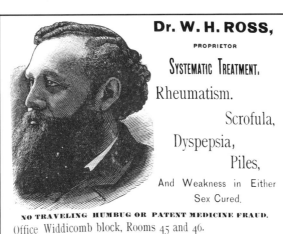

▲ Walter E. Reid offered "magnetic treatment" at the turn of the century. [*Grand Rapids City Directory*, 1888, p. 1021]

◄ The short-lived Grand Rapids Hospital advertised advance registration to those anticipating illness. [*Grand Rapids City Directory*, 1887, p. 147]

◄ Dr. W.H. Ross took pains to assure potential patients his services were neither "traveling humbug or patent medicine fraud." [*Grand Rapids City Directory*, 1888, p. 1003]

The New City Hall

As the size of city government grew, the need for a city hall became apparent. For decades, city offices had no central home. The Common Council met in various rented quarters, and other offices were often kept at the incumbents' places of business. As early as 1854, council members had spoken of the need for a city hall, but no further action was taken. Eventually, a site at the corner of Lyon and Ottawa was selected, and in May 1873 the Board of Public Works declared a city hall a necessary public improvement. The plan was tabled, however, until 1879, and then moved forward only by fits and starts for four more years, until, finally, in April 1883, a $150,000 bond issue was approved by voters.

Once funding was authorized, the pace picked up. In October 1884, architect Elijah E. Myers of Detroit was selected, and the following April, W.D. Richardson of Springfield, Illinois, was awarded the construction contract for the sum of $185,641.68. The cornerstone was laid on September 9, 1885, and in a little more than three years an impressive three-story stone building, with full basement, was completed. Housed in the building, which was to serve as the focus of city government until 1969, were all city offices, including the superintendent of schools, the superior court, and the recently organized public library.

A proud citizenry gathered on September 26, 1888, to tour the new building and hear Mayor Isaac M. Weston declare it formally open for business. Even the fact that final costs totaled $290,338.61 — nearly double the first bond issue and well beyond provisions of the initial construction contract—did not dampen the spirit of the day.

Acceptance and Formal Opening by Mayor Weston.
Mr. President:

In behalf of Grand Rapids I am pleased to accept this handsome and commodious edifice, and as chief executive of this city I hereby declare it open for public use.

It is a grand monument to the generous enterprise of our citizens; to the taste, the ability and the integrity of the Board that built, the architect who planned and the contractor and superintendent charged with its erection. Graceful in design, solid in construction, ample in accommodations, it stands a source of pride to every one of our 75,000 inhabitants.

For the first time our city government owns its home. Following the practical conservatism which has ever characterized the administration of our municipal matters, we first provided ample and elegant school structures; a complete system of necessary public improvements; and now, in the full tide of prosperity, when the tax is scarcely felt, we build an official residence creditable to our rank among cities, where we can dwell in comfort and entertain with pride.

But while proud of our new and elegant home, I am far prouder of the record made by Grand Rapids during her fifty years' existence as a municipal government. The aim of her officials has been to give a pure, able and economical administration of public affairs; to advance morality, promote enterprise, protect labor, administer justice and combat ignorance. During this half century there has been no definite charge of misconduct against an official of Grand Rapids. This fact is remarkable and should be an incentive for all to maintain the enviable reputation we have so thoroughly earned. Let us hope that all future legislation and official acts within these halls will be for the common weal—doing exact justice to all, remembering that the good done will survive long after these walls are in decay.

▲ *Grand Rapids City Hall Dedication Program, 1888*, p. 29, Grand Rapids Public Library.

▲ The Grand Rapids City Hall, built in 1888. [GRPL, *Grand Rapids Illustrated* Collection]

◄ Mayor Isaac M. Weston. [GRPL, Photo Collection]

The public library had ► rooms on the second floor of city hall. [GRPL, James R. Hooper Collection]

"You Have Outraged Every Sense of Honor..."

Perhaps part of the citizen excitement over the impressive city hall edifice was a hope that it would have a cleansing effect on the practice of local politics. In the early summer of 1888, Kent County prosecuting attorney Samuel Clay had been bounced from office amidst allegations that he had solicited bribes, worked for special interests, and obstructed rather than expedited the work of the police department.

Not long afterwards, the mayoral election, held on August 3, marked the culmination of a nasty, hotly contested campaign that was decided by a mere nine votes. Some said

Mayor Weston's victory over Charles Belknap was secured only after tampering with the ballot boxes. Others responded that the cheating was evenly divided between the two sides, and the election ought to stand. Eventually the Michigan Supreme Court concurred and Mayor Weston remained in office.

Four years earlier, a similar no-holds-barred congressional campaign had resulted in an open rift between two of Grand Rapids' best-known families. Although he won the election, Charles C. Comstock could not forgive the editorial comments that appeared in Aaron B. Turner's

Grand Rapids *Eagle,* and penned a bitter letter venting his rage. The fact that the two men shared a granddaughter — Comstock's son, Tileston, who died in 1870, had been married to Turner's oldest daughter — did not deter them from carrying on their bitter public feud. One can only wonder how Mary Comstock, who was 16 years old at the time, felt about the charges printed in her grandfather Turner's newspaper (only a few examples are reprinted here), and her grandfather Comstock's responding letter that spoke of a chasm "that will never be bridged over."

▲ A.B. Turner (top) and C.C. Comstock, in-laws and enemies. [GRPL, Photo Collection, Russell Family Collection]

The *Leader* concludes that a man is a hog if he runs for an office for a second time when once defeated by the people. Comstock is now running for Congress the third time, and will be beaten more next Tuesday than ever before.

▲ *Grand Rapids Daily Eagle,* October 30, 1884, p. 2.

The more astute leaders of the Fusion party, especially the Democratic portion, in their confidential moments, concede that Comstock will be overwhelmingly defeated, and rather rejoice over it. They are tired of burdening their consciences by supporting such an incompetent man, and of the false pretenses involved in calling him the poor man's friend or the friend of the

laboring man. They want him buried under the biggest possible majority and completely finished.

▲ *Grand Rapids Daily Eagle,* October 31, 1884, p. 2.

As one proof of Comstock's special friendliness to the poor man, it is stated by some of the fishermen of the city who catch suckers in the spring, from the river, that he charges from $25 to $50 per season for the privilege of fishing from the banks on his property, or from the river alongside such banks. The fishermen say that in so charging Comstock proved the biggest sucker they ever caught, for several of them are now working for his defeat.

▲ *Grand Rapids Daily Eagle,* November 1, 1884, p. 2.

Grand Rapids, Mich.
Nov. 4th 1884
A. B. Turner,
Your conduct during this campaign has created a chasm between your family and mine, that will never be bridged over. You have outraged every sense of honor and attempted to destroy my good name, which by a life time of toil has been honestly earned a better legacy for my children than any thing also to have to give them. When defamatory falsehoods were published in the *Eagle* and pointed out to you, you refused to correct them and heaped other insults upon slanders, and lies such as ought to drive any living creature out of humanity's reach. It matters little to me which way the election turns but your lies will burn in my brain till my pulse ceases to beat although you may have been dead and in your grave a score of years. My family are more indignant if possible than myself. If my blood is mixed in a posterity with yours, they will feel the effects of your conduct if I should be fortunate enough to leave any thing as a birthright to my children.
C. C. Comstock

◄Russell Family Collection, Grand Rapids Public Library.

Honoring Our Nation's Birth

Politics was only one form of recreation for the citizens of Grand Rapids. Those who preferred their theatrics with a little more refinement enjoyed the performances of local and traveling stage companies, while those who cared to make their own entertainment could choose from any number of games, sports, and public events.

Probably the greatest of the public spectacles came in 1876 with the centennial celebration of the Declaration of Independence. Thanks to half-price railroad fares, visitors traveled great distances to Grand Rapids to participate in the centennial's Independence Day activities. Among the observers was a wide-eyed 13-year-old named Cornelius Louwerse who later wrote his recollections of the celebration that began on Sunday, July 2, and continued for three exciting days.

Even the year before, 1875, we were being stirred up by the papers about what was going to be done at Philadelphia. Spring came on. Our lively lumber town of the middle west was all stir and bustle. A great many people had plans they wanted to see carried out.

Those in command finally decided to build a triumphal arch, and it was a dandy. It was constructed this way: a large frame affair about 100 feet broad, 15 feet thick and three stories high. Up aloft to finish off, a level surface about 15 feet as a cap. Both sides alike. Flat roof cupola on top. Large arch cut in the street level for carriage traffic. Smaller ones at the ends for pedestrians. The whole draped with evergreens. Don't you wish you could have seen our arch...?

Then the four of July, or rather third. We celebrated three days. Street parade in the morning. Downtown was all fussed up with bunting and flags. Our own Germania band was out on the street playing the fine music they so well knew. The man who played the big horn worked in the same shop with my brother, and I could go down there and look at him....

On that day I tasted my first banana.

Our fire department was headed at the time by Gen. Israel C. Smith. After our luncheon on the Fourth I went down to the main street and looking around saw General Smith on his little black saddler, stripped of bit and bridle, guiding his mount by the kick of his heel. He was dressed as an Indian chief. After that came the Horribles. Old time affair like a carnival, disguised folks with clown white or burnt cork on their faces... floats, music, etc. In the afternoon they pulled a sham battle on the island. I was not allowed to go there.

It is six o'clock and we are all fed a substantial meal. On this day my mother had green peas and new potatoes flavored with parsley and lamb stew. My brother and his wife are to take me to see the fire works. We start out, saunter west until we reach Ball's Hill....

Crowds are gathering and selecting locations to sit down. We find a place. The crowd is jolly. Darkness finally falls. We hold our breath as the first piece is touched off. The only pieces I remember were George Washington on horseback and a sham battle. Roman candles and skyrockets galore. The crowd goes wild. Finally all is over. I, a youngster, am a bit drowsy, have to be shaken up a bit to get in walking order. We reach home and "to bed". Happy times.

▲"Cornelius Louwerse Memoirs," Grand Rapids Public Library.

▲Campau Square's Centennial Arch. [GRPL, Photo Collection]

▲ A "Parade of the Horribles." [GRPL, George E. Fitch Collection]

◄ The Bridge Street Centennial Arch. [GRPL, Guy Johnston Collection]

Batter Up!

Baseball games were a standard part of Fourth of July celebrations in the years after the Civil War. The game had been played in the camps of both the Union and Confederate armies, and returned soldiers formed teams in all parts of the country. After an attempt a year earlier had failed, the Kent Base Ball Club of Grand Rapids was established on April 4, 1867, with Silas Perkins as its president. Within a few weeks, the Kents announced that they were at work constructing a playing grounds "on a hill east of the city in Coit's Addition," somewhere near today's Kent Country Club. On April 20, 1867, the club played a demonstration game, and a short time later announced an upcoming two-game series with the Custer team of Ionia.

The Kents were a determined lot. Because club members had varying work schedules, and in order to accommodate them all, practices were held at unusual hours, including at least one session at 5 o'clock on a Saturday morning. Practices were announced in the newspaper so that all players and interested spectators could turn out.

The rules of the game were different then. An out was recorded if a ball was caught on the fly or on the first bounce, and "leading off" by base runners was not permitted. Overhand pitching was not allowed, there was no such thing as a walk, and no limit had been placed on the number of pitches a hitter could take before swinging. Three strikes constituted an out. Profanity was not permitted, and umpires immediately assessed a 25-cent fine to any offending player.

At their first game, played in Grand Rapids, the Kents lost 48-19 to the Custers, who had been organized the previous year and were more experienced. They fared little better in the rematch played in Ionia, losing 62-33.

Though they were not an artistic success, the Kents quickly gained a following for baseball. Several other teams were formed after the first game with the Custers, and by the Fourth of July, 1867, Grand Rapids boasted four teams that marched in the parade and played two games in the afternoon. This time the Kents were victorious, defeating the Centrals 88-39 for a silver ball prize. In the other game, the Dexters annihilated the Hickorys 86-7 to win a silver cup.

Baseball had come to Grand Rapids. The following excerpt from the Grand Rapids *Eagle* describes the Kents' first game with the Custers, and captures some of the interest and excitement still generated by the game.

A high wind prevailed during the entire game, interfering to some extent with the players. The concourse of spectators was large, about two thousand ladies and gentlemen and juveniles being present.

In personnel the two clubs are about evenly matched, both being composed of young athletic men with muscles hardened by the exhilarating exercise of the game. The Custers' uniform is black pants, white shirt, azure fatigue caps trimmed with white, and canvas shoes. The uniform of the Kent Club is black pants, white shirt tastefully embroidered in blue, leather belt, white caps trimmed with blue, and canvas shoes. Both clubs made a fine appearance, and won the frequent plaudits of the large concourse by their excellent play.

The Custers had the first innings and made nine runs. Some excellent batting — Cash making a home run on first bat. The Kent Club evinced the benefit of their recent practice by good fielding, several splendid stops and fly-catches being made. Kent Club then went in — white-washed — considerable skill was shown with the bat, but the Custers were ubiquitous and seldom failed to catch a fly ball, when there was a possibility of doing so.

The Custers having the experience of a season are more than a match for the Kents, although the latter has excellent material

▲Workmen playing baseball during their noon break at the Couple Gear Company, ca. 1900. [GRPL, Photo Collection]

and already possesses good players; the short stop — Porter, was exceedingly well executed.

At the conclusion of the game the clubs adjourned to the Rathbun House and partook of an excellent supper, prepared by "mine host" [proprietor Truman H. Lyon]. The Kent nine entertained their opponents in good style, and everything passed off pleasantly and agreeably. The Custers left for home on last evening's 7 o'clock train.

▲ *Grand Rapids Daily Eagle,* May 24, 1867, p. 1.

BOX SCORE

Custer		RM	HL	Kent		RM	HL
Cash	C	7	2	Withy	1stB	2	7
Tower	3dB	6	4	Avery	3dB	2	7
Stevenson	1stB	5	4	White	2dB	3	6
Bliss	SS	6	4	Earle	RF	3	6
Taylor	LF	6	3	Joslin	P	3	6
Worden	2dB	5	4	Hulbert	C	2	7
Reep	P	5	5	Pierce	CF	2	7
Tucker	RF	5	5	Hubbard	LF	0	9
Cornell	CF	4	5	Porter	SS	2	9
Total		48	36	Total		19	64

Home Run -- Cash, 1

RM = Runs made.
HL = Hitters left (outs and left on base).

▲ Grand Rapids plays Saginaw in an early league game, 1882. [GRPL, Photo Collection]

Watering the Tree of Knowledge

For those who preferred quiet lectures and musical interludes to brass bands and fireworks, Grand Rapids offered several attractive options. As the city grew, so did the craving for a greater variety of cultural activities. With more human and financial resources available, cultural organizations sprang up to offer both private and public lectures, theatrical performances, and musical concerts. Among the earliest of these organizations was the Ladies Literary Club, founded in 1869. Meeting in members' homes at first, the club marshaled its forces and less than two decades later broke ground for a large clubhouse on Sheldon Avenue with a 400-seat auditorium. A history of the club written at the end of its first decade describes the type of topics covered at its weekly meetings.

During the winter of '69-'70, Mrs. L. H. Stone, of Kalamazoo, organized in this City a class of ladies in history. She met them from time to time as she was able, and in the intervals six or eight of them met at private houses for mutual improvement. At length they resolved to organize a literary society. Having drawn up a constitution, they called a meeting of ladies who wished to join them. A large number responded, and the association was duly officered, and named "The Ladies' Literary Club." The first meeting was held in April, 1872. . . .

Ladies of all ages are included. . . .

Much sound, satisfactory work is done. The Club owns a large number of photographs, selected with great care. It is also a member of the Palestine Exploration Society, and receives such photographs and documents as are published under its auspices. Since the autumn of '75, the Club has had a member, at its expense studying under the direction of the Boston "Society for the Encouragement of Study at Home." (Several others have studied, also, under its auspices, at their own expense.) The results have been given to the Club, accompanied with specimens of natural history, on the Saturdays assigned to Science and Education. No longer than one hour, is ever allowed to these scientific talks or lectures, lest some listeners might weary, or the lecturer encroach on her prerogative. These lectures have proved highly instructive, and highly creditable to the ladies who have given their time to the studies, and the results to the Club.

Religion, politics and social questions, upon which different members are known to have different views, are ignored by common consent.

▲ *History and Plan of the Ladies Literary Club,* Grand Rapids Public Library.

▲ Caroline Williams-Putnam, first president of the Ladies Literary Club. [*Our Presidents: Ladies Literary Club,* p. 10]

◄ The Ladies Literary Clubhouse, built in 1887. [GRPL, *Grand Rapids Illustrated Collection*]

A Building Devoted to Music

On September 7, 1883, nine women who preferred music study and performance to literary pursuits gathered to form a music society "free from selfish interests, devoted to musical improvement, and to the development of the art in the community." The Saint Cecilia Society (it did not become the Saint Cecilia Music Society until 1970) founded that day quickly became a major source of musical enrichment for the community. A decade later the club had broken ground for a large building with room for classes, a ballroom, and an auditorium.

Who ever imagined a few short years since, when a small number of enthusiastic ladies met and discussed plans for the consolidation of their mutual interests, that, out of these quiet little Friday afternoon meetings, one of the most unique and celebrated musical societies of the present age would eventually rise into existence and proudly wave its banner before the admiring gaze of the whole musical world. All these have come to pass and the end is not yet....

It is an historic fact that, nowhere in the world at the present day has a society of women alone, by women's efforts, succeeded in erecting such a building as now ... ornaments this city—a building to which the loyal citizens can point with feelings of utmost pleasure and pride....

Few of the citizens of Grand Rapids are aware of the scope and importance of this splendid temple of art that has sprung into existence as it were, under the inspiration of the muses, elevating its imposing facade toward the setting sun, and reaching, in solemn dignity far back in massive proportions. But the day is drawing nigh — the day of dedication, when its grand corridors and spacious halls will be opened to the astonished and wondering eyes of the public, a day that will not be soon forgotten in the history of musical art in this fair city....

In wonder the eye will be astonished; who ever dreamed of such a perfect auditorium; roomy, high, admirably and perfectly ventilated; lighted from above by a skylight occupying almost the entire ceiling, heated by the latest and most appealing apparatus, seated on a scale of generosity which puts to shame any other auditorium in the state — a hall cheerful, bright and healthy. Then the ball room, with its great depth and breadth, its fascinating spring floor, vibrating to the rhythmic step and pulsation of Terpsichorean festivities. Those who have once bent the knee to the goddess to the dance upon this delightful bounding plane all know how to appreciate its superiority to any of the dead surfaces heretofore used for dancing clubs and parties.

Thus let everybody enthuse over the foyer, the wide airy halls, the library and reception room, and the various details for social comfort and enjoyment. Whoever anticipated such a kitchen or supper room such as the basement offers, with its gas ranges, hot water tanks and economic culinary devices? But there is only one way to appreciate the elegance and utility of the entire structure. Come and see for yourselves. Words are utterly inadequate to do justice to the situation. And why should not the St. Cecilia's have the best building of the kind in the whole wide world? Why not reap the harvest of their untiring thrift and industry? Is there any banded society who has a better right....

◄ *Grand Rapids Evening Press,* Special Edition, May 5, 1894, p. 2.

▲ St. Cecilia Auditorium, built in 1893. [GRPL, Catherine Colby Swanlund Collection]

▲ Ella Matthews Pierce, first president of the St. Cecilia Society. [St. Cecilia Music Society Archives]

The Merry Men of the Schubert Club

For many years men who enjoyed group singing gathered informally in private homes and occasionally, on summer evenings, took to the streets to serenade in front of the houses of the city's most attractive young women. Eventually, they, too, decided to impose order on their singing activities, and after due consideration adopted Schubert as their namesake. Although informal singing sessions like the one described here continued to be a favorite activity, the Schubert Club also gave public concerts, including joint sessions with the Saint Cecilia Society.

It was in the spring of '84, a few months later than the formation of the St. Cecilia society that the Schubert club was organized. At the invitation of Henry C. Post thirteen young men met at his home and before they departed the club was well under way. The name Schubert, suggested by Mr. Post, was the one decided upon, after some discussion as to the fitness of Liszt, Schumann and others. William H. Loomis, who has always showed an active interest in things musical, with the assistance of H. Arthur Stuart, now of Minneapolis, were prime movers in the club, for they circulated the list of names and secured 16 charter members....

Henry Post was the first director of the club and Lucius Hoyt its first president.

Previous to the eventful night which marked the birth of the Schubert club there were meetings, not exactly preliminary to the formation of the society, but which in a way led up to it. One occasion which still glows as a bright spot in memory to those who took part happened on a beautiful evening in the late fall of 1883, soon after Henry Post had returned from his studies in Germany. He invited several of "the boys" to come up to the house and have a "sing," and there they met at the old Post family home on Ransom street, which still stands on the brink of the hill and is marked by its large, old fashioned front pillars. This was a night when all nature seemed in harmony with youth and joy, for the trees still retained some of their warm autumn tints and the stars twinkled down from a clear sky, still there was a chill in the air and the blaze from the open fireplace lent a sense of cozy comfort to the evening. With the host at the piano to give the key and the company grouped in the bay window, they joined in song after song typical of the time. A feature of that evening which has not been forgotten was the pitcher of brown cider as clear and rich as old wine, with which the guests were refreshed, and mirth and jollity reigned. It was largely these same young men who met the second time in the same place and formed the society.

▲ *Grand Rapids Herald,* February 14, 1909, Society Section, p. 5.

◄ The Schubert Club, ca. 1890. [GRPL, James R. Hooper Collection]

Michigan's Sweet Singer

Of all the local talent that performed on Grand Rapids stages, the most notorious may well have been Julia A. Moore, the "Sweet Singer of Michigan." A simple farm woman, Moore was a determined poet whose energy exceeded her talent. Her naive, maudlin verse attracted a nationwide following that included the likes of humorists Mark Twain and Bill Nye, although writing poetry was, for Moore, anything but a humorous enterprise. Yet the harder she tried, the greater the mirth she provoked. Twain claimed he read Moore's work in order to learn the art of delivering lines to make them funny. Nye wrote that he thought she had abused her poetic license and that it ought to be revoked.

Moore selected accidents for her topics, along with the deaths of children and similar tragic episodes, and then in her earnestness, proceeded to make them a source of merriment for her readers. In 1877 and again the following year, she was persuaded to give public readings of her poems in Grand Rapids' Powers Opera House. Although she treated the evening with the utmost seriousness, her sponsors did not. For them it was a lark. On both occasions, her introduction and the behavior of the audience were clear evidence of the intent to make fun of her presence on the stage. The *Daily Morning Democrat's* account of her second performance leaves little doubt about the audience's intent on coming to the reading. But Moore maintained her dignity and at the end of the evening is supposed to have said, "You people paid fifty cents to see a fool, but I got fifty dollars to look at a house full of fools."

Later, Julia's husband stepped in and forbade her to present any more public readings or publish any more of her verse, a decision she respected until his death in 1914. Thereafter, she returned to her writing.

As a nation advances in civilization, the amusements of the people become more intellectual. It is for this reason, perhaps, that a large audience assembled at Powers' Opera House last night to hear Mrs. Julia A. Moore, known as the "Sweet Singer of Michigan," read selections from her poems. The event had been well advertised, and the audience were prepared for a fine treat.

The performance commenced with an overture from the orchestra, presumably written in honor of the occasion. Then there was a wait of several minutes, but at last Mrs. Moore was led upon the stage by Mr. J.H. Mason Reynolds, who with a few well chosen words introduced her to the audience. Mrs. Moore took a seat upon the sofa when Mr. Reynolds began his remarks, and the seat being a little deeper than she expected, had a narrow escape from a tip over backwards. She was attired in a black dress, with a black hat and red feather, white gloves, and roomy shoes....

Mr. Reynolds then retired and Mrs. Moore stepped up to the table, and opening her volume of original poems, remarked that it was "partly full of mistakes" and "therefore not correct." She also said the book was written to "Catch the public" and she thought she had succeeded. "Literary is a work very hard to do," remarked Mrs. Moore, and the audience grinned assent.

The first poem read by the talented lady was entitled "Willie and Nellie's Wish." One stanza will do for a specimen:

Willie and Nellie, one evening sat
 By their little cottage door;
They saw a man go staggering by-
 Says Willie, "that's Mr. Lenore;
He is just going home from town, where
 He has been in a saloon.
When Maggie and I came from school,
 Said Maggie, 'please papa, come home.'

When the reading of the poem was finished, the lady, without stopping for breath, announced the title of the next which was, "I Wonder Where my Papa Is?" This sounded so much like a conundrum that the audience gave it up. The sentiment was very fine, and there wasn't a wet eye in the house. Then came "The Southern Scourge," a touching description of the ravages of the yellow fever, which displays so much poetic fancy and genuine feeling that we are obliged to print the opening verse:

The yellow fever was raging,
 Down in the sunny south;
And in many of the cities,
 There was a death at every house.
This plague a war was raging.
 With the lives of people there;
The young and old were stricken down,
 And lay in sad despair.

During the readings Mrs. Moore made frequent incursions to behind the scenes, where an occasional muffled wail told of infantile innocence pining for maternal sustenance.

"To My Friends and Critics," was the only poem in which the lady permitted herself to become overpowered with emotion, and "she stopped short," at the end of the line:
"Dear friends I write for money."

This was quite a shock to those of the audience who had permitted themselves to think that Michigan's favorite poet wrote only for fame. Her mercenary disposition was passed over, however, and the delighted auditors stamped, applauded, and whistled for her appearance. The Sweet Singer then came to the side of the stage and by expressive pantomime gave the audience to understand that the show was over, and they reluctantly left the hall. No words can do justice to the subject. "We ne'er shall look upon her like again."

▲ Grand Rapids Daily Morning Democrat, December 24, 1878, p. 2.

▲ Julia A. Moore. [GRPL, *Papers of the Bibliographical Society of America*, Vol. 39, p. 111]

> My childhood days have passed and gone,
> And it fills my heart with pain
> To think that youth will nevermore
> Return to me again.
> And now kind friends, what I have wrote,
> I hope you will pass o'er,
> And not criticize as some have done,
> Hitherto herebefore.

▲ Julia Moore's poetic plea for understanding. [Julia A. Moore, *Sentimental Songbook*, p. 56]

CHAPTER 6
A New Century

As the hands of the giant city hall clock struck midnight 1901, church bells throughout Grand Rapids rang in the new century. (Numbering the modern centuries had begun with "1" rather than "0"; therefore, 1901 marked the 20th century's inaugural year.) Citizens everywhere looked to a future filled with the promise of technological wonders. But would the marvels of taller buildings, flying machines, and labor-saving devices assure them a world of peace and prosperity, or would human ingenuity be turned to exploitation and destruction? The coming years would find truth in both views.

In the opening decades of the 20th century, growing numbers of Grand Rapids residents buzzed along downtown streets in new automobiles and took to the sky aboard barnstorming airplanes. Trains were bigger and faster, and tracks seemed to lead everywhere. Passenger trains entered and left the Furniture City as many as 30 times each day, taking more residents than ever before to places far beyond West Michigan.

Telegraph and telephone lines carried news of distant events virtually as they happened. Three daily newspapers kept the populace well informed, and weekly papers in several languages served the city's Dutch, German, Polish, and Scandinavian residents.

Imported goods and visitors from distant lands further emphasized Grand Rapids' place in a shrinking world. Appearances by such internationally renowned performing artists as Irish tenor John McCormack dazzled local audiences. Exotic woods like mahogany and teak supplied veneers for the furniture industry, and few days passed in the city without news of the arrival of some overseas businessman or foreign government representative.

The dramatically shrinking globe also had its negative side. The United States was becoming an increasingly important international power. At the turn of the century, local soldiers fought in Cuba, the Philippines, and later in Mexico and Europe, a reminder to those at home that America was no longer isolated from the quagmire of international intrigue and war. Small, violent sneezes in faraway capitals could not be ignored, for fear they might become part of a dangerous virus and spread unchecked across many borders.

By the early years of the 1900s, technology had permanently changed the workplace. With an increasing supply of electrical power available, labor-saving machines became a standard factory feature. Workers' hours were still long, and pay rates had not improved, but now, the speed of the machines controlled the work, and greater risk of injury loomed over every workman. Unions were one obvious response to the changing conditions, but management fought bitterly against all organizing initiatives, beating back most union efforts, including a city-wide strike by furniture workers in 1911.

Technology even intruded into recreation. On warm summer weekends, increasing numbers of citizens took to the roadways on their bicycles or in automobiles. And on one summer evening, fans were even able to see a baseball game played under electric lights.

Down at city hall, local government changed in response to a more diverse population and to attitudes shaped by new technology. Businessmen were the heroes of American society, and a rising chorus called for a "Progressive" reform to impose modern management practices and make city government more efficient and less costly. The result, in 1916, was a charter amendment, passed by a narrow margin, that replaced the old aldermanic system with a city-manager form of government.

Grand Rapids exemplified what was taking place all across the United States: The country was growing up and moving to the city. No longer was America a nation of rural towns and yeoman farmers. Cities, with their factories and industrial wage earners, were now the national norm.

The Future Is Now

The special significance of January 1, 1901, did not escape notice in Grand Rapids. The dawn of the new century represented an ideal opportunity to shake free of the problems of the past and start anew. In honor of the occasion, local newspapers were filled with stories of the New Year's celebration and speculations about the changes the next 100 years would bring.

▲ The *Grand Rapids Press* announced the new century with this banner headline. [*Grand Rapids Press,* January 1, 1901, p. 1]

The Red Cross watch-night entertainment presented last evening at the Auditorium was a delightful success, both in point of attendance and in the manner in which the numbers on the program were received. There was a good audience inside the hall when the Evening Press Newsboy band played the opening number, "Mosaic Overture," about 8 o'clock, and the number was increased later.

The entertainment was held for the Red Cross fund, at the same time that hundreds of similar entertainments were being held in cities of size all over the country. In New York, it is said the celebration was carried on a grand scale, but the observance of the occasion while less pretentious here was none the less sincere and worthy of commendation. The purpose here, as in the country over, was the raising of a fund for the Red Cross in America. Incidentally the Children's Home was helped out here through the sale of tickets.

A military drill presented by a squad from the Grand Rapids battalion under the command of Captain Blickle was well received. A chorus of sixteen voices from the Schubert club, under the direction of J. Francis Campbelt, the director of the club, and a chorus of sixteen St. Cecilia singers under the direction of Mrs. Aldworth, rendered several selections in a very pleasing manner. "Trelawney" and "Schubert Serenade" were both given by request, and the usual hearty manifestation of appreciation of the music of the Schuberts and the St. Cecilia chorus was not lacking. The illustrated songs and stereopticon views made a hit with the audience, especially the "Star Spangled Banner." It was sung by the Schuberts and the St. Cecilia students' chorus and was illustrated on the screen as the story progressed in the song, by Leo A. Caro and George E. Fitch. Perhaps as interesting as anything on the program was the illustration of the work of the Red Cross nurses on the battlefields.

▲ *Grand Rapids Evening Press,* January 1, 1901, p. 1.

AS IT MAY BE
One Hundred Years Hence.

Printed books will be cheap and abundant, and the art of illustrating and embellishing them will reach high perfection.

International difficulties will be settled by commissioners or conventions, instead of by appeals to arms to end in the destruction of life and property.

Air ships will be a regular method of transportation, passengers from "fliers" being dropped at cities under the route by means of parachutes.

Photography in colors will be well understood and practiced, and the camera will contest with the type-setting machine in the manufacture of books and newspapers.

Scientific discoveries and appliances will do away with dangers to health incident to the massing of vast numbers in the cities. Water will be pure, temperature will be equalized, food will be scientifically prepared for use, and men and women will live longer by obeying the common sense laws of health.

Capital and labor will be at peace by the prevalence of the golden rule, which enjoins us to do to others as we would have them do to us. The working people, it is hoped, will be shareholders, in the farm or factory where they work, and draw dividends from the profits. They will lose by all strikes, because the strike will be against their own interest.

By 2000 the phonographic principle will have been so perfected that the best books will appear in records or plates for use in many different styles of speaking machines. The exact tones of the elocutionist in speaking the words of the poet, teacher, philosopher and novelist will be reproduced in the library or parlor of every home. The exact tones of the sweet singer will also be faithfully reproduced.

◄*Grand Rapids Evening Press,* December 28, 1900, p. 2.

▼ Downtown Grand Rapids looked like this in 1901. Straight ahead are Campau Square and Sweet's Hotel (site of today's Amway Grand Plaza). [GRPL, George E. Fitch Collection]

Private XY

Not every Grand Rapids citizen was at home to enjoy the New Year's celebration. Even before the turn of the century, the United States had embarked on a course of foreign military adventures, including a "splendid little war" with Spain. In 1898 several local young men, answering the call to action led by Teddy Roosevelt and his "Rough Riders," volunteered for duty fighting Spanish troops in Cuba. A few weeks later they found themselves in a hot, muggy land where life-threatening diseases were a greater danger than enemy soldiers.

During the Spanish-American War, yellow fever became a source of great concern to American military leaders. Long lines of soldiers serving in Cuba were answering sick call. And, all too often, commanding officers had to write letters home to the families of men who had died from the disease. No one knew what caused yellow fever, but with so many Americans among its victims, the Army was determined to find out.

In 1900, Major Walter Reed, an army physician, was sent to Cuba to study the disease. According to one hypothesis put forth by Cuban doctors, yellow fever was carried by mosquitoes and could be contained by eradicating the insects' breeding grounds. Reed approved plans for a monitored study to establish the mosquito's culpability.

Reed's initial study focused on a single individual, Private William H. Dean of Grand Rapids, who neither sought nor enjoyed the role of hero. An itinerant house painter before the war, Dean was not cut from an heroic pattern. At the time Reed asked him to participate in the pilot experiment, he was an army hospital patient, recovering from a case of gonorrhea. Offered a chance to stay in the hospital for another month or more if he consented to being bitten by a mosquito, Dean readily agreed.

Five days after the bite, he came down with yellow fever.

The experiment using Dean as a guinea pig clearly established mosquitoes as the carrier. But because testing on a human subject had not been authorized by the military, the Grand Rapids soldier could only be identified in official records as Private XY.

It was not until 1927 that local leaders learned of Dean's role in the experiment and decided to afford him the recognition he deserved. Plans were made to name the newly constructed Fulton Street Bridge in his honor, and a gala ceremony was arranged. Unfortunately, Dean's health had long suffered from recurrent bouts of the yellow fever he voluntarily contracted for Dr. Reed, and he died shortly before the ceremony was scheduled. Few people know of the bridge named in his honor or the story behind his brush with history.

▲ Private William H. Dean. [GRPL, *Grand River Valley Review* Collection]

In June 1900, Maj. Reed was sent to Cuba as president of a board to study the infectious diseases of the country, but more especially yellow fever. Associated with him were Acting Asst. Surgs. James Carroll, Jesse W. Lazear, and A. Agramonte.

Lazear began to breed, dissect, classify and infect mosquitoes, in which work Carroll and Agramonte took little or no part. Now and then Lazear would apply them to whoever allowed it. Most of the mosquitoes died early in captivity. Lazear, Carroll, and several other persons had been bitten several times by mosquitoes which previously had fed on yellow fever blood, without result,

so then the theory of mosquito transmission was gradually being discredited, until Carroll fell sick, on the 30th of August (1900).

Suspecting the origin of his infection and its real gravity, Drs. Lazear and Agramonte decided to test the mosquito which presumably had caused Carroll's attack by applying it to the first nonimmune individual who might allow it.

Therefore, on the afternoon of August 31, the same mosquito and three others, were applied to an American soldier who had not left Columbia Barracks (which was free from yellow fever) for 57 days prior to his inoculation; nor did he go out of said reservation before he

fell sick with yellow fever, five days afterwards, thus confirming in our minds the fact that he had been infected by the mosquito bites.

The name of the American soldier, XY, who was the subject of the second experiment, was concealed at the time, because the experiment was made without military authorization. It has been recently ascertained to be William H. Dean, private, Troop B, Seventh Cavalry. He has never received any reward. He was discharged August 17, 1902, by reason of expiration of term of service, and there is no further record of him at the War Department. His residence at enlistment was given as Grand Rapids, Mich. His case has special importance as having been the first experimental case which was complete in the matter of control, for Dr. Carroll's, which came four days earlier, was defective, by reason of his going into the infected zone during the period of incubation.

▲ "Yellow Fever," *Senate Document No. 822, 61st Congress, 3rd Session, Serial No. 5919*, pp. 26-27.

◄ Citizens filled Campau Square to see local volunteers off to the Spanish-American War. [GRPL, Photo Collection]

Putting the City on Wheels

Two-wheeled bicycles had first appeared on the local scene in the 1880s. By the turn of the century, the demand for them had become a craze. Convenient transportation for workmen, they also gave rise to touring clubs and races attended by large crowds. With so many cyclists taking to the roadways aboard their two-wheeled steeds, the *Press* attempted to explain the craze to its readers.

▲ A women's bicycle club pauses for a rest at the Crescent Park fountain. [GRPL, Photo Collection]

It is estimated that five out of every one hundred residents of Grand Rapids are bicycle riders, and the season for buying wheels has only just opened.

Every manufacturer and dealer in the country is behind with his orders and the demand continues unabated. The reason for the unprecedented boom in the wheel business lies largely in the fact that the prices of high grade bicycles have been reduced 20 per cent below what they were last year. Of the estimated 4,000 riders in this city fully 500 are women and girls. The use of the wheeled steed by professional men of all classes is becoming more general every day. Doctors especially find them useful in making professional calls. No less than a dozen physicians in this city have discarded the use of horses, as a rule, and many of them have sold their animals. The bicycle, they say, does not "eat its head off" and it is always ready for use. The services of a hostler are dispensed with, along with all the annoyance and exasperating delays of this servant's inefficiency. The idea that a professional man lowers his dignity when he gets astride of a bicycle is now fast wearing away, although it has taken a long time for this impression to be overcome. Among a certain class of people who proverbially cling to old things, just because they are old, the bicycle is still unpopular. In this class may be found some physicians. They are saying nothing now, though, seeming to prefer to jog along all the ruts made in the bygone ages as man has fought his way to higher places in every department of his manifold and complex nature. The

ox-cart and wooden plow were good—in their day—but the steel plow and locomotive were better, even as the steam plow and electric motors are superior to the later inventions. In America where energy and unceasing activity are such factors of our civilization the bicycle is bound to be the vehicle for business and pleasure. Its cheapness at the present time has enabled hundreds of Grand Rapids mechanics to put them into use in going to and from their work. The investment is found to be economical, too, as the saving of car fare is alone a large rate of interest upon the amount of money represented.

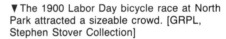

◄ *Grand Rapids Evening Press,* April 20, 1895, p. 1.

▼ The 1900 Labor Day bicycle race at North Park attracted a sizeable crowd. [GRPL, Stephen Stover Collection]

Make Way for the Motorists

Railroads were the dominant form of public transportation at the turn of the century, but forces were gathering that would soon challenge the preeminence of the iron horse. No one was more convinced of this than Clark Sintz. Owner of the Sintz Gas Engine Company, the former Ohio farm boy had been building steam and gasoline engines for more than 30 years. Like other tinkerers and inventors working around the country and in other nations at the time, his goal was to develop a functional, gasoline-engine-powered automobile.

Sintz produced a very serviceable vehicle, but was unable to market it successfully. For every entrepreneur like Henry Ford who managed to engage in large-scale production, countless others like Sintz struggled along until they had to abandon their efforts. Before he gave up the chase, however, Clark Sintz was certain that his motor cars would soon be seen hurrying about the city streets in noisy, exhaust-belching profusion.

▲ Clark Sintz's motor car was the first of several built in Grand Rapids. [GRPL, James R. Hooper Collection]

After six months of close application of study and painstaking work Clark Sintz of this city has produced an automobile which he feels confident will prove one of the most useful and practical machines of the kind yet placed on the market. This machine has already been sufficiently tested to demonstrate its worth, and others of the same type will be constructed at once. It is not the present intention of Mr. Sintz to form a company, though this will doubtless be done eventually, but for a time he will manufacture in a small way. When a few have been placed in successful operation, and the genuine merit of them is shown he feels confident capital will seek the investment. He has several plans in regard to their manufacture and marketing which are now in such embryonic shape that he does not wish to disclose them.

The particular point in the new machine which gives it value over those already on the market, says the inventor, is the engine and the transmission gear. The motive force is gasoline and the power is transmitted in such a manner that the machine can be changed from full speed forward to reverse, almost instantaneously, and without catching any speeds between. This is a marked advance in security and safety of operation. In case of obstructions or when danger menaces in shape of collisions, or in any form. This is an essential which will be appreciated not only by the driver, but by the general public as well. So far as Mr. Sintz knows there is no other engine yet invented by which this result can be obtained. The machine is also unique in that all the working parts can be reached without the necessity of crawling under the car. Both the hood and the floor may be removed and every part of the working gear reached from above. It is in nowise a racing machine. It is geared to thirty miles an hour, but is intended strictly for road work and the average speed at which it is intended to be driven is not more than twenty miles. Mr. Sintz is not a believer in the high speed fad, and declared that if he had his way no machine that was to be used for road work should be permitted to be built for anything more than this speed.

The machine will be known as the Sintz motor car, manufactured by Clark Sintz of Grand Rapids and was built in his shop at Fulton and Front streets. Technically it is described as the French Tonneau type, propelled by a double cylinder gasoline engine, 16 horse power, and placed under the hood. The transmission has three speeds, forward and reverse, operated by one lever. It has but one clutch and all speeds are changed and the clutch operated by this lever. The working parts are fastened to an angle iron frame which can be operated when the body of the car is removed. This is a convenience in case the driver should see fit to participate in races.

In addition to the novel features which have been enumerated the car is provided with fenders or mud guards which afford protection to the occupants. The weight of the car is 2,000 pounds and its cost $2,000. The car which has been completed will seat six persons. It is 10 feet 6 inches over all and 5 feet 1 inch in its highest part, which is the back. The wheel base is 7 feet and the wheels 30 inches in diameter with 4 inch tires. The gauge is 4 feet 6 inches. The tanks will hold fifteen gallons of gasoline and ten gallons of water when loaded and this is sufficient to carry the car one hundred and fifty miles at a speed of eighteen miles an hour.

Grand Rapids Press, ▶ December 27, 1902, p. 7.

▲ Three different motor cars were parked in front of the Michigan Automobile Co. on the northwest corner of Ottawa Avenue and Louis Street in 1903. [GRPL, Photo Collection]

Wings Over Grand Rapids

In 1903, Wilbur and Orville Wright proved that heavier-than-air vehicles could fly, thereby demonstrating that the potential of the internal-combustion engine was not limited to ground transportation. In the years after the first successful flight at Kitty Hawk, aviation took off on the wings of barnstorming daredevil pilots who toured the country, showing off their planes and their flying prowess. Large crowds turned out whenever barnstormers visited Grand Rapids.

One such visit in 1913 sparked Tom Walsh's lifelong love affair with aviation. Walsh was a 12-year-old orphan living with a farm family and working for his keep when he learned an airplane was coming to the West Michigan Fair. Sneaking away from his home, he managed to meet pilot Hilary Beachey and get an airplane ride. Several years later, after a stint in the Army during World War I, Walsh helped build Kent County's first commercial airport and served as its manager for nearly three decades. After retiring in 1957 he recalled his introduction to flying.

Well, back in 1913 I was working on a farm up between Sparta and Casnovia. I read in the paper that there was going to be an airplane at Comstock Park. Course, I didn't have any chance of getting there, like most kids did, but I did borrow a bicycle from one of the neighbor kids. I went over the wood shed roof about 11 o'clock when they were all asleep and I pedalled to Comstock Park. I got there just at the right minute. This plane was setting there and the pilot came over to the fence and said, "Does anyone have a bicycle?" and I said, "Yep, here I am." Well he had broken a rocker arm and he had it in a piece of burlap and he gave me a five dollar bill and told me to take it to a foundry and have it cast. And I remember he said, "Cool it in oil, not water." So I went off and I did the job, finally found a foundry. When I got back there it was after dark, and I think I had 80¢ left out of the five bucks and he said "Keep it." Well that was a fortune in itself. But the important thing was he said, "How would you like an airplane ride, kid?" And I said, "Boy, I sure would." Well he said, "You come back here tomorrow morning and I'll give you a ride. We'll have this together." Well, I didn't need to come back, I slept under the bleachers.

It was in September and my memory of that first airplane flight was that I damn near froze to death. I set up there on a board, they didn't have seats like they have today. We took off in the wild blue yonder. And I got down and I thanked him, pedalled back to the farm. But, that ride fascinated me. I could see not only what was on the ground, I could even pick out cattle. But the noise was terrific, you had everything blasting back at you. Well, that really was the key to my becoming interested in aviation.

▲Tom Walsh Interview, 1984, Grand Rapids Public Library.

▲ Sixteen-year-old Tom Walsh (right), pictured here with his buddies Westrau and Purdy, lied about his age in order to enlist in the Army in 1917. [GRPL, Walsh Collection]

◄ Aviator Hilary Beachey brought his biplane to Grand Rapids in 1913. [GRPL, Walsh Collection]

The Water Scandal

Some turn-of-the-century Grand Rapids figures, like City Attorney Lant K. Salsbury, gained notoriety through misadventures that embarrassed and angered the community. Heavily in debt as the result of some investment schemes gone bad, Salsbury had first of all contrived to cover a $30,000 loss by conspiring with Old National Bank bookkeeper S.V. McLeod to misappropriate funds from the bank. At the same time, he was the point man in a shady plan to build a pipeline to bring Lake Michigan water to the city of Grand Rapids.

In those years, the Grand River did double duty — supplying city residents with drinking water and carrying away raw sewage. Outbreaks of disease caused by heavy river pollution, especially in the spring, made Lake Michigan an attractive alternative for a fresh drinking water supply.

The plan Salsbury was pushing called for a pipeline to be funded by city-backed bonds and built by a syndicate headed by New York promoter G.H. Garman and his financial backer, H.A. Taylor. The problem was that bonds were to be issued in a sum much greater than the actual cost of building the pipeline and a pumping station, with Garman and his associates pocketing the surplus. To secure favorable action on all necessary city commission votes, Salsbury doled out $100,000 of Taylor's money as bribes to Mayor George Perry, the city clerk, 16 of the city's 24 aldermen, members of the board of public works, and even members of the state legislature. In a bid to assure public support for the project, payments were also made to the managing editors of the city's three daily newspapers, and at least one reporter.

The elaborate scheme began to come apart in 1901, when rumors of foul play led to grand jury indictments of Salsbury and the New Yorkers, who were tried and convicted of bribery and conspiracy. Salsbury received a prison sentence and a fine, which he appealed, and the others paid fines of up to $2,000. In a subsequent federal court action in Grand Rapids, Salsbury and McLeod were found guilty of violating federal banking statutes, and served two-year sentences at the Detroit House of Corrections.

Initially, no charges had been brought against the local officials to whom Salsbury had made payments. However, as he faced the prospect of several more years in prison on the pipeline bribery and conspiracy charges, Salsbury agreed to tell all he knew. Armed with information from the former city attorney, prosecutors initiated a series of arrests, trials, and legal maneuverings that lasted from the end of 1903 until early in 1906. By then, the list of those who had been imprisoned, fined, or charged in the scandal filled nearly a page in a local history book.

One of the last loose ends in the water scandal prosecutions was the case of Mayor George Perry, who had been fingered by Salsbury as having accepted a bribe. Using a variety of tactics, Perry's attorney managed to prevent a successful prosecution. Finally, on February 10, 1906, a frustrated Charles E. Ward, assistant prosecuting attorney, went into district court in Grand Rapids and offered a motion to dismiss all remaining cases. His motion was granted 12 days later. Grand Rapids' worst political scandal was over.

In 1906, historian Dwight Goss used court records to compile the following list of cases, defendants, and dispositions. The list does not include federal court action against Salsbury and McLeod.

▲ Charles E. Ward prosecuted the perpetrators of the water scandal.
[GRPL, Oversized Photo Collection]

Lant K. Salsbury, city attorney. Bribery and conspiracy. Fined $2,000.

Thomas F. McGarry, attorney. Bribery and conspiracy. Sent to Ionia for four years. Paroled in the spring of 1906.

Stilson V. McLeod, banker. Bribery and conspiracy. Acquitted.

Gerrit H. Albers, attorney. Bribery and conspiracy. Acquitted.

Henry A. Taylor, millionaire promoter. Conspiracy. Fined $2,000.

George R. Perry, mayor. Bribery. Jury disagreed. Never retried.

Corey P. Bissel, member Board of Public Works. Bribery. Fined $400.

Malachi Kinney, alderman. Bribery. Pleaded not guilty. Never tried.

David E. Burns, state senator. Bribery. Acquitted.

John Muir, alderman. Bribery. Pleaded not guilty. Never tried.

Peter De Pagter, alderman. Bribery. Pleaded not guilty. Never tried.

James Mol, alderman. Bribery. Convicted. Granted new trial. Acquitted.

Jacob P. Ellen, alderman. Bribery. Fined $300.

John T. Donovan, alderman. Bribery. Fined $500.

Adrian Schriver, alderman. Bribery. Fined $100.

Charles T. Johnson, alderman. Bribery. Fined $200.

Reyner Stonehouse, alderman. Bribery. Fined $100.

Daniel E. Lozier, alderman. Bribery. Fined $500.

John McLachlin, alderman. Bribery. Fined $200.

Gerrit H. Albers, attorney. Perjury. Convicted. Granted new trial. Never tried.

William F. McKnight, attorney. Attempted perjury subornation. Never tried.

Abraham Ghysels, alderman. Bribery. Fined $300.

Clark E. Slocum, alderman. Bribery. Fined $500.

James O. McCool, alderman. Bribery. Fined $500.

E.D. Conger, newspaper publisher. Conspiracy. Tried and acquitted.

C.S. Burch, newspaper manager. Conspiracy. Never tried.

J. Russell Thompson, newspaper reporter. Conspiracy. Never tried.

Isaac F. Lamoreaux, city clerk. Pleaded guilty. Never sentenced.

Ed. Wierenga, attempting to corrupt juror. Never tried.

George E. Nichols, attorney. Perjury. Dismissed by court.

William Leonard. Bribery. Never tried.

J. Clark Sproat, newspaper publisher. Conspiracy. Never tried.

▲ Dwight Goss, *History of Grand Rapids and Its Industries*, Vol. II, pp. 1032-33.

▲ Alderman John Muir (left), and Mayor George Perry, were among those charged with accepting bribes. [GRPL, Photo Collection]

Take Me Out to the (Night) Ball Game

In 1909, the Grand Rapids Ad Club was looking for a way to raise funds for a pageant planned for the following summer. Someone in the club learned about a promoter who traveled the country with a portable, carbon-arc lighting system, sponsoring night games. Electric lights were less than three decades old at the time and noted as much for their power failures and burnouts as they were for brilliance. But baseball was a popular attraction, and playing a game at night under lights was an almost guaranteed crowd-attracting gimmick.

Sure enough, the novelty of the show drew an audience of more than 4,000 to see the home team take on Zanesville in a game that would not count in league standings, even though the two teams were battling for Central League leadership. According to newspaper reports, the spectators were treated to a closely contested, if not particularly well played, performance.

Thought to be the first night game ever played by two recognized professional teams, the Grand Rapids experiment did not lead to a sudden shift to night baseball. Two more decades would elapse before the first major league night game was played, and another 80 years would pass before Chicago's Wrigley Field, the last bastion of daytime baseball, would be outfitted with lights.

▲ Judging by this newspaper photograph, playing under the lights was risky business in 1909. [*Grand Rapids Herald,* July 8, 1909, p. 1]

Baseball at night, at least the game played by Grand Rapids and Zanesville under the glare of the electric lights at Ramona Athletic park last evening was voted a huge success by one of the largest crowds that ever attended a baseball game in Grand Rapids. Grand Rapids won, 11 to 10, which means that the local club was better at marathon running than the visitors, for no player dare go into a night game who is not in condition to go the full route of the distance runners.

Drawn by the novelty of the play by artificial light, 4,500 spectators found their way into the park for the Ad club entertainment, and when the game ended with the Grand Rapids club one run to the good at the end of the first half of the seventh inning there wasn't a member of this great crowd but what was willing to declare that they had more fun in one hour than at any previous time in their young, or old, lives.

Night baseball is a novelty which has been much talked about, but little played during the past year. The offering of the Ad club last night was the first that has ever been put on between two league teams in the history of the sport. There were some ardent fans who wanted to know whether the contest would count in the league standing. It will not, for there is a baseball rule which says that a league game cannot be called later than two hours before sunset, and this will stand until such a time as the rulemakers feel that the night game is feasible.

Now the fan who went out last night and started to keep a box score had to hustle some. The hits came so frequently and for such distances and the runners went around the bases so fast that a few assistants were needed in fixing up the tabulated form. Home runs numbered half a dozen, three baggers were but two less, while doubles were strong. Outfielders had their troubles in judging the balls hit in their direction but the light was perfect for the batters, and how they did land on the ball.

The averages in the moonlight league would make .400 hitters in the daylight organizations. There wasn't anything to getting a single, double or triple when you laid against the ball.

All in all the game was run in regulation style. Even the peanut boys were on hand, and they delivered the goods in a way that made some of the youngsters who sell at the regular games stand around in open-eyed astonishment. But of course they had the added attraction of the chance to win a prize on their peanuts. Then canes were sold, 500 walking sticks being furnished by Herpolsheimer's and disposed of at the game. The spectators who haven't a souvenir of the first night game are few and far between.

You had to be in on the rulings to get wise to the scoring secrets. It was decided before the game that all grounders and misjudged flies should go as hits and errors be given only on dropped thrown balls. Under these conditions Grand Rapids secured just 20 hits, with Zanesville but one behind.

Mayor George Ellis was the umpire. He kept his eyes on the game and worked in regulation style. The mayor was so much onto his job that Larsen was called out for cutting first base in the last inning.

When it was all over the greatest question asked was, "Do you think league baseball at night will ever be a success?" Certain it is. The game is practicable. It can be played.

However, in the successful games the lights must be placed in a position where they will not interfere with the fielding. Glaring in the players eyes makes it almost impossible to see a ball. It is certain, however, that a field can be prepared for a night game. Players who took part in the game enjoyed it immensely, and they believe that a system can be devised whereby the lights can be placed at the backs of the fielders and at the same time not interfere with the batter. The national game will do after dark.

▲ *Grand Rapids Herald,* July 8, 1909, p. 8.

◄ "Frenchy" Larue's line drive nearly decapitated the Zanesville center fielder. [*Grand Rapids Herald,* June 3, 1909, p. 8]

◄ "Buster" Brown was the winning pitcher in Grand Rapids' first night baseball game. [*Grand Rapids Herald,* June 2, 1909, p. 8]

The Michigan Assassin

Night baseball may have held the sporting public's attention for a moment, but it was boxer Stanley Ketchel (Stanislaus Kiecal) who put the city on the sports map. With an aggressive, slugging style that thrilled fight fans, the West Side native battled his way to the world's welterweight and middleweight championships in 1907 and 1908. Declared by many to be, pound-for-pound, the century's greatest fighter, Ketchel was best known for two things, the speedy manner in which he knocked out most of his opponents, and his thirst for the bright lights and a good time.

It was this second characteristic that was his undoing. On October 15, 1910, only 23 years old and at the peak of his fighting prowess, Ketchel was shot and killed at his recently purchased Missouri ranch by the jealous boyfriend of his housekeeper and companion. His funeral, held in Grand Rapids, was one of the most widely attended send-offs in the city's history.

▲ Stanley Ketchel was at his prime when he struck this classic boxer's pose for a publicity photograph. [Photo courtesy John Rappelyea]

◄ Ketchel's funeral in 1910 brought unprecedented crowds to St. Adalbert's Catholic church. [GRPL, Photo Collection]

The last bell has sounded for Stanley Ketchel, middleweight champion pugilist of the world.

Funeral services over the body of the murdered ring general were held yesterday morning at St. Adalbert's church, which was packed to its greatest capacity; while the streets about the church were crowded with men, women and children, eager to catch a glimpse of the funeral procession and to gaze upon the gray hearse in which the one time idol of fistiana was being taken on its last journey. It is estimated that in the vicinity of 7,000 or 8,000 persons, from old men to infants in arms, a good many of whom were prompted by curiosity, gathered in the vicinity of the church long before the funeral cortege arrived and every available porch and step was pressed into service as a resting place. Never before in all of Grand Rapids' history had such a crowd turned out to view the funeral procession of any man, no matter how great or famous he may have been.

A drizzling rain set in early in the morning, but it did not serve to thin the ranks of the crowd. The Polish Military band and carriages containing girls, dressed in white, who carried flowers, waited for more than half an hour at the corner of Leonard and Canal streets for the hearse and cortege, which came overland from the family home at Pine Island lake, near Belmont. The procession arrived about 10 o'clock, the gray hearse, drawn by four gray horses, followed by members of the local order of Elks and relatives in carriages.

With the band playing a funeral march, the line continued down Canal street to Bridge, where it turned west and proceeded to Jefferson street, thence to the church at Fourth and Davis streets.

Along the route of the procession the curbs were lined with hundreds of curious spectators, many of whom followed along to the church, anxious to look upon the face of the slain fighter.

When the cortege arrived at the church it was with difficulty that the mourners and bearers of the casket made their way through the crowd into the little edifice, which could not have held another person. The band played Chopin's funeral march while the body was being carried into the church, and not only the mourners, but many who had known Ketchel only slightly, wiped their eyes as they realized it was the last service for the man. The solemn mass funeral service was said over the body by Father Skory and throughout the church complete silence reigned.

The services lasted until about 12:30, but the crowd outside did not diminish, for it was believed that a view of the dead man was to be obtained. But the casket was not opened and immediately after the service the body was removed to the Polish Catholic cemetery on Walker avenue and interred.

▲ *Grand Rapids Herald,* October 21, 1910, p. 6.

The Great Flood

While the water scandal cases cast a deep shadow on the integrity of Grand Rapids municipal government, the great flood of 1904 did serious physical damage to the city. The worst flood in Grand Rapids history, the 1904 deluge remains the standard by which all potential flooding is measured today.

As spring approached in 1904, hints of trouble were already threatening. There had been no mid-winter thaw, a good snow pack was on the ground, and river ice was so thick that city engineer L.W. Anderson had begun dynamiting to prevent ice dams from forming in the event of a quick thaw. Such precautions had been taken before, so residents were no more concerned about spring flooding than usual. However, when the weather turned unseasonably warm at mid-month, the first words of caution sounded. With only a few dams to hold back meltwater from upstream, the Grand River rose steadily, and when heavy rains began falling, officials prepared for the worst. On March 25 the river passed flood stage and, as thawing and rain continued, reached a peak of 20.4 feet — more than five feet over flood stage — three days later.

Despite warnings, the river's sudden rise took many West Side residents by surprise and left them stranded in their homes. Many citizens were removed to safety by a flotilla of rowboats commandeered from nearby lakes under the direction of Police Chief Albert A. "Ab" Carroll. They were taken to residences and hotels on the city's east side where higher ground limited the damage to flooded basements and first floors in shops and factories along the river.

Before the waters receded, 8,000 people had been thrown out of work, an uncounted number of homes were damaged — some so badly that they were torn down rather than cleaned up — and east-side hotels and public buildings were taken over by the relief effort. Initial, unofficial estimates placed the damage at $1 million. Although a final appraisal was never done, actual damage was undoubtedly much higher.

Even before the waters had completely receded, residents began calling for the construction of concrete flood walls to prevent such disaster in the future. Promises were made, but little action was taken. However, when floods in 1905 and 1907 caused additional hardship and financial loss, the clamor grew louder. The building of flood walls to contain the river within its banks became an important election issue, and finally, in 1911 construction was complete.

We lived on West Wealthy Avenue at the very last street where there weren't any more houses built. I would judge that we were about a mile from the river, but I don't think much farther than that. I can remember the water started pouring in around three or four o'clock in the afternoon, and we little kids stood out in the yard and just let it pour in on us, and it was warm enough that we were having fun. It continued to rise until it reached the second window sash in our house. We had a stairs that went upstairs right opposite the door, and we were there upstairs a week in the flood when the city officials came to our house in the night and told us that our house was going to lose its foundation and that they would have to evacuate us. So we just got up and put on whatever clothes we could find at the moment and rushed downstairs. We had put all the furniture and everything that we could get upstairs so it was terribly crowded. We got downstairs and they rowed the boat up to the stairway and we got into the boat and they rowed us over a couple of blocks and we got into a hack that carried us down to the Clarendon Hotel and we stayed there probably about two or three weeks. We took our meals right at the hotel, but my father had to go out and buy me a dress and my brother a shirt to wear before they would take us in that dining room. The Clarendon was located at the corner of Monroe and Bridge Street, and the Grand Trunk Depot was just on the other side of it.

[When we got back to our house] it had inches of mud—just loads of mud in it. We cleaned it out, and I know that we were there for a little while, but oh, the odor was terrible.

◄ Stella Warfield Interview, August 19, 1983, Grand Rapids Public Library.

▲ The Grand River's sudden flooding in 1904 left many people stranded in West Side homes and boardinghouses. [GRPL, Guy Johnston Collection]

Never in the history of Grand Rapids did the West Side come nearer to being the scene of a lynching than Sunday night. Refugees from the Gunnison swamp district were being landed by boatmen at the corner of Gold and Shawmut.

The people of that neighborhood had been enraged over the report that many of the men who had boats were charging poor people large prices for conveying them to safety and, in most cases, collecting their exorbitant fees in advance. The rumor that there was a regulation price of $1.50 per head for ferrying is probably not a fact, although this price was charged in many instances and in some cases more was asked. The average thus would fall not far short of $1.50.

Late Sunday night a boat drew up to high ground and a shivering woman and two little children stepped out. The woman, when she reached the little party of anxious watchers on the corner, broke down and stated that the boatman had forced her to give up her last half-dollar for bringing herself and children to safety.

She intended to buy some food for her hungry family with the amount and was so overcome by its loss that the crowd was instantly worked up into a mood for hanging.

Some one suggested this course in a loud voice and the dreaded call for a lynching was heard. Several men made a dash for the boat containing the wretch who had robbed the woman. He rowed quickly away in the direction of Bridge street and the men, encumbered by their heavy boots, ran as fast as they could in the swift current, but were unable to overtake him. The man in the boat was not recognized and the woman stated that she had never seen him before.

▲ *Grand Rapids Press,* March 29, 1904, p. 6.

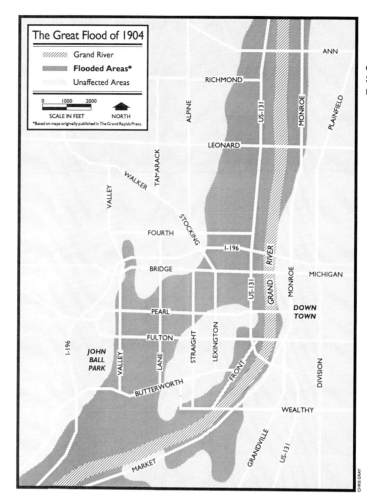

◄ Most of the 1904 flood damage was on the West Side, where waters reached nearly to John Ball Park.

▲ With rescuers out in rowboats, the West Side took on the look of Venice. [GRPL, Photo Collection]

◄ East Side buildings close to the river, including the *Evening Press,* were also flooded. [GRPL, Guy Johnston Collection]

"Rowing, Not Drifting"

On November 10, 1904, a group of African-American women gathered at the home of Mrs. Louisa Gaines to form the Grand Rapids Study Class. Their purpose, as stated in the constitution they adopted shortly after that first meeting, was to "unite all efforts towards individual, home, and community betterment through study and civic cooperation in all things, which portends the advancement of all groups." "Rowing, not drifting" was their motto, and they agreed to meet regularly to discuss pertinent issues of the day.

Renamed the Grand Rapids Study Club shortly after its founding, the group explored topics that reflected the depth and breadth of members' concerns. The printed programs, now in the Grand Rapids Public Library's historical collections, reveal interest in such wide-ranging subjects as "The Negro Woman's Contribution to History," "Education of the Handicapped," and "The Unpublished History of the Negro Versus the Published." The club also brought nationally known speakers to Grand Rapids, including poet Langston Hughes who presented a program titled "Poems of Negro Life."

In 1935, the club purchased a house at 427 James Avenue that continues to serve as its headquarters today. Celebrating its 75th anniversary in 1979, the club committed itself to renovating its clubhouse and building a larger membership base by recruiting young black women professionals — perhaps the daughters, granddaughters, or nieces, of past and present members — to carry on its traditions and its work.

April 11, 1912—School Laws of Michigan.
　　ROSA PETTIFORD
April 18, 1912—The Temperance Question as we see it.
　　GRACE GREEN
March 8, 1917—Possibilities of Alaskan Farming
　　MRS. MYRTLE LASHA
March 15, 1917—Negro Poets Negroes in the Musical World
　　MRS. LOUISE GAINES
January 16, 1917—Pioneer Days of Grand Rapids
　　MRS. WINIFRED PORTER
January 30, 1919—Woman's Invasion of the Business World
　　MRS. HATTIE PINKNEY
April 21, 1921—Healthful Living, One of the Fine Arts.
　　MRS. IDA ELLIS
March 20, 1925—Effects of World War Upon Negroes of America and Elsewhere.
　　MRS. MYRTLE LASHA

▲ Grand Rapids Study Club Collection, Grand Rapids Public Library.

▲ Grand Rapids Study Club members (left to right) Kathryn Nickerson, Edith Rambeau, Ethel Coe, Virginia Glenn, and Sara Glover plan for an appearance by poet Langston Hughes. [GRPL, Grand Rapids Study Club Collection]

The Grand Rapids ▶ Study Club, 427 James SE. [GRPL, *Grand River Valley Review* Collection]

"Of the Women, For the Women, By the Women"

Calls for political and social action took many forms in the early 20th century. One of the most interesting advocacy vehicles was *Woman,* a short-lived weekly newspaper founded in 1908.

Local pressure for women's rights, heralded by the founding of the pioneer Women's Rights Club in 1874, increased markedly in the first two decades of the 1900s. Grand Rapids women who played leading roles in the state and national women's rights movements also found ways to assert their quest for equality at home. *Woman* was one of their most ambitious efforts. Its managing editor, Helen Ashton Williams, was an experienced journalist who worked on several other newspapers before and after her stint at *Woman.* Also on the staff were contributors Addis Farrar Andre of the Chicago *Daily News* and Mary D. McFadden of the Duluth *News Tribune,* and business manager Caro Parks Blodgett of Grand Rapids. The newspaper's inaugural editorial set out the assumptions that had led to its founding and the standards that were to guide its production.

Published for a year before failing revenues shut it down, *Woman* was an important voice used by local women to communicate with each other, and to speak to the entire community.

WOMAN will cover, from week to week, every phase of women's occupations in this city, in this state, and in this country. . . .

Among the professional women, doctors, teachers, lecturers, writers and librarians abound. *WOMAN* hopes to print from week to week, news items which will interest all of these women in the great "woman-heart" of America, and the world.

WOMAN will cover, as quickly as possible, the local society, club, social, fraternal and musical news, fully. Space in these columns is offered gratuitously to those church and fraternal societies which will make it possible for the editor to have their news, all their news, and have it on time. Space is also offered to every woman in the city who has an idea which she wishes to give to, or share with other women.

Any woman in Grand Rapids who desires to administer a boost or a knock to men in general or things in particular is cordially invited to use these columns.

This paper belongs to the women of Grand Rapids, it was conceived for them; at the cost of much labor and anxiety it has been launched out for them, and despite the fact that we are beaten by the Chinese, we at least offer you a paper unlike any other in America, as far as we know.

While this is distinctly a newspaper, we realize that a great many women enjoy reading of a more domestic character and from time to time, in the nature of feature stories, helpful suggestions along that line will be added. We shall also maintain a page for men, thereby repaying in some measure the "Women's Realm" department, universally found in the men's newspapers.

Of the management of *WOMAN* it may be said, that we are exactly what we claim in our subhead, a weekly newspaper "Of the women, for the women, and by the women." The owners are women, the editorial staff, business manager, contributors, illustrators and special writers are all women. We know that women are engaged in every occupation under the sun, and we had hoped to keep the, not defiling, exactly, but superfluous touch of masculinity away from this enterprise, but alas, were confronted with a foreman of the composing room, rather than a forewoman, and we were obliged to stop the tide of feminity there. The linotype work, however, is done by women and the big press on which we are printed is run by electric power, and is, therefore feminine while printing *WOMAN* anyway; the stitching, etc., is all in the hands of women. A few printers and a foreman are all that stand in the way of our announcing that no man has been, is, or will be, identified with this paper.

▲ *Woman,* November 21, 1908, p. 8.

▲ For a time, *Woman* provided an alternative to male-dominated newspapers and magazines. [GRPL, *Woman* Collection]

War Against Flies

One of Grand Rapids' biggest concerns in the early years of the 20th century was the outbreak of disease that plagued the city each spring and summer. In an average year, it was not unusual for the city board of health to report several hundred cases of diphtheria, typhoid fever, cholera, and tuberculosis. Unsanitary conditions were a primary cause of disease, and each summer's assault by mosquitoes, flies, and other insects caused local leaders to take dramatic steps.

In 1911, the Anti-Tuberculosis Society enrolled the city's youth in an all-out war on flies. High school industrial arts classes built special wooden fly traps, and cash prizes were offered to the youngsters who managed to trap the most flies. Today's readers may be amused at reports of mounds of dead flies and wild estimates of the number of germs eliminated, but at the time, the campaign against flies represented a serious effort to make the city a healthier place to live.

With 100 quarts of dead flies the total catch of two weeks of fly extermination closed last night. Grand Rapids has 885,500,000,000 less germs than before the contest began. This figure is obtained by multiplying the number of flies caught, 35,420,000,000, by the number of germs each fly is said to carry, 1,250,000. Burton Smith is the champion killer.

Thirty children entered the contest by bringing in flies. The prizes were won by the following: Burton Smith, first, 26 quarts and 7 gills [a gill is 1/4 of a pint], awarded $10; Ernest Monnett, 25 quarts and 4 gills, $8; Roland Dewitt, 14 quarts and 5 3/4 gills, $5; Lawrence Dark, 8 quarts, $4; Edward Riordan, 5 quarts, $4; Walter Stowe, 3 1/2 quarts, $2; Robert Taylor, 3 quarts, $1.

On account of the lack of interest shown in the contest on the part of the girls the prizes in this case will be held over until the contest in the spring. Four girls turned in flies, Margaret Blair, who had 1 pint, will get $3; Florence Tennis, 3 gills, $2; Gertrude Papque, 1/2 gill, $1; Cassie Scherpenisse, 1 gill, $1; Hazel Heseltine, $1.

▲ *Grand Rapids Press,* September 15, 1911, p. 19.

▲Burton School's manual training class built traps to assist the fly extermination campaign. [GRPL, Kent County Tuberculosis Society Collection]

▼ Winners posed with a part of their catch. [GRPL, Kent County Tuberculosis Society Collection]

▼ Displays emphasized the effectiveness of the campaign. [GRPL, Kent County Tuberculosis Society Collection]

Extra! Extra!

For those young boys who chose not to pursue the bounty on flies, "hawking" newspapers offered another way to make money. Sidewalk newspaper selling was extremely competitive, and fights for especially lucrative corners were commonplace. Newsboys, many orphaned or abandoned, lived in a dormitory at the newspaper. Having no other means of income or support, they were prepared to defend themselves against all challengers. George Welsh, who was active for five decades in Grand Rapids politics as alderman, city manager, and mayor, was an orphan who worked with his brother as a newsboy for several years. As he recalled the experience in a 1972 interview, his rough life as a newsboy prepared him well for his later political career.

The *Press* had a great deal to do with my boyhood. I went to work for them when I was 12 when the *Press* was just starting in opposition to the *Eagle*....That was the big paper. The *Press* had some great pioneers that did a job and they drove the *Eagle* out of business, and they did it through their work with boys. Grand Rapids had the first newsboys band in the world. I remember that John Sousa came one time and offered medals and congratulated them.

I remember on the corner of Monroe and Pearl street where Woolworth's is now, we had a "Taffy John" who pulled taffy in the wintertime and sold popcorn balls in the summer—made them there. The kind of competition the *Eagle* was up against was that you had to have boys to sell "Extras," and in those days the newspapers got "extras" out at the drop of a hat. Whatever came along, why there was an extra on the street. But you had to have boys to sell them, and the *Press* had a circulation manager by the name of Charles Halstead who was very vigorous and on one occasion when they got word that there was going to be an extra, he went up to "Taffy John's" and bought a bushel basket of popcorn balls and put them on his shoulder and went up and down Monroe street telling all the kids that he saw that there was going to be a party at the *Press* hall, and when he got them down there they locked the door. When the extra came out there were no boys to sell the *Eagle*. The *Press* had all the boys. They did a lot of sharp things. The *Press* staged an annual newsboys' race where the boys started out with a bag of papers. I think they had 20 papers in their sack and there were 20 spots. The *Press* was located on Pearl Street by the bridge. That was the address of the *Press*: Pearl Street by the bridge. They would start there, and they came up Monroe to Division, crossed over and went way down to Michigan and then back, and they had 20 spots where they had to stop and leave a paper. The winner of these races was ridden on a white horse with the *Press* newsboys band playing. It was a big occasion. It seems to me we had more occasions of that kind. Today nobody looks at a parade. In a way it seems as though we've gone down hill....

...The *Press* sold for a penny and you made a half a cent on every one you sold. But you had to be something of a warrior to hold a good position. There was a lot of street fights. If a boy got a good corner he wasn't going to give it up. So the *Press* met that problem by holding boxing matches every Saturday morning. They put four benches together and made two rings, and the circulation manager Joe Taylor would say "Hey you and you get in there." And you put on the boxing gloves and he made everybody fight everybody else. Well, it isn't long before you find out who you can't lick, and if you can't lick 'em, you don't argue with 'em. When you had a paper route or a corner that was doing well, you didn't let infiltrators take it away from ya.

Well, Sunday was a great day for tourists—for excursions—they ran excursions to Detroit and the best place to sell papers was down at the depot. On a Detroit *Free Press* you made two cents on a Sunday paper and you shined shoes. But there again came the fact that we were horning in on somebody else's corner. We had quite a time. It took us two or three weeks before we could break in. We used a little strategy. My brother loved to fight. He just enjoyed every minute of it, and he did a pretty good job. So, I hid around the corner of the G R & I building and he would go down and tease them, and they'd chase him, and when they finally got up close the two of us would take care of them. It took us about three Sundays to fight our way into the depot.

▲George Welsh Interview, 1972, Grand Rapids Public Library.

◄Newsboy George Welsh took his turn swabbing the deck of the *Grand Rapids Press'* houseboat. [GRPL, James R. Hooper Collection]

▲*Press* newsboys gathered in front of a newsstand at the turn of the century. [GRPL, Photo Collection]

The Great Furniture Strike

In the first decade of the 20th century, Grand Rapids dominated the U.S. furniture industry. New York and Chicago had more furniture factories and produced a larger volume, but the large companies concentrated in Grand Rapids set the tone for design, manufacturing standards, and marketing. The industry's largest company — Berkey and Gay — and scores of others, large and small, were headquartered in Grand Rapids, where 10,000 workers cut, carved, glued, and planed the city's signature products.

As Grand Rapids furniture companies grew in prominence, they attracted imitators, some of whom attempted to capitalize on the Grand Rapids name. The Grand Rapids Furniture Company of Chicago, for example, had no connection with the Furniture City other than its name.

To combat this unwelcome flattery, a group of the largest local firms created an organization called the Furniture Manufacturers of Grand Rapids, and developed a trademark that would be placed on all their products. This trademark assured potential buyers that they were putting their money down for the genuine made-in-Grand Rapids article.

For as much as they felt threatened by outsiders using their name, Grand Rapids furniture makers were even more concerned about the efforts to unionize their workers. For the most part, theirs were non-union companies, a circumstance they were determined to maintain. Unfortunately, the industry experienced some years of slow sales between 1905 and 1910, and companies gave their workers only minimal raises or none at all. Fueling the growing unrest was the fact that recently arrived workers from eastern and southern Europe had a greater heritage of labor radicalism than the predominantly Dutch, German, and Scandinavian immigrants of the previous generation. Feeling themselves powerless in the face of owners who could hire or fire them at will, set hours and working conditions as they saw fit, and unilaterally determine pay rates and raises, workers listened receptively when union organizers came to town.

In October 1910, the simmering kettle of trouble came to a boil when an estimated 4,000 workers sent a proposal to the owners calling for a nine-hour work day, a 10 percent wage increase, and the abolition of pay based on piecework. Refusing to acknowledge the workers' communique, the owners announced they would conduct their factories on an "open-shop" basis and declined to bargain collectively with the workers. It was high noon and workers and management stood face to face, waiting for the other to blink.

Grand Rapids' mayor at the time, George Ellis, owed much of his political success to the support of West Side working-class neighborhoods. Fearing the stand-off between workers and management would lead to a strike idling thousands of workers, Ellis offered to name a committee to arbitrate the dispute. His proposal was accepted by the District Council of the Carpenters Union, which spoke for the skilled furniture workers, but it was flatly rejected by the owners who steadfastly held to their "open-shop" position.

On March 25, 1911, workers overwhelmingly ratified a proposal to strike on April 1 if their proposal was not accepted. Despite the workers' intense negotiating efforts, the deadline passed without an inch of movement by the owners. On April 19, at 9 a.m., more than 3,000 workers laid down their tools and left their work benches. Grand Rapids' great furniture strike was on, and four months would pass before it was over. During those four months, several small factories would settle, and many workers would return to their jobs as their strike benefits ran out. But the core of the strikers and the big companies maintained their head-to-head posture to the bitter end.

Although the strike was eventually broken when the national Carpenters and Joiners Union withdrew its support and the Christian Reformed Church declared that union membership was contrary to church policy, the wounds it caused were deep. Shaken company owners made grudging concessions on working conditions and wage rates, but many good workers either left or were blackballed from the industry, and those who returned never forgot their bitterness over management's unwavering position. Some have argued that the Grand Rapids furniture industry never fully recovered, and the strike of 1911 was one of the first slips in a downward slide that gained momentum in the 1920s and 1930s.

▲ Mayor George Ellis walked a tight-rope between strikers and owners during the 1911 furniture strike. [GRPL, Photo Collection]

The trouble started when Harry Widdicomb with a closed automobile filled with men who are said to have gone to work since the strike began came out of the factory grounds shortly before 6 o'clock.

When the automobile came into sight it was the signal for an attack by the 300 or more in the mob which had collected about the plant. First it was jeers and insults. Then started a rain of rocks and stones.

As the machine carrying Widdicomb and three workmen drew across the tracks at Fifth street crossing a rock went through one of the windows. It was the signal for a fusillade and in a moment a perfect storm of missiles enveloped the machine.

The car drew out of the danger zone, going east, and Patrolman Sprague grabbed one of the men who had thrown the first stone. With his gun out the patrolman backed the man toward the John Widdicomb offices. A stone cut the officer's head open and took off his hat. The windows in the plant were shattered as he dragged the man safely inside.

Farther east on Fifth street Patrolman Lennon of the motorcycle squad picked one of the men who threw a stone at the center of a howling mob. He waved them back with his drawn gun and finally fired a shot in the air. The crowd retreated a moment, but a woman stepped to the front and yelled: "Take him away, the cop hasn't any bullets." This was the signal for a hail of stones and the patrolman fired his first shot into the crowd. If it hit any one no one paused. Another patrolman grabbed one of the strikers and another storm center was under way.

At 6:30 there were fully 2,000 persons surrounding the plant.

Supt. of Police Carr when informed of the seriousness of the trouble detailed every available man in the station to duty at the plant and soon there were about twenty-five men on the scene, with Lieut. Howell and Sergeants Conlon and Whalen in charge.

Abbot Widdicomb of the William Widdicomb company attempted to help the neighboring factory by taking one man away in his machine. Some one threw a stone at his car and he got out and gave pursuit. Running the fellow down he was forced to let him go when the crowd surged around.

Patrolman Lennon in attempting to rescue Widdicomb was struck in the abdomen with a rock. He was knocked out and suffered considerable pain.

Another and another patrolman grabbed his man and the officers bravely fought their way together in the middle of the street. The shooting began to be in volleys, the men hiding behind the corner of the William Widdicomb factory, until another more bold than the others walked right down the middle of the street, yelling: "They can't hit nothing." Then every one came out from shelter and rained stones on the policemen.

It became apparent from the lessening revolver fire that the policemen were running out of ammunition. They retreated slowly down the center of the street, using their prisoners as shields as best they could. At the corner of Broadway the last shot was fired and the click of falling hammers told the crowd there was no more ammunition.

There was a yell of delight and fully 300 closed in. Literally carrying their men the officers retreated almost to Turner street and took refuge in a yard.

The mob fought its way close and took away one of the prisoners in the hand to hand fight, in which a dozen heads were laid open by clubs. Before more of the prisoners could be released the honk of the police automobile and the warning cries of sympathizers drove the remainder of the crowd away. As the police auto came up, however, there was another mad surge on the part of the mob and the rest of the prisoners were torn from the hands of the patrolmen. The riot was then transferred to the point where it began. The street was filled with madly running and cursing men and women and almost every other face seemed to be streaked with blood from an injury or from the injury of another.

The fighting spirit of the mob was up and the police automobile no longer had an cowing effect. It was greeted with a perfect rain of rocks and clubs and a dozen patrolmen sallied forth with drawn revolvers and clubs. Once more there was the sound of shots and the spit and whir of the bullets

◄ Led by metal workers carrying tin umbrellas, Grand Rapids workers were out in full force in the 1900 Labor Day parade. [GRPL, Stephen Stover Collection]

as they cut through the foliage that overhangs Fifth street.

Then it was that the police clubs began to get in their ugly work. One of the mob hurled a stone and was grabbed from behind by a policeman. In a moment the bluecoat was down under a score of madly striking and kicking persons. Another patrolman came to the rescue and grabbed one of the men, who turned and hit him full in the face with his fist. He went out of the fight immediately, for a third policeman hit him across the face with all his might, and the man spun around with a cry and dropped. He was up in a moment, screaming, and his face was bathed in blood. It was like setting a match to powder when the crowd caught sight of that bloody face.

Women fought with men for an opportunity to get into the fray. The wife of the stricken man led the mob and called upon them to take vengeance. A policeman gently tried to keep her back. She hit him twice in the face with her fist and he went down under a big brick, but came up again, fighting gamely.

This was only one of a dozen incidents that were taking place simultaneously. There was no more chance for the use of guns, even had there been ammunition. At this juncture the big Austin car owned by William Widdicomb and driven by his son came up with a load of reserves. These jumped out and mixed in the fray. Young Widdicomb stood up in his automobile, a fine mark for the rocks that were aimed at him, and calmly surveyed the scene of the strife and carnage. The man whose face seemed to have been

battered in by a club was taken into the car. His wife fought the officers right up to the moment the man was taken into the tonneau and the bricks that flew hit the injured man as often as the patrolmen.

Another who had been hit in the face by a club continued to fight desperately with five bluecoats trying to keep him down. His wife called upon other women and while the crowd applauded a dozen women fought their way up to the struggling group. The man finally was dragged into the automobile and it sped away. The continued arrival of reserves seemed to have no effect on the mob and a call was sent in for the fire department, the intention being to use the streams on the crowd and drive them back. The firemen were not used, however. Repeated trips by the police automobile massed all the available men and quiet was restored.

Mayor Ellis reached the scene at this juncture and made a speech urging the crowd to disperse. The crowd cheered him, but never moved. The police auto took the last of the prisoners out of the Widdicomb factory under a guard of at least thirty men, with drawn revolvers.

After the mayor had made his speech and it was found that the crowd would not listen to the advice it was decided to call the fire department again and this time No. 3 hose company got into real action. The steamer was run up directly in front of the Widdicomb plant, the connection made and soon a powerful stream from the big nozzle was playing on the crowd.

Hundreds were drenched, but they retreated reluctantly and their mood was made more ugly.

It was just at this time that Albert Schuiteman, ladderman of No. 3 company, was injured. He was standing near the factory building when suddenly he dropped as if shot and the blood spurted from a wound just above his temple. Where the stone came from no one knows. Evidently it was thrown from a distance. He regained consciousness speedily and was assisted into the factory office, being removed to his home later and attended by Dr. S. Porter Tuttle.

During the lull following the use of the water the five or six workmen, who were the indirect cause of the outburst, were taken in automobiles and hurried to their homes. Upon the running boards of the machines stood the officers with drawn revolvers, but the cars were followed by jeers and showers of stones.

The scene of last night's rioting today was as quiet as a church. No attempt was made on the part of the John Widdicomb factory management to continue operations today. There was no attempt to take workmen into the plant and therefore no incentive for rioting or demonstrations.

The police started out this morning on the ground that no crowd should have an opportunity to gather. Autocop Wilson and Patrolman Sprague were on duty at 7 o'clock. No one was permitted to loiter except the pickets and these lent every assistance in keeping the curious from congregating.

▲ *Grand Rapids Press*, May 16, 1911, p. 2.

◄ Union leader Gerritt VerBerg (right) and an unidentified compatriot met at the Union Hall to discuss the progress of the 1911 furniture workers strike. [GRPL, Photo Collection]

▲ Local furniture makers adopted this trademark in 1900 to identify products made in the "Furniture City." [GRPL, Furniture Manufacturers Association Collection]

The "New" Immigrants

In the first decades of the 20th century, Grand Rapids became home for increasing numbers of immigrants from eastern and southern Europe. Poles, Russian and Polish Jews, Greeks, and Italians followed the path of immigrants from earlier generations, seeking jobs in the furniture industry or dreaming of owning a business and enjoying the opportunity America promised. Their presence did not go unnoticed by local newspapers, which devoted many stories to the activities of new arrivals.

Grand Rapids may well feel elated over the Greek element of her population. These as a class possess the elements which produce excellent citizens. They are high minded, progressive, dignified, law abiding, allying themselves with every movement which aims to produce better conditions. They command the respect of all right minded persons who come to know them. No race should rank higher as such. Invariably they succeed financially. No benevolent organization has to support them. They give close attention to business, are alert to grasp promising opportunities, make the most of these and live within their means.

In recent years they have taken a prominent part in building up the smaller trades and commercial enterprises of this city, and are giving it a cosmopolitan spirit it would not be likely otherwise to obtain.

Grand Rapids has no more noble or loyal citizen than the Greeks; and the sooner they are recognized for their true worth and given the recognition and social standing their merit deserves the better it will be for the community. . . .

Without hardly an exception every person of this nationality who came here and went into business has succeeded financially. The Greeks carry on an immense quick lunch and restaurant business, as well as confectionery, soft drinks, baked goods, fruits and in late years they have spread out into other lines, meeting with phenomenal success. There are several wealthy Greeks in Grand Rapids and they are attracting the best class of citizens from their homes far across the sea. The Greeks are intensely patriotic.

No better indication of this could be cited than that a short time ago a number left their homes and positions in this city to return to the mother country and take up arms in her behalf, prompted by pure patriotism. They love no less, though, the land of their adoption and should this country ever have to face a foe upon the battlefield her Greek population would be as prompt as any to enlist for service.

◄ *Grand Rapids Press,* March 1, 1913, p. 10.

▲ Grand Rapids Public Schools citizenship classes were announced in four languages. [GRPL, Unprocessed Manuscript]

◄ This 1920s Greek christening celebration featured a patriotic motif. [GRPL, Hellenic Horizons Collection]

Grand Rapids Thursday sent its first quota of men to fight for Italy in the great European war, ten reservists leaving on the Pere Marquette for Detroit at 7 a.m. From Detroit the party intended to go by boat to Buffalo and then on to New York from which port they will sail Aug. 1 for Naples. Next week another squad will leave the Furniture city for the Italian front.

Among those in the party leaving Thursday was John De Bernardis, a United States citizen of Italian birth, who heard the call of his country and who immediately offered himself and his three years' experience in the Italian army, gained while he was a resident of Italy, to his former country. De Bernardis was importuned by his mother, who is in Italy, to go back to Europe and join the fighting. The young man is a cabinetmaker at the plant of the Grand Rapids Showcase company, and confidently expects to return to his bench after the war.

Also in the party were John Dagostern, L. Fiorvanti, C. Giulos, Tony Odola, Tony Cassini, Pete Lorenzo, L. Salvati and Pietro Vannucci, who was in charge of the party.

De Bernardis is the only one of those leaving Thursday to be able to claim the rank of an officer, and he is a corporal major, according to his statement.

▲ *Grand Rapids Press,* July 29, 1915, p. 13.

FIRST ITALIAN CONTINGENT LEAVES TO TAKE PART IN EUROPEAN CONFLICT

Left to right: John Dagostern, L. Fiorvanti, C. Giulos, Tony Odola, L. Salvati, Tony Cassini, John De Bernardis.

▲ When war broke out in Europe, several recent immigrants like these Italians, returned to fight for their home countries. [*Grand Rapids Press,* July 29, 1915, p. 13]

▲ Citizenship classes, like this one at American Seating, were regularly held in factories. [GRPL, Photo Collection]

The Great War

Grand Rapids watched along with the rest of America as war unfolded in Europe following the assassination of Archduke Francis Ferdinand of Austria in 1914. Newspapers and magazines published graphic accounts of the fighting, but so long as the United States was not directly involved, few comprehended the magnitude of the death and destruction that were overtaking Europe. Officially, the United States was neutral, and Woodrow Wilson had been reelected president in 1916 on the claim that "he kept us out of war." However, as the fighting dragged on, the United States moved slowly toward direct participation as one of the Allied belligerents. The final straw came in 1917 when German submarines sank several American ships. Congress quickly said yes to President Wilson's request for a declaration of war, and the call went out for volunteers.

Some volunteers had enlisted in the Allied cause, either as members of foreign armies or with the Red Cross, before the United States officially entered the war, and many others volunteered for duty once war was formally declared. However, these volunteers were not enough to meet the military's needs, and a draft of eligible men was implemented in June 1917. Three Grand Rapids men, Stanley Kubiak, Jacob Hampton, and Clare Cooper, were selected in the first draft lottery. Kubiak and Hampton were exempted from service, and Cooper was inducted on September 7, 1917, at Camp Custer. By the time the war was over, 2,901 local men had been drafted, and another 1,500 to 2,000 had entered the military as volunteers. At war's end, 244 area servicemen were counted among the casualties.

The United States military also needed nurses, and throughout the nation nurses responded to the call for volunteers. Among them was a group organized by the Grand Rapids Red Cross that joined early in 1918 and served for the war's duration. A total of 155 area nurses responded to the call for volunteers.

Folks back home kept up with activities overseas through letters sent by loved ones. The *Grand Rapids News* regularly printed letters from soldiers, including the following examples from Arthur DeVries, Matthew Siegel, and Leo R. Wolff.

DeVries, who wrote "At last we are doing what most of us enlisted for," was killed in action on August 18, 1918. Siegel provides a vivid account of life in the trenches, and Wolff provides an account of the dangers faced by ambulance drivers.

May 29, 1918

Dear Mother,

Tomorrow is Memorial day, and no doubt you folks back home will be observing it in the customary way. We, too, will observe it, but in an entirely different manner than you. There will be air battles, and, in fact, a regular Fourth of July fete. Machine guns will be singing their usual songs in strings of three, or in the clip fire, and the much-dreaded shrapnel will no doubt be bursting near our dugouts.

At last we are doing what most of us enlisted for. We are occupying the front line of a certain sector, the name of which I cannot disclose. I understand that things were at a deadlock before our arrival, but they sure are livening up the past few days. In fact, there is a noticeable change.

Everything is mighty interesting, and it is a novel experience for us. Of course, we all have our scares frequently, but they are forgotten in a short time. This A. M. a number of us were walking down a road in the rear of the lines, and our friend "Fritz"

dropped a few 105's, which burst not a great ways from us. If Dan Patch or any other of our famous race horses could have seen us race for our dugouts, it would have made them green with jealousy.

The other night a number of us visited No Man's Land on an ambush party and stayed there most of the night. One soon learns to make friends with Mother Earth, and it is wonderful how close one can hug her when "Fritz"

turns his machine guns loose on you.

Today we had an artillery bombardment. First he would drop a few over near us, and then we would return the compliment by way of showing him that we are still here. One Grand Rapids boy, a sergeant in K company, was shot the day before yesterday, but, believe your son, mother, I am the most cautious boy in the world.

Arthur [DeVries]

◄ *Grand Rapids News*, July 3, 1918, pp. 1, 3.

▲ Soldiers from the 339th Ambulance Corps, most of whom were from West Michigan, enjoyed a meal and relaxed for a moment while on duty in France. [GRPL, 339th Ambulance Company Collection]

▲ Ambulance drivers often had to contend with near impassable conditions. [GRPL, 339th Ambulance Company Collection]

Somewhere in France, June 9.

Dear Sister and Brother - The farmers are making hay now. It is all cut by hand and is drawn in by oxen.

We have been in the trenches for a while, but are out again in a rest camp.

The trenches are a great sight. It is somewhat noisy when the artillery begins to fire. I was up in the first line trenches one day. All one can see is barbed wire entanglements and shell holes.

The nights are the worse. I did night duty mostly, and, believe me, I did not think much about sleep. It is just like a Fourth of July every night. The star shells and the roar of the big guns afford excitement.

There are a large number of rats in the dugouts. They are so thick that they come out in the day time and run around. They even carry off tobacco and gloves and such things to build nests.

I was at a church one Sunday that had been shelled. It was a beautiful church, but the shells destroyed the steeple. They have mass there just the same, and it is not far from the lines. I was at mass this morning. I have been in about 25 different churches over here.

They have plenty of wine over here, but it is too sour for me.

Matthew [Siegel]

▲ *Grand Rapids News,* July 5, 1918, p. 11.

▲ Flyer Daniel Waters Cassard of Grand Rapids was shot down over France on July 16, 1918. [GRPL, Walsh Collection]

▲ Lulu Cudney served with distinction as a World War I nurse. [GRPL, Lulu Cudney Collection]

▲ These nurses served in France as a part of Medical Unit Q, a volunteer medical corps organized by the Grand Rapids Red Cross chapter. [GRPL, Lulu Cudney Collection]

Dear Jacob,

Just came back from post after doing 24 hours duty. The lieutenant came over to our dugout and handed me five letters dating from Feb. 15 to March 25, and to my amazement they were from you, "home." What a wonderful world? My first letter or letters I have received from you since being in France. Oh, how I waited for news from you and it certainly makes me one happy "Sammy" to receive your letters all in a bunch. Now, I don't want you to worry, because everything is going fine.

We are located in a small village which the Germans have held five times. The houses are pretty well intact in some parts. I am living with three others in a house, one half of which has been bombarded away, but we have patched it up so it is practically waterproof. We have a big fire place, and at night we build a fire therein and sit around and swap stories, telling of all the good times we had "back home."

Outside a dark night we go and lay in the grass outside our quarters and watch the star shells and various lights go up in "No Man's Land." Oh, what a wonderful sight. They light up the whole landscape. They are also a big help to us when we are driving at night, as we are not allowed to use any lights.

The roads are always filled up with troops and artillery going and coming from the lines, which makes driving very difficult. On extremely dark nights we now carry with us an extra man, and he walks ahead of the car, pointing out the way.

Have been up on the third line trenches, which is our advance post, and it isn't nearly as dangerous as back some distance, because of artillery action. The only narrow escape I've had was when I was called to one of the other posts for some very seriously wounded. On arriving I went inside the dugout with the intention of helping with the stretcher and while inside my car was hit by a shell and wrecked. So I telephoned back for another car.

Leo [R. Wolff]

▲ Armistice Day was marked by a jubilant parade through downtown. [GRPL, Photo Collection]

◄ *Grand Rapids News,* July 8, 1918, p. 8.

The Polar Bear Expedition

Godfrey Anderson had a different wartime experience from most soldiers. After being drafted into the 337th Field Hospital Unit in May 1918, Anderson assumed he was headed for duty in England or France. However, President Wilson had something else in mind. He assigned American forces, including Anderson's field hospital unit, to join British and Canadian toops in an expeditionary force sent to Archangel, in northern Russia, to assist the anti-Bolshevik (or Menshevik or White) faction in its effort to prevent the Bolsheviks (or Reds) from taking control of Russia's revolutionary government. Anderson and his fellow unit members were assigned to an effort to keep open vital supply links between the Mensheviks and the West.

An avid historian all his life, Anderson wrote a memoir that begins with an account of his brief boot camp training at Camp Custer and concludes with his unit's service in Russia. The folly of meddling in Russia's internal affairs becomes painfully clear when Anderson describes the combined U.S., Canadian, and British forces' retreat through the forest during the coldest days of a bitter Russian winter of 1919 with the Bolsheviks nipping at their heels. Anderson captures the fear and misery of the retreat in a manner that could only have been done by one who was there.

▲ Godfrey Anderson had no idea his Army duty would take him to northern Russia. [GRPL, Godfrey Anderson Collection]

The years have passed and memories fade with fleeting time, but some events are so deeply graven on the mind that they can never be forgotten. Such are the memories of that fateful nineteenth of January and the events that crowded upon each other in such rapid succession in the days that followed. It was in the darkness that preceded the dawn when we were awakened by that first sullen boom from up Ust Padenga way. It sent the echoes rattling about town and reverberating across the flats beyond the river. We lay in our bunks, alert and straining our ears to listen. Again came that sustained roll, like distant thunder. What the ---! What's going on up there, anyway. Again and again the thunder continues. The night man, clattering up the stairs, carrying a lantern, burst into the room to wake us up for breakfast; the reveille bugle had long been discarded. "There's hell at Ust Padenga," he said.

[The advance unit was driven back and a decision was made to retreat from Shenkursk.]

[It was] no easy task to tuck some of those wounded patients into sleeping bags. Some of those were so badly injured that the slightest touch would cause excruciating agony. But there was need for urgent haste and we had no alternative but to stuff the patient in the bag as best we could despite his agonized screams. Then there were those shell shock cases, who raved and struggled and fought, and finally had to be overpowered by brute force. The patients were tucked in the straw, in pairs, in the bottom of each sleigh, covered with blankets and then checked by the medical officers, given a shot of medication or a swig of rum, as the case might be. We could but wonder where they had managed to commandeer all those sleighs and ponies. They were filled up as soon as they moved into place, and then moved on to halt in a long line to await the orders to move out. Those lying dead in the room upstairs were to be left behind.

It was sometime after one o'clock when the convoy got the go ahead signal. Because of a report that a couple hundred of the enemy were posted astride the main road, it had been decided, as a sort of desperate gamble, to leave town by way of a little used back-woods road which disappeared into the woods to the north and rejoined the main road some twelve miles beyond. Mounted Cossack scouts had reconnoitered this unbroken trail for some distance and reported no enemy obstruction ahead, they, no doubt, considering this primitive trail hopelessly snow bound and impassible.

The Cossacks were now in the lead, already buried somewhere in the gloom of the forest, followed by the Canadian artillery. Now at last the hospital convoy got under way, more than fifty sleighs with over a hundred (now) sick and wounded. When the last of these had passed along the monastery wall, the foot soldiers, British, American and Russian, numbering about a thousand, who were halted on Vologda St., now fell into line and passed through the maze of barbed wire entanglements strung about the town. They passed the last of the outlying blockhouses at the edge of town.

Civilian refugees, about 5000, brought up the rear. Jittery and terrified, they struggled to get their topheavy sleighs into line. All were plodding along beside their rigs, men, women and children alike, except for the tots, who were bundled atop the sleigh, staring wide-eyed and frightened. Sometimes a rig would get stuck in the drifts and the whole family had to get behind and push. Sometimes a rig would tip over and strew the contents of the sleigh around in the drifts and the driver would throw up his hands wailing and imploring assistance from one or all of the Byzantine saints.

The ordeal was especially tough for those men of Co. A. bringing up the rear. They had been active for nearly a week, with little sleep. They had started out in double file but could not keep that formation, eventually straggling along as best they could, some falling asleep as they stumbled along, falling down again and again, unable and even unwilling to rise and having to be helped and urged to continue. Soon all excess baggage was thrown to the side, in a desperate effort to survive that terrible march.

As for myself, I struggled blindly along slipping and skidding in those unbroken-in Shakleton boots, which though indeed warm, had shiny leather soles, with no traction whatever. Time and time again I found myself taking nose dives and sprawling in the ruts because of the impossible footing....Although it was around 35 degrees below zero and an icy draught swept through the passageway, I had soon worked up a sweat. Nevertheless the muffler covering my mouth and nostrils soon clogged with icicles, which had to be cleared away to permit breathing. During all that agonizing peregrination, unaware of where any of my company were, I did not once sneak a ride on the sleigh I followed. However, whenever the terrain sloped downhill I got a bit of relief by stepping on the runners. I had developed a respect and consideration for those tough little

▲ Members of the 337th Hospital Unit posed with one of the small Russian ponies and sleighs that helped them escape from Russia. [GRPL, Godfrey Anderson Collection]

Russian ponies and felt ashamed to add to their burden, (although some did.)

It was late afternoon, approaching dusk, when we finally reached Shegovari. This village is over twenty miles straight north of Shenkursk as the crow flies, but of course much longer when following the circuitous trails we had followed.

◄ Godfrey J. Anderson Collection, Grand Rapids Public Library.

The Furniture Industry Goes to War

Those who remained at home also contributed to the war effort. There were bandages to be rolled, weapons and munitions to be manufactured, and unlikely though it may seem, there were bomber aircraft to be built. Over 300 two-engined, wood-frame, Handley-Page airplanes — the largest aircraft used in the war — were produced by the Grand Rapids Airplane Company, a consortium of 15 local furniture manufacturers. Made by skilled furniture workers using the woodworking machinery of their peacetime trade, the British-designed planes had a range of 800 miles and were meant to deliver their explosive cargo deep behind enemy lines.

Full of patriotic fervor, and eager for the opportunity to prove their commitment to the Allied cause, local workmen — and women — produced all of the parts except the engines. Production was ahead of schedule, with 356 planes completed and on their way to England, when the November 1918 armistice rendered the aircraft unnecessary. The role of the Grand Rapids Airplane Company in the Allied war effort was subsequently reported in the *Furniture Manufacturer and Artisan* magazine.

Not one of the 356 complete Handley-Page airplanes — the largest and most powerful bombing machine used by the Allied forces, which were made in the 15 plants of the Grand Rapids Airplane Company, had reached the fighting front when the German quit cold. And yet those gigantic machines, each of which carries a crew of six men with two and one-half tons of the most destructive explosives, undoubtedly contributed to that full measure of retribution about to be precipitated upon the Hun, which led his shrinking autocrats to plead for leniency and sign the armistice on November 11, 1918. For it is conceded by those familiar with America's preparation for the anticipated campaign of 1919, that Handley-Page airplanes made in Grand Rapids formed an important part of that huge quantity of war materials being produced in this country — the menace of which did more to end the war than any exhaustion of Germany's military strength, fancied or real. Thus Grand Rapids, through the conscientious application of its industrial resources and manufacturing ideals to a patriotic end, served to save the lives of some 200,000

American doughboys who might have been sacrificed had the war continued.

The work of the Grand Rapids Airplane Company is done, and soon after these words see print its existence, like the war it was created to win, will have been closed. But in the history of that war and the industrial accomplishment it inspired, the names which follow will be written — the same names which are attached to the furniture which is displayed within hundreds of representative stores throughout the country:

The Berkey & Gay Furniture Co., the Century Furniture Co., the Grand Rapids Chair Co., the Grand Rapids Furniture Co., the Johnson Furniture Co., the Luce Furniture Co., the Macy Co., the Royal Furniture Co., the Phoenix Furniture Co., the Sligh Furniture Co., the Stickley Brothers Co., the John Widdicomb Co. and the Wilmarth Show Case Co.

It was in the factories of those institutions, one-third of the facilities of which were devoted to the production of the Grand Rapids Airplane Company at the height of its activity, that the only Handley-Page airplanes made in America were built.

Less than three months after its contract for 1,000 Handley-Page airplanes and spare parts for the Aircraft Production Division of the United States army was signed, finished planes were being delivered by the Grand Rapids organization. At the close of the war the company was considerably ahead of its shipping schedule, having produced 356 complete planes in all, every one of which represented labor and materials sufficient to build five ordinary training planes. Of these aircraft, 110 were "over there," in process of assembling at Oldham, England, and soon would have flown across the channel on their way to the western front. More than 200 machines were ready to ship and 150 were in work, representing a schedule of production that would have reached 40 planes a week, complete with spare parts, a month after the armistice was signed.

What that production involved is reflected in the manufacturing

▲ Main plane ribs for the Handley-Page bomber were assembled at the Wilmarth Showcase Company. [GRPL, Furniture Manufacturers Association Collection]

◄Metal tips were put on propellers at the Phoenix Furniture Company. [GRPL, Furniture Manufacturers Association Collection]

facilities it required; of the 5,800 employes of the associated factories, with 3,500,000 feet of floor space, 2,000 workers and 1,000,000 feet of floor space were devoted to the making of aircraft. Those facts are better understood when the magnitude of the plane itself is considered. The Handley-Page, which bears the name of the English manufacturer by whom it was first produced and from whose blue prints that Grand Rapids planes were built, has a wing spread of 100 feet and measures 63 feet from the nose to the tail of its huge fuselage. It is propelled by two Liberty motors of 410 horse-power each (the only part of the plane, ready-to-fly, which was not made in Grand

Rapids) and it has a cruising radius of about 800 miles. Sixty gallons of gasoline are required for each hour's flight and its customary crew includes a pilot, an observer, a front gunner, a rear gunner, a bomber and a mechanic. Approximately 98 per cent of the lumber used in its construction is western spruce, which in Grand Rapids was dried in 38 batteries of kilns, with a capacity of 300,000 feet of spruce each week. Mahogany and walnut are used as material for its propellers. The cost of the plane, as it was built in England, was approximately $75,000 — an estimate which was considerably reduced by the economies of the Grand Rapids manufacturers.

◄ The Furniture Manufacturer and Artisan, Vol. 17, No. 6, June 1919, pp. 306-9.

Doing Away With Demon Rum

Successfully concluding the war to "make the world safe for democracy," and watching their president sail off to France to fashion a lasting peace, put many Americans in the mood to take up the unfinished business of social reform at home. Prohibition had been on the national agenda for many years, but prior to the war, supporters of the cause had been unable to muster the Congressional votes necessary to place a Constitutional amendment before the American people. Advocates picked up support during the war — alcohol sales had been restricted near military camps — and took advantage of their newfound strength to secure ratification of the Prohibition Amendment in 1919.

Michigan citizens who had voted to make the state dry on May 1, 1918, a year before prohibition became national law, attracted the attention of social scientists and media commentators exploring the implications of a booze-free society. In 1920, shortly after the Eighteenth Amendment was ratified, *Survey,* a national magazine of opinion and feature stories, sent a team of writers to Grand Rapids to prepare a lengthy article determining "What Elimination of the Liquor Traffic Means to Grand Rapids." Their findings, published in November 1920, presented a rosy assessment of life after liquor, and contributed to the widespread initial optimism that the "Grand Experiment" would succeed.

DRINK: Two years before most American industrial centers Grand Rapids became sober. State prohibition closed its 160 saloons and its forty or fifty "halls" equipped with private bars. Its wholesale liquor houses went out of business and its three breweries turned into soft drink factories. Grand Rapids today is free from drunkenness if not from drink.

THE HOME: Families spend more time together. The front porch and the garden have come up as the corner saloon has gone down. Children are better cared for. Mothers know, some of them for the first time, what it is not to be on the grocer's books. Fathers take notice of shabby furnishings and help save up to replace them. The whole town is better dressed. China shops and piano dealers have engaged new assistants. Home purchase, always popular in Grand Rapids, flourishes even more.

THE FACTORY: Mondays are no longer blue or black. Absenteeism because of "severe headaches" has decreased; industrial accidents likewise. The trouble-making barkeeper is now not the first to welcome the newcomer to the city or the homecomer on his way from the pay-window. Philip, sober, has begun to realize that some men are worth more than others; to take a livelier interest in shop concerns, to express himself more freely and intelligently on the processes of which his work is a part. The change has, however, also made for restlessness, especially among the younger workers, and in some cases it has slackened effort and swelled the labor turnover. Faced with the necessity of retaining experienced employes, manu-facturers are coming to study more closely the conditions of work and human relationships within the factory.

HEALTH: Tuberculosis and infantile mortality, two good indices of the public health, are on the decline in Grand Rapids. Though primarily this is due to effective popular education, wiser spending and more food have played their part. Folks go to see the doctor, dentist and oculist before they are forced to do so by pain of disability; they insist on the best treatment; they pay more attention to small ailments. The vital statistics in the years to come will show the results of this shifting from cure to prevention.

RECREATION: The demand for automobiles, for fishing tackle, tents, and other sporting goods can hardly be met. The boat clubs have long waiting lists. Facilities for both indoor and outdoor recreation have been outgrown. The one big improved park of Grand Rapids on Sundays is crowded to overflowing. The roads leading out of the city are filled with happy family parties out for picnics. More vacations are taken and longer vacations. Moving picture and vaudeville theaters have full houses.

"When prohibition first came," said the proprietor of a retail store selling toilet articles and chemicals, "the old toppers in town started runs on some of my goods. As soon as they'd find something with a kick in it, they'd spread the word around. For a while it was Westphal's Hair Tonic. Then they switched to Pinaud's Vegetal Lilac Toilet Water, and for a while they tried Pinaud's Quinine Tonic. I got tired of it after a while and fixed up a game on 'em. I changed some of the formulas. For example, I put more oil in my tartar emetic — there was a run on that for a while — and the effect was to make 'em sick. They quit and tried something else. Now they seem to be discouraged and don't come in often. I'm doing legitimate business here and don't want that kind of trade in the store."

The largest dealer in fishing tackle in the city gave it as his unqualified opinion that prohibition had caused a new era in fishing. Unlike more vigorous pastimes, fishing, he said, seemed to be attracting men past middle-age, men whose appearance gave color to the conclusion that they were former saloon devotees, now solacing themselves with rod and hook. Never within his memory, he said, had fishing been as popular as it had within the past two years. The golden age of the angler seemed to have returned.

▲ Winthrop D. Lane, "Prohibition: What Elimination of the Liquor Traffic Means to Grand Rapids," *Survey Magazine,* November 6, 1920, pp. 189-204.

▲ Police Chief Albert A. Carroll filled a closet with different bootleg alcohol samples he seized. [GRPL, Photo Collection]

▲ Women and children led the crusade against "Demon Rum," including this Sparta group led by Anna Grawn (behind flag). [GRPL, Dorothy Keister Collection]

Votes for Women

The women's suffrage movement gathered support during and after World War I. Persistent lobbying and educational efforts by women's organizations began to alter national opinion. Once-resistant newspaper editors used their pens to aid the cause. The Grand Rapids *Press,* which in 1890 had declared that "politics belong exclusively to men," argued years later that women voters would be no better or worse than their male counterparts. In fact, *Press* editorial writers contended that women were behind many recent social reforms and were entitled to citizenship.

Women contributed countless volunteer hours to the war effort, even though mothers and wives had not had any say in the decision that sent their sons and husbands to fight and die. The combination of their war service, together with the cumulative work of women's suffrage activists for more than half a century, finally turned the tide, and in 1920 the Nineteenth Amendment guaranteeing women's suffrage was passed.

FIRST PRIZE SONG
(By Fred G. Engle.)
Tune, "Battle Hymn of the Republic."
Equal Suffrage.
Everywhere, the clouds are breaking and the darkness disappears,
And the splendor of the morning ushers in the golden years.
Women are no longer chattels, but are recognized as peers;
    Our cause is marching on.

Equal suffrage is our slogan and the burden of our song,
For the mothers, wives and sisters, who have toiled and suffered long.
In this age of human progress right shall triumph over wrong,
    For truth is marching on.

Let us battle with injustice and uphold the pure and good;
Let us work for equal suffrage and enfranchise womanhood,
Mighty evils then will vanish that so long have grimly stood —
    God's cause is marching on.

Chorus.
Glory, glory hallelujah,
    Glory, glory hallelujah,
Glory, glory hallelujah,
    Our cause is marching on.

▲ *Grand Rapids Press,* May 2, 1914, p. 16.

Husbands in Grand Rapids Wednesday morning got their own breakfasts, dressed the children and in their idle moments shoveled a path down the front walk for friend wife, who was going out to vote. Beds were left unmade, breakfast dishes lay unwashed on the table and front parlors went untidied, for it was election day and Grand Rapids women for the first time practiced the gentle art of voting as full-fledged citizens.

Many a working woman got up a half hour early in order that she might have time to go around the corner to call on the board of election inspectors before going to work. But the women who visited the polls between 7 and 8 o'clock were not all working women. Many of them obviously were wives and mothers.

"It comes just as natural as dressing one's hair and it's a lot simpler," declared one women who was asked how it felt to be a voter. "I think we women have dreamed of voting and imagined ourselves doing it for so long that it doesn't seem at all strange. Then, too, so many of us have voted on school questions and have been at the polls when suffrage was being voted on that voting isn't quite as much of a mystery to us as it is supposed to be. Besides, there have been so many schools of instruction that we could hardly avoid learning how to vote even if we wanted to."

Election clerks in one of the Third ward precincts had to look twice Wednesday morning to make sure it was a group of women instead of men who had come early to vote. The group consisted of women employes of the Sligh Furniture factory—and they wore their bloomers.

▲ *Grand Rapids Press,* March 5, 1919, p. 9.

▼ The Grand Rapids women's suffrage headquarters was a busy place. [GRPL, Photo Collection]

◄ Among other activities, the Grand Rapids Equal Franchise Club staged suffrage parades. [GRPL, Postcard Collection]

A Vision for the City's Future

Grand Rapidians might have been forgiven if they spoke with excessive optimism about their city's future in the 1920s. After all, the Great War in Europe was over and the German-led Central powers had been defeated. Prohibition was the law of the land, and women had voted for the first time in a general election.

On top of these developments, the nation's premier city planner, Harland Bartholomew, had come to Grand Rapids and drawn up a plan for the city's future that included wide, tree-lined streets and boulevards; a modern transportation system; a restored and beautiful riverfront; and a vigorous downtown that was the retail and commercial center of West Michigan. Although some of his assessments, such as the importance of railroad and streetcar transportation, were wide of the mark, other visions, like the importance of the riverfront, will strike a responsive chord among modern residents.

A Beautiful River Front and New Retail District

For years we have neglected the beauty possibilities of the Grand river flowing through the city, until it has degenerated into a sluggish, weed-grown stream. But now plans are underway to make it one of our most valuable civic assets.

Already the city has acquired the east side power company canal interests as the first and major step in a river front esplanade, and appropriations have been established for the building of small dams between Bridge and Pearl street bridges in order to keep the river at a proper level.

Campau street, between Monroe avenue and the river, now has no retail value whatever, and is given over to loft and manufacturing buildings. It finally terminates in an alley at the north. It is proposed to make this into a high grade avenue, lined with retail stores. In time it will open up frontage now of little worth and make it extremely valuable for retail purposes. The imposing 34-story Furniture Capitol Exhibition building now under way at the foot of Lyon street fits into this plan nicely and will add to the attractiveness of the street.

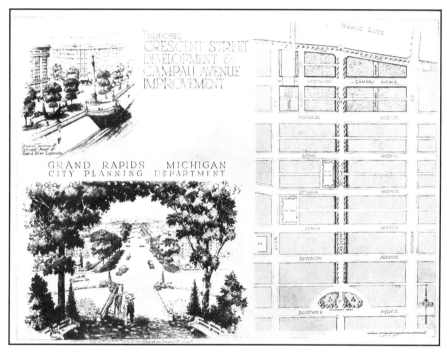

▲ Planner Harland Bartholomew envisioned a city with broad boulevards and walkways along the Grand River. [Harland Bartholomew, *The Grand Rapids City Plan*, p. 32]

◄ Harland Bartholomew, *The Grand Rapids City Plan*, 1927, p. 9.

Future Street Railway System Here Proposed is Planned to Serve a City of 300,000 by 1975

To lay new tracks and pull up others is a costly proceeding and the improvements proposed can be done profitably only in the course of time, as earnings permit and the various sections of the city grow enough to provide sufficient patronage for extensions. Improvements most needed will be effected first and already some of those in the business district have been brought about. Sections of the city needing service but not justifying track extension at present are being served by buses, such as Bridge street hill, Alpine, North College and North Lafayette, Eastern and Kalamazoo, and Market and Godfrey streets.

The plan proposed requires 139 miles of track, including 51 miles of the 66 in the present system, involving the abandonment of 15 miles of present trackage.

▲ Harland Bartholomew, *The Grand Rapids City Plan*, 1927, p. 18.

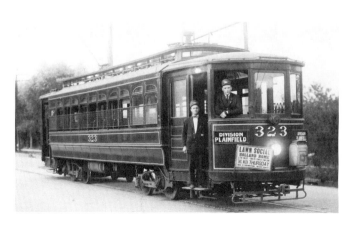

◄ In Bartholomew's plan, the city would be served by an extensive street railway system. [GRPL, Photo Collection]

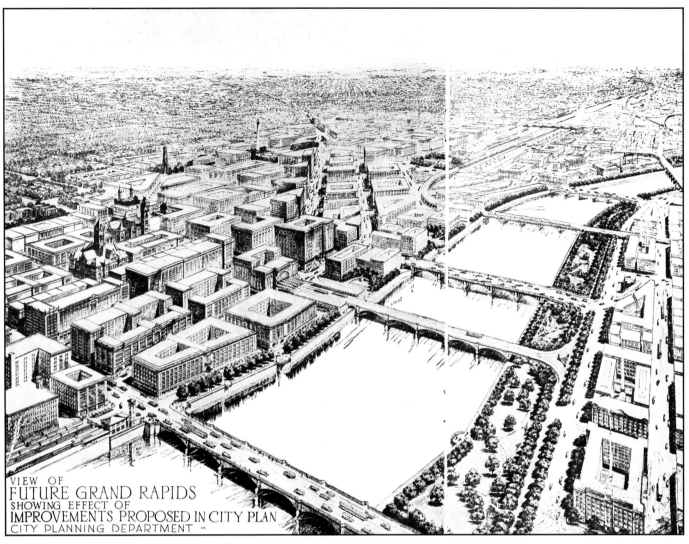

VIEW OF
FUTURE GRAND RAPIDS
SHOWING EFFECT OF
IMPROVEMENTS PROPOSED IN CITY PLAN
CITY PLANNING DEPARTMENT -

▲ Harland Bartholomew's view of downtown Grand
Rapids, with large office buildings and parkways on both
sides of the river, looks much like the city of the 1990s.
[Harland Bartholomew, *The Grand Rapids City Plan*,
pp. 10-11]

CHAPTER 7

Economic Depression and War

At times it seemed the prosperity and excitement of the 1920s would go on forever. Factories hummed with activity and buyers went eagerly to the stores, confident their growing incomes would accommodate their appetites for automobiles, appliances, and the other consumer goods that made their lives so different from those of their parents.

Most Grand Rapids consumers paid scant attention to declining furniture orders or to dropping farm prices that left many farmers in debt at the end of a year's work. Talkies playing at downtown theaters, dancing, amusements at Ramona Park on Reeds Lake and the North Park Pavilion, automobile rides in the country or out to Lake Michigan, and a host of other distractions masked dark clouds gathering on the horizon. Placid certainty persisted that tomorrow would be better than today, and that each year would improve on the last.

By 1927, however, the economic danger signs were becoming so obvious Grand Rapidians could no longer ignore them. In a city whose economy was built on furniture, the closing of the Nelson Matter Company during World War I was an ominous but unheeded harbinger. A decade later the decline of the giant Sligh Furniture Company could not be ignored. Coming as it did at the time of the 1929 stock market crash that ushered in the Great Depression, Sligh's closing marked the transformation of the 1920s' exuberant dance into the 1930s' dispirited shuffle.

Unless experienced firsthand, the hardships of the Great Depression are difficult to comprehend. At its peak, the depression left one of every four Grand Rapids workers unemployed. Local churches, charities, and city government provided relief to the most destitute, but their ability to help fell far short of the need.

Faced with so many unemployed workers, Grand Rapids officials fought back with a jobs program. In 1930 and 1931, scrip wages paid by the city for work on roads, parks, and numerous construction projects enabled thousands of local families to get by until federal New Deal programs were enacted.

It took World War II and a total commitment to military production to end the nation's economic doldrums. The bombs that dropped on Pearl Harbor solved America's employment problems. Young men and women entered the military by the hundreds of thousands, while on the home front, local factories turned out war matériel ranging from parachutes and glider wings to gun stocks and metal ship's furniture.

The flame of patriotism burned as brightly in Grand Rapids as anywhere in the nation. When war came, local citizens rallied to President Franklin Roosevelt's call. For the next four years, no event was awaited with as much eagerness and anxiety as the arrival of daily news reports from the theaters of war.

Not until 1945 when the war's outcome no longer seemed in doubt did residents permit themselves to think of the postwar future. Peace, however, carried a price that would not soon be forgotten. Estimates ran as high as 35 to 40 million dead in Europe and Asia. U.S. forces suffered over a million casualties, including 400,000 dead. In Kent County, 30,403 citizens had volunteered or been drafted to military service, and 1,022 made the ultimate sacrifice.

"No Home Should Be Without One"

Electrical appliances led a 1920s revolution in consumer buying. Where furniture had once held almost exclusive sway, now refrigerators, washing machines, vacuum cleaners, radios, and phonographs competed for consumers' durable-goods dollars. Thomas Edison demonstrated the labor-saving potential of electricity, and before long a host of engineers and innovators flooded the market with devices designed to save time, put an end to drudgery, and provide households with new forms of entertainment.

Novelties at first, electrical appliances quickly became essentials in a well-appointed home. By the 1920s, local merchants filled newspaper pages with advertisements touting the virtues of their wares. Some carried brand names that would remain familiar to households two generations later. Others were destined to pass from the scene as they lost the perpetual battle waged for consumer loyalty.

Make Wash Day a Play Day

Have you ever wondered how that certain neighbor of yours has her washing all done before you are fairly started and how she manages to have so much spare time on wash days? Here's the answer:

She is the proud possessor of a THOR Electric Washer. All she does is to fill up the tub and turn the switch.

Let us put a Thor in your home on trial. If you like it keep it. If it does not render satisfactory service we will take it away and you will be nothing out and a washing ahead.

Thor Electric Shop

H. D. O'BRIEN, Mgr.

130 Pearl St. Citz. 62497. Opp. Consumers Power Co.

The Hoover for the Home

It beats as it sweeps, as it cleans.

A leading English scientist recently discovered that dust exerts a harmful chemical effect upon the body, in addition to carrying the germs of disease.

When you use a Hoover you are sure of eliminating the dust from rugs, draperies and upholsteries.

We are headquarters for Hoover Sales and Service.

—Daily Demonstration Main Floor.

MUSICAL INSTRUMENTS

BUY

Victrolas -- Pianos

Watches, Diamonds, Jewelry

On Time, at Cash Prices

L. E. PHILLIPS

TWO STORES—1365-67 Plainfield Ave. N. E.
414 Leonard N. W.

FANS

Happy and cool the home where there's an Electric Fan wafting the delicious breezes of the refreshing seashore climate. Get an Electric Fan tomorrow from Michigan's Largest Electric Store - low prices.

John S. Noel

112-114-116-118 DIVISION AVE. SOUTH

◄ By the 1920s, time-saving electrical appliances seemed to be available for every domestic chore. Newspapers and other publications were full of advertisements for vacuum cleaners, washing machines, fans, record players, and similar devices that were forever altering American life. [Clockwise from upper left: *Grand Rapids Press*, July 19, 1922, p. 17; *Grand Rapids City Directory*, 1923, p. 90; *Grand Rapids Press*, July 15, 1922, p. 5; *Grand Rapids City Directory*, 1924, p. 68; *Grand Rapids City Directory*, 1922, p. 66; *Grand Rapids Press*, July 13, 1922, p. 3.]

Electrical Contractors

CONSULT	Proper Lighting
US	Correct Wiring
FOR	Motors and Repairing

Complete Fixture Display

Meyering Electric Co.

915 LEONARD, N. W.
AUTO PHONE 69974

APEX HOME APPLIANCE STORE

E. L. McCAUSEY, Propr.

Washing Machines
Ironing Machines
Hoover Vacuum Cleaners

117 DIVISION AVENUE SOUTH
CITIZENS PHONE 51834

Radio Days

A successful broadcast demonstration in 1907 ushered the United States into the age of radio. By 1915, the new technology was well established locally, and the Grand Rapids Radio association was holding weekly meetings to

make a joint study of the intricacies of wireless telegraphy, to discuss the various phases in connection with the receiving and transmitting of messages and to keep in touch with the latest experiments and improvements being tried out in other parts of the country.

In August 1920, WWJ in Detroit became the nation's first commercial broadcast station. Two years later, Wurzburg's department store in downtown Grand Rapids purchased a receiver and set up a radio listening room. There, area residents were welcome to come and hear the concerts, speeches, and dramas being broadcast by WWJ and stations in Pittsburgh and New York.

On September 16, 1924, the first radio broadcast by a Grand Rapids station, WEBL, captured local imaginations, if not large audiences. Few people owned receivers at the time, and those who wanted to catch the broadcast came by the improvised studio and listened to the performance live. A month later, its call letters changed from WEBL to WEBK, Grand Rapids' first radio station received its permanent operating license.

To the blare of the saxophone and the staccato rattle of the snare drum Grand Rapids' first radio show was opened in the Klingman building, Pearl-st. and Ottawa-av., Tuesday afternoon and that it was a popular event was evidenced by many visitors who gazed upon radio apparatus ranging from the makeshift, schoolboy manufactured affair to the ornate, complicated and expensive receiving set—the very latest in the art of radio production.

Three carloads of radio apparatus were neatly arranged in the exhibition space, showing development of the radio from the time of its inception to the present, and experts from the Radio Corporation of America and the C.J. Litscher Co., Grand Rapids distributors, were on hand to explain the devices to visitors.

From 2 to 3 o'clock Tuesday broadcasting took place from the big station brought here in connection with the show. Radio programs were received in the afternoon and enjoyed by the visitors through the medium of amplifiers. At 8 o'clock Tuesday evening Mayor Elvin Swarthout is scheduled to speak and a concert by artists from the Grand Rapids Conservatory of Music will be broadcast. The station will be known as WEBL, Grand Rapids.

Wednesday Mrs. Frances Morton Crume, contralto, will sing, accompanied on the piano by Miss Florence Malek. A talk on Butterworth hospital guild and music by the Jungle Kings, a Negro jazz orchestra, will feature the afternoon program. Wednesday evening The Ritzema trio, a

male quartet, the Louis-Dietrich orchestra and the Wolverine Four will furnish the broadcasting program. The Beatrice Lewis orchestra will play and there will be talks by representatives of Butterworth hospital, which receives the proceeds of the show.

▲ *Grand Rapids Press*, September 16, 1924, p. 2.

▲ "Uncle Jerry" (Hugh Harb) entertained children over radio station WASH. [GRPL, Murch S. Morris Collection]

◄ Several radio sales stores vied for Grand Rapids customers by the mid-1920s. [*Grand Rapids City Directory*, 1926, p. 99]

"Who's Playing at the Powers?"

Radio may have been the entertainment curiosity of the 1920s, but legitimate theater was still the staple. Grand Rapids boasted three stock companies: the Broadway Players at the Regent, Marguerite Field's Theatre Company at the Orpheum, and the Wright Players at the Powers Theatre on Ionia next door to the Waters Building. Brightest star for the Wright group was its handsome young leading man, Spencer Tracy, who moved on to Broadway and then films. A glance at programs and publicity photographs shows that Tracy was not alone; others in the group who came to enjoy distinguished stage and film careers included Selena Royale, Georgia Backus, Dean Jagger, and Porter Hall.

Mounting production costs, the Great Depression, and then World War II spelled the end of stock companies in Grand Rapids. But for a couple of years in the late 1920s, the answer to the question: "Who's playing at the Powers?" was "Spencer Tracy."

▲ Above and below: Programs from the Powers Theater on Pearl Street, the center of West Michigan drama and music productions in the 1920s. [GRPL, Powers Theater Program Collection]

◀ Spencer Tracy was cast in the lead role as Paul Jones in the Wright Players' 1925 production of "The Cat and the Canary." [GRPL, Emily Deming Collection]

◀The Wright Players. Spencer Tracy is far left, back row. [GRPL, Emily Deming Collection]

From Iron Rails to Rubber Tires

During the 1920s, family dollars not budgeted for appliances were often set aside for the purchase of an automobile. By 1925, cars were commonplace on the Grand Rapids scene, and the Grand Rapids *Press* reported that 79 percent of Kent County households owned automobiles.

As they became the primary mode of transportation, automobiles clogged city streets originally built for horse and streetcar transportation, creating rush-hour traffic jams and a flurry of accidents. Intersection police, directional signs, and, eventually, stop-and-go lights brought a measure of control to the traffic.

The growing acceptance of the internal combustion engine signalled the ultimate demise of electrically powered streetcars. In 1935, the transition from iron rails to rubber tires was complete when 100 green and scarlet buses began operating over 12 routes, making Grand Rapids the second city in the nation (San Antonio was the first) to shift completely from streetcars to bus service.

Street cars, in Grand Rapids, are a thing of the past.

Early today, when the "J. Boyd Pantlind" with the veteran Motorman Miles McDonald at the controls, made the last run from Campau square to Ramona and was finally put in the barn, Grand Rapids became the second largest city in America without surface cars.

This morning, for the first time since the days of the Civil war, the iron rails were out of service. Shortly they will be torn up.

Waiting for the final run and preparing for his first vacation in 41 years, Motorman McDonald last night reminisced of the past, going back to Jan. 7, 1895, when he started out on the front end of a "bald-face" car.

"What I mean by bald-face cars is cars with no vestibule. I believe the cars ran just as fast as they do now and for a man to stand out on one of those and push them along on schedule time when the temperature was 10 or 12 below zero was, I assure you, anything but a pleasure.

"We worked 'swing runs,' the day run about 11 hours, the swing about 12, and the long, say, about 14.

"People rode the cars then to and from work, to ball games and to the park on Sundays, to the theaters, and it was a big problem for the railroad to furnish them something to ride on. I have seen them going out to Reeds lake up on top of the cars. People had to ride the cars then, if they got anywhere, as there was no other means of mass transportation. But, oh, how times have changed. Little did we ever think those days of ever seeing these car tracks torn up for good, but I suppose we will have to arrange our lives to meet the changing conditions."

◄*Grand Rapids Herald,* August 26, 1935, p. 1.

▲ Although the contest seemed a standoff at times, automobiles eventually won their battle with streetcars for the streets of Grand Rapids. [GRPL, Photo Collection]

◄ Campau Square was filled with streetcars in 1925. [GRPL, Photo Collection]

Ten years later, the ► streetcars had all been replaced by buses. [GRPL, Photo Collection]

An Aviation Milestone

Aviation came of age in Grand Rapids in the 1920s. Kent County's first airfield, built by the Grand Rapids Aero Club but used by nonmembers as well, was dedicated on October 29, 1919. Over the coming years, the club worked to upgrade the facility by constructing a small headquarters building and hangars, and installing fuel tanks.

In 1925, Detroit engineer and inventor William B. Stout appeared before the Grand Rapids Rotary Club to promote his idea of regularly scheduled intercity passenger air service. Approached by business and civic leaders to establish such a line between Detroit and Grand Rapids, Stout accepted the proposal. A community-wide fund drive financed a variety of improvements at the airfield, from graded runways to construction of a passenger terminal.

On July 31, 1926, a Ford Stout monoplane rose into the clear afternoon sky, and Grand Rapids laid claim to the "first strictly passenger airline in the United States." Planes were scheduled to arrive from Ford airport in Dearborn at 11:45 each morning and leave at 1:40 in the afternoon for the return trip. The fare was $18 each way or $35 round trip. Passengers were assured of a comfortable flight no noisier than "a pullman car with the windows open in the summer, [and] windows can be opened in the plane if desired for extra ventilation...."

Although it was still a novelty, Grand Rapidians were excited by the prospects of regular air travel. That excitement was reinforced when Charles Lindbergh, the "Lone Eagle" who soloed across the Atlantic in a single-engine plane, made the Furniture City a stop on his 1927 cross-country tour to promote air travel. After his visit, many Grand Rapids business and government leaders became firm believers in the future of aviation.

▲ The North End Paint Shop prepared this banner to welcome Charles Lindbergh in 1927. [GRPL, Murch S. Morris Collection]

The Lone Eagle of the air swooped into Grand Rapids Friday afternoon and was acclaimed by all western Michigan.

Never has Grand Rapids nor this section of the state seen a demonstration such as greeted Col. Charles A. Lindbergh as he alighted in his Spirit of St. Louis plane at the local airport. Nor did the noted flyer receive all the applause, for Mrs. Evangeline L.L. Lindbergh, schoolteacher mother of the world famous pilot, preceded her son, arriving at the airport at 1 o'clock.

True, the demonstrations given the trio, the son, mother and plane, may not have equaled in size those of Washington, Detroit and New York and St. Louis, but certainly the warmth of the reception has not been surpassed. It was western Michigan at its best.

From the minute the silverwinged plane was first sighted in the sky until the "unofficial ambassador" climbed into a waiting automobile and started on his trip through the downtown district to John Ball park, where 100,000 persons heard him, he was cheered as no other person has been in Grand Rapids.

After Col. Lindbergh was greeted at the airport by Mayor Swarthout the reception committee in its car started the long trek to John Ball park, while The *Press* Newsboy band played. At Madison-av. and Burton-st. there was stationed the Grand Rapids Railroad Co. electric railroad coach named in honor of Col. Lindbergh. It was manned by William Meinke. Mayor Swarthout called the Lone Eagle's attention to the car.

At the park Welfare Director A.E. Davidson arranged space for children under 15 years of age and special attention also was given to 12 crippled children who were in the parade.

"I believe that the basic principles of flying should be taught in schools, for the children must become interested in aviation in order that it may be developed along proper lines," declared Col. Charles A. Lindbergh. "This best can be accomplished by teaching the children to build the models of planes. It is my opinion interest in aviation will be aided tremendously through the teaching of aeronautics in the schools."

◄ One of the nation's first regularly scheduled passenger airlines was launched in Grand Rapids when this plane took off on July 31, 1926. [GRPL, Photo Collection]

▲ *Grand Rapids Press*, August 12, 1927, pp. 1-2.

Emmett N. Bolden v. Grand Rapids Operating Corporation

One of the many battles waged by local African-Americans in their struggle for equal protection under the law was launched in the winter of 1925 at the B.F. Keith Theater in downtown Grand Rapids.

On the evening of December 14, Dr. Emmett N. Bolden, D.D.S., Dr. Eugene E. Alston, M.D., and two companions planned to attend a vaudeville show and a film at the Keith. The four men were turned away, however, when they requested seating on the main floor. One of several local theaters to draw a color line, the Keith restricted individuals of African descent to seats in the balcony.

Two days later, supported by the Grand Rapids Chapter of the National Association for the Advancement of Colored People (NAACP), Dr. Bolden filed suit in Superior Court against the Grand Rapids Operating Company, the theater's holding company. Attorney for the plaintiff was Oliver M. Green, and assisting with the legal research was Floyd H. Skinner, then in his final year at the University of Michigan's law school.

In presenting Bolden's case to the court, Green argued that under Michigan law and the Civil Rights Act of 1885 (amended 1919), discrimination in public accommodations in any form was unconstitutional. The holding company, on the other hand, maintained that a "theater is a private enterprise,... and may exclude therefrom any person whatsoever." The decision came down in favor of the theater operator.

On June 6, 1927, the Michigan Supreme Court reversed the lower court ruling. Although no damages were awarded to Bolden, the victory was nevertheless his when the supreme court justices upheld the principle of civil rights by requiring the Keith Theater (and by extension, all others) to provide integrated seating. Green and Bolden both died within a few years of the case, but Floyd Skinner went on to a distinguished legal career in Grand Rapids.

STATE OF MICHIGAN
SUPERIOR COURT OF
GRAND RAPIDS
Emmett N. Bolden, Plaintiff
v.
Grand Rapids Operating
Corporation
PLAINTIFF'S AMENDED
DECLARATION
The Plaintiff Says:

1. That he is a native born citizen of the United States, a colored man of African blood, a graduate of South High School of Grand Rapids, Michigan and of Howard University, Washington, D.C., and was at the time hereinafter named a duly licensed dentist, and practicing dentistry in the City of Grand Rapids, Michigan.

2. That on said 14th day of December, 1925, said defendant, the Grand Rapids Operating Corporation, did directly refuse, withhold from and deny to plaintiff full and equal accommodations, advantages, facilities and privileges of said theater, to-wit: that on said 14th day of December, 1925, said defendant, the Grand Rapids Operating Corporation, did directly refuse, withhold from and deny to plaintiff a seat in said theater downstairs (on their first floor), and did then and there willfully and unlawfully prevent plaintiff from buying a ticket of admission to said theater, downstairs (on the first floor), solely because of his color and because of his race.

▲ Left to right: Emmett Bolden, Oliver Green, and Floyd Skinner all played a role in the Keith Theater case. [*South High Annual*, 1919, p. 16; *Michigensian*, 1923, p. 134; *Michigensian*, 1926, p. 127.]

Keith's Theater interior. Before Emmett Bolden's successful challenge, African-Americans were permitted to sit only in the balcony. [GRPL, Robinson Collection]

◄ *Emmett N. Bolden v. Grand Rapids Operating Corporation,* Case No. 3043, State of Michigan Superior Court of Grand Rapids.

"We All Worked and Worked Hard"

On "Black Thursday," October 24, 1929, a dip in the stock market turned to panic when a record 13 million shares were sold in one day's trading. Efforts to stem the slide failed, and "Black Tuesday" followed on October 29, when an additional 16 million shares were sold at rapidly falling prices. Coming as it did in the wake of declining industrial earnings and increased consumer debt, the 1929 stock market crash ended several years of unprecedented speculation and triggered a decade of economic depression.

By the end of 1930, an estimated 4.5 million Americans were out of work, and 1,300 banks had closed their doors. In Grand Rapids as elsewhere, people relied on wit and ingenuity to provide for themselves and their families.

For me, thinking about the Depression brings back memories of people—also fear and, oddly enough, along with the fear, laughter and sense of community—folks helping each other.

Actually we were relatively well-off. My dad worked for the Grand Trunk Railroad, owned by the Canadian National—always got his pay check on time and never lost his job.

He came close. On the railroad if you are laid off you can "bump" (take the job of) the man youngest in seniority if you have even one day more seniority than he has. At one point, there were only three men lower on the seniority list than my dad and with a wife and four little kids to support, he was scared. What did he do? I think his response to the situation was typical of the Depression. He went out, on his own time, and sold freight—convinced companies and people to ship their goods on the GTW. He knew that selling freight could not defeat the seniority system if it got to him but, maybe, just maybe, it would help the company keep jobs open that they might otherwise have closed out and, thus, possibly the seniority system would not reach him. Something worked, 'cause he never lost his job.

When we bought the house for seventeen hundred dollars (payments of $10.00 per month) there was about 3/4 acre of raspberries there, planted in rows, in good condition. Mother often told me that the first few years we were there, after paying for boxes and paying the pickers 2 cents a box, they cleared over $120.00 for the season on raspberries. So, the berries more than met the house payments.

Dad put in overhead irrigation, designing the system himself, and did a large part of the construction work himself. With that available, he switched part, or all, of the

land from berries to food stuffs which did best if they got lots of water: tomatoes, watermelon and muskmelon, among others.

I remember, at a very young age (5 or 6) helping measure the distance between when tomato plants were set. We planted them 3 feet apart each way. Nothing in the world tastes quite as good as a dead-ripe tomato, warm from the sun, a little salt sprinkled on (and the added taste thrill that we weren't supposed to do this). However, every kid had a salt shaker in a pocket of his or her bib overalls and Mother had a hard time keeping salt shakers in the house for table use.

The years we grew melons, I could take my tablecloth, or just the cloth, outdoors and have a melon party for my friends. We could have as much, or many, melons as we wanted and could eat. You see, there was fun then too, along with the problems.

Dad often told me that during the heart of the Depression he cleared $300 to $500 a year from truck gardening his irrigated land. Those were net, or clear profit, figures and represented an enormous amount of money in those days.

Lest I give the wrong impression, not everything Dad tried succeeded and none of it happened

without hard work. We all worked and worked hard, but that's what the world was all about then and everyone worked.

And so we struggled, a contest that went on and on: My father and our family using every ounce of strength, guts and mind we had against succumbing to the financial and emotional depression of the times. Always we knew that if Dad lost his job, the whole effort would come apart and God only knew what horrors would come about. However, although there was fear, and from time to time, lots of it, we kept going and, as we did so, we even helped other people in their struggle.

I've often thought that one definition of courage is "scared to death and doing it anyway."

"The City Where Every Man Has a Job"

By 1932, faced with rising unemployment and growing dissatisfaction with his policies, President Herbert Hoover conceded that the federal government had to do more, because state and local agencies could not provide adequate relief. For many citizens, however, Hoover's concession came too late, and his proposed programs offered far too little.

In Grand Rapids, City Manager George Welsh took the initiative in providing relief to the unemployed. His solution was a city-funded program that hired workers to do a variety of public works jobs ranging from shoveling snow to cleaning up the Grand River to constructing buildings in city parks. The workers were paid in municipal scrip that was redeemable at city-run stores for everything from foodstuffs to clothing and furniture.

While not unique, Welsh's program was one of the most extensive of its kind in the country. Not only did the Grand Rapids plan draw the notice of officials from other cities and attract the attention of the newly elected Roosevelt administration in 1932, it also prompted the editor of *American* magazine to send writer Neil Clark to Grand Rapids in 1931 for a story on the "city where everyone has a job."

▲ City Manager George Welsh was the architect of Grand Rapids' scrip labor program. [GRPL, Photo Collection]

Marty Mullane, of Grand Rapids, Michigan—a dead-broke human being, if ever there was one. He admitted he didn't have two dimes to rub together the day I saw him. But he was lugging home a hefty bag of groceries which he had bought over the counter at the city store, using city certificates for money; and he looked me straight in the eye, his big face blooming with good nature, when he said:

"Sure, I eat well—but I earn it."

Grand Rapids gave Marty a job. Not much of a job. Helping to cut back the curb and lay cement to widen a downtown street. But enough to feed him and his family. and what a difference it makes...!

How did the plan come about, and why can't every city do it? For the answers, go back about three years. Grand Rapids was broke, then. The city had run into a deficit of more than a million dollars. George Welsh was called in as new city manager to try to put the city on its financial feet.

Welsh is red-headed. Or was. For now the red has turned prematurely white. On his own from early boyhood, he had known hard times himself. He had served as a city alderman, state representative, Speaker of the House, lieutenant-governor. When he took up the reins as city manager he did the job he was asked to do. By rigid economies he wiped out the deficit and piled up a surplus.

Then the depression started. The furniture factories, which are the backstay of Grand Rapids industry, speedily called a halt on their operations. A great number of people were thrown out of work. The city welfare depart-

▲ The city store, operated by and for scrip laborers, provided basic food staples to many local families. [GRPL, City Welfare Department Scrip Labor Collection]

ment found itself suddenly called upon to give help to an increasing number of able-bodied workers who could find nothing to do....

"Is it going to last long?" [Welsh] queried.

At that time, many were predicting that the worst would be over in a few weeks. But Welsh consulted experts.

"It may last a long time—years!" they told him.

So he began thinking about a solution that would last—years. The germ of his idea developed slowly. First, he used unemployed men for snow removal, as most cities do. Snow, unluckily, doesn't always fall when wanted! Welsh needed something more dependable. He called in the head of one of the city departments.

"Frank," said he, "there must have been times when you asked the city for money and didn't get it. I mean, for some worthy project you wanted to undertake."

"Plenty of times!"

"Well, then, think! What

project of this sort could you tackle right now, provided all the labor were supplied to you free? Think it over—let me know."

"I can tell you right now what I'd do," said the other.

"What?"

"I'd clean out the river bed above the Pennsylvania Railroad bridge...."

"What would the job need besides labor?" Welsh asked.

"Pickaxes, shovels, wheelbarrows."

"Got 'em?"

"Plenty. If I need more I can get 'em from the water department."

"All right, I'll get you the men."

The news went out. Able-bodied men applying for relief were to be given jobs, at fifty cents an hour. They turned to on the task. Hand-shovels, muscles, wheelbarrows. Not one power machine on the job.

The plan has been in operation now for about two years. It has been financed by two emergency bond issues amounting in all to

$650,000, involving an assessment of only about a quarter of one per cent on city property.

And look at what it has done for the city!

On the chosen site for a new civic auditorium, for example, were several old buildings. These were demolished by the city's needy workers. Afterwards the dismantled brick, lumber, plumbing, and steel work were cleaned and salvaged by the same workers.

An outdoor swimming pool had been demanded for years. So city workers built the swimming pool — one of the largest of its kind in the country....

The City Hall was dingy. City workers cleaned and painted it.

These are a few of the jobs: Sewers have been laid, and miles of water mains. Streets have been widened and dangerously sharp street corners cut back. These jobless men, in a word, are beautifying their own city, making it a place permanently better to live in, both now and when good times return.

Such a plan, of course, requires rules and regulations. Every man who applies for city work must have lived in Grand Rapids for at least a year. He is given a thorough physical examination, and is certified as fit for "light" work or "heavy" work, as the case may be. If he himself cannot work, there may be someone else in the family who can. The family's circumstances are thoroughly investigated. Where there are several children in a family, a man is allowed more work than if he has only one or two persons to support. Nobody is given more than six half-days of work a week. At forty cents an hour, the present rate of pay, this yields just about sustenance wages.

The wages are paid in city certificates, or scrip, redeemable in groceries, dry goods, and various other basic supplies at the city store, at prices on a par with the lowest priced cash stores carrying similar qualities.

But the really big outcome of the plan I found in the pick-and-shovel men themselves—in what it is doing to them....

I stood outside the city employment office. A group of scrip workers had gathered around me. They didn't like the times at all. Wished they had their own good old jobs back again....

Someone mentioned scrip. Naturally, they didn't like everything about that, either.

"But I'll tell you this," boomed a brawny chap, who looked as if he could give orders to a gang; "I'd ten times rather work like this than have 'em give me my grub, like I hear they do in most of these places."

And that, precisely, is the point!

▲ Neil M. Clark, "A City Where Every Man Has a Job," *American,* January 1932, pp. 28-31, 86.

▲ Above: Shoe repair was one of several services that could be purchased with scrip. Below: Scrip labor workers canned fruits and vegetables for the city store. [GRPL, City Welfare Department Scrip Labor Collection]

◄ The banks of the Grand River were cleared and stabilized by scrip workers. [GRPL, City Welfare Department Welfare Scrip Labor Collection]

▼ A city bond issue was passed in 1932 to provide funds to build the Civic Auditorium. [GRPL, Photo Collection]

◄ Scrip workers cleaned bricks from demolition of old buildings at the Civic Auditorium site, and prepared them for other projects. [GRPL, City Welfare Department Scrip Labor Collection]

The Committee of 100

Not everyone agreed that Welsh's scrip labor program was a success. The Rev. Alfred W. Wishart of Fountain Street Baptist Church was one of the program's more strident critics. In January 1932 he unleashed an attack that condemned Welsh for "mixing politics with business management of the city." Concerned that city scrip laborers would be used in the construction of Grand Rapids' new Civic Auditorium, Wishart argued that the program should not compete with private construction contractors or grocery store operators and other retailers.

Ever the politician, Welsh issued a prepared statement denying Wishart's charges and offering the minister the recently vacated position of city social service director. Wishart, quite naturally, declined.

Wishart's objections led to a decision by the city commission to investigate the entire Grand Rapids social service program. At first Welsh resisted the criticisms and denied any wrongdoing. Finally, sure of vindication, he and his supporters on the commission agreed to an investigating Committee of 100 made up of a representative cross-

section of the city's social and business leadership.

The committee's report, issued on August 28, 1932, contained no allegations of wrongdoing. But only one member, furniture company owner Robert Irwin, saw no reason for change. The rest were unanimous in their recommendation that the entire program be completely overhauled.

Several changes were made in the weeks and months that followed. The issue was finally laid to rest as the New Deal programs of President Franklin Roosevelt brought more and more relief programs under the aegis of the federal government.

There is no profit in the City Store to the City of Grand Rapids; therefore if this business were given to the local merchants it would benefit them and be no more costly to the city.

It might be possible to give scrip workers orders on nearby merchants for their supplies of food, etc., and it would be a move in the right direction if this could be done, because it would bring this business back to the merchant.

1. *SCRIP*:

After careful investigation, which covered the methods in use in various cities, as well as Grand Rapids, your committee recommends the discontinuance of the use of scrip, and that cash be paid instead, for the following reasons:

(a) We believe the scrip to be payment for labor, and therefore wages.

(b) It is not negotiable. As such it greatly disturbs the economic balance of a community.

(c) It causes unemployment. Recipients of scrip are obliged to limit their purchases to wares offered by the city store. This causes merchants in localities where there are many scrip workers to reduce their working force.

(d) It is wasteful. Whatever is spent for printing, issuing and checking the back scrip is wasted. . . .

(e) It is destructive to morale—both of men receiving it and their families.

(f) It causes discontent on the part of those receiving it. Scrip workers appearing before your

committee testified they no longer went to Church or Sunday School—that they could only barter the food they received for such service as hair cutting, etc. — that they could live better satisfied if they received the same amount of money as they did scrip.

2. *WORK RELIEF*:

Your committee recommends the continuance of work relief, but it is not in favor of the continuance of the present methods used. Much of the work is wasteful and inefficient. The manner in which the men work is very detrimental to their morale, and an actual waste of time and money.

It is our contention that there are two classes of people now receiving aid. One, the indigent who probably would be receiving aid regardless of conditions—and the other, those who are out of work and asking for aid for the first time in their lives. It is our contention that the second class of people do not need the aid of welfare workers or investigators; the only thing they need is wages.

Your committee is not concerned whether the usual indigent class under the supervision of the Social Service Department has any work or not. It is their opinion that the less they contaminate the good workmen, the better. . . .

In conclusion, it is the opinion of your committee that while relieving distress, the morale and citizenship of our citizens must be saved. . . . wages should flow through normal channels, thereby benefiting as large a number of people as possible.

▲ Rev. Alfred Wishart of Fountain Street Baptist Church was a leading critic of George Welsh's social programs. [GRPL, Photo Collection]

▲ Furniture manufacturer Robert Irwin filed a dissenting, minority report as a member of the Committee of 100. [GRPL, Furniture Manufacturers Association Collection]

▲ The city social center for unmarried men was a target of the Committee of 100's criticism. [GRPL, City Welfare Department Scrip Labor Collection]

◄ GRPL, "Report of the Committee of One Hundred Including Sub-Committee Reports and Minority Report."

Turning the Tap at the Big Lake

Hard times persisted in Kent County throughout the 1930s. In mid-decade, 63,600 individuals — over 25 percent of the total county population of 240,500— were receiving some form of public assistance, most of it coming from federal New Deal work programs. Probably the most significant local public works project of the 1930s was the Lake Michigan pipeline, secured through the efforts of Mayor George Welsh.

Welsh, who had resigned as city manager shortly after the Committee of 100's investigation, made an unsuccessful run in the Michigan Republican gubernatorial primary. He returned to the local political scene in 1938 and was elected mayor. Welsh, city manager C. Sophus Johnson, and a majority of the city commission pursued $1,845,000 in federal Works Progress Administration (WPA) funds for the construction of a $4.1 million pipeline for

Lake Michigan water that would put hundreds of unemployed to work.

Pipeline construction began in 1939, with as much as a half-mile laid on some days, and completion of the 30-mile tube was scheduled for May 1940. The opening of the valves on May 26, 1940, right on schedule, began a steady flow of fresh Lake Michigan water that continues to serve Grand Rapids to this day.

"Extremely satisfactory."

Thus did Service Director Peter A. Kammeraad and other city officials characterize the initial test of the Lake Michigan pipeline project Saturday afternoon.

City Commissioner James C. Quinlan, whose resolution to the city commission, May 26, 1938, brought about the pipeline project, turned on a huge pump at the lake shore pumping station at 2:30 Saturday afternoon. Some 30 miles away, at the municipal filtration plant in Grand Rapids, Thomas Grady, plant superintendent, gave 120 turns on the wheel of a huge valve to permit pressure from the distant pump to push water into the filtration plant. It was Grady who opened the valve that let the first Grand river water into the filtration plant in 1912.

Marcus C. Davis, PWA engineer, announced that Saturday's test showed the project "substantially complete," according to Kammeraad. Saturday was the deadline set for completion of the job by the PWA, which gave a $1,845,000 grant toward the $4,100,000 pipeline job.

Kammeraad reported the big pump at the station on the Lake Michigan shore "purred right along" and that pressure was satisfactorily maintained along the 30 mile line as the initial test was started. Lake water forced into the big line by the pump was expected to reach the filtration plant late Saturday night. The 30-mile main transmission line was two-thirds filled with water which had been pumped in for testing and sterilization purposes in recent weeks, and the pump was forcing this out of the line at the filtration plant here late Saturday afternoon at a rate of more than 500,000 gallons per hour.

When the pipeline project is completely hooked into the city's water system it will have two days normal supply of water constantly stored in reservoirs. The pumping station on the lake shore also will be able to provide 108,000,000 gallons of water every 24 hours if necessary, several times the average daily consumption over the year.

▲ *Grand Rapids Herald*, May 26, 1940, p. 1.

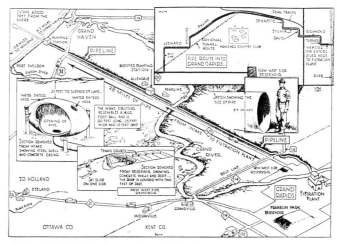

▲ Artist Kreigh Collins produced this picture map of the Lake Michigan pipeline. [*Grand Rapids Press*, January 2, 1939, p. 1.]

▲ To make the Lake Michigan water pipeline, sections of cement pipe, four feet in diameter, were produced at a central facility, hauled to the site and lowered into place. [GRPL, Photo Collection]

◄ Each pipeline segment was carefully hand sealed to insure against leaks. [GRPL, Photo Collection]

"A Date That Will Live in Infamy"

On December 7, 1941, one of the most fateful days in American history, the Japanese bombed America's naval base at Pearl Harbor, Hawaii. Though diplomatic relations with Japan had strained and then broken, no one was prepared for the shock of the devastating attack on the United States' Pacific fleet. Nineteen U.S. ships were sunk or disabled, some 150 planes were destroyed, and 2,403 soldiers, sailors, and civilians were killed.

Across the country, citizens tuned their radios to President Franklin Roosevelt's speech declaring December 7 a date that would "live in infamy." As soon as they were on the street, newspaper extras were snapped up by readers eager for any details. With these editions came the first stories of actual events at Pearl Harbor, and news of local residents suddenly thrust into war.

U.S. entry into World War II announced itself to Grand Rapidians in many ways. Radio, newspapers, word of mouth — word spread quickly. For some, like Mr. and Mrs. George E. Downs, the news was immediate. In Hawaii visiting their daughter and son-in-law, Lieutenant Colonel G.I. Hoppough, they realized the Japanese had attacked when planes flew over the house so low that the rising sun insignias were clearly visible on their fuselages. Mr. and Mrs. Downs left Hawaii as soon as transportation was available. Once back in Grand Rapids, they shared their experience with a Grand Rapids *Herald* reporter.

Drone of motors overhead, interpreted as the sound of American planes at maneuvers, was succeeded by the sound of shattering tiles as machine gun bullets struck the roof of the house. That was the first warning George E. Downs and Mrs. Downs of 1713 Division ave, SE, who have just returned from six weeks spent with their son-in-law, Lieut. Col. G.I. Hoppough of the U.S. air force, and daughter. . . .

The morning of Dec. 7 everybody was sleeping late in Honolulu, it seemed.

When the planes came overhead, Mr. Downs said, many persons got their first realization of the identity of the aircraft by looking up and seeing the rising sun insignia, which was plainly visible, so low were the planes flying. They machine-gunned Hickam field, where many officers' homes were, relentlessly. The car standing at the back of the Hoppough home was damaged by machine gun fire. Meanwhile bombs could be seen landing in the channel 200 yards away.

The noise was terrific and the whole house shook from the force of the explosions.

Chandeliers, Mrs. Downs says, fell from the ceiling or hung by a single strand of wire. . . .

While Col. Hoppough rushed away to his military duties, Mrs. Hoppough got her parents into the shattered automobile and drove them to the home of her friends in Manoa valley, some 10 miles from the harbor. The Downs remained there more than a week. At once they experienced the wartime necessity of blackouts.

Hawaiian homes were not equipped with heavy draperies to shut out light. Some people painted their windows black but in most homes the blackout was observed simply by not turning on lights at all. This meant that all meals had to be eaten during the daylight hours with sufficient margin to allow for washing the dishes afterward before night fell.

Before bedtime, families sat in utter darkness and people retired in the dark, undressing at night without light and if they arose before the tardy winter daylight, also dressing in the dark in the morning.

After their week in Manoa valley, the Downs returned to Honolulu for a short time. . . . Soon came the order that women and children from the military posts were to be evacuated. With their daughter, Mr. and Mrs. Downs embarked on a liner of army families and wounded soldiers. . . .

Leaving Hawaii on Christmas day the ships pursued a zig-zag course across the Pacific landing in San Francisco. . . .

The Downs. . .came to Grand Rapids as soon as they could get train reservations.

They speak of their experiences in Hawaii only with the utmost reluctance.

▲ *Grand Rapids Herald*, January 11, 1942, p. 3A.

▲ The *Arizona* burns in the background of this scene of destruction after the Japanese attack on Pearl Harbor. [National Archives]

Artillery Day and Night

itler's 1939 blitzkrieg of Poland ignited the war in Europe. While its Axis ally Japan marched across Asia and Mussolini's Italian troops invaded North Africa, Germany saw its armies sweep across the European landscape, occupying virtually every nation in their path.

Within days of Japan's attack on Pearl Harbor, Germany also declared war on the United States. Almost immediately, planning started for the Allied retaking of Europe sometime in the future.

While building up troops and supplies for the final European assault, the Allies drove Axis forces from North Africa and successfully campaigned up the Italian boot. Follow-

ing the invasion at Normandy on June 6, 1944, Allied forces fought across France toward Germany, while their Soviet counterparts attacked from the east. The going was tough on both fronts, with dug-in German troops contesting every acre of ground.

Some of the most vicious fighting occurred from September 1944 to February 1945 in the Hurtgen Forest, 50 square miles of dense, hilly woods on the Belgian-German border, where eight U.S. infantry and two U.S. armored divisions attempted to dislodge German soldiers from their network of concrete bunkers. Later historians questioned the Allied high command's decision to continue an assault that was pro-

ducing casualties as high as 50 percent in some rifle companies. But at the time, soldiers like Clarence Blakeslee knew only that day after day they had to battle fear, fatigue, and the elements, as well as their German foe.

Born in Grand Rapids, Blakeslee grew up in the Rockford area, and was a married 27-year-old by the time war broke out. That did not keep him from army service, and November 1944 found him in the heart of the Hurtgen fighting. Many years later, Blakeslee published his recollections in a book titled *A Personal Account of WWII by Draftee #36887149.*

When the Allies broke through the German defenses in August, the Germans withdrew behind their famous West Wall and Sigfried Line where they felt impregnable. Thousands of huge pillboxes and dragontooth tank barriers stopped the allied forces along the borders of Germany. After a month of stalemate, the 28th Infantry Division was chosen to spearhead the big attack on the Sigfried Line. The 9th Infantry had tried, but were slaughtered. The 5th Infantry Division was to support us on our left, and we did get through the Hurtgen Forest to Schmidt on the Roer River, but had to withdraw back into the forest. Our losses were described by war historians as horrific. We were told later that we had accomplished our mission in breaking through by forcing the Germans to bring all of their reserves to stop us. This gave the 1st Army the opportunity to attack and break through north of us. We were called a diversionary thrust—a decoy.

The Germans brought everything they had to stop us when we broke through — including 119 battalions of artillery. This was the most artillery ever concentrated on a single army division in the history of warfare, and I got caught in the dead center of it. We decided that our position would be too exposed to be usable and were walking along the edge

of the forest at a road intersection when I learned what the term "all hell broke loose" meant. Artillery, rockets, mortars and machine guns were all concentrating on the road intersection. I made it to the edge of the woods and started to dig in with my trench knife and canteen cup. The first two feet was fast digging, but then I ran into shale that I had to peel off a flake at a time. The shells were covering me with dirt, mud and stones; the trees around me were turning to skeletons, and I could hear men screaming. The din was constant, but even above the noise I could hear one particular battery of big shells. When the shells from the battery hit nearby, it would jar you and the concussion would make you grunt. The bad thing was hearing each volley as they came nearer to you, and you just knew the next one was going to land on you. (I promised God everything during that time.)

The shelling went on from 12 noon until 4 p.m. I had not been able to dig into the shale so most of me was above ground. I was breaking down, panting like a dog; my fingers were bloody from tearing at the shale, when I prayed for the Lord to drop the shells in the field behind me. I then prayed for forgiveness, because I knew the field behind me was full of soldiers. Finally I said, "Lord, I can't take it any longer. If you

don't stop it I am going to be a disgraceful Christian."

Just then someone hollered, "It's stopped, let's go. . . ."

There were 36,000 American men killed and wounded in and around the Hurtgen Forest. If those that were shell-shocked or with combat fatigue were added, it would have doubled that number.

◄ Clarence Blakeslee, *A Personal Account of WWII by Draftee #36887149*, pp. 24-30.

▲ The bombed area around Schlieden, Germany, looked like craters on a moonscape. [Clarence Blakeslee, *Personal Account of WWII*, frontispiece]

◄ St. Sever Calvadose was reduced to little more than rubble by August 1944. [Clarence Blakeslee, *Personal Account of WWII*, frontispiece]

"Conspicuous Gallantry and Intrepidity"

alf a world away, another
Grand Rapids soldier distinguished himself near Leyte, in
the Philippine Islands. After Pearl
Harbor, and the expulsion of U.S.
troops from the Philippines, American and Australian forces had
begun retaking the Pacific island by
island, a campaign that brought
them to Leyte in October 1944. Two
months later, the Leyte campaign
was over at a cost of 70,000

Japanese casualties and 16,000 for
the Americans.

On December 15, 1944, Private
Dirk Vlug, of the 126th Infantry,
32nd Infantry Division, who had
enlisted in Grand Rapids, awoke to
another day of the campaign to
drive Japanese forces from Leyte. He
had no way of knowing that before
the sun set, he would engage in a
hand-to-hand confrontation of such

intensity that it would make him the
only Grand Rapids enlistee to win
the Medal of Honor, the highest
combat award the nation can be-
stow. The citation that led to his
award describes an experience that
seems straight from a John Wayne
movie — except the bullets, tanks,
and Vlug's rocket launcher were
real.

◄ Private First Class
Dirk J. Vlug. [Stanley J.
Bozich, *Michigan's Own:
The Medal of Honor*,
p. 164]

Stanley J. Bozich, ►
Michigan's Own, p. 165.

**World War II
DIRK J. VLUG
Private
U.S. Army**

VLUG, DIRK J., Born Maple
Lake, Minnesota. Entered service
at Grand Rapids, Michigan.

Private First Class, U.S. Army,
126th Infantry, 32nd Infantry
Division.

Medal of Honor award: Near
Limon, Leyte, Philippine Islands,
December 15, 1944. He displayed
conspicuous gallantry and intre-
pidity above and beyond the call
of duty when an American road-
block on the Ormoc Road was
attacked by a group of enemy
tanks. He left his covered position,
and with a rocket launcher and six
rounds of ammunition, advanced
alone under intense machine gun
and 37-mm fire. Loading single-

handedly, he destroyed the first
tank, killing its occupants with a
single round. As the crew of the
second tank started to dismount
and attack him, he killed one of
the foe with his pistol, forcing the
survivors to return to their vehicle,
which he then destroyed with a
second round. Three more hostile
tanks moved up the road, so he
flanked the first and eliminated it,
and then, despite a hail of enemy
fire, pressed forward again to
destroy another. With his last
round of ammunition he struck the
remaining vehicle, causing it to
crash down a steep embankment.
Through his sustained heroism in
the face of superior forces, Private
Vlug alone destroyed five enemy
tanks and greatly facilitated
successful accomplishment of his
battalion's mission.

Kamikaze!

or sailors in the United States
Pacific fleet, no single word
aroused quite as much dread as
"kamikaze," Japanese suicide planes
loaded with explosives, piloted by
men whose only mission was to
crash into American ships, offering
their lives as the price of a direct
hit. The only chance the gunners
had to save the target vessel was to
shoot down or disable the enemy
craft before impact. If the gunners
failed, and if the pilot was accurate,
the result could be devastating.

Sam Horowitz of Grand Rapids

enlisted in the Navy in 1942, and
found himself aboard the *USS
Sigsbee*, a destroyer built in 1943. In
early 1945, Horowitz and his mates
were participating in the massive effort to invade the island of Okinawa
and drive the Japanese further back
toward their homeland. From February through April, the *Sigsbee's*
destroyer squadron had experienced
heavy aircraft fire and kamikaze attacks as it supported first the attack
and occupation of Iwo Jima and
then Okinawa.

The *Sigsbee's* luck ran out on

April 14, 1945, when a single plane
struck the vessel and inflicted serious
damage. The ship's log for that attack provides an emotionless description of the explosion that injured 78
sailors and killed three others instantly. A fourth man died later
from his wounds. Sam Horowitz suffered bruises and contusions, but
stayed with the vessel as it was
towed to Apra Harbor, Guam.

1348 Enemy planes closing formation for attack, opened fire on single engine fighter which later crashed into water after grazing USS HUNT, numerous enemy planes around formation being engaged and chased by our CAP. 1354 Enemy plane closing on starboard bow, distance 2½ miles, commenced rapid fire, made emergency ahead flank speed, left full rudder. 1355 Plane crashed aft of gun five at main deck level, heavy dull explosion occurred, considerable shrapnel in air, lost steering control, stopped all engines. Considerable casualties occurred as a result of the explosion. The following material damage was sustained; stern above 1st platform deck, except gun five, aft of frame 170 including shell plating missing, compartments below 1st platform flooded and damage undetermined, port propeller probable missing, no steering control, compartments C-262-E and C-201-L open to sea, gun 4 and 5 inoperative, bulkheads and after deckhouse dished and pierced due to shrapnel and concussion. Other material damage throughout the ship due

◄ The *USS Sigsbee* was a bombed-out hulk after the kamikaze plane hit. [Photo courtesy Sam Horowitz]

▲ Sam Horowitz (right) and a buddy. [Photo courtesy Sam Horowitz]

to concussion. 1400 CAP on station outside gun range. 1405 Commenced to jettison depth charges and torpedoes, using starboard engine to alter heading, port engine out of commission.

▲ *"U.S.S. Sigsbee* Diaries for the Period January 23 thru November 1943," p. 4.

"Have Seen a Lot of Country, Haven't I?"

Grand Rapids women were present in every theater of the war. Nurses who had been working in local hospitals were quick to join up, and students from the three local nursing schools enlisted as their classes graduated. After training at U.S. military hospitals, the nurses were sent throughout the United States, Europe, and the Pacific to serve in evacuation hospitals, recuperation facilities, and wherever else they were needed.

As she saw her nurses leave for war, M. Annie Leitch, head of the Butterworth Hospital School of Nursing, encouraged them to write to her regularly. She saved the letters she received and as the following excerpts show, her former charges saw plenty of action. Two of the first to head overseas, Laurine Smith and Frances Bacon, had their transport ship blasted out from under them in mid-Atlantic.

Later letters from Joy Shepard Hosey in Luxembourg and Virginia Miller "somewhere in Germany" describe work on a hospital train and in an evacuation hospital.

July 19, 1941

Dear Kate and all,

We were really lucky — we were only in the life boat a couple of hours. Of course it was raining and it wasn't exactly pleasant (it was so rough and I was seasick for the one and only time). Smith and I were together all the time. There were four other girls with us. One was a dope but the other three were heaps of fun and we laughed a lot even at the worst moments. There were eight marines and some of the crew (thirty-four of us in all) were with us. We were picked up by the same boat. We went into Iceland because we had four wounded with us. None of us girls were hurt at all so we were able to go right to work, or at least five of us did. The dope of course fainted. She wasn't much of an asset at any time....

We had a nice two weeks in Iceland even though we didn't have any clothes and we were restless to be on the way. We won't forget the fourth of July we spent there — it was never celebrated better by so few Americans.

We started out with a bang here

in London. In fact before we even got here we had movies taken of us arriving on British soil, so watch the newsreels. . . .

We have been to two very fancy teas with all sorts of lords and ladies present. You can imagine how we feel. Of course, they all know we are survivors and they cluck over us and call us "poor dears" and tell us how brave we are. Next week is full to the top with social activities. Wednesday we are going to Noel Coward's new play and meet him afterward. We had to pass up a chance to have coffee with Vivian Leigh yesterday because we had to go see some Red Cross business which we weren't even interested in but three of the girls went and they said she was charming and she asked about the six of us and said she would come down to the hospital to see us. The other girls have met the Queen and walked in the garden with her too. We are hoping she will send for us too, (I sent her a special message by one of those people who knows someone who knows someone telling her how anxious we were to meet her) but I hope we look more decent by the time she does. They also met the Prime Minister which we are hoping to do too.

Frances Bacon

▲ GRPL, M. Annie Leitch Collection.

◄ Laurine Smith (left) and Frances Bacon waved goodbye from the train as they left for active duty on June 8, 1941. [GRPL, M. Annie Leitch Collection]

▼ GRPL, M. Annie Leitch Collection.

February 13, 1945
Pentage, Luxembourg
Dear Miss Leitch,

As you already know, I'm working on a hospital train and will try to tell you something about it. . . .

We have 15 cars in all including officers quarters with a day room, an office car, E.M. car, kitchen and mess hall car, and ambulatory for 64 sitting patients, eight ward cars with 30 litters in each, a pharmacy car with a complete operating room and a baggage car where our two maintenance men sleep. There are four nurses, 2 doctors, one administration officer, and 33 enlisted men including wardmen, cooks and surgical technicians. It's really very complete Miss Leitch, just like a hospital on wheels. The nurses wear fatigues, boots and helmets and the only time we're exposed to skirts and stockings is when we manage to have a day or so off in Paris which is our headquarters for the present.

I have charge of two litter cars and the ambulatory patients with five wardmen that do the actual work. The nurses serve mostly in a supervising capacity and as morale builders more than anything else. Some of these poor fellows haven't seen American girls for months and months and we take quite a razzing but like it!

So far we've operated in Scotland, Wales, England, France, Belgium, Luxembourg, and made one trip to the southern part of Holland. Have seen a lot of country in one eight months overseas, haven't I?

Joy Shepard Hosey

◄ M. Annie Leitch, director of nursing at Butterworth Hospital, corresponded with military nurses from Grand Rapids throughout the war. [GRPL, M. Annie Leitch Collection]

April 12, 1945
Somewhere in Germany
Dear Miss Leitch,

I have been going to write for quite some time but just never have. Perhaps you have heard from some of the girls about a 750 bed Evacuation Hospital but if not I think some of this may interest you.

Imagine a 750 bed hospital complete with Surgery, X-ray, Central Supply, etc. all of its personnel living in tents, you know it's really an accomplishment. Then to have and take care of patients without running water, limited number of wash basins, and all of the necessities we take for granted. We had quite a time getting used to this type of nursing.

Everything is taken out of wooden boxes, then the boxes are turned into desks and cabinets to be used in that particular ward. All of our wards we attempted to standardize with desk, beds, cabinets so it will be easier whenever nurses change wards.

However it's rather difficult to keep things completely standardized as some corpsmen have more initiative and ideas than others for making desks and chairs.

Our surgery is set up in tents but we have material to cover the ceiling and wooden flooring for the OR. We have definite teams with the same surgeon, assistant, two nurses and enlisted men and these teams stay the same as much as possible. Our Pre-op and Shock tents are also connected with our Surgery by smaller connecting tents, as are X-ray and separate tent for cast application.

Virginia Miller

▲ GRPL, M. Annie Leitch Collection.

Grand Rapids Gliders Over Germany

To those engaged in the production of war matériel, southeastern Michigan became known as the "Arsenal of Democracy." Three hours to the west, Grand Rapids furniture factories struggled to find a role for themselves in war production; wood products were not in nearly as much demand as trucks, tanks, and airplanes. But securing military business was just one more challenge to Grand Rapids' furniture

company owners who through innovation and determination had brought their companies near the pinnacle of the industry, and then survived the Great Depression.

Under special wartime legislation designed to promote efficiency, 15 local companies combined to form Grand Rapids Industries, Inc., and set about finding government production contracts. Soon, they were employing an estimated 5,000 to

6,000 workers in the production of wooden gun stocks, parachutes, and a variety of wooden airplane parts. Highlight of their efforts was the CG4 glider, for which they made wings and other assemblies. The following excerpt and illustrations are taken from a booklet Grand Rapids Industries, Inc., produced describing the project.

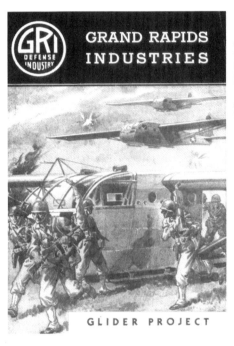

◄ Gliders were designed to deliver troops silently behind enemy lines. [GRPL, Furniture Manufacturers Association Collection]

One of the major innovations of the present world conflict has been the use of glider borne troops in battle.

The chief reason that the United Nations have been able to improve and develop this new weapon lies in the now famous CG-4A, the standard fifteen place glider of the Troop Carrier Command, which has turned out to be as sturdy a flying machine for its purpose as could be desired.

The CG-4A is so tough that it can be literally wrapped around trees or slammed into barns with little or no damage to personnel and equipment. This durability is a tribute to the workmanship which has been put into its manufacture by the finest precision woodworkers in America.

In practice maneuvers during the past months, CG-4As have been deliberately landed on lakes, in the tops of trees, thick underbrush, and tiny plowed fields

about the size of backyard victory gardens. Almost without exception the troops, safely encased in their closely knit wood and tubular steel cage, have jumped out to join the "attack" without a scratch. Sixty of these gliders can carry a whole battalion of airborne infantry with its artillery and, timed for takeoff at 30 second intervals behind their C-47 tow planes, can be put into the air from one runway in a few minutes.

The mission of gliders in war will probably always be much the same...surprise attacks on the enemy staged behind his lines and frequently at night. Glider attacks have one salient advantage over parachute attacks in that the CG-4A lands its troops in a compact package ready to attack or defend themselves as a unit, whereas paratroops land somewhat spread out and need a certain breathing spell after landing in which to organize.

With its intricate nose lifting mechanism, which allows a jeep, pack howitzer or other equipment of similar size and weight to be stowed inside in lieu of its standard load of thirteen fully outfitted troopers, its great load lifting capacity and gliding range of almost fifteen times its altitude when cut loose, the American built combat glider and its highly trained crew is a silent and formidable weapon of war. A monument to United States ingenuity and resourcefulness, it will be heard from during the great operations which are to come on battlefronts throughout the world, and its contribution to victory is assured.

▲ GRPL, "Grand Rapids Industries' Glider Project" Furniture Manufacturers Association Collection.

▲ Large gliders could carry equipment and even vehicles, as well as troops. [GRPL, Photo Collection]

We Did It!

Many of the people who worked for Grand Rapids Industries had little or no previous manufacturing experience. With young men and women in military service, factory jobs were available for anyone who was willing to work. Teenagers, housewives, and retirees came to the factories where they learned the mysteries of heavy machine tools and assembly-line production. Among those hired for factory work was Nora Lawrence who went to work for the Irwin-Pederson Arms Company making M-1 carbines.

▲ The American Aircraft Trade School prepared men and women for positions in local factories. [GRPL, Robinson Collection]

I was put in the Trigger Housing Department, on operation 17, a Milwaukee milling machine. There were about 130 operations in that department — although some operations had more than one machine and operator. The number of the operation apparently designated a specific thing we did to that 3 pound 9 ounce block of metal to make it into a trigger housing, rather than the number of machines.

We were making M-1 carbines. This gun was designed for accurate, close work in brush. It was light-weight, 3 pounds and 9 ounces complete, and could be completely taken apart, cleaned and repaired in the field by using parts of the gun itself. If you got one from a company that had made guns before the war started and, therefore, knew how to do it, you had an excellent gun. If you got one made by a company that had NOT been a gun-maker, you would be lucky not to get your head blown off. The design, however, was excellent for its purpose....

I started working there at 50 cents an hour and thought I was going to be rich!

...There were very few others working in the department when I started there — we were just getting geared up. It was heavy work — that close to the beginning of the line the pieces were still quite heavy — very few chips had been taken off. Chips were long, sharp pieces of metal that were shaved off. With bare hands, they had to be cleaned out of the chip tray. They cut my hands. I remember once I put red methiolate on all the cuts on my hands and counted just the fresh ones which hurt when I put the stuff on. That day I totalled 56 fresh cuts on my hands. They worked their way through our work shoes too. I remember sitting on the curb on Campau Square one Sunday morning about six o'clock (I'd worked all night but they had to let us go home early on Sunday because there was a state law limiting the number of hours a woman could work). Anyway, there I sat on the curb with my shoes off, taking the steel slivers out of my shoes, my socks and my feet.

The machines we had to work on were old and it was necessary on some of them (including mine) to "sling a solder hammer." This meant you had to hammer the jug securely shut. If it wasn't properly closed it would "chatter," a term everyone who has worked on machines knows. This would result in a piece which had waves across the cut surface. There was a great deal that went on in that factory which just would not be allowed nowadays but it was then. We all felt that the injuries we suffered were very minor in comparison to the possible wounds of our brothers, fathers, boyfriends and sons. We didn't really complain.

More and more people of all sorts were hired. As one of the early hires I was used to teach women how to run these machines — in addition to doing my own work. I taught many middle-aged housewives who were so unmechanical they couldn't fix a light plug. I taught my first-grade school teacher, Miss Tiffany, and failed miserably when she asked me to call her by her first name. I just couldn't do that! I remember that one of the violinists from the Grand Rapids Symphony ran a machine. I don't remember for sure but I rather think he was the Concert-Master. They were really quite careful of HIS hands....

As I think back, I am absolutely amazed at the magnitude of the task, the ineptitude of the work force which had to be used (it was all there was available) and the fact that we succeeded!!!... We became the arsenal of the free world and I do believe we surprised most other people as much as we surprised outselves.

◄ GRPL, Nora V. Lawrence Collection.

◄ Women like Clara Bush stepped into factory jobs while the men in their families served in the military. [GRPL, Robinson Collection]

Grease Goes to War

War production used up the nation's reserves of many raw materials. Before the U.S. war effort was many months old, Americans were being asked to save scrap metal and discarded paper, rubber products, and cloth rags. Even cooking fat was reusable. Under the direction of the Kent County Salvage Committee, the local scrap campaign was a huge success.

▲ Scrap drives were a regular home front activity during World War II. [GRPL, Robinson Collection]

Housewives in Grand Rapids and throughout the nation are being asked by the government to save kitchen fats to be turned into glycerine for war purposes.

The fat salvage campaign will continue throughout the war, housewives are requested to save all animal, vegetable or poultry greases in their kitchens. This must be strained through fine mesh kitchen strainers to remove all meat particles and foreign materials and placed in a coffee can or some other container.

When the housewife has collected one pound of grease, she is asked to take it to her regular meat dealer, who will pay her in defense stamps or cash for the salvaged grease. The paying price will be 5 cents a pound, subject to changes in the market. The retailer will be given 1 cent a pound for handling it.

From the retailer the grease will go to a renderer, who will use it for making soap and glycerine. Approximately 12 percent of animal and vegetable grease is composed of glycerine, needed for making dynamite and other explosives.

▲ *Grand Rapids Press,* July 6, 1942, p. 15.

With monotonous regularity reports of activities of the salvage committee of the Kent county defense council, recorded in news columns and committee files, show results beyond the quotas set — either by the local committee or by state headquarters.

It is roughly estimated that in the last year Kent county has produced more than 75,000 tons of scrap and salvage material, including waste paper, rubber, metals, kitchen fats, discarded silk and rags and other useful material.

Skeptics might wonder if goals were deliberately placed at a low level, but Lawrence F. Calahan, chairman of the salvage committee, sees another reason for the uniformly high performance.

"It's the spirit of the people," he said. "Throughout the year we've found not only the committee members, community chairmen and other regular volunteer workers enthusiastic but the general public has responded quickly to every special appeal."

First major salvage campaign undertaken in the county in the year following reorganization of the defense council and formation of the salvage committee was a drive for waste paper to relieve a critical situation facing the paper consuming industries. Gordon Bonfield of the conservation office of the paper industries co-operated in this drive which filled the yards of the mills and dealers and established a stockpile that lasted through the summer.

In response to President Roosevelt's appeal for a nationwide rubber salvage campaign, to be conducted with the aid of the petroleum, rubber and automotive industries, Kent county residents produced 1,012 tons for an average of 8 pounds per capita. This compared with the quota set by state headquarters of 5 pounds per capita and with a national collection of 3 pounds per person.

Collection of keys, a special autumn project of the Paper & Twine club on a nationwide scale, brought thousands of pounds of old nickel and bronze keys out of hiding and into the stream of critical metals flowing toward the war plants. This was carried out independent of the salvage committee.

Processed tin cans are now being collected monthly in Grand Rapids and the collection is being extended to the entire county. Figures for a typical month in which there were no special campaigns or drives were:

Iron and steel, 4,329 gross tons; nonferrous metals (copper, brass, bronze, etc.), 91 tons; wastepaper, 1,514 tons; rags, 119.5 tons.

▲ *Grand Rapids Press,* January 1, 1943, p. 27.

◄ Aluminum was one of many commodities sought for war production. [GRPL, Robinson Collection]

Lights Out!

Although they were oceans away from the nearest belligerents, Grand Rapids leaders took no chances that enemy aircraft could identify key locations at night. As in other parts of the nation, the city held scheduled blackouts.

One of the earliest "lights out" orders came in 1942 when Police Chief Frank J. O'Malley informed residents that sirens would sound at 10:57 p.m. on August 12, three minutes before the blackout would begin. For the next half hour, all city lights were to be snuffed, except those necessary to continue around-the-clock operations in plants holding war products contracts. At 11:30 sirens would once again sound, announcing the all clear.

By the day of the blackout, however, local officials decided that more time was needed, and the actual "lights out" lasted from 10 to 11:30 p.m. The next day, blackout managers reported to the *Press* that the effort was an almost total success. Only a few violators were reported, and they had been dealt with quickly.

A downtown tire and service station blazed away for most of the blackout period. Efforts of auxiliary police to get into the place failed and a telephone call to the owner brought the response that he couldn't drive down and his employee "must have forgotten to turn off the lights."

While those at the control center appreciated the owner's plight the violation was too brazen to be allowed to continue.

Chief Electrician Peter Camp of the safety department, at his station for any emergency, was ordered to the station. He cut the electric cable and fixed the wires so no other damage would result.

Manager Fred Barr of Ramona park complied with every requirement of the blackout rules — and yet kept some attractions going.

Using dark blue lights to furnish the lighting, he kept the roller skating rink in full action while the show continued in Ramona theater. No light escaped the theater.

About 10:20 p.m., however, a man sitting on the bank opposite Reeds lake struck a match to light a cigarette. As East Grand Rapids police later said: "The park was so dark one lighted match fairly illuminated the whole place." By the time an auxiliary policeman reached the scene there was no light — and the violator went unchallenged.

▲ *Grand Rapids Press,* August 13, 1942, p. 23.

▲ Michigan Bell Telephone Company employees received gas mask training in case of an air attack. [GRPL, Robinson Collection]

▲ During the blackout exercises, a medical headquarters was maintained to practice for responses in case of a real air raid. [GRPL, Robinson Collection]

An Ideal Place to Study Weather

For eight months in 1943, Grand Rapids played a unique role in the war effort. The Army Air Force's Weather Training School took over the Civic Auditorium and several downtown hotels, turning the city into a "college town" for hundreds of fledgling forecasters. The school came to Grand Rapids through the efforts of airport manager Thomas Walsh and Mayor George Welsh, who expected leasing contracts with the military to pump sorely needed dollars into the local economy.

After several months of negotiations, word came that classes would begin in January 1943. All the facilities of an army post sprang up to meet the soldiers' needs. Several downtown buildings were turned into barracks, mess halls, classrooms, and offices. The school had its own hospital, laundries, newspaper, recreation rooms, and police and fire protection. Even a musical review called "On the Beam" was produced by the soldiers and presented to the entire community. Former student Wilton G. Hawes, who returned to Grand Rapids, married a local girl, and taught at Grand Rapids Junior College, later wrote about his Weather School days.

We forecasters learned our skills by practice. Our classes used weather maps prepared from non-current data. There was a printing department on the ground floor of the Exhibitors Building which turned out United States maps about 20 by 30 inches. Every school day, each pupil received one of these maps with different data dates. Reporting stations were indicated on the map by numbers. Surrounding the one-sixteenth-inch circle marking each station were symbols for atmospheric conditions — the air pressure, temperature, humidity, mixing ratio, cloud type, wind speed and direction — as reported there. The observers were required to fit all this into a space the diameter of a dime. We students then used this data to chart weather fronts across the map.

As we Weather School students were in the military, the handling of arms was part of our training. Since weather personnel are not normally fighting men, the firearm issued us was the .45 caliber Colt automatic pistol. On a cheery May day, our class in the use of this weapon was held, of all places, on the sidewalk in front of the Civic Auditorium. As we sat along the curb, an instructor explained the pistol's parts and their function. The next step was for us to take apart and reassemble our own guns. Our rather unmar-

tial group struggled with this task and was timed on it. No doubt it could have been worse; some soldiers were required to do the job blindfolded.

For calisthenics and physical training, we marched in formation to Reservoir Hill, now Belknap Park. From Huron Street on the north side of the Pantlind Building, our route went up Monroe north to Michigan, east up the hill to Fairview, and north to the park.

Near the end of my tour of duty in Grand Rapids, word came one day that the Grand Rapids Weather School would be closed and the operation moved back to Chanute Field. The Pantlind personnel who served our food had become quite attached to us, and several of the middle-aged women actually cried to see us go.

The story of my part in the Weather School ends here, but not my interest in Grand Rapids. During that second tour of duty in the city, I had met and fallen in love with a local girl, Barbara Watson. Following my overseas duty in Ascension Island in the mid-Atlantic, we had our wedding at St. Mark's Episcopal Church, where Dean Higgins remarked that he did not at all mind marrying a Boston Congregational Yankee to one of his parishioners.

▲ Wilton G. Hawes, *Grand River Valley Review*, Vol. 19, pp. 22-28.

▲ Weather school students kept fit running up and down Belknap Hill. [GRPL, Mary A. Medendorp Collection]

▲ U.S. Army Air Force Weather School students studied local weather with the aid of instruments carried aloft by balloons. [GRPL, Mary A. Medendorp Collection]

War's End

War ended in Europe on May 8, 1945. But as one resident reminded a *Press* reporter during the subdued celebration that accompanied the announcement of the end of hostilities, "There's still a lot of fighting on the other side of the world." *Press* accounts of the local VE-Day observances make it clear that a sobering reminder of the job not done hung over the city as citizens gathered to mark the occasion.

Four months later, on August 14, 1945, when news came that Japan had surrendered, the celebration was more exuberant. This time, everyone knew that rationing, military service, scrap drives, and war industry work were over. Within a few minutes of President Truman's announcement, people began gathering downtown to share the excitement and thanksgiving. By all accounts, VJ-Day marked the largest downtown gathering Grand Rapids had ever seen. Without becoming either rowdy or violent, the party lasted into the early hours of the morning.

There was much to celebrate, but there was also the sad awareness that, according to Grand Rapids *Press* accounts, 654 men from the Grand Rapids area had died, and another 1,425 had been wounded. When prisoners of war and those missing in action were included, over 2,100 of the area's citizens had been killed, wounded, or captured. Few in the crowd celebrated the end of fighting without remembering some personal price that had been paid. A party marked the moment; memories would last for decades.

▼ A large crowd gathered in Campau Square to celebrate "VJ-Day," August 14, 1945. [GRPL, Robinson Collection]

Grand Rapids greeted official VE-day early with more prayers than cheers.

Indications were that the downtown area might see more dense crowds toward evening, but it was equally certain that thousands would flock to the city's churches in a spirit of humility and thanksgiving and with a grim appreciation of the task that lies ahead in the Pacific.

Virtually every church in the city is holding evening services, under the prearranged plans. By order of Bishop Francis J. Haas all Catholic churches in the diocese are having holy hour from 7:30 to 8:30.

Absenteeism and restiveness upset the plans of numerous war plants and some schools to continue operation. At noon, this had resulted in suspension of operation in approximately three-fifths of the factories and in all high schools. Grade schools continued in session.

"The lights go on again" tonight in Grand Rapids.

Lifting of the "brownout," in effect here several months, will take place at once, Herbert S. O'Brien, war production board manager, announced Tuesday.

During the day banners of red and gold and blue and gold, bearing the legend: "Tokio next! Buy war bonds" were placed on the street light posts along Monroe-av.

▲ *Grand Rapids Press,* May 8, 1945, p. 1.

Happy bobby-soxers and their male contemporaries set the pace for and "kept the heat on" the VE-day relaxation in the downtown section Tuesday morning. Their ranks were augmented by some of their elders as the day progressed.

Workers' cars with horns blasting had created a traffic jam on lower Monroe-av. by 8:30.

First of the cheering, dancing youngsters to appear apparently had cut classes, but before the morning was far along their numbers had been swelled by high school students who had belatedly yielded to the celebration urge or had been officially dismissed.

Crowds grew as offices, public and private, suspended work and as factory employees made their way to the downtown section after their plants had closed, but at no time did the celebration begin to approach the Armistice day hilarity of 1918.

Unseen, of course, but there — just as surely as the flags and the shredded paper floating down from office buildings — was the grim knowledge that VJ-day is still a long, hard way ahead and that many of "the boys" in Europe will have to come home by way of Japan.

▲ *Grand Rapids Press,* May 8, 1945, p. 7.

Jubilation over the end of the war was marked here Tuesday night by the greatest outpouring of citizens to Monroe-av. in the city's history. The celebration continued far into the night. The fact that the surrender of Japan had been delayed several days and that the news had been "brewing" for many hours detracted not one whit from the pandemonium.

Police estimated 50,000 persons stormed the downtown section — not all at one time but in a continuous stream.

A few minutes after President Truman's announcement of the war's end, crowds started to swarm onto Monroe-av. from all directions. First, of course, came the automobiles with blaring horns, deliberate backfires and screeching brakes. For the first time in years, four-lane driving was necessary on Monroe-av.

Within 30 minutes pedestrians started to "take over." Thousands within walking distance reached the main thoroughfare first. Then came cars from the outlying areas to discharge their hordes into the throng. Hundreds of cars dragged cans loaded with stones. Many of the vehicles were draped in paper bunting.

At 7:10 — 70 minutes after the official peace announcement — regular police, aided by 350 specially-trained auxiliary officers, succeeded in clearing Campau square of all motor vehicles so that the downtown district could be turned over to the exuberant throngs afoot.

In less than half an hour after the first announcement police had placed traffic barricades to control and divert traffic. All these measures had been planned in advance by Police Chief Frank J. O'Malley and his assistants. Because of the imminence of the surrender news over a period of several days, O'Malley had had little sleep for four nights. He paid tribute to his hard-worked department members and to the fine service of the auxiliaries.

Because the news came an hour after usual closing time for offices and big stores, there was little paper-tossing from windows of the larger buildings, but other expressions of wild excitement were many — tin horns, flags, firecrackers, whistles, bells, shouts, dishpans, drums and at least one toy cannon. Some persons even used spoons and pans to add to the clatter. Merchants who had anticipated an early end of the war sold out quickly on stocks of flags and horns.

There was a reverent note to the celebration, too. Thousands went quietly and humbly to churches. In the earlier phase of the celebration bells and chimes of downtown churches rang out above the din.

◄ *Grand Rapids Press*, August 15, 1945, p. 1.

◄ Many sought the quiet reflection of a church sanctuary when they heard the news that the war was over. [GRPL, Robinson Collection]

CHAPTER 8

Postwar Changes

For a brief time, as it celebrated the end of World War II, Grand Rapids was unified as never before. Distinctions of class, race, culture, and geography were forgotten as residents shared the joy that followed victory and savored the knowledge that the troops were coming home. Adding to the excitement were announcements from Washington that rationing of scarce products would be lifted and production of peacetime goods would commence as soon as possible. Now that peace had come to the nation, prosperity seemed just around the corner.

For returning veterans and civilians alike, the first order of business was resuming the domestic lives that had been postponed for the duration of the war. When all hostilities finally ceased in August 1945, those who served on the battlefields and those who had labored on the home front looked forward with a mixture of exhilaration and exhaustion to a future in which marriage and children, home purchases, job promotions, and family vacations provided all the excitement they desired.

The austerity imposed by a decade and a half of depression and war was finally coming to an end, and with savings in hand from defense jobs, many consumers were poised for a spending binge. At the same time, depression and war had also forced businesses and city government to postpone needed changes and improvements. Now, community leaders looked forward to new construction and renovation financed by the revenues that prosperity would bring.

A Battle Plan for Postwar Prosperity

Even before the war was over, Grand Rapids area business and government leaders began planning for the postwar years. Thousands of young GIs hungry for jobs would soon be coming home, and city officials knew they had to be ready for a rapid transition back to a peacetime economy. Grand Rapids was geared up for war production, but government orders would stop the minute the surrender was signed. Once the war ended, new jobs would have to be created — quickly.

Unable to compete with lower labor costs and cheaper raw materials, Grand Rapids had relinquished its claim as the "Furniture Capital" to southern manufacturers, and local leaders knew that, the southerners would continue to strengthen their hold. In 1944, a University of Michigan study done for the Chamber of Commerce suggested that Grand Rapids would create as many as 19,000 new jobs by 1950, and nearly all of them would come from outside the furniture industry.

To meet the challenges of the postwar era, local leaders were working to build a highly diversified economy. Determined never again to be dependent on a single industry, they looked to the area's 3,600 non-furniture businesses to provide 17,000 of the 19,000 new jobs, and they aggressively recruited other businesses to provide additional employment. The result of their efforts was not only a successful transition to a peacetime economy, but the foundation for a diverse economic base to fuel economic growth through the remainder of the 20th century.

Grand Rapids business and industry leaders estimate there will be industrial jobs for nearly 9,000 more local workers than are now employed within 18 months after the end of the war against Germany and Japan [and 19,000 new jobs by 1950] — enough to "take care of our own" but not offering employment for any influx of large numbers of workers from other cities.

The jobs are in sight for returning war veterans, civilians employed in local war plants, and local men now employed elsewhere.

New industries located here since 1940 and contemplated new industrial products figure importantly in this prediction. . . .

It is based on a survey of 405 plants, representing more than 95 per cent of the total industrial employment in the Grand Rapids area, by the international division of the CED, followed by a resurvey made by a representative of the University of Michigan's business research bureau which confirmed the findings of the local groups.

The report states there may be a temporary drop in employment immediately following the war in the period required for reconversion of local plant facilities from production of war materials to manufacture of civilian goods after all war contracts have been canceled and the jobs they created eliminated.

It is stressed that the forecasts are based on expected cooperation by the federal government in a program which will make the period of reconversion a relatively

short one. This includes prompt settlement of canceled contracts, removal of government controls on prices, wages, and commodity distribution and modification of the present tax structure. . . .

Estimated increases would come on top of an increase of 9,809 industrial jobs here since 1940, according to the report. Increases in the four-year period include 9,444 metal workers, 186 wood workers and 179 employed in diversified industries.

Half the increase in metal working employment comes from the presence of concerns which have been located in Grand Rapids since 1940 through efforts of the Chamber of Commerce, it is pointed out. These concerns plan both to continue and to expand their local postwar employment estimates and the expansion plans of a few prewar Grand Rapids plants accounts for the entire indicated postwar metal working employment increase of

approximately 3,000 over the June, 1944, level.

Prospective postwar increase for the woodworking industry is 1,966 and for the diversified group, 3,458.

◄ *Grand Rapids Press*, September 2, 1944, p. 1.

◄ Job announcements often offered special consideration for veterans. [*Grand Rapids Press*, November 3, 1945, p. 5]

▲ This counseling center operated by the Chamber of Commerce helped returning veterans find work. [GRPL, Robinson Collection]

▲ Hot metal casting at Michigan Wheel Company. Most of Grand Rapids' wartime jobs had come in heavy metal industries, but postwar growth was more diversified. [GRPL, Robinson Collection]

"Look Mom, No Cavities!"

On August 2, 1944, while American forces still battled in Europe and the Pacific, a nine-word telegram from Dr. William Dekleine, commissioner of the Michigan Department of Public Health, to Dr. H. Trendley Dean of the International Institute of Health marked the beginning of one of the 20th century's quietest but most successful battles for better public health. The telegram's wording was simple — "Grand Rapids City Commission voted to approve Fluorine Study" — but its impact on the dental health of millions of children was worth volumes.

Youthful tooth decay had long concerned dentists and public health officials, but until they discovered a much lower incidence of dental caries (cavities) in areas with naturally fluoridated water, the problem defied solution. Now, in 1944, Grand Rapids had agreed to an experiment to see if fluoride added to the city's drinking water would reduce tooth decay among children.

Nearly six months after the initial telegram, a short note from W.L. Harris, chief chemist of the city, announced the experiment was underway. "Sodium fluoride application to the local water supply started 4:00 p.m., Thursday, January 24," he wrote, "a total of 107 barrels, each holding 375 lbs. of fluoride was received in [railroad] car PRR 35981 on the morning of the above date."

Before the water was fluoridated, 32,000 city school children, plus a control group of 8,000 children from Muskegon and 8,000 children from Aurora, Illinois, were given complete dental examinations. Thereafter, the children were examined once a year to determine if the fluoride was having an impact. The results were dramatic. After eight years Grand Rapids children showed reductions of 50 percent to 70 percent in their tooth decay rate, while rates for children in the other cities remained constant. Impressed by the results, Muskegon officials insisted that the ten-year experiment be stopped after six years so that they too could begin fluoridating their water supply. The following interview with W.L. Harris tells how Grand Rapids was selected for the experiment.

The Rockwell Water ► Journal, January, 1957, pp. 4-5.

The actual introduction of a fluoride compound into the water started January 25, 1945; but there was a lot of study previous to that. If you want to go back to the point where it was actually decided to investigate a pilot study on fluoridation, you'd have to go back to about 1941....

We were the first to add a fluoride compound to a municipal water supply. There were two others that started that same year, but some months later.

Dr. Trendley Dean of the United States Public Health Service talked before the American Water Works Association National Convention in the early forties. He outlined the problem that the dental profession had in regard to tooth decay, using as his example the fact that more men were rejected for the army in the early part of World War II because of dental defects than for any other disease.

From there he went on to point out that in the Chicago suburban area a study had been set up to show that in communities using well waters containing the right amount of fluoride, tooth decay was greatly reduced over that of neighboring communities using Lake Michigan water supplied by Chicago. He then went on to say that perhaps the time had come to institute a pilot study where a carefully controlled amount of fluoride was added to a municipal water supply and the results precisely recorded over a ten-year period....

The fact that so much work had been done previously on Lake Michigan water made them very much interested in some community using Lake Michigan water....

Grand Rapids was fortunate in that we started the program before there was any gathering of opposition forces. We were supported right from the start by the public press and civic organizations....

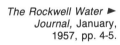

◄ W.L. Harris (right) and two unidentified men look on as Grand Rapids Water Department worker Jerry Gunther adds fluoride to the city's water supply. [Grand Rapids Archives and Records Center]

▲ W.L. Harris checking fluoride levels in the water filtration plant testing laboratory. [Grand Rapids Archives and Records Center]

A Monument to the Thrifty Dutch

In the 1950s, the popular stereotype of Grand Rapids as a city of conservative Dutch furniture workers was repeated regularly. When the *Holiday* magazine writer John Tebbel came to town in 1952, he too fell victim to that widespread perception of Grand Rapids. Taking as his theme the traditional Dutch values that he believed defined the city's history, Tebbel compared them to the values of a postwar generation that was already moving to the suburbs, where lifestyles were less constricted by tradition and religion.

Tebbel sought to counter the idea that Grand Rapids was a sleepy backwater by showing that those things for which the city was criticized were in fact its greatest strengths. In so doing, he mistakenly perpetuated popular stereotypes about the dominance of the Dutch population and the furniture industry, while overlooking the city's increasing racial, cultural, and economic diversity.

▲ Though leadership was passing to a new generation, Grand Rapids' older generation of "thrifty Dutch" still set the standard by which the city was known. [GRPL, Robinson Collection]

▲ Calvin College students offered older citizens reassurance that Grand Rapids' post-World War II generation was not likely to abandon the values of its elders. [GRPL, Robinson Collection]

The Dutch.

In those two words is the key to the city's personality. Originally The Dutch made Grand Rapids a solid, ultraconservative city laid out on the strictest moral lines, an island of Old World culture and resistance to change. Today, though their way of life is changing, slowly, stubbornly yielding to a world they never made, their influence is still felt.

To understand The Dutch, to understand Grand Rapids, to understand the conflict between old and new and the changing scene which is the city today, you have to know Willem...he stands here for the Average Dutch Man in the street.

Willem's family has been in America for a century, but time has done little to change his physical type. He is inclined to have a broad face, a square, sturdy build and light hair. His wife is likely to be short and plump. Together they have helped populate Grand Rapids with some of the best-looking blondes to be found in the United States. In the last two or three decades, marriage has diffused this type, as sons and daughters have gone outside the once closely-knit Dutch hegemony to establish homes. But the Dutch and their descendants still make up roughly a quarter of Grand Rapids' population, far outnumbering the Germans, Lithuanians, Poles and Irish who comprise most of the remainder, and wielding a social and civic influence well above their numerical strength.

Willem's people are clean, hardworking and clannish. As merchants, they are utterly honest, and utterly devoted to the dollar and its uses. As citizens, they believe that the manners and customs their forebears brought to America will never be improved on by man, least of all by non-Hollander man....

Sunday in Grand Rapids is a potent reminder of how successfully the Dutch have resisted change. Grand Rapids has some two hundred churches of all denomination, but the most powerful religious force is the Reformed Church, in its half-dozen incarnations: Christian Reformed, Dutch Reformed, Holland Reformed, Holland Christian, True Reformed and simply Reformed.

This church is responsible for much of Grand Rapids' high moral character. Its members do not believe in going to movies, card-playing, dancing, drinking or smoking....

The children of Willem and his neighbors show signs of withdrawing from the old strict ways. These youngsters have joined young newcomers in the new developments that have sprung up around the fringes of the community....

There are some gloomy observers who believe that old Willem and his children will quarrel each other into a state of civic desuetude. Actually, the two generations should be able to work out the future of their city without overmuch treading on each other's toes.

"We're a conservative town," Old Willem says, "People here like their homes and churches. No matter what happens you don't change things like that."

▲ *Holiday,* February, 1952, pp. 97, 102, 106-9.

Los Hispanos

Grand Rapids' Hispanic population traces its local roots to the earliest years of the 20th century when several young men of Mexican descent decided to stay on after spending a summer working for area vegetable farmers. The Great Depression slowed migration during the 1930s, but by 1940 an estimated six to ten families had moved to Grand Rapids, and as many as 100 more families arrived during World War II. In the years immediately following the war, the availability of industrial jobs and the recruiting efforts of factory owners in need of workers continued to attract Hispanic newcomers, swelling the ranks to what was conservatively estimated at more than 200 families. Most of the early arrivals were Mexican-Americans, although Cubans, Puerto Ricans, and South American nationals have also been part of the migrant stream.

As Dutch, Polish, German, and other groups had done before them, Hispanic families clustered together at first in the same neighborhood, turning to more established families and institutions such as the Catholic Church for assistance in finding homes and work. They also formed clubs and societies for recreation and social activities. Many began their life in Grand Rapids by settling around Grandville Avenue and vicinity, but as their circumstances permitted, they followed the resettlement pattern of other immigrant groups, diffusing throughout the city as their financial situations improved.

Like other immigrants before them, Grand Rapids Hispanics have established a newspaper so they can read of local and national events in their native language. *El Hispano* also prints interviews with pioneer residents who remind more recent arrivals of the growth of Grand Rapids' Hispanic community and the experiences common to all immigrants, no matter what their country of origin.

In 1941 Daniel and Guadalupe Vargas left Texas to visit Guadalupe's sister who was living in Wisconsin. She encouraged them to get to know Grand Rapids because it was a good place to look for work and to settle down.

"We stayed because we liked it," says Dona Guadalupe, explaining the couple's reasons for coming to visit the city and deciding to stay.

Daniel agrees with his wife. Immediately after arriving he began to look for work. The first job he found wasn't the best, but at least it met their needs. The job was shoveling snow.

The following year Daniel got a better paying job where he cleaned thousands of bricks from the demolition of a west Grand Rapids business. . . . [Later, he found a permanent job with the American Seating Company.]

Meanwhile, his wife, Guadalupe, did domestic work in the home of wealthy people. She was paid 40 cents an hour plus an additional 25 cents for bus fare.

The Vargas' life is characterized by cooperation with their compatriots and other Hispanic immigrants who were arriving in Grand Rapids during those early years. . . .

As a volunteer for the city's Office of Human Relations, Daniel assisted other Spanish speaking people. He helped those who arrived in Grand Rapids without a place to live, search for housing and helped others with driver's license exams. . . . Vargas [also] gave Spanish classes to Mexicans who neither knew English nor were literate in their native language. . . .

Only one time was he denied certain rights of economic and social progress. That was when he went to work for the railroad. He wanted to be trained as a mechanic, but the workers' union of the company opposed his training.

Now Vargas is retired. He lives with Guadalupe in an apartment replete with awards, plaques, and other trophies of recognition for their long years of community service.

◄ *El Hispano,* March 30, 1991, p. 9.

◄ Daniel Vargas helped many Hispanics settle in Grand Rapids. [Photo by © *Grand Rapids Press,* July 28, 1986, p. A4]

▼ Mike and Isabel Navarro, successful owners of the El Matador Tortilla Factory, came to Grand Rapids in 1948. [Photo by © *Grand Rapids Press,* July 28, 1986, p. A4]

Paco Sanchez didn't have the least idea in the world where a place called Grand Rapids was in May of 1950. He encountered it for the first time in a New York employment office, where he went to look for work.

He came [to Grand Rapids] as a cook for a crew of agricultural laborers who were harvesting cherries, onions, apples, and other crops in the area of what is now Wyoming and Standale. He started at $2.79 an hour for his work.

...Sanchez immediately arranged to bring his relatives and friends....This is how his brother-in-law, Leopold Figueroa, arrived in Grand Rapids in 1951....

Figueroa found a good job that assured him a level of savings simply unimaginable for him at the time. When he left Puerto Rico he was earning 25 cents an hour as a construction laborer. In Grand Rapids he started at $1.18 for the same work.

The significant increase in his savings permitted him to send for his wife, Guadalupe, and his three children in relatively little time....

The Mexicans were well established in the city, organizing two baseball teams that played teams later formed by the Puerto Ricans....

Sanchez remembers "as if it were yesterday" when in 1951 he got a job with the railroad company cleaning snow and ice from the tracks in order to keep them from freezing.

That same year he quit the railroad to start at Michigan Bakery, "where the only person of color was me." [said Sanchez] Later, he was able to recommend other Puerto Ricans, Mexicans, and even Chinese for employment in the cleaning department which he had charge of for [several] years.

As does Figueroa, Sanchez recognizes that the Mexicans came first,...[and] that it was the Mexicans who gave them a place to stay when he arrived in Grand Rapids. He specifically mentioned the Chavez family, in whose home he stayed for a good length of time until he could establish himself with his family who came later from Puerto Rico.

▲ *El Hispano,* March 15, 1991, p. 8.

◄ Francisco Vega became a successful businessman and served with numerous community organizations after his arrival in 1946. [Photo by © *Grand Rapids Press,* July 28, 1986, p. A4]

◄ Activist Martin Morales became the city's first Hispanic mayoral candidate in 1991. [Photo by © *Grand Rapids Press,* July 27, 1986, p. E1]

▲ Zoraida Sanchez, director of Latin American Services, shares a happy moment with Puerto Rican senior citizens Anjelita DeLeon and Rafaela Lopez in this 1986 photo. [Photo by © *Grand Rapids Press,* July 29, 1986, p. A7]

War in Korea

In the early years of the Cold War between the United States and the Soviet Union, home-front preparation for response against air attacks was accompanied by a foreign policy designed to contain the expansion of Communism. That policy was put to the test in 1950 when, on June 25, North Korean Communist forces launched a full-scale attack across the 38th Parallel into non-Communist South Korea. The attack was condemned by the United Nations Security Council, which called for member nations to provide troops to help repel the Communist advance.

Troops from 16 nations were in Korea by 1951, with nearly half coming from the United States. Reserve troops and National Guard units from throughout the United States were called to active duty. Led by 200 Grand Rapids Marine Reservists who were called up in late July, local men who thought they had seen their last combat suddenly found themselves headed back to war.

For the next three years, local soldiers were in the thick of the fray, serving with honor and distinction. Pvt. Robert B. Dickson, whose Second Cavalry Division was rushed to Korea from Japan following the invasion, was the first local soldier to be wounded in action, struck by a hand grenade on July 21, after only four days in Korea. Later, on August 24, he was interviewed by a Grand Rapids *Press* reporter at Great Lakes Naval Training Station Hospital where his right arm had been amputated. His comments reflected the attitude of most Americans as they once again faced the prospect of involvement in a foreign war. "The American troops aren't worried and morale is high," he said. "We're just over there fighting the Reds so we won't have to fight them over here."

By the time the war ended on July 27, 1953, 3,181 Kent County men had enlisted, and another 2,918 had been drafted. Of the 33,629 American deaths in the war, 40 were local soldiers.

There was small talk over the breakfast tables in the homes of more than 100 Grand Rapids Marine Reservists, Friday, but as soon as the men put down their empty coffee cups, they began packing, and even infant members of the families knew without being told, this day was different from any other.

Called to active duty a few weeks ago, the Marines had been spending the days at the Naval Reserve Armory training and getting their equipment ready. Nights at home, they had tried to keep conversation away from Friday, Aug. 25, their personal D-day, which came just two months after the Communists invaded Southern Korea.

After packing, the next-to-the-last goodbyes were said at home, and the Marines reported to the Naval Armory in fatigue uniforms, because there was a long train ride ahead of them.

After last-minute orders and briefing, they filed into buses which took them to Union Station where the real goodbyes were said to mothers and fathers, wives and children and other relatives waiting to wave as the special sleeper cars moved slowly out of the station.

Maj. C.J. Tydzewski, Commander of the unit, said the morale of his men was "very good." It was helped by a recent report of an impending increase in pay for dependents, about whom many privates and corporals had worried. Some of them were leaving homes unpaid for, and several children to be supported on low salaries.

But right then — when the train pulled out at 5:45 p.m. — nobody was thinking about how much money the Marines would be making. And although there were smiles and jokes, nobody said very much because there was a lump in the throat of almost everyone at the station.

▲ *Grand Rapids Herald,* August 26, 1950, p. 9.

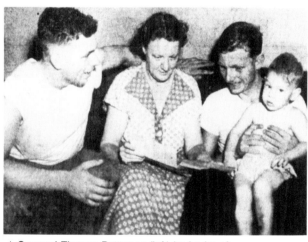

▲ Corporal Thomas Patterson (left) had a lot of catching up to do with his mother and brothers when he returned to Grand Rapids in August 1953, after 32 months as a prisoner of war. [Photo by © *Grand Rapids Press,* August 31, 1953, p. 1]

◄ Fr. Edward L. Eardley, chaplain at St. John's Home, left behind the city's largest family when he reported for Korean War duty. [GRPL, Robinson Collection]

Not One of the Boys

At its first session in January 1961, after 110 years of sameness, the Grand Rapids City Commission took on a new look. Evangeline Lamberts, a community activist and organizer who had helped elect other commissioners, used her skills to win election to a seat on the commission for herself. Although women had served on the school board as early as 1888, and women had been eligible to vote and hold office in Michigan since 1918, Lamberts was the city's first elected woman office holder.

No stranger to politics, Lamberts had gained recent prominence for her part in the successful effort to reform practices at the Kent County Juvenile Home. The reorganization of the juvenile court and juvenile home that ensued helped to establish an entirely new facility by 1966.

Lamberts built a strong community support base and was a force to be reckoned with during her two terms on the commission. After taking her seat, she organized a 4-3 commission majority that challenged many of the actions of Mayor Stanley Davis. Her successful tenure laid a strong foundation for several women commissioners who have followed.

▲ Robert Blandford served several terms as city commissioner before losing his seat to Evangeline Lamberts. [GRPL, News Photograph Collection]

▲ Stanley Davis was mayor when Lamberts took her seat on the city commission. [GRPL, Delbert W. Blumenshine Collection]

A group of men asked me if I would run for the city commission, which I hadn't even thought about. They wanted someone to [run against] Bob Blandford. He had served three terms.... They said you do it and we will get the money and we will help you. So I did....

The campaign was sort of interesting. I don't know why I won when I think about it, 1961 was before women's lib. What the real issues were at the time is not what gave me the problem. It was what went on underneath.

Because of the census, Grand Rapids had increased in population and there were a significant number of liquor licenses that were available, and that was an item. At first the rumor was that if elected, I intended to see that the Polish clubs in the second ward would be closed. So one of my supporters was Polish, and he said, "Vangie, here's what we're going to do. I'm going to take you over to the Polish clubs; we'll go over there at noon. No one is going to be there but the bartender. So we will go in and I'll order a beer and you order a coke, and we'll chat with the bartender, and everybody in the Polish club will hear about it, and I'll give him a nice tip." And that's what took care of that rumor....

Poor Bob, since I was the first woman to ever try this, he didn't know quite how to proceed. We would appear together at meetings and he would say something like "my opponent is a very nice lady. She has a very nice husband and family, but...but...."

My thinking was first to not say anything, but then it became so annoying that I finally answered him and I said, "My supporters have a slogan, 'Don't send a boy to do a man's job, send a woman, you'll get the job done.'"

That was the last damning with faint praise I got.

We had a little trouble getting [newspaper] space....

So what we did was once a week, we would engage a room at the YMCA and my supporters, maybe five, maybe ten of them would go down there and listen to me give a speech..., and they would print it.

That's what I had to do to get publicity.

So I got elected....

They had a lot of chit-chat about what I should be called. Bunny [Commissioner Bernard S.] Barto, said to me, "Well, Vangie, now you're just one of the boys."

I said, "Not on your life, buster."

▲ Interview with Evangeline Lamberts, August 13, 1991.

ELECT

Mrs. Austin Lamberts

SECOND WARD COMMISSIONER

*A progressive, open-minded community worker
Her positive un-biased attitude is needed!*

◄ Evangeline Lamberts became Grand Rapids' first woman city commissioner when she defeated Robert Blandford in 1961. [GRPL, Evangeline Lamberts Collection]

City Growth by Annexation

Much of the land available for new homes lay outside the city limits, but that posed little hindrance either to builders or home buyers. In some cases, developers sought annexation to the city in order to secure utilities and streets; in other instances, they provided wells and septic tanks, lobbied for improved township and county roads, and kept their communities independent of the city. Whatever the chosen alternative, so long as there were buyers, construction went on.

As Grand Rapids leaders watched the suburbs grow at the expense of the central city, they resorted to a time-honored method of preserving the city's tax base — they began annexing adjacent areas. A rush of annexations in the later 1950s and early 1960s expanded the city's total area from 23.5 square miles, the same as it was in the late 1920s, to 44 square miles.

This growth might have continued even longer, and drastically altered the shape of modern Grand Rapids, had not a Michigan Supreme Court decision changed the annexation rules. Existing law based annexation decisions on a vote of the annexing city and the voters in the area to be annexed. That law was put to the test in 1963 when Grand Rapids sought to annex the Kent County Airport property that had become available for industrial development now that the airport was moving to a new site. The city of Wyoming also bordered the annexed area and claimed that it, too, had an interest in the property and should have been part of the vote. The court ruled that the municipality that stood to lose land also had a voice. If it said no, the annexation failed.

The state court's ruling that Grand Rapids had to return the airport property brought the era of annexations to an end. But the previous successful annexations had provided Grand Rapids with abundant property for industrial, commercial, and residential development.

Grand Rapids' greatest growth in 35 years becomes official Saturday morning as its long struggle to expand its boundaries comes to fruition.

The historic moment for this 100-year-old Michigan metropolis is 12:01 Saturday when vast suburban areas of Grand Rapids and Walker townships — including 13.72 square miles and 19,880 new citizens — join the city as a result of annexations Aug. 2 and Nov. 8.

The transition for the biggest annexation since 1925 will be smooth, say city officials.

The last major annexation in Grand Rapids was on Nov. 23, 1925, when the so-called Alger Park district between Division and Kalamazoo avs. and Twenty-eighth and Burton sts., SE, joined the city.

There were subsequent annexations of sizeable areas in the Second and Third wards on April 4, 1927, and in the First ward on June 7, 1926.

Takeover of fire facilities in Grand Rapids township started Friday morning and agreements to provide uninterrupted fire protection for Walker areas have been approved by Walker and city officials.

Street maintenance — specifically snow and ice removal — also is assured because of agreements to provide this service between the city and Kent county road commission until next October. The road commission filed notice with the city commission Thursday it is relinquishing legal control of Grand Rapids township streets, alleys and highways effective Jan. 1.

Police cruiser service in newly-annexed areas starts Saturday morning, City Manager Rypstra announced.

Garbage pickup also will start in new areas immediately.

Pamphlets explaining city services and listing emergency telephone numbers were distributed within the last two weeks to residences of the areas as well.

▲ *Grand Rapids Press*, December 30, 1960, p. 17.

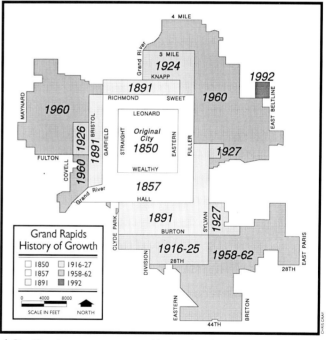

▲ Significant new areas were added to the city of Grand Rapids in the late 1950s and early 1960s.

◄ *Grand Rapids Press*, December 30, 1960, p. 17.

City Mushrooms

Here's how Grand Rapids looks statistically as a result of annexations in 1960:

Population: 197,193

Area: 38.02 square miles.

Size: Second largest in Michigan. Sixty-second largest in the United States.

State Equalized Valuation: $626,000,000 (estimated).

1960 Tax Rate (total): $41.06 per $1,000 of assessed valuation.

Street Millage: 585.

Voter Precincts: 123

Registered Voters: 100,823 (estimated).

Refuge From the Ravages of War

War's end left a totally disrupted Europe in its wake. Families everywhere had lost loved ones and had seen their homes, businesses, and communities devastated. Displaced persons were gathered in camps all across Europe. Many lacked the means to return home, and others, particularly Eastern Europeans, were denied the opportunity because their countries were now in the hands of Communist governments. The United States offered refuge to multitudes of those displaced by war.

With the help of newly elected Congressman Gerald R. Ford and other members of the West Michigan delegation, many Latvians, Lithuanians, and Estonians who had seen their countries swallowed up by the Soviet Union made their way to Grand Rapids. Local families, churches, and social agencies worked hard to find housing and jobs for the hundreds of new arrivals who asked nothing more than a chance to put the war behind them and start over. The recent arrivals often took menial jobs, but through hard work, careful saving, and self-help organizations, they were soon able to purchase their own homes and establish comfortable and secure lives. Grateful for their welcome, Latvian leaders issued a public "thank you" to the people of Grand Rapids.

"Our Prayers Answered."

After years of despair and tragedy, the forceful splitting of families and the tragic despair of an aimless existence in exile our prayers have been answered by you good citizens who have devoted so much time, energy and thought to extending a helping hand.

To the Grand Rapids - Kent Council of Churches' Aid to Displaced Persons corporation which, through its president, J.H. Roeper, has done so much and is doing so much in this behalf and to all citizens of this community we extend our undying thanks. Such thoughtfulness and generosity in assisting and giving us the opportunity to begin a new life seems like a dream and creates a great ray of hope for our many unfortunate brothers who still live in fear and despair in the displaced persons camps of Europe.

Being on the threshold of a new year we Latvians now settled in your community are lifting our grateful hearts to Almighty God and praying that every blessing may fall upon you and yours and that we will prove to you our gratefulness and that we shall humbly be worthy of becoming citizens of your country.

Sincerely and in behalf of the Latvians in Grand Rapids and Kent county,

    Victor Purins,
    Ernest Petersons,
    Artur Gregors.

▲ *Grand Rapids Press,* January 3, 1950, p. 4.

◄ Grand Rapids' Latvian immigrants gathered in 1951 to celebrate the purchase of their Latvian Association Hall, where they would study and teach their Latvian language and culture to their children. [GRPL, Lucia Erins Latvian Collection]

▲ Latvians spent years in displaced persons camps, like Camp Valka in Germany, before being allowed to emigrate to the United States. [GRPL, Lucia Erins Latvian Collection]

A Home to Call Their Own

Single-family home construction reached an all-time high in Grand Rapids in the years immediately after World War II. Young couples who had seen their plans of home and family postponed by half a decade wasted no time securing the home of their dreams. No matter if it stood on a stark lot devoid of grass or landscaping, or that access roads were little more than dirt trails. As modest as the dwelling was, it was a place to be called home.

Building materials were scarce in the early postwar years. In order to meet the housing demand, builders resorted to "prefab," or "factory-built" structures that had a look-alike, cookie-cutter sameness dictated by mass-production techniques copied from the automobile industry. Pieces were cut to order in lumber yards, packaged, and delivered to the housing site where a waiting crew had prepared the foundation and was ready to assemble the structure. Over and over the process repeated itself wherever open land was available in areas served by sewer and water utilities. Spurred on by federal mortgage guarantees to veterans, banks and savings and loan institutions approved loans in record-breaking time. Several hundred unit-housing developments sprang up in a short time within the city and in the surrounding area.

To date in this postwar period, efforts to meet the nation's housing needs have manifested themselves primarily in a splurge of new one-family homes. . . .

Long-term records compiled by the national bureau of economic research and the bureau of labor statistics show that seven out of every eight nonfarm dwelling units built from 1945 through 1947 were one-family homes. . . .

Numerically, more single family homes were built last year and the year before than in any other year for which records are available.

In contrast, the number of multi-family dwelling units constructed since 1945 represents less than one out of every ten nonfarm dwelling units built in the postwar period, an abnormally low proportion, the institute reported.

The city issued 6,286 building permits with a valuation of $12,408,505 in the period from July 1, 1947, to July 1, 1948, Building Inspector Ralph E. Seger reported Friday.

Of that amount $5,087,950 was for 813 permits issued for new one-family houses, while valuations totaling approximately $1,300,000 were set on permits for 66 factory additions and 11 new factories in the same period.

Multiple housing to ease the housing shortage was a black mark on the record, however. Seger reports no permit was issued for a house containing three or more dwelling units and only 11 permits were issued for two-family houses.

◄ *Grand Rapids Press*, August 14, 1948, p. 9.

▲ Veterans were often given preferential treatment when they sought home mortgage loans. [*Grand Rapids Press*, April 13, 1946, p. 3]

◄ Small, affordable homes that could be built quickly to serve veterans' housing needs sprang up all around Grand Rapids immediately after World War II. [GRPL, Albert Collection]

All's Not Quiet on the Home Front

By the 1940s, many Grand Rapids residents were growing tired of the manner in which local politics were conducted. Party boss Frank McKay had secured a tight grip on both local and state Republican politics in the late 1920s, and continued to hold on for most of the next two decades. From his position as state treasurer, McKay was regularly accused of involvement in all manner of corruption including kickbacks on state contracts and selling overpriced, shoddy merchandise to state agencies. McKay was never convicted because key witnesses had a way of changing their minds, or moving out of state, before the cases came to trial.

Finally, in 1944, a group of local reformers known as the Home Front began calling for change. Headed by dentist W.B. VerMuelen; businessmen Stanton Todd, Ekdal Buys, Edsko Hekman, John D. Hibbard, and Paul Goebel; Irving Pennington, chairman of the Kent County Board of Supervisors; and attorneys Fred Searl, Fred Wetmore, and Gerald Ford, the Home Front wrested control of the local Republican party from McKay. As part of its reform effort, the group also succeeded in unseating longtime Fifth Congressional District incumbent Bartel Jonkman and securing the 1948 nomination for Ford's son, Gerald Ford, Jr., who went on to win the first of 13 Congressional elections.

The Home Front's success encouraged a second, nonpartisan group, known as Citizens Action, to set its sights on Mayor George Welsh. In office since 1938, Welsh was allegedly linked to the McKay machine, and Citizens Action wanted him out. The group galvanized around the issue of a new assessor to clean up the city's politically dominated property assessment system, charging that wide discrepancies in property valuations were based on party affiliations and contributions.

On May 12, 1949, more than 4,000 citizens attended a mass meeting in Fulton Street Park. Speakers included Dr. Duncan Littlefair of Fountain Street Church; Professor Donald Douma of Calvin College; Mrs. Dorothy Judd, a well-known civic leader; labor leader Edward W. Kosten; and businessman Jack Stiles. A recall committee was formed, and before long Citizens Action had more than enough supporters to force Mayor Welsh and city commissioners Joseph Haraburda and Lester Wagemaker to resign. Welsh sent his resignation via telegram from Rome, where he was junketing on behalf of the National Conference of Mayors. Commissioner Carl Richards was recalled in a special election.

Welsh, however, did not go quietly. Believing Citizens Action to be a one-issue group that would break up as quickly as it had been formed, he announced his candidacy for mayor in the 1950 primary. Citizens Action responded with a spirited, tightly organized campaign, coordinated by Mrs. Dorothy Judd, that placed local businessman and University of Michigan football star Paul Goebel in the mayor's chair. After the campaign, Judd wrote a letter thanking all the volunteers for their effort.

CITIZENS ACTION
359 Houseman Building
Grand Rapids, Michigan

February 26, 1950

Dear C.A. Contributors,
  C.A. Ward Committeemen,
  C.A. Neighbors,
  C.A. Telephoners,
  C.A. Office and Home
    Volunteers,
  C.A. Drivers and Baby
    Sitters,

"You dun it". So read one congratulatory telegram after election. But the fact is, "*You* dun it". Or perhaps it would be still nearer the truth to say that each and every one of you 1,800 workers and contributors "dun it"....

The 360 contributors have made it possible for C.A. to finance this campaign without leaning too heavily on large contributors....

The 100 Ward Committeemen made possible C.A.'s wide block organization of C.A. Neighbors....

The 700 C.A. Neighbors — well, you have read what the newspapers said: You were the foundation of the big vote...And the voting statistics prove this. The biggest C.A. vote was in the precincts where the most thorough block work was done.

But then — there were you telephoners — 450 of you who called the 27,000 C.A. members, all signers of recall petitions and therefore all registered voters who had asked for better government. Did you happen to notice that Paul Goebel's vote of 26,000 almost exactly equalled the number of signers of the Welsh recall petitions? Looks like you telephoners won this election.

And you drivers and baby sitters were the ones that got out all the old folks who hadn't gone to the

▲ Following the Fulton Street (Veterans Memorial) Park rally, Citizens Action volunteers went door to door with petitions calling for the ouster of Mayor George Welsh and several commissioners. [GRPL, Robinson Collection]

polls in years, but were glad at last to have a chance to vote for upright, able men. And some of you, we hear, even dressed and fed babies while determined young mothers rung up their votes for a better Grand Rapids.

And as for you 200 office and home volunteers, who have spent weeks and months typing and alphabetizing card files, addressing and stuffing thousands of envelopes, making maps and packing and mailing work kits and telephone cards — well, the C.A. Neighbors and the telephoners and the drivers and the baby sitters just couldn't have done their jobs without you...

You — all of you — have the opposition puzzled. They think C.A. is rich because they see all of this work being done...

The fact is, you did do work worth hundreds of thousands of dollars to Grand Rapids in better government. But each of us knows that we did it, not for a handful of powerful, self-seeking politicians, but for Grand Rapids.

And so here are the heartiest congratulations,

Dorothy L. Judd
First Vice President
and Chairman of the
Organization Committee,
Citizens Action.

▲ GRPL, Citizens Action Collection (unprocessed).

◄ A large crowd of supporters gathered in Fulton Street Park on May 12, 1949, to hear Citizens Action speakers. [GRPL, Robinson Collection]

◄ Calvin College students showed up at the rally with signs to make their feelings known. [GRPL, Robinson Collection]

A Free Election--(CA Style)

◄ Citizens Action leader Dorothy Leonard Judd was a prominent speaker at the rally. [GRPL, Robinson Collection]

◄ Not everyone agreed with Citizens Action, as this cartoon from a West Side weekly shows. [*West Side News,* February 15, 1950, p. 10]

A Game of Their Own

In 1943, major league baseball owners, including Philip K. Wrigley of the Chicago Cubs, were concerned that President Franklin Roosevelt would cancel their 1944 season because it was not essential to the war effort.

Wrigley was not about to accept such news passively. To insure that his Wrigley Field ballpark would be filled with spectators, he set about organizing the All-American Girls Professional Baseball League (AAGPBBL), made up of the best women softball players in the nation. Initially the women played a hybrid game that was part baseball and part softball. Bases were 75 feet apart, the ball was nearly the size of a softball, and pitchers could throw only underhand or sidearm. To emphasize their femininity, the women were outfitted in skirts with knee-high stockings, rather than the knickers worn by men. Later, the rules and equipment of baseball were adopted, but the uniforms did not change.

Although the threatened cancellation of men's major league baseball never occurred, women came from all over the United States and Canada to try out for the teams. Instead of Chicago and Wrigley Field, the women ended up playing in several small midwestern cities, including Springfield, Milwaukee, Peoria, South Bend, Kalamazoo, Muskegon, and Grand Rapids, on teams with nicknames such as the "Lassies," "Belles," "Sallies," and "Chicks."

At its peak, the league drew more than a million spectators, and the Grand Rapids Chicks played before crowds as large as 10,000 at their South High School home field. They won the league championship in 1953, and were in the final playoffs on two other occasions. Television, competition from other summer recreation, and poor management sounded the women's league's death knell in 1954, not the quality of play. Several Chicks players stayed in Grand Rapids after the league folded and recalled their experiences in a later television interview.

Dorothy Hunter (player and later chaperone): I was a Canadian. I got picked up by scouts going through Canada.... We were interviewed in a downtown hotel and they picked several local players to come and I happened to get chosen as one and I'm telling you, you might as well have given me a million dollars. I thought I was on my road to stardom.

Darlene "Beans" Risinger (pitcher): I'm from Hess, Oklahoma....

The first year, 1947, they wanted me to go to Rockford (Illinois) and I borrowed the money, went on the train to Chicago, and I got homesick and turned around and went back home. Then I had to pick cotton again to pay off the bank loan.

So I made it in 1948 and that was the good part. In 1949, I came to the Grand Rapids Chicks.

Marilyn Jenkins (bat girl and catcher): I think the first thing I did was pick stones out of the diamond when they cut the infield, and then cleaned up under the bleachers, which was great because you found money. I was nine or ten years old at the time. [Jenkins went on to become bat girl, and then the Chicks' catcher.]

Dolly (Niemec) Konwinski (infielder): Speaking of rookies, I joined the team in French Lick, Indiana. [Team captain Alma "Gabby" Ziegler] was saying "Boy wait until that Niemec gets here. She's a rookie, just wait until she gets here. She's going to shine every shoe on this club." And I'm sitting there eating. She didn't know I was there and I kept thinking, "one, two, three,... How many pairs of shoes do I have to shine tonight?"

"Beans" Risinger: I had a good high and tight pitch. You'd better be loose. The girls expected that, they didn't go running out to the mound and charging you if you gave them a high and tight pitch. I get so angry when I see that in a men's game today, I think "Stand up there and hit the ball." For $3 million, we would have. That's just part of the game.

◄"Grand Rapids' Girls of Summer," videotape, 1991.

▲ The Chicks pleased large crowds with the skill and enthusiasm they showed on the baseball diamond. [GRPL, Robinson Collection]

▲ The 1953 Grand Rapids Chicks were champions of the All American Girls Professional Baseball League. [GRPL, Robinson Collection]

What's on the Tube?

Television came to Grand Rapids at 8 p.m. on August 15, 1949, forever changing the city's leisure patterns and the way news and information were disseminated.

The 20th-century dream to broadcast both voice and moving images had become a reality in 1928, but it was not until after World War II that efforts to establish national networks realized widespread success. Larger cities were the first to avail themselves of the new technology. Detroit's first television station went on the air in 1947. Although some local residents had seen these broadcasts, most had to await the establishment of a local station.

Leonard A. Versluis, already the owner of WLAV AM and FM radio, led the local television effort. In August 1947, he applied for one of the two licenses allotted to Grand Rapids. Construction began the following spring, but Versluis had decided he would not begin broadcasting until he was able to receive and rebroadcast network programs. According to the accompanying newspaper account, securing network programming required construction of a series of towers between Grand Rapids and Chicago. Work was not completed until the summer of 1949, and after two weeks of seeing nothing but test patterns, local residents were more than ready for their first two hours of television programming. If any viewers contemplated the full impact of the new technology, their voices were lost in the general excitement over that inaugural broadcast.

Construction of a television transmitting station here has progressed so far that sending "test patterns" to local sets is scheduled to start next week and television programs will be broadcast from the station on schedule Aug. 15, officials of WLAV-TV asserted Friday.

Completion of the relay stations and further adjustments in the setup here are being rushed so that by Aug. 15 the programs at Chicago can be transmitted here via relay stations. Broadcasts will consist of film features from 6 to 7:30 p.m. and of "live" network features from 7:30 to 10:30 or 11 p.m. No live local programs are planned immediately....

From Chicago the signals will be beamed across Lake Michigan to Stevensville, 55 miles distant. A 220-foot tower at Stevensville, which is 700 feet above sea level, will provide "line-of-sight" transmission from Chicago. In fact, not only must the top of the Chicago tower be visible from the Stevensville tower, but the line of sight must be 25 feet higher than all obstacles, according to the federal communications commission.

From Stevensville the television signal will be transmitted again 37 miles to another relay station at Cedar Bluff, north of South Haven and also 700 feet above sea level. There a 200-foot tower will pick up the signals and send them out again by "line-of-sight" transmission to the Ninety-second-st. station....

Local set owners should not worry about having a solid obstruction such as a hill or building between them and the station, as "the signals fill in behind the obstruction."

◄ Grand Rapids Press, July 8, 1949, p. 2.

▲ These proud winners of a new television from Wolverine Distributors looked on with pleasure as their daughter enjoyed the new set. [GRPL, Robinson Collection]

TELEVISION
Thursday Schedules.
5:45—Test Pattern.
6:00—Cactus Jim.
6:30—Events.
7:00—Kukla, Fran, Ollie.
7:30—Events.
7:55—Varieties.
8:00—Stop the Music.
9:00—Kay Kyser Show.
10:00—Big Ten Football.
Friday Daytime.
3:00—Test Pattern.
4:00—Homemaker's Exchange.
WLAV—Channel 7.

▲ Television programming was limited to one station and about six hours per day in 1949. [*Grand Rapids Press,* December 1, 1949, p. 24]

▲ WOOD TV's Buck Barry hosted a popular children's program for many years. [GRPL, Robinson Collection]

Let's Hit the Malls!

Grand Rapids' shopping patterns changed dramatically in the late 1950s and 1960s. For decades, downtown Grand Rapids — with its department stores, "dime store block," and specialty shops — had been West Michigan's shopping destination. Every August, families made the trek downtown to stock up on back-to-school clothes and supplies, and no year was complete without a Christmas shopping expedition, preferably on the weekend of the Santa Claus parade.

A whole generation of residents remembers its first ride on the train that circled the basement-floor ceiling of Herpolsheimer's department store. And before the advent of suburban drive-ins and "multiplex" movie houses, youngsters from miles around made their way downtown to see the latest movies and to spend an hour or two "cruisin'" the Monroe-Division circuit as they looked for the evening's action.

Change began in 1958, with the opening of Rogers Plaza Shopping Center on 28th Street, and swiftly accelerated with the arrival of three new malls — Eastbrook in 1967, Woodland in 1968, and North Kent in 1970.

Shoppers flocked to the new retail centers that were closer to their suburban homes and surrounded by acres of free parking space. By 1970, downtown stores, theaters, shops, and restaurants were closing, and downtown cruisin' had become an almost solitary exercise. Planning for the regular influx of downtown shoppers was replaced by anxious discussions about how to "save" downtown and bring customers back to struggling stores.

▲ Ample free parking made Rogers Plaza, Grand Rapids' first covered shopping center, an immediate hit. [GRPL, Photo Collection]

▲ Old Kent Bank president Carl Morgenstern (second from left) joined Kentwood Mayor Peter Lamberts (second from right) and several others to break ground for Woodland Mall in 1968. [GRPL, Chamber of Commerce Collection]

The $20 million Woodland Mall officially opened Wednesday, welcoming 47 retail merchants to West Michigan's newest shopping area.

With managers of each store standing by, owner-developer Alfred Taubman turned a key in a four-foot padlock in the culmination of a four-year project.

Addressing about two thousand onlookers, Taubman said the complex at 28th St. and the East Beltline SE was an "achievement of great moment for Grand Rapids and, indeed, for the entire Middle West."

Dignitaries assisting Taubman in dedication ceremonies included Archie Siegel, partner with Taubman in the Taubman Co. of Oak Park, Mich.; Culver J. Kennedy, vice president of Sears, Roebuck & Co.; Kentwood Mayor Peter Lamberts and Joseph Van Blooys, president of the Greater Grand Rapids Chamber of Commerce.

"Woodland Mall represents the first true regional shopping center in Western Michigan," Van Blooys said, "and will prove to be a great tourist attraction for the Grand Rapids area as well."

The crowd of onlookers, and a busy line of shoppers entering the 5,200-car parking area, bore out predictions of most of the retailers.

The first crowd of customers was accompanied by marching bands from Kentwood and Forest Hills High Schools moving from store to store down the 952-foot-long mall.

The bands, of course, will not be a standard attraction, but to many of the retailers it won't make a great difference.

"With the attraction of the mall itself, we expect to do more business here than in any of our other stores," one manager commented.

▲ *Grand Rapids Press*, March 13, 1968, p. 1.

▲ Signs like this appeared in many downtown store windows in the late 1960s and early 1970s. [GRPL, Tom Reges Collection]

Connecting Ribbons of Concrete

On July 23, 1961, Grand Rapids entered the age of freeway transportation as state officials joined city leaders to celebrate the opening of the first mile of US 131 to downtown. While suburban areas grew rapidly in the postwar years, many industries and jobs were still located within city limits. Streets and roadways built in the 1920s became clogged with traffic each morning and evening as commuters made their start-stop way to and from work. Clamor for a better highway system grew in the postwar years as the semi-trucks and trailers of freight-hauling companies displaced railroads, and as weekday business travelers took to the road with their families for weekend excursions and vacation trips.

The answer was a system of highway financing that placed more of the burden on the federal government. The Federal Aid Highway Act of 1956 provided federal funds for up to 90 percent of the cost of freeway construction, with the remainder shared by the states and local units of government. Grand Rapids leaders had wanted better connecting links with other Michigan cities since the end of World War II, and when the 1956 act was passed, they acted quickly. The first local contract was issued in 1957. Four years later, residents witnessed the first of a series of highway openings on their small section of the more than 41,000 miles of national interstate roads built between 1956 and 1972.

Although it speeded transportation and made automobile travel safer, the freeway system through the city was a mixed blessing. The price for convenient, speedier, and safer transportation was disrupted lifestyles, destroyed businesses, and bulldozed landmarks in the wake of great concrete canyons and ridges built through well-established neighborhoods.

A colorful chapter in West Michigan road building history will be written Monday when the first mile of the $50 million Grand Rapids north-south freeway is opened to traffic.

State Highway Department and Grand Rapids officials will join hands at 9 a.m., in a brief ribbon cutting ceremony opening the freeway between 28th St. (US16) and Burton St.

"Completion of this section of freeway is a milestone in efforts to give Grand Rapids one of the finest city freeway systems in the nation," State Highway Commissioner John C. Mackie said Saturday.

Nearly 18 miles of freeway within the city will link downtown Grand Rapids with areas to the north, south, east and west when the entire system is open to traffic by the end of 1964.

"This new system will enable Grand Rapids to realize its full economic and industrial potential," Mackie said.

The ceremony Monday will write an end to nearly three decades of dreams, indecision, court fights, charges and countercharges.

People first began dreaming of a freeway network in Grand Rapids nearly 30 years ago.

Initial planning was started in 1947 when State Highway Department studies showed the need for an express route through the city was eminent.

But the need for new highways didn't mean the way was clear for contractors to begin work.

It took 10 years of negotiation before the first contract for work inside the city could be awarded.

The first contract was awarded in 1957 to L.W. Lamb Co. of Holland. It called for construction of a bridge to carry the north-south freeway over Plaster Creek and the Pennsylvania railroad tracks between 28th and Burton Streets.

Work on the span started in July, 1957, and was completed in December, 1958.

Construction of the first mile of roadway was delayed nearly three years, however, because of right of way problems.

This is the mile of freeway that will be opened to traffic Monday.

◄Grand Rapids Press, July 23, 1961, p. 1.

▲ Freeway construction dramatically changed the Grand Rapids landscape in the late 1950s and early 1960s. Familiar landmarks had to be torn down and whole neighborhoods disrupted in order to accommodate automobile transportation. [GRPL, Chamber of Commerce Collection]

◄ Miss Michigan, Karen Jean Southway (left), joined State Highway Commissioner John C. Mackie (at microphone), and local officials to dedicate U.S. 131 on December 22, 1961. Greater Grand Rapids Chamber of Commerce president Marvin Blackport is at Mackie's right. [GRPL, Chamber of Commerce Collection]

A Modern Airport

Increased automobile travel was matched by the growth of air transportation. World War II had greatly improved aviation technology, demonstrating the potential for long-range transportation at high speeds, and introducing jet airplanes. Wartime developments quickly found domestic uses after the fighting ended. Passenger travel multiplied from over 650 million scheduled miles just before the war in 1939, to nearly 31 billion miles in 1960. In city after city, pressure grew to upgrade airport facilities to serve the growing army of airline passengers.

Kent County's airport, built during the Great Depression with help from several federal programs, could not accommodate the increased traffic and the newer, larger, faster airliners. Complaints about the inadequate facility from passengers, and objections to the noise and constant traffic heard from residents, convinced county aeronautics board members it was time to seek a new location and funds for a completely new facility. Federal and state funds would account for nearly $3 million of the new airport's estimated $7 million cost. The remaining $4 million would come from a 17-year bond issue financed by an increase in taxes.

Airport officials had to work hard to secure county voter approval of the increased property tax proposal that was passed on June 30, 1960. Three and a half years later the new airport in Paris Township was scheduled for a grand opening. Set for November 23, 1963, the festivities were canceled at the last minute, when news arrived the day before that President John F. Kennedy had been assassinated in Dallas. Without fanfare, flights in and out of the new airport began as scheduled, but it was not until the following June that a lavish air show and crowds estimated as high as 50,000 formally dedicated the new facility.

THESE ARE THE FACTS:
- Grand Rapids needs a better airport.
- The Federal Government will contribute $2,188,000 toward the new airport.
- The State of Michigan will contribute another $587,000 to the new airport. That leaves a balance of $3,973,632 to be supplied by the county through the issuance of 17-year general obligation bonds. To retire these bonds, taxpayers throughout the county will be asked to pay a maximum of 40 cents per year on each $1,000 of the state equalized value of their property.
- It is expected that the present airport will be sold within two years for $2,000,000. This will then reduce the tax levy to 10¢ for each $1,000 of your property's market value.
- The county's economic future is at stake. Industry, with the valuable taxes it contributes and the valuable jobs it creates, seeks progressive communities in which to locate. Air transportation is a very important requirement.

CAN'T WE FIX UP THE OLD AIRPORT?

Yes, but only with great difficulty and high cost. To make the old airport acceptable for today, it would cost the county $7,340,834 — nearly twice what our share of the new airport will be.

▲ GRPL, Thomas Walsh Collection.

▲ A modern air traffic control tower dominated other buildings at the new Kent County Airport. [GRPL, Thomas Walsh Collection]

▲ Airport manager Robert Ross spoke at the June 1964 dedication of the new Kent County Airport. [GRPL, Thomas Walsh Collection]

▲ An airshow was part of the Kent County Airport dedication that was delayed from November 1963 until the following summer because of President Kennedy's assassination. [GRPL, Thomas Walsh Collection]

Urban Renewal

In the 1960s, development on Grand Rapids' periphery was a steady drain on downtown retailers. Some had pulled up stakes and moved to new locations closer to suburban housing developments. Others were considering the move, and some had closed their stores. On Monroe Avenue, between Pearl and Michigan streets, 19th-century buildings that had once been the pride of the city fell into neglect and disuse.

Similar circumstances prevailed in most other American cities, and across the country mayors turned to the federal government for help. Revisions in the federal Housing Act of 1954 permitted one-third of the appropriated funds to be used for nonresidential, central business district revitalization projects. By designating Central Business Districts (CBDs) for renewal, local leaders could secure funds for acquiring and demolishing vacant or deteriorated properties, and preparing them for new commercial and government structures.

In 1960, Grand Rapids city planning director J. Paul Jones and his staff had designated a 230-acre area as the city's central business revitalization district. Inside this tract, generally outlined by Bridge and Michigan streets on the north, Scribner on the west, Weston on the south, and Jefferson and Division on the east, land was designated for commercial, parking, wholesale, residential, civic, cultural, and public uses. A three-phase financial plan estimated total costs at $17.5 million, with $2.7 million in federal funds to be paid for land acquisition and demolition in the first phase, and $15 million in municipal bonds to fund construction of sewer, streets, and parking. Bond retirement would come from an increased tax levy, income from parking, and Civic Center rental. With Jones as its leading proponent, and city leaders working closely with the Chamber of Commerce, the plan got underway with city commission approval in January 1962.

At that time *Harper's Magazine* editor Russell Lynes was visiting the city and interviewed Grand Rapids city planner John Paul Jones about the project.

▲ As a Chamber of Commerce member and then mayor, Christian H. Sonneveldt played a key role in Grand Rapids' urban renewal program. [GRPL, Chamber of Commerce Collection]

I spent my first morning in Grand Rapids with J. Paul Jones, the director of city planning of the community, and with John Knapp, an architect. Mr. Jones's office is on the top floor of the City Hall and commands a view of urban demise.

"Almost everything you can see from here," he said, "is going to come down."

Above warehouses and business blocks I could see the red tower of the County Building. "That too?" I asked. Mr. Jones obviously thought that it was not worth saving and that it was economically unsound, even though the structure was probably good for another inconvenient hundred years. He showed me maps of the city with tissue overlays on which were drawn in bright crayons the bright future he hoped for it. Forty acres of "blight" (including the City Hall) would give way to the wrecking ball and the bulldozer, and a civic center would open like a flower on plazas leading down to the river. "Parking and alternate uses" would surround the commercial district of the city, and a cultural and educational area would gradually emerge from what is now a combination of houses and schools and museums and what seem to be called "miscellaneous occupancies." Mr. Jones is in no hurry; he will move a step at a time but, unless I am mistaken, he will eventually get what he primarily wants, which is the revitalization, as he calls it, of the downtown area.

▲ *Harper's Magazine*, January, 1962, p. 22.

▲ These two shots, taken before (left) and after urban renewal, offer graphic evidence of the dramatic changes it brought to downtown Grand Rapids. [GRPL, Robinson Collection]

Battling the Wrecking Ball

Just after dawn of an early November day in 1969, as sleepy commuters headed for their automobiles and the drive to work, Mary Stiles set out for downtown Grand Rapids on an unusual mission. Her destination was the corner of Lyon and Ottawa, where a tall stone tower stood as the last remnant of Grand Rapids' magnificent 19th-century city hall. Designed by Elijah E. Myers, who had also designed the state capitol in Lansing, the city hall had already met its doom, and now the tower was being torn down as part of the downtown urban renewal.

Stiles and others objected to the total demolition of several blocks of older buildings, arguing that many of the structures, like the city hall, should be rehabilitated and used for new purposes. The Kent County Council for Historic Preservation, organized with the help of the Junior League of Grand Rapids in 1967, sued in United States Federal Court in Detroit, but the case to save city hall was dismissed. When it became apparent that the building would be destroyed, the council tried to save the clock tower, its most prominent feature. For a time city commissioners seemed willing to grant their wish, but the final vote was 4-3 in favor of tearing down the tower.

Protesters made two final, symbolic statements. Late one night, two men, Donald Fassen and William Bouwsema, climbed the tower and clanged on its bell, creating an eerie dirge for the old structure, until police managed to remove them. Later, on the day the tower was scheduled to come down, Mrs. Stiles made her statement. Arriving before the wrecking ball operator reached the site, she climbed onto the ball and secured herself with a chain and padlock. Only after photographers had recorded her statement for posterity did she consent to get down and permit the ball to do its work.

EDITOR OF THE PRESS: Demolition of old City Hall would deprive the Grand Rapids community of one of its richest and most irreplaceable heritages. In this age of rapidly accelerating change, it becomes more necessary than ever that selected symbols of our past remain with us as reminders of our progress....

The richness of materials and the artful craftsmanship of the old City Hall no longer can be duplicated today. To abandon these in the name of progress is to impose an injustice on the community which can never be corrected.
WALTER B. SANDERS
Director, Michigan Region,
American Institute of Architects
Jackson, Mich.

▲ *Grand Rapids Press,* August 23, 1969, p. 14A.

EDITOR OF THE PRESS: Since when do Grand Rapids taxes have to be decided by people living elsewhere...? The downtown urban renewal program was approved by the people, who assumed the burden of higher taxes.

Now we are being bombarded by letters from all over the country, letters obviously solicited, petitioning us to "Save City Hall," a structure which somehow has assumed historic status (probably due to the fact that it hasn't collapsed of its own dead weight, decay, rot and grime)....

Enough of this nonsense about saving old City Hall....

Let's get rid of it — and soon. Get on with the beautification of our city.
ARLENE M. FERINGA

▲ *Grand Rapids Press,* August 30, 1969, p. 14A.

◄Mary Stiles registered one final protest by chaining herself to the wrecking ball before the city hall clock tower was demolished. [GRPL, Photo Collection]

◄With most other buildings gone, wrecking equipment prepared to move in on Grand Rapids' Victorian-era city hall. [GRPL, Chamber of Commerce Collection]

▲ Detailed ornamentation, like these floor tiles, was one reason preservationists fought to save the old city hall. [GRPL, Marius Rooks Collection]

Trouble in River City

Tensions between people of different racial and cultural backgrounds grew in Grand Rapids in the 1960s. In the 19th century, immigration had produced an ethnically diverse population that had strong differences of religion and culture. Polish Catholics and Dutch Calvinists found much to disagree about, but over time, their similarities tended to outweigh their differences, and second- and third-generation immigrant families lived, worked, and played together with diminishing concern about their divergent European backgrounds.

This process of assimilation did not work for the African-Americans who came to Grand Rapids. Their color set them apart, making them the target for discrimination in housing, jobs, and many social activities. Local blacks saw the postwar years bring improved lifestyles to whites, while their own situation remained unchanged. Many suburban housing developments had restrictive covenants prohibiting home sales to blacks. Employment opportunities remained limited, and black students were concentrated in a few inner-city schools.

Resentment over this second-class condition spread across America in the 1960s. In the summers of 1965, 1966, and 1967, inner-city ghettos exploded in violent orgies of looting, burning, and shooting. From Los Angeles to Detroit, Chicago, and Newark, major cities saw dozens of deaths and hundreds of millions of dollars in damages. Smaller cities like Grand Rapids experienced less violent confrontations that served to remind their leaders that they, too, must confront problems associated with discrimination and *de facto* segregation.

Local trouble began early in the morning of July 25, 1967, two days after riots had erupted in Detroit. Rumors abounded that carloads of troublemakers were on their way to Grand Rapids, and police and local citizens were on edge. A crowd quickly gathered on Delaware Street when police confronted a carload of youths in a stolen car. Within minutes, the incident touched off nearby violent outbursts. By the time order was restored two days later, 44 people had been injured, 213 arrests had been made, and damage estimates stood in the hundreds of thousands of dollars.

In the aftermath of violence, several steps were taken to correct inequities. The city's Human Relations Commission, organized in 1955, became an important forum for communication, and local programs reflected national efforts to provide improved housing, education, and job opportunities. Grand Rapids elected its first African-American city commissioner the next year, and the Rev. Lyman Parks went on to become mayor in 1971.

◄ William Pritchett (left) and Richard Donley revisit the Division Avenue area north of Franklin, where they worked in the summer of 1967. [Photo by © *Grand Rapids Press*, July 26, 1987, p. B1]

▲ Heavily armed police patrolled Grand Rapids streets for several days in July 1967. [Photo by © *Grand Rapids Press*, July 26, 1987, p. B1]

Richard Donley didn't know he had a nickname when he agreed to trade the West Side for the streets along South Division Avenue in the summer of '67.

The others hired as part of a federally funded United Community Services youth program, called him "The Saint."

Donley was one of two whites. William "Cowboy" Pritchett, who grew up in Chicago and Allegan, was assigned as his partner. Already a Ferris State College graduate, Pritchett was employed at Franklin-Hall Complex. . . .

"We all knew something was going to happen," Donley says. "There were rumors of guys coming from Detroit. . . and those kind of rumors, whether they're true or not, just accelerated that whole week. . . .

"I remember driving in front of Franklin-Hall Complex and there was a rental truck in front of one of those stores they were looting, and these were grown men."

Pritchett agrees that "looting was the biggest attraction."

Pritchett recalls trying to stop looting at a grocery store.

"Some of them were listening (to Task Force members). And then the police arrived and people started scattering every which way," Pritchett says.

"People were screaming and women started screaming and people were hiding meat. Police were grabbing them by the jackets, hair, anything they could, and trying to shake whatever they had out of their hands. People were going out doors that I didn't even know existed on that building, with shopping carts loaded up with meat."

By the third night, when the Michigan State Police arrived to aid the beleaguered local police and sheriff's deputies, the riot had changed.

"You didn't see a lot of people out, but every once in a while you'd hear a bunch of guns shooting off," recalls Donley.

"It was still, like after a storm has ended," Pritchett adds. "Police were driving in the street with their headlights out. . . ."

". . . guns sticking out the window," Donley says, finishing Pritchett's sentence.

▲ *Grand Rapids Press*, July 26, 1987, p. B1.

The City's New Symbol

Save for the construction of a new Convention Center and Performing Arts Auditorium, the initial phase of Grand Rapids' downtown urban renewal was complete by the end of the 1960s. Marking the conclusion of those first efforts was the dedication of a remarkable piece of public sculpture in 1969. *La Grande Vitesse* by Alexander Calder was paid for with a combination of private funds and a new public sculpture grant program of the National Endowment for the Arts (NEA). Many were surprised when Grand Rapids was the first city to receive one of the NEA grants, but those who knew of the city's pride and longstanding support of the arts saw the move as a logical extension of traditional community interests.

Arts advocate Nancy Mulnix, who spearheaded the effort to acquire the Calder stabile later recalled the initial approach to the NEA, and the dedication of the sculpture.

▲ Alexander Calder posed with a portion of *La Grande Vitesse* at his Sache, France, home in 1969. [GRPL, Nancy Mulnix Collection]

◄Nancy Mulnix was among the speakers at the dedication. [GRPL, Nancy Mulnix Collection]

◄ A large crowd gathered for the June 14, 1969, dedication of Alexander Calder's *La Grande Vitesse*. [GRPL, Nancy Mulnix Collection]

On May 10, 1967, I sat down at my kitchen table and wrote a letter to my Congressman. Nothing unusual about that. But the letter concerned making a request for a federal grant to be used to commission a giant piece of sculpture for Grand Rapids, and the Congressman was Gerald R. Ford.

It was common knowledge that Jerry Ford always responded promptly to requests from his constituents, but I was a little unprepared for the subsequent lightning-fast action! Within the week Jerry replied that he had phoned Roger Stevens, then chairman of the National Endowment for the Arts, and had formally requested his personal attention and assistance for our embryonic idea. Less than five days later, Mr. Stevens himself called to tell me that he was convinced that Grand Rapids should be the first city in the country to receive a federal grant to be used for commissioning a monumental piece of sculpture by an American artist for a specific civic site.

Two years and much agony and ecstasy later, we dedicated the Grand Rapids Calder, LA GRANDE VITESSE, in Vandenberg Center. Gerald Ford shared the platform with the sculpture committee, Roger Stevens, and Alexander and Louisa Calder. Even through my heady euphoria, I remember what Jerry said: "...art gives quality to life. And so it is that this sculpture dedicated here today raises the quality of life in our community. It speaks to us of the fundamental truth of human existence: that man is a being with noble aspirations and high ideals. For in creating this stabile which now graces Vandenberg Center, Alexander Calder has imparted to us and to all who may gaze upon his work, the best and highest feelings of which man is capable. This is the work that proceeded from a beautiful incentive, that of bringing forth the spirit of a city, to take metal and to shape it into a form that speaks from one man's soul to the soul of others. The dedication of this sculpture today brings a new dimension to our lives here in this part of Michigan. I think it leaves with us a deep sense that everything passes, that art alone is eternal."

Jerry eventually spoke from the floor of the House in support of an increased appropriation for the arts endowment. He was quoted as saying, "At the time I didn't know what a Calder was, but I can assure the members that a Calder in the center of the city in an urban renewal area, has really helped to regenerate Grand Rapids." In retrospect Grand Rapids probably received that premier grant because Gerald Ford, the Minority Leader of the House, was our representative. The National Endowment undoubtedly wanted his powerful support and endorsement. But because all the circumstances and ingredients were there, we created an enormously successful project and literally wrote the book on art in public places. Roger Stevens had been dealt a royal flush, and Grand Rapids had not failed our Congressman's faith in us.

▲GRPL, Nancy Mulnix Collection.

CHAPTER 9

Today's Community – Tomorrow's Vision

By 1970, Grand Rapids was defined by its diversity. The city that had once been the nation's furniture capital and home to succeeding generations of European immigrants was now distinguished by a broad economic base and a racially and culturally diverse population.

The 1970s dawned on a note of optimism. The downtown urban renewal project launched the previous decade was dramatically changing the face of the urban landscape. No longer having all its economic eggs in one basket, the city took pride in a broad-based, post-furniture economy that featured a prosperous blend of complementary manufacturing, commercial, and retail enterprises. And the racial tensions that had erupted in the '60s were being eased by federally funded neighborhood revitalization programs supported citywide by organizations whose leaders believed racial and cultural harmony and coexistence were not only necessary, but achievable.

As the decade wore on, increasing causes arose for concern. Runaway inflation in the late 1970s precipitated a loss of federal and state funds in the 1980s. Equally troubling was the lack of population growth and industrial development in much of the central city. While surrounding localities such as Kentwood and Wyoming were enjoying high rates of growth, Grand Rapids' tax base was stagnating.

Without adequate resources for maintenance and repair, the city's infrastructure was starting to crumble, and the escalating cost of maintaining streets, utilities, and government and school buildings became topics of general concern and conversation. But no one had ready answers. Social problems — from poor educational achievement to job and housing shortages, an overburdened criminal justice system, and the rise of illegal drug trafficking — were proving more complex and resistant to solution than many citizens had anticipated.

As a result of this sobering dose of reality, Grand Rapids residents approached the 21st century in an ambivalent mood. On the one hand, they celebrated the construction of new buildings and honors such as All-America City recognition; on the other they faced a long list of challenges. Most citizens still believed that the city's problems could be resolved, but they also acknowledged there would be no quick fix. It was a time for rolling up shirtsleeves and getting on with the work.

One of the greatest challenges was Grand Rapids' diminished role in relation to surrounding cities. No longer the region's only political and economic force, Grand Rapids was still the dominant player, but its strength was waning. The central city was now the largest in a cluster of municipalities that counted as many people living outside its borders as within. And in the face of this changing metropolitan order, the key question had become: Would the existing system of very loosely linked municipalities persist, or would as-yet-unforeseen developments force a greater degree of cooperation through an area-wide commitment to metropolitan planning?

Although most of the area's commercial and cultural activities were still centered in downtown Grand Rapids, each neighboring municipality had its own educational system and provided most of its own public services. Many outside the central city felt little need to participate in large-scale, area-wide planning efforts. Even though utility and public transit services linked much of the area, few who lived and held jobs in the suburbs were interested in seeing their tax dollars at work in Grand Rapids. Downtown may have been an interesting place for an occasional visit, but fewer and fewer wanted to live in the city or help pay for its rehabilitation.

As the new century drew near, metropolitan planning advocates stubbornly persisted in their efforts to secure cooperation from neighboring municipalities. At the same time, Grand Rapids citizens were being encouraged to offer their own voices and visions to create a more viable, livable downtown. Most observers agreed that a clear sense of direction for the metropolitan area was still in the formative stages. What had become increasingly apparent, however, was that Grand Rapids would have to build on new strengths, rather than rely on old virtues.

Celebrating the Arts in Grand Style

With bands playing and banners flying and performers ready to take the stage, Grand Rapids' arts festival gets underway with great fanfare on the first Friday of every June. Over the three days that it lasts, the gala celebration of the visual and performing arts, run entirely by volunteers, draws throngs of fun seekers to the heart of downtown to enjoy what has become the largest such event in the nation.

The idea of an arts festival first surfaced back in 1962, when a dedicated group of arts boosters began holding a modest event, first in the parking lot of the Art Museum and then, for several years, at John Ball Park. Discontinued when interest waned, the outdoor arts festival took on new life with urban renewal and the installation on Vandenberg Plaza of Alexander Calder's *La Grande Vitesse.* Proposing to make the Calder stabile the centerpiece of a vastly expanded arts celebration, organizers managed to muster the necessary support and launched the first downtown Festival in 1970.

By today's standards, Festival '70 was a modest affair, but in the context of its time, it was a huge success. Over 7,000 people turned out to view the art, listen to and watch the performers, and purchase a snack at one of the food booths operated by various local nonprofit organizations. The ethnic delicacies served up at that first Festival proved to be genuine crowd pleasers, and the percentage of the profits turned over to Festival helped offset the estimated $15,000 operating costs.

With one confirmed success under their belts, Festival organizers were back the following year — and so were the crowds, which swelled to 100,000 within a few years and eventually reached a record-setting 500,000. As it grew ever larger and even more popular, Festival overflowed the plaza and filled the surrounding streets.

Each year's Festival brings forth its own memories and the moments of humor and poignancy that exemplify the resiliency and happy, carefree attitudes that pervade the entire weekend. Consider, for example, the recollections of Festival '74 co-chairs Lois Poppen and Buck Matthews, and volunteers Vance Orr and Jo Wills.

Rain squalls dominated Festival '74 and provided Buck Matthews with his most memorable moment — the drowning of the debut of Festival's specially commissioned theme. Later, mellowed by the passage of time, Buck recalled the moment with humor and no bitterness toward the caprices of nature:

We had commissioned Chuck Buffam to write a theme for us, and it was to be played by the symphony during its traditional Saturday night concert. As emcee of the Calder Stage for the occasion, I distinguished myself by embellishing my announcement. My speech runneth over...by three minutes to be exact. The piece itself runs about three and a half minutes under dry conditions. Well, they got just thirty seconds into it when the skies opened up with an instant downpouring of all the rain in the world.

The music died with a gurgle in mid-note as the musicians fled for shelter. I was never so embarrassed in all my life.

Lois Poppen remembered those early Festivals for one of the more unusual fads of the 1970s:

Nineteen seventy-four was the year of Streaking, and Buck and I secretly hoped we would be honored with one. We even talked to the police about being compassionate should such a character appear. Sure enough he did! He pulled up in a car off the Monroe entrance to the County Building, which served as our Coffee House. He somehow made it all the way through that teeming mass of humanity, up the stairs past my amazed children, and all the way to the Calder Stage before two plainclothesmen hustled him into a nearby cruiser.

We were really pleased to have him. I often wonder what he's doing today?

▼ Sprawling across Vandenberg Plaza and onto adjacent parking lots and streets, Festival has become West Michigan's most popular outdoor event. [GRPL, Photo Collection]

Long associated with the heavy labor of production, Vance Orr, who later took his turn as Festival co-chair, could usually be found on the deserted plaza late Sunday night and early Monday supervising the cleanup:

I was backing a 27-foot moving van off the Plaza, when I saw this man running after me waving wildly. I was still moving rather slowly and by the time he caught up to me shouting for me to stop I had literally backed over the trunk of his parked car. I remember it vividly to this day...a bright red Pontiac.

I still have the chrome taillight ring from it hanging on my wall at home. That's probably the only guy in town who thinks ill of Festival.

Festival veteran Jo Wills remembered how the spur-of-the-moment enrollment of a small corps of volunteers speeded setting up hundreds of folding chairs:

Suddenly this bus brought a class of first grade schoolchildren down to the Plaza for lunch.

We recruited all those little kids to help carry the chairs from the truck. It was like a line of ants. Each little person would carry one chair over, set it up and then get back in line to start over. It was absolutely amazing how much fun we all had, and how quickly the job got done.

▲ *Accent Grand Rapids*, Vol. 8, No. 4, May 1979, pp. 14-15.

▲ Festival has long encouraged young artists to express themselves without adult interference. [Photo by © *Grand Rapids Press*, June 7, 1970, p. 3D]

A Downtown Mall for Grand Rapids

Although Festival enlivened the cityscape for a single weekend each year, it had become clear to business and government leaders that more dramatic steps were needed to reinvigorate downtown Grand Rapids. After years of losing customers to suburban shopping malls, most downtown merchants were receptive when architect M. Paul Friedberg proposed in 1975 that they fight fire with fire and convert Monroe Avenue into a downtown pedestrian mall surrounded by easily accessible parking.

Friedberg's plan was similar to projects being proposed and constructed in other cities. Many city planners began with the assumption that downtown areas were unfriendly to users when compared to suburban shopping centers. Therefore, if downtown business centers wished to hold a share of the market, they needed grassy areas, benches, and even ornamental fountains to create a more enticing shopping environment.

The proposed mall was also seen as a critical part of the larger urban renewal initiative that included a convention and cultural center adjacent to the Welsh Civic Auditorium, and parks and parkways along the Grand River. After considerable discussion, merchants approved the Friedberg plan by more than a two to one majority.

The mall would open in 1980, with the Grand Center debuting a year later. Neither would by itself turn aside downtown's troubles, but both would receive popular acclaim and be regarded as positive steps in the right direction.

◄ Closing Monroe Avenue and making it a parking lot was the first step toward a downtown pedestrian mall. [GRPL, Chamber of Commerce Collection]

Downtown's daytime dwellers and developers have much to chew on the next few days.

The merchants and property owners know the program detailed and drawn for them by New York architests M. Paul Friedberg and Dean McClure Thursday and Friday is needed medicine if the central city shopping area — Monroe Center — is going to regain its health.

They also know that the cure is going to be costly to them now but a benefit to them and the community....

Total cost of the project, which appeared Friday to be meeting with strong enthusiasm among the merchants and the owners, would be around $2.2 million....

That figure would cover converting Monroe Ave. into a pedestrian mall from Campau Square, at Monroe Ave. and Pearl St. NW, to Monument Square at Monroe Ave. and E. Fulton St.

The $2.2 million does not include planned rerouting of Monroe Ave. in a southwesterly direction, a "must" if Monroe Center is to be redeveloped. That rerouting calls for demolishing buildings between Pearl and Market....

Acquisition of the buildings, demolition and rebuilding of the "new" part of Monroe Ave. would cost "another $2 to $3 million...."

An enlarged Campau Square — it would appear at least six to eight times the size of what the city now knows as "the square" — has captured much attention.

If the principal proposal of the architects is picked, it would be a Campau Square of multilevels with a large fountain as the feature attraction. Water from it would spill over into a moat or onto a court that could be frozen in winter and used as an outdoor public skating rink....

The area would have an "amphitheater" appearance with steps leading down into the platform area. The steps could serve as concrete bleachers.

Also on the square would be an information building, a second fountain, plantings, decorative "street" furniture and a section for flags....

Monroe Center would tie into two other major projects at the lower end of Monroe — expansion of Civic Auditorium and development of parks along Grand River.

▲ *Grand Rapids Press,* November 10, 1975, p. 1B.

The formation of the Mayor's Project Study and Coordination Committee in 1974 might be designated as the time when the city's downtown improvement turned from the 1960s urban renewal "bulldozer" approach to plans to lure people back to the heart of the community....

[In 1965] Christian Sonneveldt, then-mayor, appointed a cultural committee, which for three years studied proposals for various cultural facilities in different locations, particularly in the Jefferson Avenue-Fulton Street area. That was the location of the old Junior College-Jefferson Connector Plan.

Ideas ranged from construction of an auditorium in conjunction with expansion of Junior College to building an addition at the north wall of the Civic which would allow use of the large stage both by the large multipurpose auditorium and fixed-seat hall.

Some of those same ideas were reviewed by the Study and Coordination Committee appointed by then-mayor Lyman S. Parks in 1974.

"We had all kinds of plans going on by different groups," recalls Richard M. Gillett, board

◄ Several buildings were demolished to make space for the Campau Square amphitheater at the north end of Monroe Mall. [GRPL, Photo Collection]

chairman of Old Kent Bank and who was Parks' choice to head the study committee....

Gillett says the committee's first responsibility was sifting through the myriad of plans to set priorities so that the entire community would benefit....

Gillett recalls at least two factors that gave impetus to the plans which have resulted in the Grand Center.

One was the inclusion of Richard M. DeVos on the planning committee, the other approval of a hotel/motel tax by the Kent County Board of Commissioners.

A couple of members of Gillett's committees kept a log:

April, 1975, Mayor Lyman Parks appointed Design Committee to interview and select architectural firm for Civic Auditorium expansion....

August, 1975, George C. Izanour of George C. Izanour Associates, hired as consultant for expanding Welsh Civic Auditorium. Received federal Economic Development Administration grant of $3.2 million....

February, 1976, Harry Weese of Harry Weese Associates, Chicago, signed contract as architect, Daverman Associates of Grand Rapids hired as local architect for project.

June, 1976, Lothar Cremer, acoustician for Berlin Philharmonic Hall, Sydney, Australia Opera House and others, hired by Weese as acoustical consultant for auditorium....

September, 1977, Received the [$5.438 million] Public Works grant.

February, 1978, Richard Gillett and Richard DeVos, co-chairmen of the auditorium fund-raising, top the $5 million goal for private donations....

Probably as important as [those] donations was Mary Ann Keeler's persistence in battling to have a fixed-seat auditorium as part of any downtown improvement plan. She now admits great satisfaction, but recalls a few

▲ Construction of the Grand Center and the DeVos Hall for the Performing Arts marked the final step in the downtown renewal process. [GRPL, Photo Collection]

battles she fought against plans in the past which did not include the auditorium....

If the abbreviated history were to be continued an entry must be made for October 12, 1980. For tonight, the first official program — an interdenominational Festival of Praise and Thanksgiving — will be held at DeVos Hall of the Performing Arts Center.

◄ *Grand Rapids Press,* October 12, 1980, p. 1.

▲ Monroe Center pedestrian mall, with its open walkways, clustered seating areas, and shrubbery, was completed in 1979. [GRPL, Photo Collection]

Heritage Hill

The flight to the suburbs that devastated downtown businesses also affected residential neighborhoods. The "Hill" district that bordered the downtown had been a popular residential area since the city's earliest days and contained many elegant homes built during the heyday of the furniture industry. By the 1960s, however, many of these fine old Victorian homes had fallen upon hard times and been divided into apartments. Property values were falling, and plans were afoot to tear down whole blocks in order to accommodate a central health-care complex and Grand Rapids Junior College's expansion plans.

Having watched the urban renewal projects of the 1960s level entire city blocks, historic preservationists were determined that Grand Rapids' finest 19th-century residential neighborhood would not suffer the same fate. In 1971, Hill area residents working in concert with several preservationist groups succeeded in lobbying Washington for the creation of the Heritage Hill National Historic District. At the same time, they persuaded the Grand Rapids City Commission to pass an historic preservation ordinance and to establish an Historic Preservation Commission to see that the ordinance was properly observed.

Although Heritage Hill has continued to be the focal point of much of the preservation efforts in Grand Rapids, the preservation commission has designated other historic landmarks and districts throughout the city. Inspired by these successes, preservationists continue to work diligently to assure that the community's historic legacy is preserved.

▲ The distinctive stone facade of lumber baron Thomas Friant's house (601 Cherry SE) makes it a standout among the homes of Heritage Hill. [David and Marilyn Hanks, *The Homes of Heritage Hill*, p. 14]

▼ Damon Hatch's home (445 Cherry SE), built in 1844, remains a Heritage Hill and city landmark nearly 150 years later. [David and Marilyn Hanks, *The Homes of Heritage Hill*, p. 4]

Interview ▶
with Barbara Roelofs, June 9, 1992, GRPL, Oral History Collection.

The banks weren't writing mortgages and the S&Ls weren't lending money to people to buy houses in the "Hill" area, partially because of pressure from developers who envisioned having a big medical complex in the southern portion of the district....It was called "Project Recap," and when you wake up on a Sunday morning and see those big plans on the front page of the newspaper and realize that your own home is going to be open to developers to buy upon city condemnation and be destroyed, you get angry and decide to do something about it. Project Recap extended down Jefferson to the museum, up State Street to Union, down Union to Wealthy and back to Jefferson. That was a large area with some magnificent homes.

There was another area under contemplation for urban renewal that was called the College Park Urban Renewal Project, which was on the north part of the district. The ultimate plan for that would have extended between Fountain and Lyon streets all the way to Houseman Field.

A group of neighbors got together and formed a neighborhood public relations group. We had well over 100 people at our organizational meeting in 1967, including city commissioners William Worst and Carl Eschels. That's when the snowball started....

We knew that [we had]...to do something positive to stop the wrecking ball. In 1966, President Johnson had signed the National Historic Preservation Act. Section 106D of the act said that you could not demolish anything with Federal money that was listed on the National Register of Historic Places. So we thought we must get listed on the National Register.... (Congressman) Jerry Ford was very helpful. He had his office on Cherry Street, just around the corner.

In the meantime the Board of Education was going ahead with an application for Urban Renewal to HUD for College Park. On March 11, 1971, we were entered on the National Register....They tried to get around the Register, but Washington said, "This area is on the National Register, you go back and have a compliance conference and deal with those ladies from Heritage Hill." In June, 1971, we held the first compliance conference in the United States under the Act of 1966, and when all was said and done, the advisory council...said to the Board of Education and city officials, "Thy project shall stop, thou shalt not tear those houses down." You should have seen the look on their faces.

An Increasingly Unpopular War

From about 1963 to 1972, the United States was engaged in an undeclared war in Vietnam that claimed over 55,000 American lives. The war became a reality for Grand Rapids residents on Thanksgiving Day, 1965, when they learned of the death of Dale Funk, Kent County's first casualty. Direct local involvement in the war ended more than seven years later when Major Joseph Shanahan returned to Grand Rapids after more than four years of confinement as a prisoner of war. In between, 131 Kent County men died, many more were wounded, and others brought home scars they carried for many years thereafter.

As it dragged on, Vietnam became an increasingly unpopular war. On the surface, life went on at home with very little disruption, but strong feelings were emerging that would turn the conflict into one of the most divisive issues the nation had ever faced. Draftees and enlistees left for their tours of duty with little fanfare and returned later to a country and a community that seemed embarrassed to acknowledge their service. A weekly peace vigil began near the Calder on Vandenberg Plaza in 1970 and lasted, rain or shine, warm or cold, for the next 34 months. In May 1971, the Grand Rapids City Commission passed a resolution calling upon the president and Congress to be "courageous in extricating us from the hostilities in Indo-China [and to]... begin reversing the priorities established by this war."

Like the civilians at home, soldiers who fought in the war had many ambivalent feelings. Kenneth Tepper, who was wounded and cited for bravery at the battle of "Hamburger Hill," talked freely with a reporter about what he saw as the battle's lack of purpose. In a Grand Rapids *Press* article, families of soldiers shared letters home that expressed emotions ranging from frustration for the lack of their countrymen's support to graphic descriptions of conditions in Vietnam.

By the time the war ended, it was opposed by a majority of the population, and relief, more than jubilation, accompanied the signing of the truce document on January 23, 1973.

"It just wasn't worth it. I saw too many of my friends get killed, and when we got up there, nobody was around."

So does Spec. 5 Kenneth Tepper, 1137 Eastern Ave. NE, describe the controversial battle of Hamburger Hill in which he was wounded May 18.

The 24-year-old squad leader was hit by shrapnel in the right leg just below the knee during a charge up the hill.

"It's what they call a million-dollar wound," he said. "Bad enough to be evacuated but luckily not too serious."

Tepper was a member of the 3rd Battalion, 187th Infantry, 101st Airborne Division, that was involved in the capture of Dong Ap Bia — Hill 937 or Hamburger Hill. The battle has become a political football, with many war critics calling it "senseless and irresponsible."

"I am not protesting the fact that we are involved in Vietnam," he said, "but I do consider the battle for that hill a waste.

"It was like a turkey shoot, and we were the turkeys. They would send one or two companies up the center and leave the flanks wide open making us easy targets. And now after all that fighting we've left the hill."

▲ *Grand Rapids Press*, June 9, 1969, p. 1.

Air Force Capt. Charles Griffin, 28, was the first U.S. Air Force Academy graduate from Grand Rapids....

Last December, he wrote his folks, saying, "I know that you may be caught up in the disillusionment concerning the war, (but) freedom is something which must be constantly fought for and preserved — to turn the other way when we can reasonably preserve that freedom for another is eroding and destroying, for who can place a price tag on the liberties we take for granted...."

Besides the [dangers of war] there is the lack of comfort. Pfc. Atkins wrote his wife Joyce, of 1148 Ionia Ave. SW, "We just got back from a 10-day patrol. Out of those 10 days I think I got about 8 hours sleep. We have been at this new base camp for about 15 days now and I have only slept in my bed 2 days...."

Pfc. Alexander J. Vigh, 20, of 1044 Eastern Ave. SE, wrote home, saying, "Our bodies are constantly wet from sweat.... Also there are bees, flies, spiders, mosquitoes and other real small bugs whose names I do not know. With sweat and bugs I'm always scratching myself."

Marine Lance Cpl. David B. Nelson, 21, of 283 Netherfield St. SW, wrote: "We hit here just after the start of the monsoon season (1966) and everything, including me, is waterlogged. Believe me it's miserable."

▲ The longer it lasted, the more the Vietnam War inspired protest at home. This Grand Rapids group journeyed to Lansing in an effort to persuade state legislators to adopt a resolution opposing the war. [GRPL, William M. Glenn Collection]

▲ Over 1,000 well-wishers gathered to welcome Maj. Joseph Shanahan of Kentwood home after four and a half years of imprisonment in North Vietnam. [Photo by © *Grand Rapids Press*, April 4, 1973, p. 1E]

◄ *Grand Rapids Press*, "Wonderland," November 9, 1969, pp. 3-9.

A Long Trip to Freedom

When American soldiers withdrew from Vietnam, they left behind South Vietnamese soldiers and civilians vulnerable to the oncoming Viet Cong forces. Many of these people escaped any way they could. Families were separated in the confusion, and years often passed before they were reunited.

As in the days following World War II, local church leaders organized to help refugees resettle in Grand Rapids and begin a new life. Freedom Flight Task Force, a project run by the Rev. Howard Schipper of Bethany Reformed Church, brought several hundred Vietnamese refugees to Grand Rapids and found them jobs and local sponsors. Among the new arrivals in November 1976, were the wife and daughter of Pham Huu Duyet, reunited with the former Vietnamese army officer 17 months after he had been forced to leave them behind as he fled Vietnam.

Since April, Do Tih Hong, her 9-year-old daughter and her sister have been starved, robbed, shot at, imprisoned and starved some more.

But Friday night, after a reunion with her husband at Kent County Airport, Mrs. Hong wiped her tears with the back of her hand and told him: "It is all forgotten. I am happy now."

The 45-year-old woman, her husband, Pham Huu Duyet, 44, daughter Pham Thi Phung Nga and her sister, Do Thi Ven, 48, were hustled by a local refugee resettlement agency to an undisclosed 48th St. SE apartment to enjoy their first hours together since May, 1975.

That was when Pham, a South Vietnamese Army lieutenant colonel, boarded a U.S. Army helicopter in Long Bien, Vietnam, and fled for his life ahead of advancing North Vietnamese and Viet Cong troops.

Freedom Flight Task Force, the resettlement organization run by local churches, brought him here from Camp Pendleton Refugee Center in California two months ago.

He has a job now as a sheet metal worker with Quality Trane Air-conditioning Co. He also has a new, Americanized name, Philip Pham.

"I didn't think they would ever get out," Pham said Friday, his family huddled around him. "So many things could have happened. With many families, the husband got out and the wife and children are still behind."

For a year he heard nothing about his wife and child, then through the refugee grapevine, he began getting scraps of information about their escape.

He didn't hear the full story until the airport reunion.

With food rationed at six pounds of rice a month for each person in Saigon, the three worked their way north.

At one point, Viet Cong soldiers found the three hiding in a rural graveyard, took what the family had with them and let them go.

They crowded into a small fishing boat for a frightening seven-day trip to Thailand. They sailed unharmed past bullets fired from the shore by Cambodian Communists.

"In Thailand," Mrs. Hong said, "the minute we touched the ground we were taken to a criminal prison. Conditions there were very, very miserable. Sixty persons shared a small cell and the food was a small amount of dried fish, once a day."

She suffered bouts of paralysis in her legs from not being able to move around, she said.

Meanwhile, Rev. Howard Schipper, pastor of Bethany Reformed Church and chairman of the refugee aid group here, was beginning the frustrating diplomatic process of bailing the Pham family out of the Thai prison.

First, through the grapevine, then from a behind-bars photo of Mrs. Hong and Nga in a refugee magazine, Pham had learned where his family was being held.

After six months of letters and phone calls from Grand Rapids to the State Department in Washington, D.C., and from Washington to Bangkok, Thailand, Pham finally received a cable from his wife.

The federal refugee relief program set up and paid for travel arrangements for the family when Thai authorities agreed to the release.

▲ *Grand Rapids Press*, November 6, 1976, pp. 1A-2A.

◄ This behind-bars photograph was Pham Huu Duyet's first look at his wife and daughter since he fled Vietnam. [Photo by © *Grand Rapids Press*, November 6, 1976, p. 1A]

▲ Pham Huu Duyet had a joyful reunion with his daughter and wife at Kent County Airport in 1976. [Photo by © *Grand Rapids Press*, November 6, 1976, p. 1A]

Lyman Parks Becomes Mayor

The Rev. Lyman Parks turned down three better-paying offers to accept a position as pastor of Grand Rapids' First Community African Methodist Episcopal Church in 1966. Later, he explained that he picked the Grand Rapids church because the congregation specifically wanted someone "who was willing to become involved in the community." Parks' commitment to community action was tested shortly after his arrival when several days of racial violence threatened to tear the city apart. In the wake of the disturbance, Parks and others from many different parts of the community rallied to replace friction with understanding and cooperation.

Deciding that 1968 was the right time for political action, Parks decided to run for the Grand Rapids City Commission. In his successful campaign to become the first black elected to city office, he presented himself as a conventional public servant who was interested in good government and safe streets, and paid attention to voter concerns. Three years later, in May 1971, he was elected president of the city commission, a largely honorary position that entailed presiding over committee of the whole meetings and acting as mayor in the absence of the mayor.

At that point, fate intervened to make Parks the city's first black mayor. Robert Boelens, who had been elected in 1970, resigned his post, and because Parks was commission president, he became acting mayor. Wanting to prove that the time had come when a black person could be elected mayor, Parks successfully ran for a full four-year term in 1972.

◄ Lyman Parks took great pride in downtown revitalization efforts begun during his term. [GRPL, Chamber of Commerce Collection]

I came to this church because they wanted somebody to be involved with young people and with the community. I don't think they ever thought I'd get as involved as I did. I asked their permission to run for office for the city commission because I felt politics did a lot toward controlling our lives. They said we'll permit that, but you'll never be elected.

The timing was right. I recognized that. . . .

I announced that I was going to run without really giving a lot of thought to all that was involved. I had a friend here who was from the same school that I was from, Wilberforce University, Judge [John] Letts. So I went to see him and he steered me in the direction of some people. Norm DeGraaf was one of them. . . . He was not sure how many people would give him a hard time for even supporting a black. But nevertheless he agreed to become my campaign

◄ After completing the unexpired term of Robert Boelens, Lyman Parks was elected mayor in his own right and sworn in on January 2, 1974. [Photo by © *Grand Rapids Press*, January 3, 1974, p. 1A]

manager, and Alden Walters was my treasurer, and Bill Eerdmans of Eerdmans Publishing Company was a member of that group, and two blacks, Martha Reynolds who was a union member, and Ed Mabin who was just beginning with Michigan Bell. They made up my little inside group. I was running against Herb Soodsma. The theme of my campaign was unity — unifying the third ward. . . . I went into many, many homes, many Dutch homes. . . , and I just talked about my background, and where I had come from, and what I felt I could contribute toward making this a better place. . . .

The powers that be in the city never thought it would come to pass, and I'm sure there were a lot of other people who didn't think it would happen. But. . . I won the election outright in the primary. People began to see the need for black people being involved. . . .

I'm a dreamer, and after I became city commissioner. . . I kept dreaming, and I said to myself, "If I can be a city commissioner, why can't I be the Mayor?. . ."

At that time I was the mayor *pro tem*, and Boelens resigned, and I became the acting Mayor. We held several ballots to select a mayor until the next election, and the vote was always the same, two for Pat Barr, two for me, and two for Abe Drasin. And the city manager suggested to me that I have a secret ballot. And we had a secret ballot and I got all the votes but one. And I was elected.

Interview with ► Lyman Parks, November 19, 1985, GRPL, Oral History Collection.

A Ford (Not a Lincoln) Becomes President

For nearly 25 years, Gerald R. Ford had been Grand Rapids' favorite son. First elected to the House of Representatives as a reform candidate in 1948, Congressman Ford had been returned to office 12 times by comfortable majorities. Known for the promptness with which he responded to constituent needs, Ford never lost touch with his home base. His conservative views were closely aligned with the majority of voters in his district, and he took care to maintain a regular presence between elections. In 1965, Ford had been named House Republican leader, and if his party had ever been able to win a majority of the House seats, he would have achieved his longtime ambition to be Speaker of the House.

Ford did not become Speaker, but a series of events beginning in the fall of 1973 intervened to set him on a course for a higher office. When Vice President Spiro Agnew resigned in the wake of charges of scandal and kickbacks during his years as governor of Maryland, Ford was nominated to take his place. In his December 7 acceptance speech, the new vice president emphasized his desire to return the office to a business-as-usual status as quickly as possible. "I am a Ford, not a Lincoln," he said. "My addresses will never be as eloquent as Lincoln's. But I will do my best to equal his brevity and plain speaking."

Ford's tenure as vice president was short lived. Even as he was being sworn in, President Richard Nixon was in trouble for his role in the cover-up of the break-in at Democratic party headquarters in the Watergate apartment complex. Eight months later Nixon resigned in the face of impeachment by the House of Representatives, and the likelihood of conviction if he were tried by the Senate.

On August 9, 1973, Ford stood before the American people to take the oath of office as the 38th president of the United States. Speaking to a small group of business and political leaders in the East Room of the White House, and to a large national television audience, Ford gave what many regard as his best speech.

Mr. Chief Justice, my dear friends, my fellow Americans. The oath that I have taken is the same oath that was taken by George Washington and by every President under the Constitution.

But I assume the presidency under extraordinary circumstances never before experienced by Americans. This is an hour of history that troubles our minds and hurts our hearts.

Therefore, I feel it is my first duty to make an unprecedented compact with my countrymen. Not an inaugural address, not a fireside chat, not a campaign speech, just a little straight talk among friends. And I intend it to be the first of many.

I am acutely aware that you have not elected me as your President by your ballots. So I ask you to confirm me as your President with your prayers. And I hope that such prayers will also be the first of many.

If you have not chosen me by secret ballot, neither have I gained office by any secret promises. I have not campaigned either for the Presidency or the Vice Presidency. I have not subscribed to any partisan platform. I am indebted to no man and only to one woman, my dear wife.

As I begin this very difficult job, I have not sought this enormous responsibility, but I will not shirk it. Those who nominated and confirmed me as Vice President were my friends and are my friends. They were of both parties, elected by all the people and acting under the Constitution in their name.

It is only fitting then that I should pledge to them and to you that I will be the President of all the people.

Thomas Jefferson said the people are the only sure reliance for the preservation of our liberty. And down the years, Abraham Lincoln renewed this American article of faith, asking is there any better way for equal hopes in the world.

I intend on next Monday to request of the Speaker of the House of Representatives and the President pro tempore of the Senate the privilege of appearing before the Congress to share with my former colleagues and with you, the American people, my views on the priority business of the nation and to solicit your views and their views.

And may I say to the Speaker and the others, if I could meet with you right after this — these remarks — I would appreciate it.

Even though this is late in an election year there is no way we can go forward except together and no way anybody can win except by serving the people's urgent needs.

We cannot stand still or slip backward. We must go forward now together.

To the peoples and the governments of all friendly nations, and I hope that could encompass the whole world, I pledge an uninterrupted and sincere search for peace. America will remain strong and united.

But its strength will remain dedicated to the safety and sanity of the entire family of man as well as to our own precious freedom.

I believe that trust is the glue that holds governments together, not only our Government but civilization itself. That bond, though strained, is unbroken at home and abroad.

In all my public and private acts as your President, I expect to follow my instincts of openness and candor with full confidence that honesty is always the best policy in the end.

My fellow Americans, our long national nightmare is over. Our Constitution works. Our great republic is a government of laws and not of men. Here, the people rule.

But there is a higher power, by whatever name we honor him, who ordains not only righteousness but love, not only justice but mercy.

As we bind up the internal wounds of Watergate, more painful and more poisonous than those of foreign wars, let us restore the Golden Rule to our political process. And let brotherly love purge our hearts of suspicion and of hate.

In the beginning, I asked you to pray for me. Before closing, I ask again your prayers for Richard Nixon and for his family. May our former President who brought peace to millions find it for himself.

May God bless and comfort his wonderful wife and daughters whose love and loyalty will forever be a shining legacy to all who bear the lonely burdens of the White House.

I can only guess at those burdens although I witnessed at close hand the tragedies that befell three Presidents and the lesser trials of others.

With all the strength and all the good sense I have gained from life, with all the confidence of my family, my friends and dedicated staff impart to me and with the goodwill of countless Americans I have encountered in recent visits to 40 states, I now solemnly reaffirm my promise I made to you last Dec. 6 to uphold the Constitution, to do what is right as God gives me to see the right and to do the very best I can for America.

God helping me, I will not let you down.

Thank you.

▲ *New York Times,* August 10, 1974, p. 3.

◄ All of Grand Rapids looked on with pride as Gerald R. Ford was sworn in as the nation's 38th president. [Gerald R. Ford Library]

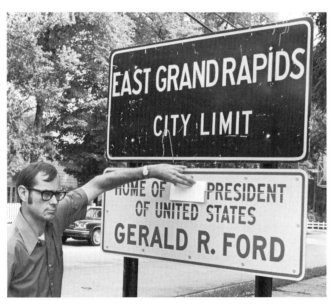

◄ Signs saluting the hometown of Vice President Ford were quickly changed after he became president. [Photo by © *Grand Rapids Press,* August 9, 1974, p. 17A]

Advice to Salmon: "Look Before Leaping"

In response to urging by environmentalists and the state Department of Natural Resources (DNR), Grand Rapids had begun cleaning up the Grand River in the 1960s. By 1970, with the dumping of sewage curtailed and toxin levels reduced, the DNR began planting hundreds of thousands of steelhead trout and coho and chinook salmon in the Grand and Rogue rivers. Salmon and steelhead runs made the Grand one of the nation's hottest game fishing spots, especially at the Sixth Street Dam in the heart of the city where the fish were blocked in their upstream spawning migration.

To help the fish bypass the dam, DNR officials proposed a fish "ladder" that turned the big jump over the dam into several smaller, more manageable steps. Art and civic groups joined the DNR to turn the ladder, dedicated in 1975, into a sculptural viewing area that enhanced the downtown landscape and became a tourist attraction as well. Unfortunately, the sculpture was sometimes hard on the fish. After its unveiling, its designer, local artist Joseph Kinnebrew, and project supporters were chagrined to learn that many fish were cracking their skulls on the overhanging viewing area as they leaped up the steps.

To their relief — and no doubt the fishes' as well — planners found they could deepen the channel and redesign the sculpture without major alterations to its viewing stage or artistic integrity.

Grand Rapids motorists and Grand River fish now have something in common: Both can find bypassing downtown hazardous at times.

Many a rushed motorist knows what it's like to fishtail through the US 131 S-curve. Not far from that spot, some unsuspecting rainbow trout are being knocked head over tail on the new ladder at the Sixth St. dam.

The unique, $240,000 ladder was designed as a functional sculpture. Sightseers can walk on the sculpture to watch the fish use the ladder to clear the Grand River dam and continue upstream to spawn.

For the time being, however, it appears that what's functional for the public may be a bit unpractical for the fish.

Biologists here for the Michigan Department of Natural Resources have discovered that some steelhead are jumping smack into one side of the sculpture that faces and extends low over the second to last step from the top.

The fish do look before they leap, said John Trimberger, chief DNR biologist here. However, during high water periods, water turbulence and velocity narrow the passage between the sculpture and fifth step. These conditions also obscure the overhanging wall as the fish gauge their last leap, he said.

And like the S-curve in a freeze, ice has been found to build up under the overhang to make fish passage virtually impossible.

The DNR hasn't recorded any trout killed by the impact, but some steelhead have been knocked back a couple of tiers in a state of semi-consciousness, he reported.

Biologists also are concerned about the fall salmon run. Trimberger said salmon leap higher and with more thrust.

Without modifications to the sculpture by then, the ladder may record its first fatality.

◄ *Grand Rapids Press,* April 5, 1975, p. 2A.

◄ Intended to help salmon and trout migrate upstream, Grand Rapids' fish ladder sculpture turned out to be temporarily hazardous to their health. [GRPL, Photo Collection]

A Bicentennial Time Capsule

In 1976, Grand Rapids joined with the rest of the nation to celebrate the 200th anniversary of the Declaration of Independence. A local committee coordinated local activities, including parades, fireworks, and ethnic festivals, as well as lectures, television programs, and the publication of history books.

Capping off the year-long observance, on December 31, 1976, was the sealing and dedication of a time capsule that would be opened in 2076 as part of the nation's tricentennial celebration.

NASA donated a training capsule from the Apollo moon exploration program to be used as the time cap-

sule, and members of Steketee's department store Teen Board, assisted by people throughout the community, proceeded to fill it with artifacts they thought would be of interest a century later. Items were still arriving as the time for sealing the capsule drew near.

Ever so carefully, Weldon Frankforter of the Grand Rapids Public Museum wedges the white, 1976 modernistic chair made by American Seating Co. among the heavy-duty cartons and partitions in the Grand Rapids Time Capsule. . . .

There are letters from [President Ford], Mayor Abe Drasin of Grand Rapids, U.S. Sens. Hart and Griffin, state Sens. Otterbacher and VanderLaan, U.S. Reps. VanderVeen and VanderJagt, and state Reps. Mathieu, Monsma and Sietsma.

The Ford letter, "To The People of Grand Rapids in 2076," points out that he personally participated in the opening of a time capsule sealed in 1876.

"Americans in 1876 had absolutely no doubt that an American president in 1976, under the Constitution of a free government, would be here in Washington to receive their message," is part of President Ford's 305-word letter to be opened in Grand Rapids on July 4, 2076.

Frankforter, the museum director, is concerned about inclusion of items from the art world. . . .

Will artist Paul Collins come up with something in time? He arrives as the deadline for packing is running out with framed sketches he made of the President while Ford was being interviewed by longtime friend — Press reporter Maury Dejonge, at Vail, Colo. . . .

Anything in the time capsule about Chaffee and Grand Rapids-born astronaut Jack R. Lousma? A frantic phone call to the *Press* results in the newspaper library sending over a National Air and Space Administration photograph of Chaffee, Virgil I. Grissom and Edward H. White II in training before they died in a flash fire on

Jan. 27, 1967, at Cape Kennedy — plus photographs and other stories about Chaffee and Lousma. . . .

What about some items of Jerry Ford in addition to his letter?

Arthur G. Brown of 3423 Badger Ave. SW, secretary of the 1930 South High championship team, provides a 1930 South yearbook, pennant, Ford congressional election button, and a letter written by Ford to Brown in 1976. . . .

What about TV representation in the time capsule? Phone calls Friday bring material from WZZM and a color videocassette of the Buck Matthews show, "Barns: A Loving Look at an American Landmark. . . ."

What's this? Sudden worrisome realization that the time capsule is carpeted. The welders fear fiery sparks as they weld the hatch shut will start a fire in the carpeting.

Is everything going down the drain with a last-minute fire?

The welders take a swatch of the carpet to the back of the truck and put a torch to it. They scorch the swatch. No fire. Says Steketee:

"For a 100-year trip we go first-class."

▲ After welders sealed the hatch, the capsule was ready for its 100-year journey through time. [Photo by © *Grand Rapids Press*, December 9, 1976, p. 1A]

◄ *Grand Rapids Press*, December 12, 1976, pp. 1A-2A.

▲ Girls from Steketee's Teen Board coordinated the collection of material for the bicentennial time capsule. [Photo by © *Grand Rapids Press*, December 9, 1976, p. 1A]

Running (And Rolling) Along the Grand River

Physical fitness became increasingly important to Americans in the 1970s, and running became a popular conditioning exercise. Entire families could be seen out jogging along roadways and through parks, and each year more cities seemed to be offering organized distance races for serious runners to enter. Grand Rapids joined the party in 1978.

The Old Kent River Bank Run was a success from the start. An estimated 1,250 runners participated the first year, running through downtown Grand Rapids and along the banks of the Grand River over the 25-kilometer (15.534 miles) course designed by the Grand Rapids Track Club. An equal number participated in the 3,000 meter (1.86 miles) fitness run.

Seeing the event as "another way to bring people to downtown Grand Rapids," Old Kent Bank provided the corporate sponsorship. Volunteer help came from track club members, medical professionals, scores of clubs and organizations, and hundreds of interested individuals, all earning praise from the runners and the thousands of spectators who lined the course. Further proof of the run's popularity came with increasing numbers of runners — 3,000 by 1980 — and appearances by many well-known, world-class competitors.

A new wrinkle, wheelchair racing, was added in 1979 and has been a fixture ever since. In the first outing, 15 wheelchair racers completed the 3,000-meter course and announced they would do more in the future. True to their word, a dozen wheelchair athletes showed up in 1980 and entered and completed the full 25K course. By 1990, wheelchair racers numbered in the hundreds and participated in both the 25K and shorter fitness course.

▲ From the beginning, the Old Kent River Bank Run has attracted athletes of all descriptions. [Illustration by © *Grand Rapids Press*, May 13, 1979, p. 3A]

Marathon runners all worry about blisters on their feet.

Tom Helder, 16, a participant in Saturday's Fitness Run, was more concerned about the blisters on his hands.

Helder was running the 3,000 meters (1.86 miles) in his wheelchair. He borrowed his dad's handball gloves. They worked well on the friction-hot rubber.

Helder, an Ottawa Hills High School sophomore, was one of 15 who raced in a wheelchair.

Tom Partanen, 28 — like many of the contestants, a member of the Pacers wheelchair basketball team — practiced for the run by doing laps twice a week at Ottawa's track.

His objective was to finish the race. All 15 finished.

Steve Payne, 15, a resident of Grand Valley Nursing Center, said he practiced at school, too. He's a 7th grader at Iroquois Middle and his strategy for the run was "just push and go."

John Batten, 30, of 349 Woodmere SE admitted he didn't practice as much as he should have, "I should practice every day," he said. "But I just wanted to finish the race."

Tom Kelderhouse, 40, of 311 Forest Hills Avenue SE, got in shape the way most of the other guys in the wheelchair division did — by doing laps and basketball....

Lee Montgomery, 21, of 346 Jefferson St. SE, felt tired after coming in second with a time of 16 minutes and 22 seconds. He said the team practiced every Wednesday to get in shape for the race.

David Kroon, 17, of 221 Edison Park Avenue NW, a student at West Catholic High School, finished first with a time of 15:07.

Kroon, also a member of the Pacers said he felt "pretty good" but said he could have done better if he had smaller rims on his wheels.

Special wheelchairs are available for marathon participants, said Kelderhouse. He said the sport chairs are built low to the ground and are a lot lighter.

He pointed out that those chairs cost approximately $700. A street chair also costs that amount and those who have one rarely can afford the other, said Kelderhouse.

He finished with a time of 22:25 and said he'd like to see next year's wheelchair division increased to four or five miles. "A two-mile run is more a sprint than endurance," he said. "Next year, we'll plan better for it."

▲ *Grand Rapids Press*, May 13, 1979, p. 3A.

Old Kent River Bank Run Records
(as of 1991)

Women: Joan Benoit Samuelson, 1:24:43 (1986)

Men: Mark Smith, 1:15:56 (1988)

Wheelchair: Robert Fitch, 1:09:57 (1989)

Please Take Your Garbage to the Nearest Park

On August 9, 1980, 850 city workers, members of AFSCME Local 1061, walked off the job, beginning the longest municipal strike in U.S. history. When they returned to work 88 days later, they had secured a 25 percent wage and fringe benefit increase over two years.

Impetus for the strike was a wage-and-classification survey, conducted by the Yarger Company in 1979. Recommended in the survey were new pay scales for all non-union, middle-management employees, who would receive an average 10.3 percent raise on top of a 10 percent annual wage hike, or about a 20 percent, one-year increase. Union members demanded equal treatment in the form of a 20 percent one-year increase and a cost-of-living increase in the second year. With so much money at stake, positions hardened, and the ensuing deadlock led to a strike call by union president Edwin Muste.

Supervisors filled in and provided basic services during the three months that workers stayed off the job. In order to have their garbage collected, city residents were asked to bring it to trucks that were stationed at a different city park each day. Negotiations continued throughout the strike, but even with state mediation efforts, no progress was made until October when city commissioners M. Howard Rienstra and Mary Alice Williams became directly involved in the talks. Thereafter both sides slowly edged away from their original positions. On November 3, union members voted to accept the city's offer of a 16 percent raise in wages and benefits the first year, and 9 percent the second.

Later, after the strike had been settled, Rienstra described the critical point in the negotiations to members of the Breakfast Club of Grand Rapids.

So, finally what happened was that as city commissioners we... decided that we had to intervene directly to see what was going on. Now, that's a very dangerous thing to do, for politicians to get involved in labor negotiations.... About October eighth I believe we made a decision that two city commissioners would participate in negotiation, first of all as observers to see what was happening at the bargaining table. And we did that....

I was one of them and Mary Alice Williams was the other. The two of us joined and what we did first was to sit back in a motel room...and watch those at the table talking to each other. We came back from that session with impressions from both sides and we wrote those impressions to our colleagues and used them for basis of further negotiations....

Number 1: There is on the part of both negotiating teams a siege mentality. Defensiveness and suspiciousness is clear, and a distinct barrier to effective communication of any sort....

Number 2: It's our perception that both parties are concerned to save face....

Well, after being non-participant observers, the city commission authorized Ms. Williams and me to go one step further, although we got our nose in a wringer for doing so, and that is to begin to speak. Those of you who know me, know it was an incredible act of self-discipline to sit there and not speak in the first day. And so we began to speak and to present the reason for the city's position to the union.... We did get a better understanding of our proposal, not agreement with us; but a better understanding of what we were talking about as a policy body of the city. We had that presented, and in the course of two or three sessions, we finally, by a four to three vote in the city commission had agreement to make a limited cost of living proposal in the second year. That was presented to the union and they rejected it....We thought we had moved from night to day in making that offer and then the union rejected it to our surprise. It was at that point that Mary Alice and I did something which got some commissioners very angry with us. We asked for a session with just two union bargainers, the chief ones, apart from our staff and apart from the union bargaining team. We said, "Can we talk to you, person to person, to try to find out where the problem is here?" We did that, we talked to them, we sat in rooms separately from them. They got authorization from the rest of their bargaining committee and tried to find out why they were rejecting at this point yet....

...The strike has been settled and now we have serious difficulties of working to get morale back into our work force.... There is a lot of work to be done, if we're not going to have another strike in two years and I certainly don't want one.

▲ Union leader Edwin Muste joined with rank and file members for a toast after ratification of a new contract ended the three-month city worker's strike. [Photo by © *Grand Rapids Press*, November 4, 1980, p. 1A]

◄ M. Howard Rienstra, "Speech to Breakfast Club," November 26, 1980, GRPL, Oral History Collection.

An All-America City

In 1981, for the third time since the award was established by the National Municipal League, Grand Rapids learned that it had been designated an All-America City. First honored for its Citizens Action campaign to clean up city politics when the award was created in 1949, the city gained All-America status again in 1960 for its downtown urban renewal effort. The 1981 award came in the wake of a decade of citizen involvement to find solutions to such post-World War II problems as the increase of urban crime, the closing of many neighborhood and central city businesses, and the seeming lack of community spirit.

When the award was announced, proud residents led by Mayor Abe Drasin and Chamber of Commerce leaders moved quickly to call attention to the city's new status. All-America city signs went up around town, and efforts were made to attract new business and convention groups by highlighting the award. While they knew that All-America honors would not resolve any of the problems the city still faced, for the moment leaders were encouraged to think others felt they were on the right track.

▲ City High School student Charlie Wallace won an All-America City student art contest and saw his work painted on the wall of the Purchase Electric building. There it greeted motorists as they entered the "S" curve on northbound U.S. 131. [Photo by © *Grand Rapids Press*, June 29, 1981, p. 00]

Grand Rapids is again an "All America City" — thanks to the thousands of citizens involved in the arts, neighborhood business revitalization, and crime prevention program.

The Furniture City is one of 10 communities across the nation to win the honor, given annually by the National Municipal League....

Though the national award is chiefly symbolic in nature, city and Chamber of Commerce officials said it could boost community pride, display the unique nature of the community and perhaps even help attract new business.

In winning the honor, "people power" triumphed where expensive building had failed....

Mayor Abe L. Drasin is expected to receive the All America city award in ceremonies June 5, the opening day of Festival 81.

Festival was one of three local projects cited in an All America City nomination form put together by a Chamber of Commerce committee....

The other projects cited were community crime prevention programs and the revitalization of the Burton Heights business district.

Some 6,000 city residents are participating in the "Child Watch" crime prevention program established by the police department and the public schools; another 13,000 volunteers and performers worked together to put on the annual Calder Arts Festival last year....

Mary Alice Williams, a neighborhood activist and 2nd Ward city commissioner, stressed the importance of winning the All America City honor for citizen participation, rather than for construction projects.

"I have a fear that it could get all hyped out of proportion from what this city really means," she said. "If Grand Rapids means anything it is that people can get involved at various levels and have an impact...."

The city and chamber already have begun planning promotions to spread the word about the honor. Ellis Outdoor Advertising Co. has agreed to place the message on billboards, and the chamber plans to sell custom front auto license plates with the words All America City.

In addition, an All America City poster — to be chosen through a city-wide school contest — will be reproduced on a building that faces the U.S.-131's downtown S-curve....

▲ *Grand Rapids Press*, April 9, 1981, pp. 1A-2A.

▲ As soon as word of the honor arrived, symbols of Grand Rapids' status as an All-America city began springing up all around town. Mayor Abe Drasin led the way by installing All-America City license plates on his car. [Photo by © *Grand Rapids Press*, June 1, 1981, p. 2C]

Celebration on the Grand

For a few days in September 1981, Grand Rapids residents were as close to the center of power in North America as they are ever likely to be. The occasion was "Celebration on the Grand," a collection of about 100 separate happenings centering on the dedication of the Gerald R. Ford Presidential Museum, the new Grand Rapids Art Museum facility, and the opening of the Amway Grand Plaza Hotel after a $24 million remodeling. So many people attended the events that guests had to be housed as far away as Holland and Kalamazoo.

The greatest excitement was generated by the crowd of dignitaries who gathered for the dedication of the Ford Museum. President Ronald Reagan and Vice President George Bush both came to town, along with Canadian Prime Minister Pierre Trudeau and Mexican President José Lopez Portillo. Congressional leaders of both parties did their part to help honor Ford, as did entertainers like Bob Hope, and leaders from the business community. An estimated 900 print and broadcast media representatives made sure that the rest of the nation knew what was going on in Grand Rapids.

Adding luster to the moment was a summit meeting in which the three North American heads of state met face to face to discuss economic concerns and the development of North American markets for products of the Caribbean basin.

For those not interested in international diplomacy, there was the movement of the Art Museum into its new home in the renovated Federal Building. There were concerts, television specials, and picnics, too, along with the first opportunity to see the totally remodeled Amway Grand Plaza Hotel, which diehards still insisted on calling the Pantlind.

It was something of a letdown when all the dignitaries and media personalities headed for home, but local folks found Celebration on the Grand to be so much fun that they made it an annual summer-ending event. The bigwigs are long gone, but the fireworks and other festivities return each year.

The air was crisp and cold, but spirits were warm this morning as a crowd estimated at 100,000 gathered to witness the dedication of the Gerald R. Ford Presidential Museum.

The $11.5 million structure received its formal opening amid a torrent of praise for Ford.

President Reagan — once a bitter opponent of Ford — paid tribute to Grand Rapids' most famous resident, saying the former president served the nation well during a difficult time in history.

"Gerald Ford healed America because he so thoroughly understood America," Reagan said. "His was and is an unquestioning belief in the soundness of our way of governing and in the resilience of our people. . . ."

Reagan called Ford "a man of decency, a man of honor," and told the man who beat him out of the 1976 GOP presidential nomination: "You brought us through difficult and trying times and helped us to believe in ourselves again. . . ."

In all, 15 speakers offered remarks on a huge stage just south of the riverfront museum. They included Vice President George Bush, Mexican President Jose Lopez Portillo, Canadian Prime Minister Pierre Trudeau, former French President Valery Giscard d'Estaing and Sunao Sonoda, Japan's foreign minister.

▲ *Grand Rapids Press*, September 18, 1981, p. A1.

▼ President Reagan, former President Ford, Nancy Reagan, and Betty Ford shared the stage at the formal dedication of the Gerald R. Ford Presidential Museum. [Photo by © *Grand Rapids Press*, September 18, 1981, p. A1]

The new location of the Grand Rapids Art Museum was dedicated this morning — from across the street.

Former President Gerald R. Ford cut the red ribbon draped between light posts at the Pearl Street entrance of the museum, but that symbolic act was the only part of the ceremony that took place on the site.

The steady early-morning rain...washed out the 9 a.m. nostalgic march from the old, white-columned museum building at 230 Fulton St. to the imposing, gray, granite building at 153 N. Division Ave.

Instead, the "Art on the Move" procession was cut drastically, from 50 minutes and several blocks to about a half minute and a hurried crossing of Division Avenue to the Pearl Street door....

Ford expressed delight in having a role in the dedication, citing the great progress of the city and the importance of cultural organizations, such as the Art Museum, and lauding those who devoted the time and effort to accomplish the expansion of the arts display facilities.

Referring to the opening, Ford said, "This can be taken as another giant step forward to enrich the daily lives of our community."

▲ *Grand Rapids Press,* September 17, 1981, p. A1.

▲ During a heavy downpour, former President Ford cut a ribbon officially opening the Grand Rapids Art Museum's new home on Pearl Street. Looking on are Helen Milliken, wife of Governor William Milliken, and Art Museum president Charles McCallum. [Photo by © *Grand Rapids Press,* September 17, 1981, p. 1A]

Elegant.

That's the best way to describe the Amway Grand Plaza Hotel, formally dedicated Tuesday evening with a private party involving 600 business and political leaders.

At the top of the VIP guest list were former President Gerald R. Ford and his wife, Betty.

By week's end, the Plaza will host the heads of state from three countries: Mexican President Jose Lopez Portillo, Canadian Prime Minister Pierre Trudeau and President Ronald Reagan....

Moments before introducing Ford, [Jay] VanAndel reminded the former president that the modern-day Pantlind was completed in 1913, the same year Ford was born.

Ford recognized an excellent straight line and drew the heartiest laughter of the evening when he said that during VanAndel's remark, "Betty leaned over and said: 'You'd better get some renovation, too.'

"I didn't tell her, but I was thinking to myself that it wouldn't cost quite as much," Ford joked, referring to the $24 million price tag for the first...restoration.

Ford recalled that during his congressional career he attended many dinners and meetings at the Pantlind and consumed "more than one beer down at the old Pub in the corner...."

After predicting the Grand Plaza would begin a new downtown era, Ford paid lavish tribute to DeVos and VanAndel.

"There is no community in this great land that has two finer leaders than Rich and Jay...I congratulate them and thank them for what they have done...."

▲ A large and enthusiastic crowd witnessed the official opening of the Amway Grand Plaza Hotel. [Photo by © *Grand Rapids Press,* September 16, 1981, p. A1]

◄ *Grand Rapids Press,* September 16, 1981, p. A1.

"Let's Have a City of Delight"

At the same time that city officials faced off against union negotiators, other community leaders were gathering downtown at Fountain Street Church for a series of three "town meetings" organized by Urban Concern, Inc. Crowds of 150 to 300 turned out to listen to selected panels offer their thoughts about the community's history and its future direction, and then air their own opinions in the discussion that followed panel members' presentations. Speakers included four college professors, two elected officials, two public administrators, a minister, a magazine publisher and arts activist, and a businessman. Their topics covered a wide range of territory — from prehistory to public transit, business development, urban planning, education, and recent changes in the landscape and environment. The final speaker was Nicholas Wolterstorff, professor of philosophy at Calvin College, who offered his personal vision of Grand Rapids as a "City of Delight."

Can the city be an object of delight? We rarely ask this question, do we? We tend only to ask questions concerning the functional efficiency of our cities. "How long will it take me to get to work?" "Where's the nearest supermarket?" And, yes, some of us prize the few jewel boxes scattered about in which we can hear good music, see fine paintings, watch good plays. But seldom do we think of the city, or at least large chunks of it, as a single object. And even more seldom do we ask of that object whether it gives us delight. Rarely do we think of the city as an object which shapes space, which provides for each of us a variety of focal points for our lives and which determines our paths among those focal points. And so of course we don't ask whether that object, the city, gives us any delight. . . .

Many of you, I daresay, have now and then been to cities which caught you up with delight, which made you glad to be there. What made them objects of delight? Can we pick out the relevant factors?

It's not hard to identify several of them. For one thing, in those cities which are objects of delight there are people — large groups of people — on the streets and the sidewalks and in the plazas and centers. There is nothing so depressing as a city whose public spaces are empty of people. By contrast, there is nothing quite so exhilarating as a city whose public spaces are filled with people going about their work and leisure, a city where there are places for people to sit, to converse with one another and to watch the passing scene. Perhaps, more than anything else, what makes a city an object of delight is that there is life in its public spaces. . . .

Second, what makes for a delightful city is the way its space is shaped. . . .

What makes cities delightful is the richness of texture which comes from layers of history. . . .

Last, the delightful city is one which is filled with surprises, interesting and curious spots, sights and spaces that one relishes. The delightful city is the city that one cannot take in with a single glance. It's a city to walk around in, to savor.

And now our question: Can Grand Rapids become an object of delight? Can Grand Rapids become like those other delightful cities that you and I have known? . . .

Let us look at our city and assess the possibilities. Calder Plaza, which in the minds of its architects was probably meant to become the center of the city, will never be that . . ., [but] there are a few pleasant little secluded spots within it. The Calder itself — in my judgment the very best of all Calder's stabiles — introduces a powerful centripetal force into the plaza, giving it some character in spite of its windblown openness. . . .

By contrast, the new Monroe Mall has a chance to succeed in drawing people to it. . . . It has a human scale and an intimacy to it. It does not feel open and windswept. There are places to sit and talk and eat — and watch. . . .

The new Performing Arts Center, from an urban standpoint, is an unmitigated disaster.

Visually, its exterior surfaces are all hard and cold, offering neither warmth nor textures that are inviting. . . . Everything about the building screams to the pedestrian, "Go away. I don't want you here." I suspect that most pedestrians will do exactly that; go away. Or rather, stay away. . . .

The city also continues to display its indifference to the river. . . .

But for these disasters there are compensations. All those wonderful Victorian houses and streets in Heritage Hill are continuing sources of delight. . . . And that old area of the city, Heartside, just south of center city, is being lovingly restored rather than thoughtlessly razed. . . .

Although we've made a lot of mistakes in our city, genuine possibilities do exist for Grand Rapids to become an object of delight. Heritage Hill, Monroe Mall and Heartside hold out the promise that people will indeed say about Grand Rapids: "It is delightful to be here."

◄ Nicholas Wolterstorff, "Let's Have a City of Delight," *Grand Rapids Past, Present and Future*, pp. 65-68.

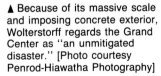

▲ Because of its massive scale and imposing concrete exterior, Wolterstorff regards the Grand Center as "an unmitigated disaster." [Photo courtesy Penrod-Hiawatha Photography]

◄ Intimate gathering places for quiet conversation on Monroe Mall help make Grand Rapids a "city of delight," according to Nicholas Wolterstorff. [T.J. Hamilton photo]

Drug Dealers Stung by Waterbeds

One of the most serious problems facing Grand Rapids police and elected officials in the 1970s and 1980s was the expansion of drug trafficking. Greater quantities of more potent and addictive substances were finding their way into the city. Larger and larger sums of money changed hands in drug deals, and dealers brazenly operated from street corners and "crack" houses.

To combat this blight, law enforcement officials sought beefed-up budgets and additional officers. They also developed more varied and creative tactics for snaring drug traffickers and bringing them to justice. In one successful mid-1980s "sting" operation, local police posing undercover as waterbed retailers arrested 145 dope dealers.

Grand Rapids police Wednesday night and early today were rounding up 145 area persons on drug and stolen goods charges in what they called the largest bust in the city's history....

According to Lt. Thomas Hendershot, whose vice unit officers conducted the six-month investigation, about 145 suspects are accused of dealing drugs including heroin, cocaine, LSD, synthetic prescription drugs, marijuana and hashish.

In Eastown, a half-dozen vice officers opened a custom waterbed shop, called Eastown Waterbeds, at 1338 Lake Drive SE. They built and sold waterbeds, light accessories, head and nightstands from the store, at the same time purchasing drugs and stolen property, police said.

Vice detectives also lived and worked in a Burton Heights home, purchasing drugs and stolen property from other suspects during the six-month period.

Most of the drug and stolen property transactions at both locations were recorded by video and audio reporting equipment, according to a department news release.

Hendershot said about 10 of the arrested drug suspects were "major" dealers capable of conducting single drug transactions worth some $25,000. All drug arrests were for sale of the substances, not possession, and all buys were made directly to vice officers, he said....

Officers chose to establish a waterbed shop because several of the vice detectives are skilled in woodworking, Hendershot said. They became friendly with other merchants and residents, even joining the Eastown Business Association and attending meetings.

They operated under the slogan: "We will build a bed for the rest of your life" and had matchbook covers printed with their name and phone number, just as a legitimate business. The business was featured in an article in the neighborhood association newsletter earlier this year.

To keep themselves from being bothered by too many customers, the detectives set their prices high, Hendershot said.

Neither patrol officers nor other residents were told the business was bogus, Hendershot said.

◄ *Grand Rapids Press*, May 12, 1983, pp. 1A-2A.

▼ Headlines announcing drug-related crimes and arrests became an all-too-common occurrence in the 1980s.
[*Grand Rapids Press*]

BATTLE PLAN: Reducing demand key to drug fight, experts argue

Drug arrests send a warning

"It's a lot less costly to prevent the drug abuse from happening. But it gets hard to convince people to spend money on kids who seem perfectly healthy."

— **Barry Mintzes**
State Office of Substance Abuse Services

Residents say sting won't stop drug dealers in area

Drug-ring figure gets 5-20 years

Chief says drug problem serious, but funding may cut back plans

Optimists push early warning on drugs

Man gets 3 years for selling cocaine

"We know there is a problem. The people calling in tell us it's a problem."
— Police Chief Barry Emmons

New 24-hour cocaine hotline available through Metropolitan's CareUnit center

All ages, classes vulnerable to drug, alcohol problems

A Landmark is Dismantled

Although the face of downtown changed dramatically in the 1960s and '70s, the weather ball atop the Michigan National Bank Building shone brightly, serving Grand Rapids residents, season after season, as an instant weather information station. Installed in August 1967, the weather ball survived countless storms, including two nearby tornadoes, with only one incident in which one of its 12-by-20-foot identifying letters blew off and fell to the street below.

In 1987, however, its demise was sealed when Michigan National officials learned that the 125-foot ball and supporting stand were causing structural damage to the bank building below. Accepting the advice of their architects and contractors, they decided to remove the ball before serious damage occurred.

Although some loyalists talked of a "Save the Weather Ball" campaign, the downtown landmark came down with little opposition. Grand Rapids *Press* writer Tom Rademacher offered a series of suggestions for re-using the ball, but it was local artist Ian Macartney who salvaged the glass neon tubes and turned them into colorful art pieces for those who wanted to own a piece of the city's most colorful landmark.

The Weather Ball Code

Weather ball blue, colder weather in view;
Weather ball red, warmer weather ahead;
Weather ball green, no changes foreseen;
Colors blinking bright, rain or snow in sight.

▲ For 20 years, the Michigan National Bank weather ball was one of Grand Rapids' best-known landmarks. [GRPL, Photo Collection]

Is nothing sacred?

This isn't the Calder stabile or the fish ladder we're talking about here — this is important stuff — the weather ball, for light's sake.

Oh, weather ball, plum, we're feeling glum.

It's the building below you that's crumbling, we're told.

Isn't there a better final resting place than the scrap heap? Isn't there enough room in the world for a slightly used weather ball? Does anybody care?

As a gesture of concern for the town's most famous sphere, we offer these suggestions as alternatives to burying the ball.

Weather ball red, you'll never be dead. . . .

—Sell the Calder for scrap iron, and replace it with the weather ball, lights and all. Dangle the weather ball on a chain, like a pendulum, between the City and County buildings. In a government setting like that, we could change the poem to say:

Weather ball blue, let's sell the zoo,
Weather ball red, new city manager ahead
Weather ball green, no surplus foreseen
Weather ball bright, Ed Muste's called another strike. . . .

—Weld it to the top of the Amway Grand Plaza Hotel's tower.

—Make it a permanent nesting site for future peregrine falcons. Raise worms in it for Grand River fishermen. My stars, make it into an observatory. A water reservoir. An Easter egg. Apartments. . . .

—Split the ball in two, plaster the insides and create a couple of new city pools to replace the bad ones.

"One if by land, two if by sea, and blinking bright if by moped." — Paul Revere

"Don't fire 'till you see the lights of the weather ball." — William Prescott

"Et tu, weather ball?" — Julius Caesar

"I have lusted in my heart for the weather ball." — former President Jimmy Carter

"It'd make a nice tie tac." — Randy Disselkoen

"I'm delighted they're taking the weather ball down. Will it give us more parking spaces downtown?" — Grand Rapids Mayor Gerald Helmholdt

"I am not a weather ball. . .am I?" — Richard Nixon

"It shall return." — Gen. Douglas MacArthur

▲ *Grand Rapids Press*, February 11, 1987, p. D1.

Celebrating Grand Rapids' 150th Birthday

On April 5, 1988, Grand Rapids marked its sesquicentennial as an incorporated municipality. On that date 150 years earlier, the Michigan legislature had granted a village charter to the small group of pioneers who had migrated west and established the community. To honor the occasion, a citizens committee planned a weeklong celebration that included a noontime birthday party in the Grand Center, downtown walking tours, museum exhibits, a sesquicentennial run through the city's historic district, and a project to outline several downtown bridges in lights.

The various events brought large crowds downtown, and left many of them with a better sense of the city's history and optimism for its future. One of those who looked to the future was *Press* editor Mike Lloyd, who wondered what had been the key to the city's development during its first 15 decades, and if that critical element would be present in the future.

Cheap land, lots of woods and running water [for transportation or power] may explain why there is a town here, but it doesn't explain why Grand Rapids turned out to be the biggest and most prosperous city on this side of the state. A publication from 100 years ago asked even then, "Why is Grand Rapids prospering?"

The article's conclusion was that the leadership of the community is what made Grand Rapids grand. The families making the big money in this community also gave a lot back. That was the point of the article. The author said there were no "old fogies" running the town.

In the decades since, that feeling of stewardship has certainly continued. Anyone who has lived in this town very long is well aware of names like Blodgett, Hunting, Butterworth, Idema, Frey, Pantlind, Meijer, Lowe, Wege, Baldwin, Cook, Sebastian, Keeler, DeVos, Eberhard, VanAndel and Pew.

In the last few years there has been a lot of discussion about what names and families will supply that philanthropic leadership for the next 150 years. . . .

"There is no question that over the years this community has benefitted by local ownership and local business leadership," said Tom Heywood, executive director of the Combined Arts Council. . . .

Diana Sieger, executive director of the Grand Rapids Foundation, told me she had the same feeling that "the leadership is changing, especially in some of our symbolically local companies. But I see that as evolutionary, not revolutionary, and I see new leaders and new businesses becoming more involved."

Linda Samuelson, director of the Council for the Humanities, welcomes the change. "Yes, I've heard all the concerns about losing local leadership and local ownership. I don't see it that way. I see progress and opportunity. We have a legacy of social responsibility in this community. If that falls off it's our fault, not some outsider's. . . ."

In the end I think Linda, who is also a city commissioner, is right. We can look back but we can't go back. As part of the sesquicentennial celebration this week there will be a giant birthday cake with (surprise) 150 candles. Let's blow out the candles but continue to carry the torch.

▲ *Grand Rapids Press,* April 3, 1988, p. F9.

◄ Fireworks over the Grand River capped a daylong celebration kicking off Grand Rapids' sesquicentennial week. [Photo by © *Grand Rapids Press,* April 6, 1988, p. A1]

▲ As Senator Carl Levin (right) looked on, Mayor Gerald Helmholdt cut a giant four-tier, red-white-and-blue cake to launch Grand Rapids' 150th birthday celebration. [Photo by © *Grand Rapids Press,* April 6, 1988, p. B1]

War in the Persian Gulf

Like most other Americans, Grand Rapids residents were stunned by the news on August 1, 1990, that Saddam Hussein's Iraqi army had invaded and occupied tiny, oil-rich Kuwait. Their sense of outrage at this aggression grew as atrocities committed by the Iraqis were reported in the American media. Support was strong for the United Nations embargo of Iraqi exports, and when those economic sanctions failed to force an Iraqi withdrawal, local citizens rallied behind President George Bush's decision to send American troops to expel the aggressors.

Only when local reserve forces were ordered to active duty did the full impact of American involvement register. Before long, area soldiers from all walks of life were saying goodbye to spouses and families and heading for embarkation points on the first leg of their journey to the Persian Gulf. From the time of their departure until they returned to a joyful homecoming, reports of their participation in "Operation Desert Storm" dominated the local news.

No single story drew more attention locally than the January 30, 1991, capture of 20-year-old Army Spec. Melissa Rathbun-Nealy of Grand Rapids and her partner Spec. David Lockett, near the Saudi Arabia-Kuwait border. Mercifully, the conflict was a short one, and less than a month after her capture, Melissa was on her way back to the United States and her family.

Army Spec. Melissa Rathbun-Nealy and her partner were lost after making a wrong turn when they were attacked and surrounded by Iraqi soldiers, according to an Army report that provides the most detailed account yet of their disappearance.

Rathbun-Nealy, 20, and Lockett, 23, were part of a two-truck convoy that came under fire Jan. 30 after the convoy mistakenly drove toward the battle at Khafji near the Saudi-Kuwaiti border, according to the report.

Two soldiers who escaped in the rear vehicle said the truck carrying Rathbun-Nealy and Lockett became stuck in the sand as they tried to flee. They summoned help, but a rescue team found only the truck, still idling, according to the report.

The drivers stopped before reaching Khafji to discuss the route they were taking, according to one of the soldiers who escaped. The report indicates Lockett insisted he knew where he was going and that it was the correct way back.

At that point, Rathbun-Nealy joined Lockett in the lead vehicle — though the report does not say who was driving — with the privates following behind. About 3 p.m., as they neared Khafji, the convoy passed a damaged Saudi M-60 tank that partially blocked the road.

"The occupants of the second HEV then heard two explosions and the sound of debris striking their vehicle, observed what they perceived to be enemy troops ahead near the archway into town, and immediately initiated a U-turn along the road," the report said. . . .

The two privates drove north along the highway to a Marine checkpoint, and a rescue team returned to where Rathbun-Nealy and her partner were last seen.

When they arrived, the vehicle was deserted and there were no signs of fighting or blood, but the soldiers' personal gear was scattered about and weapons were missing, according to the report.

According to the report, a captured Iraqi lieutenant has said he witnessed the capture of an American female and male and that both had been injured, the female having a wound in her arm.

▲ Aquinas College students favoring and opposing the Persian Gulf War gathered in front of the Press building to make their feelings known. [Photo by © *Grand Rapids Press*, January 1, 1991, p. F4]

◄ *Grand Rapids Press*, February 25, 1991, pp. A1, A8.

▲ War's reality was underlined when local soldier Melissa Rathbun-Nealy, shown here after her safe return to the U.S., was captured by Iraqi troops and held prisoner for three weeks. [Photo by © *Grand Rapids Press*, March 11, 1991, p. A1]

◄ President George Bush's visit added to the excitement of Grand Rapids' 1991 Fourth of July celebration welcoming home troops from the Persian Gulf. [Photo by © *Grand Rapids Press*, January 1, 1992, p. F4]

"Hooray, It's Snowing"

Two locally owned Grand Rapids-based companies achieved international acclaim in the 1980s. Both Steelcase, the office-furniture giant, and Amway, the home-products manufacturer, announced annual sales of over $1 billion in the mid-1980s.

Founded as the Metal Office Furniture Company in 1912 by Peter Wege, Walter Idema, and David D. Hunting, Steelcase specialized in metal at a time when most office furniture was made of wood. During World War II, the company developed a line of furniture for naval vessels, and in the postwar years its sales grew as architects designed larger and taller office buildings that required fire-safe metal furniture. By the 1970s, Steelcase had outstripped its competitors, becoming the world's largest office furniture manufacturer, with subsidiaries in several European countries and in Japan. The company controlled an esti-mated 30 percent of the U.S. market and provided employment to thousands of local workers. In 1984 Steelcase was listed as one of the 100 best companies to work for in America.

The Amway Corporation began when high school buddies Jay VanAndel and Rich DeVos decided to go into business together after they returned from Army Air Force duty in World War II. After establishing and then selling a flying school, they built a large distributor organization for Nutrilite Products, Inc. Concerned about Nutrilite's unsteady management, they created their own Amway Corporation and established a vast distributor network to market a line of Amway home products. The two were a well-matched team. VanAndel organized production and wrote promotional literature, and DeVos emphasized distributor recruitment and training. Starting out with a desk in VanAndel's basement, they built their company into a massive manufacturing and administrative complex that produces thousands of products for distributors on four continents.

Both companies continue to be locally owned and operated, and are well known as good corporate citizens of the Grand Rapids community. The Grand Center has a state-of-the-art music hall thanks to the generosity of Rich and Helen DeVos, and the Public Museum received a similar gift from Jay and Betty VanAndel. Corporately, and through its private foundation, Steelcase has given millions of dollars to cultural and social service agencies in West Michigan. Both companies stand as proof of the fundamental truth of the axiom that sound business practices and corporate success go hand in hand with good community citizenship.

HOORAY! IT'S SNOWING
(OR POURING)!!
What a wonderful day for Amway selling. Nearly everybody will be at home, planning to stay at home, catching up on extra cleaning jobs. I'll have a chance to talk to some prospects I haven't been able to tie down before.

And I have some wonderful bad-weather products to sell: Amway Dri-fab, Show Glo, Chrome and Glass Cleaner....

It's a wonderful day for cleaning the oven, polishing the silver, shampooing the rugs. And I've got what those jobs take.

This ought to be a day with that extra time in it for a promising pitch on Queen Cookware. Bad-weather days are good selling days for Amway and me.

▲ Wilbur Cross and Gordon Olson, *Commitment to Excellence*, p. 160.

▲ High school buddies Rich DeVos (left) and Jay VanAndel tried several business ventures after World War II, including a flying school, before forming the Amway Corporation. [Amway Corporation photo]

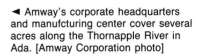

◄ Amway's corporate headquarters and manufcturing center cover several acres along the Thornapple River in Ada. [Amway Corporation photo]

▲ Steelcase's distinctive pyramid-shaped Corporate Development Center in Gaines Township quickly became a West Michigan landmark. [Steelcase, Inc., photo]

◄Steelcase trucks, with their deep blue paint and highly polished chrome trim, have become a company trademark. [Steelcase, Inc., photo]

Quality products, ► customer service, and on-time delivery have long been Steelcase watchwords. [Steelcase, Inc., photo]

THE SCHEDULE MUST BE MET!

IT IS OUR BOSS! WE MUST FIGHT TO THE ABSOLUTE LIMIT TO SHIP

QUALITY PRODUCTS, ON TIME.

ANY ACTION IS WARRANTED TO ACCOMPLISH THIS END.

The Fastest Growing County in Michigan

Numbers, it is often said, do not lie. Thus it is to numbers that analysts most often turn when seeking to understand or explain change. Population figures and economic statistics for Grand Rapids and Kent County in the past two decades are particularly instructive. While outlying areas have shown growth of 10 percent or more each decade, the totals for the central city of Grand Rapids have remained relatively unchanged. The figures also show the homogeneous nature of the suburban areas, where less than 5 percent of the population is African-American, Hispanic, or Native

American. In Grand Rapids, on the other hand, those same groups constitute slightly more than 30 percent of the total population.

Clearly, the central city and the surrounding suburbs are different. That point was driven home in 1990, when *City and State* magazine named Kent County one of the top 50 "up and coming" counties in the country at the same time Grand Rapids officials were working to shore up an aging infrastructure with limited financial resources. Citing the county's economic diversity, and high quality of living, the magazine placed Kent County 33rd

overall on the list of the 50 top counties. Making the ranking even more significant was the degree to which California with 15 counties and Florida with 12 dominated the list.

Local officials interpreted the information from different points of view. County officials saw it as an opportunity to attract additional industry, while Grand Rapids Mayor Gerald Helmholdt used the data as a strong argument for the creation of a regional metropolitan council "to manage the growth" to assure that it benefited the entire region.

A magazine survey ranking Kent County among the top 50 "Up-and-Coming" counties in the nation reflects economic diversity and quality of living likely to bring even greater growth, local officials say.

The study, published this month in "City & State" magazine, ranks Kent County 33rd in a list of 50 counties with burgeoning population and economic growth.

Oakland County, in the sub-

urban Detroit area, is ranked 37th on the list, which is dominated by Sun Belt areas. The study considered growth in population, employment and property values in ranking each county.

Richard Platte, Kent County controller, said the ranking speaks well of the county's potential to attract new industry.

"I think it's the type of thing that major employers and major industry look at," Platte said.

"When they are looking for a place to relocate — especially in the Midwest — they are going to look at us. . . ."

Grand Rapids Mayor Gerald R. Helmholdt said he was not surprised with the ranking, pointing out that Kent County's economic strength is well known. "If we can keep up that kind of good news that gets out nationwide then it can't do anything but help us," Helmholdt said.

He added the ranking further illustrates the need for an areawide Metropolitan Council to manage the growth.... Kent County Board Chairman Kenneth Kuipers, R-Grand Rapids, said he is pleased the county would rank so high nationally, particularly since most of the counties listed are in the Sun Belt.

"To be identified as a rapidly growing area is a good thing," Kuipers said. "I thought we were good, but to be in the top 50 in the United States...."

◄ *Grand Rapids Press,* July 23, 1990, pp. A1, A4.

Grand Rapids Area Recent Population Characteristics
1960-1990

1960

	White	Black	Other	Total
Grand Rapids	162,535	12,260	518	175,313
East Grand Rapids	10,903	18	3	10,924
Grandville	7,972	—	3	7,975
Kentwood/Paris Twp	19,054	161	20	19,235
Lowell	2,543	—	2	2,545
Rockford	2,069	—	5	2,074
Walker	16,346	24	11	16,381
Wyoming	45,751	28	50	45,829

1970

	White	Black	Other	Total
Grand Rapids	174,025	22,296	1,328	197,649
East Grand Rapids	12,513	22	30	12,565
Grandville	10,730	9	25	10,764
Kentwood	19,990	255	65	20,310
Lowell	3,055	1	12	3,068
Rockford	2,422	1	5	2,428
Walker	11,462	8	22	11,492
Wyoming	56,031	291	238	68,052

1980

	White	Black	Asian	Hispanic	American Indian	Other	Total
Grand Rapids	147,171	28,602	1,130	5,751	1,260	2,071	181,843
East G.R.	10,756	74	63	53	10	42	10,914
Grandville	12,158	54	75	105	20	1,928	12,412
Kentwood	28,707	1,129	280	474	108	260	30,438
Lowell	3,660	9	4	48	15	29	3,707
Rockford	3,294	1	12	15	4	2	3,324
Walker	14,796	103	766	133	49	759	15,088
Wyoming	57,493	976	329	1,218	258	658	59,616

1990

	White	Black	Asian	Hispanic	American Indian	Other	Total
Grand Rapids	144,464	35,073	2,164	9,394	1,573	3,542	189,126
East G.R.	10,520	98	126	71	16	54	10,807
Grandville	15,259	112	160	215	35	157	15,624
Kentwood	34,522	2,113	740	761	159	469	37,826
Lowell	3,909	10	18	56	16	26	3,983
Rockford	3,696	6	21	52	14	39	3,750
Walker	16,806	182	101	260	76	146	17,279
Wyoming	59,752	1,736	955	2,234	330	1,136	63,891

"Voices and Visions"

In 1990, Grand Rapids Downtown Development Authority (DDA) concluded that two decades' worth of existing downtown plans had been largely implemented, and that a new sense of direction was needed for the years ahead. Seeking the assistance of the city planning department, the DDA added a challenge: the new plan for the future of downtown should arise from a community-wide consen-sus. "Voices and Visions" was the process that evolved.

Divided into task forces that met regularly for several months, community members came together to share ideas that focused on such issues as creating a positive downtown image, establishing and maintaining a healthy environment, encouraging business development, and providing activities and facilities for citizens of all ages. Out of this grassroots process emerged vision statements developed by each task force.

The vision statement produced by the Physical Form and Image Task Force, presented by spokesperson Jean Hanks, captured the dream for the future shared by all of those who participated in the "Voices and Visions" project.

We're getting accustomed to the question, "How did Grand Rapids do it?" Every resident still smiles with a little pride when asked this, for by design we have each had a role in the city's transformation. Inspired by a deep desire to use the best of our past to make the most of our future, we committed ourselves to a grassroots effort to make our vision a reality. Old buildings were restored and lovingly maintained and new ones that are built beside them are both complimentary and progressive ....The city has revitalized its river banks and created restful green spaces.... Through creative incentives, developers have transformed vacant buildings into shops and arcades emblazoned with bold murals depicting the pride in our diverse heritage....

Today we can stroll the downtown streets and see office workers vie for a seat at a popular bistro, or a tour group studying the impressive blend of architecture. We can hear house music coming from a dance hall on a Saturday night, check out notices posted on the town hall kiosk, or see the glimpse of sunlight dancing on the rapids of the river that gave the city its name, identity, and life force.
Jean Hanks
Physical Form and Image
Task Force

▲ "Voices and Visions Workshop," November 1991, Grand Rapids City Planning Department.

▲ Jean Hanks presented the "Physical Form and Image" vision statement. [Grand Rapids City Planning Department]

▲ Grand Rapids architect Tom Nemitz (standing) leads a discussion session of the Voices and Visions "Physical Form and Image" Task Force. [Grand Rapids City Planning Department]

◄ Posters throughout the downtown area invited all citizens to participate in the Voices and Visions planning process. [GRPL, Poster Collection]

VOICES & VISIONS
COMMUNITY PLANNING FOR DOWNTOWN

A community discussion.
The VISIONS FORUM will bring together the community's hopes, fears and dreams for downtown. What will your downtown of the future be? Where should downtown be headed? What should we be striving for?

You be the judge.
Hear the exciting perspectives of groups which have discussed a number of areas of interest. Are they on track? What ideas should be added?

Get ready to act.
A variety of ways to participate and become involved... or to just be there and be a part of history.

Take hold of the future.

■ Come to the **VISIONS FORUM**

VISIONS FORUM

■ Saturday, November 23
■ 8:30 a.m. - 3:00 p.m.
■ Kent Room, Grand Center
■ Downtown Grand Rapids
■ Questions? Call 242-8400

Family Ties

Among local residents today are members of families that have called Grand Rapids home for more than a century. Their collective memories and the family heirlooms they have preserved are the real "stuff" of Grand Rapids' history. Linked by strong family ties to the past, these contemporary residents have a unique perspective on the changes that have occurred along the banks of the Grand River. Their families have seen the city at its best and worst, and have handed down to their modern descendants many lessons to be learned from the past.

Living along the banks of the Grand River, Isaac Peters' Ottawa Indian ancestors were here to greet the first Europeans to arrive in the area three centuries ago. The struggle of these earlier West Michigan residents to adapt to the presence of Europeans and Americans in their homeland, and their stubborn resistance to removal, assured that Grand Rapids would remain home to Peters and other Native Americans who are their descendants.

I am 100 percent Ottawa Indian, and my family has lived in West Michigan for hundreds of years. My father worked in the plaster mines, and died when he was still young. I was born on Butterworth Avenue and grew up with Italian, black, and Hispanic children whose fathers also worked in the mines. Before I was drafted into the Army in 1943, I attended the vocational school on South Division. Earlier I was sent to the Mount Pleasant Indian School.

After the war, I returned home and worked at odd jobs for several years before getting a job with Pittsburgh Plate Glass Company where I stayed for about 20 years. I did bull work all of my life.

As I grew up, I got used to people singling me out because I am an Indian. Just recently, I was in a store and the owner said to the son of another customer, "See that guy over there, he's a real Indian." After that the little boy stared at me like I was a freak or something.

Another time my daughter was asked to stand up in front of her school class while her teacher said this is what an Indian looks like. I complained to the principal. It bothers me when that happens. I know people do it out of ignorance, but I have always told my children they should be proud they are Indian, but people shouldn't treat us like we are on display in a museum.

Indians continue to live here, and we work to preserve our culture. I lead the opening procession each year at the Grand Valley Powwow, wearing my traditional Indian clothing. Some of the items are over 100 years old, and they are all authentic. I have a peace medal from President Millard Fillmore that was given to my great-great-grandfather, Wasaquom, in 1852. It has always been in our family, and I keep it in a safety deposit box.

When I was young, I hoped for change, but too often for Indian people, each generation seems to get more of the same. West Michigan has been my family's home for a long time, and my daughter lives here, so I expect it will continue to be our home. I just hope that one day other people will realize that Indians continue to be an important part of this community.

▲ Interview with Isaac Peters, June 17, 1992.

▲ For special events and ceremonies, Isaac Peters dresses in his traditional Ottawa clothing, including the peace medal (inset) given to his great-great-grandfather in 1852. [T.J. Hamilton photo]

Peggy Fay and her sister, Helen Ann Seger, are the great-great-grandaughters of Grand Rapids' first village president, Henry Clinton Smith. The 32-year-old Smith, known to his contemporaries as a "good and honest man," arrived at the rapids of the Grand River from Rhode Island in 1837 with several thousand dollars and a desire to open a store. Less than a year later, he was elected village president. Smith later farmed in Plainfield Township and became one of the township's first officials. He also served a term as his district's representative in the state legislature.

▲ Sisters Helen Ann Seger (left) and Peggy Fay are proud of the machinery their great-great-grandfather Henry Clinton Smith helped set in motion when he agreed to serve as Grand Rapids' first village president. [Photo by © *Grand Rapids Press*, April 3, 1988, p. E1]

When we were growing up, my sister and I were told about our great-great-grandfather being Grand Rapids' first village president. It made us proud to know that, but until the sesquicentennial of the founding of the village, we didn't realize anyone cared.

I think he would be pleased to see the way the city has grown, but he would also be very concerned. He loved the land. Sometimes when I drive past the site of his homestead (across the highway from today's Blythefield Country Club) I look at the trees he planted still standing there, and wonder how he would feel about all the growth that is occurring.

I think he would say that you have to have growth, but I also wonder if he wouldn't be concerned that the simple values of honesty and community service he knew and lived by are being lost. I think he might like to warn us not to get so wrapped up in our personal concerns that we lose sight of what is good for the community.

▲ Interview with Peggy Fay, June 22, 1992.

Linda Gietzen can trace her roots to not one but two prominent early Grand Rapids families, the Guilds and the Comstocks. Her great-great-grandfather was C.C. Comstock, who operated a furniture factory and other businesses, and was mayor of Grand Rapids from 1863 to 1865, and was elected to Congress in 1884. Comstock's second wife was Cornelia Guild, daughter of Daniel Guild and niece of Joel Guild who in 1833 built the community's first frame house on the site of today's McKay Tower. Joel, Daniel, and Edward Guild and their extended families formed the nucleus of Grand Rapids' early settlement.

▲ Holding a journal kept by her great-great-grandfather C.C. Comstock, Linda Gietzen sits at a desk that was once in his furniture factory. The brooch and earrings she wears belonged to her great-great-grandmother, Cornelia Guild Comstock. [T.J. Hamilton photo]

I have just been rereading my great-great-grandfather Comstock's memoirs, and thinking about stories about him that have been passed down in my family.

I remember being told of one instance where he was accosted by a robber as he was on his way home after working late. The man was desperate, he had no job, and his family was hungry. Mr. Comstock was a persuasive and kind person, and he talked the man out of robbery, and then told him to report for work at the factory the next day.

I think he would look at our society today and feel much as he did for the man who tried to rob him. He would like us to show compassion for those who have suffered misfortune, but he would be concerned that people be given the chance to support themselves, rather than being supported. He had a strong feeling that people in power had an obligation to see that everyone had an opportunity to provide for themselves and be productive community members.

Recently, I found a document in the papers he left my family. It is a statement signed by the men who worked for him, attesting to the fact that he was a good employer who treated them fairly. I feel fortunate to have family items like that, and I would urge everyone to preserve family photographs, letters, and other heirlooms. They will help the next generation feel a sense of continuity with the history of their family and their community.

▲ Interview with Linda Gietzen, June 23, 1992.

Curtis Jones, professor of sociology at Grand Valley State University, grew up on the family homestead in Byron Township that was settled by his great-great-grandfather, Prince Minisee, in 1866. One of the first African-American families in the Grand River valley, the Minisees came to Byron Township from New York by way of Ann Arbor.

My father still lives on the land that Prince Minisee purchased in 1866, and I was raised on that farm. My grandparents lived in the house when I was growing up, and I regret now that I did not talk with them more and learn more about my family's history from my grandmother, Mable Jones, who was Prince Minisee's grand-daughter.

I have a sister and a cousin who are now attempting to learn more about our family's history, but it would have been so much easier if we had all been better caretakers of our history along the way. I think if Prince Minisee had a chance to talk with us today, one thing he would tell us would be, "Learn your family's history and be proud of it." I hope I can pass that attitude on to my son.

I know one thing that would impress Prince Minisee if he could see Grand Rapids today would be how many African-Americans are living here now. He came to this area over 140 years ago seeking better opportunities for his family, and I think he would be pleased to see so many African-Americans taking active roles in community activities.

At the same time, I think he would also be concerned that there continue to be barriers erected on the basis of race. Prince Minisee and his family experienced open discrimination and many forms of *de facto* segregation during their lifetimes. Open discrimination certainly existed when I was growing up. The roller rink was only open to African-Americans on one night each week. I remember that I learned this by going on the

▲ Three generations of the Jones family (left to right), Curtis Jr., Benjamin Curtis, and Curtis, pose in front of the family's Centennial farm near Byron Center. [T.J. Hamilton photo]

wrong night and being told it was a private party. In fact, the only ones being excluded were African-Americans.

Prince Minisee or, for that matter, my grandmother, would be pleased to see that such open forms of racial discrimination are no longer tolerated. But I think they would say that the entire community suffers from any form of discrimination, and that we should all continue to work for equality of opportunity in all areas of community life.

▲ Interview with Curtis Jones, June 24, 1992.

Bibliography

MANUSCRIPT AND PHOTOGRAPH COLLECTIONS:

Ada Glass Plate Negative Collection, Grand Rapids Public Library

Albert Builders Collection, Grand Rapids Public Library

Amway Corporation Photo Collection, Grand Rapids, Michigan

Godfrey Anderson Collection, Grand Rapids Public Library

E.M. Ball Collection, Public Museum of Grand Rapids

John Ball Collection, Oregon Historical Society

Black History Exhibit Collection, Grand Rapids Public Library

Delbert W. Blumenshine Collection, Grand Rapids Public Library

George Catlin, "The Light," Smithsonian Institution

Citizens Action Collection (unprocessed), Grand Rapids Public Library

City Welfare Department Scrip Labor Collection, Grand Rapids Public Library

Harlan Colby Collection (unprocessed), Grand Rapids Public Library

Henry Lincoln Creswell Scrapbook, Grand Rapids Public Library

Lulu Cudney Collection, Grand Rapids Public Library

Emily Deming Collection, Grand Rapids Public Library

"Erie Canal," New-York Historical Society, New York, New York

Cadette Everett Fitch Collection, Grand Rapids Public Library

George E. Fitch Collection, Grand Rapids Public Library

Gerald R. Ford Presidential Library Photo Collection, Ann Arbor, Michigan

Furniture Manufacturer's Association Collection, Grand Rapids Public Library

William Glenn Collection, Grand Rapids Public Library

Grand Rapids Booming Company Collection (unprocessed), Grand Rapids Public Library

Grand Rapids City Planning Department

Grand Rapids Historical Society Collection, Grand Rapids Public Library

Grand Rapids Illustrated Collection, Grand Rapids Public Library

Grand Rapids Inter-Tribal Council Collection, Grand Rapids Public Library

Grand Rapids Photo Collection, Grand Rapids Public Library

Grand Rapids Press Photograph Collection, Grand Rapids, Michigan

Grand Rapids Stereo Card Collection, Grand Rapids Public Library

Grand Rapids Study Club Collection, Grand Rapids Public Library

Grand Rapids Telephone Exchange (unprocessed), Grand Rapids Public Library

Heritage Collection, Calvin College, Grand Rapids, Michigan

Peter J.G. Hodenpyl Citizenship Papers (unprocessed), Grand Rapids Public Library

James R. Hooper Collection, Grand Rapids Public Library

Sam Horowitz Photographs, Grand Rapids, Michigan

Albert Hyda Papers, Clarke Historical Library, Central Michigan University, Mount Pleasant

Guy Johnston Collection, Grand Rapids Public Library

James Keeney Collection (restricted), Grand Rapids Public Library

Dorothy Keister Collection, Grand Rapids Public Library

Nora Lawrence Collection (unprocessed), Grand Rapids Public Library

Isaac McCoy Papers, Kansas State Historical Society

Dr. Donald McDonald Manuscript (unprocessed), Grand Rapids Public Library

Map Collection, Grand Rapids Public Library

Mary A. Medendorp Collection (unprocessed), Grand Rapids Public Library

Murch S. Morris Collection, Grand Rapids Public Library

Nancy Mulnix Collection, Grand Rapids Public Library

Native American Photo Collection, Grand Rapids Public Library

News Photo Collection, Grand Rapids Public Library

Penrod-Hiawatha Company, Berrien Center, Michigan

Thomas Porter Collection, Grand Rapids Public Library

Poster and Oversized Materials Collection, Grand Rapids Public Library

Powers Theater Program Collection, Grand Rapids Public Library

M. Howard Rienstra, "Speech to the Breakfast Club of Grand Rapids," November 26, 1980, Oral History Collection, Grand Rapids Public Library

Robinson Studio Photo Collection, Grand Rapids Public Library

Russell Family Collection, Grand Rapids Public Library

Saint Cecilia Society Archives, Grand Rapids, Michigan

Steelcase, Inc., Archives, Grand Rapids, Michigan

Stoddard-Close Collection (unprocessed), Grand Rapids Public Library

Catherine Colby Swanlund Collection, Grand Rapids Public Library

Temple Emanuel Archives, Grand Rapids, Michigan

"Third Michigan Infantry," Burton Historical Collection, Detroit Public Library

Robert Thom, "Michigan Fever," Michigan Bell Telephone Company

"Walk-in-the-Water," Dossin Great Lakes Museum, Detroit, Michigan

Thomas Walsh Collection, Grand Rapids Public Library

Widdicomb Furniture Company Collection, Grand Rapids Public Library

INTERVIEWS:

Peggy Fay, June 22, 1992

Linda Gietzen, June 22, 1992

"Grand Rapids Girls of Summer." Grand Rapids, GRTV, 1991. (Copy in Grand Rapids Public Library)

Curtis Jones, June 24, 1992

Lyman Parks, November 19, 1985. Oral History Collection, Grand Rapids Public Library

Isaac Peters, June 17, 1992

Barbara Roelofs, June 9, 1992. Oral History Collection, Grand Rapids Public Library

"Voices and Visions Workshop." November 1991, Grand Rapids City Planning Department

"Thomas Walsh, Aviation Pioneer." Grand Rapids, GRTV, 1984. (Copy in Grand Rapids Public Library)

Stella Warfield, 1983. Oral History Collection, Grand Rapids Public Library

George Welsh, 1972. Oral History Collection, Grand Rapids Public Library

GOVERNMENT DOCUMENTS:

Acts of the Legislature of the State of Michigan Passed at the Annual Session of 1850, No. 247, Lansing, Michigan.

Bartholomew, Harland, The Grand Rapids City Plan, Grand Rapids City Planning Department.

Emmett N. Bolden v. Grand Rapids Operating Corporation. State of Michigan, Superior Court of Grand Rapids, Case No. 3043, June 14, 1926.

Kappler, Charles V., ed. Indian Affairs Laws and Treaties. U.S. 57th Congress 1st Session, Vol. 1, No. 452. Washington, U.S. Government Printing Office, 1903.

Letters Received by the Office of Indian Affairs, Michigan Superintendency, 1842-1845, (microfilm) No. 234, Roll 425.

Letters Sent by the Michigan Superintendency of Indian Affairs, 1845-1851, (microfilm) Vol. 4, Roll 1-40.

"Minutes of the Village of Grand Rapids." Grand Rapids City Archives and Records Center

"Report of the Committee of One Hundred Including Sub-Committee Reports and Minority Report," August 28, 1932. (Copy in Grand Rapids Public Library)

U.S. Census Bureau Decennial Population Statistics, Michigan Schedules, 1850-1900. Washington, D.C., U.S. Government Printing Office.

Yellow Fever: A Compilation of Various Publications. Washington, D.C., U.S. Government Printing Office, 1911.

NEWSPAPERS:

El Hispano

Evening Leader

Evening Press

Frank Leslie's Illustrated Newspaper

Grand Rapids Chronicle

Grand Rapids Daily Eagle

Grand Rapids Daily Morning Democrat

Grand Rapids Enquirer and Herald

Grand Rapids Herald

Grand Rapids News

Grand Rapids Press

Grand Rapids Telegram-Herald

Grand Rapids Weekly Democrat

Grand River Eagle

Grand River Times

New York Times

Woman

BOOKS:

A Tribute to Anna Sutherland Bissell by Her Children. No Publisher, No Date.

Baker, Robert, *The City of Grand Rapids.* Grand Rapids, Dean Printing and Publishing, 1889.

Ball, Kate, Hopkins, Flora Ball and Ball, Lucy, eds. *Autobiography of John Ball.* Grand Rapids, The Dean Hicks Company, 1925.

Baxter, Albert, *History of the City of Grand Rapids.* New York and Grand Rapids, Munsell and Company, 1891.

Beebe, Lucius and Clegg, Charles, *The American West.* New York, Bonanza Books, 1960.

Belknap, Charles E., *The Yesterdays of Grand Rapids.* Grand Rapids, The Dean Hicks Company, 1922.

Blakeslee, Clarence, *A Personal Account of WWII by Draftee #36887149.* Clarence Blakeslee, 1989.

Bozich, Stanley J., *Michigan's Own: The Medal of Honor.* Polar Bear Publishing Company, 1987.

Brinks, Herbert J., ed. *Write Back Soon: Letters from Immigrants in America.* Grand Rapids, CRC Publications, 1986.

Buley, R. Carlyle, *The Old Northwest: Pioneer Period, 1815-1840.* Vol. I. Indianapolis, Indiana Historical Society, 1950.

Chappell, Alonzo, *National Portrait Gallery of Eminent Americans.* New York, Johnson, Fry, and Company, 1864.

Comstock, Charles Carter, *Early Experiences and Recollections of Charles Carter Comstock.* No Publisher, 1936. (Copy in Grand Rapids Public Library)

Cook, Darius, *Six Months Among the Indians.* Niles, Michigan, Niles Mirror Office, 1889.

Cross, Wilbur and Olson, Gordon, *Commitment to Excellence.* Elford, New York, The Benjamin Company, Inc., 1986.

Dunbar, Willis F., and May, George S., *Michigan: A History of the Wolverine State.* Grand Rapids, William B. Eerdmans Publishing Company, 1980.

Emigrants' Handbook. No Publisher, 1845. (Copy in Grand Rapids Public Museum)

Everett, Franklin, *Memorials of the Grand River Valley.* Chicago, Chicago Legal News Company, 1878.

Fitch, George E., *Old Grand Rapids.* Grand Rapids, No Publisher, 1925.

Fitch, M.L., *Photographs of Furniture Made by Nelson Matter Furniture Company, Chamber Sets.* No Publisher, No Date.

Goss, Dwight, *History of Grand Rapids and Its Industries,* Vol. 2. Chicago, C.F. Cooper and Company, 1906.

Grand Rapids As It Is, Second Edition. Chicago, Illinois Printing and Binding Company, 1888.

Grand Rapids City Directories. Grand Rapids, R.L. Polk and Company (various years).

Grand Rapids City Hall Dedication Program. No Publisher. (Copy in Grand Rapids Public Library)

Grand Rapids Medical College, 1905-1906. Grand Rapids, Lecher Print Company, 1905. (Copy in Grand Rapids Public Library)

Grand Rapids Medical College Prospectus for Session of 1897-1898. Grand Rapids, West Michigan Printing Company, 1897. (Copy in Grand Rapids Public Library)

Hanks, David and Marilyn, *The Homes of Heritage Hill.* Grand Rapids, Heritage Hill Association, 1970.

History and Plan of the Ladies Literary Club. Grand Rapids, C.M. Loomis, Book and Job Printer, 1879.

Hornung, Clarence P., *Handbook of Early American Advertising Art.* New York, Dover Publications, 1947.

Hubbard, Gurdon S., *Autobiography.* Chicago, Lakeside Press, 1911.

Listy Emigrant Ow Z Brazylii I Stanow Zjednoczonych 1890-1891. Warsaw, Poland, Ludowa Spoldzielnia Wydawnicza, 1973.

McCoy, Raymond, *The Massacre of Old Fort Mackinac.* Bay City, Raymond McCoy, 1938.

McKenney, Thomas L., *Sketches of a Tour of the Lakes.* Baltimore, Fielding Lucas, Jr., 1827.

Michiganesian. Ann Arbor, University of Michigan, 1923, 1926.

Moore, Julia, *Sentimental Song Book.* Cleveland, J.F. Ryder, 1877.

Nowlin, William, *The Bark Covered House.* Detroit, William Nowlin, 1876.

Neely, Lon M, *Phoenix Furniture Company Catalog.* No Publisher, 1876.

Olson, Gordon and Holland, Reid, eds., *Grand Rapids Past, Present, Future.* Grand Rapids, Urban Concern, Inc., 1981.

Our Presidents: Ladies Literary Club. Grand Rapids, Stanton Printing Company, No Date.

Schoolcraft, Henry Rowe, *History of the Indian Tribes of the United States,* Part II. Philadelphia, Lippincott, Grambo, and Company, 1853.

South High Annual. Grand Rapids, No Publisher, 1919.

Stoddard, A.H., *Miscellaneous Poems.* Kalamazoo, A.H. Stoddard, 1880.

Verwyst, P. Chrysostomus, *Life and Labors of Rt. Rev. Frederic Baraga.* Milwaukee, M.H. Wittzius and Co., 1900.

White, Stewart Edward, *The Riverman.* New York, Grosset and Dunlap, 1908.

MAGAZINES AND PERIODICALS:

Century Magazine

Clark, Neil M., "A City Where Every Man Has a Job." *American,* January, 1932, pp. 28-31, 86.

"The Faith-Sped Victory." *Furniture Manufacturer and Artisan,* Vol. 78, June 1919, pp. 306-9.

Grand Rapids Furniture Record, October 1900, p. 166.

"The Grand Rapids [Fluoride] Story." *Rockwell Water Journal,* January 1957, pp. 2-10.

Greenly, A.H., "The Sweet Singer of Michigan Bibliographically Considered." *The Papers of the Bibliographic Society of America,* Col. 39, 1945, pp. 91-118.

Harper's Weekly, February 17, 1877.

Hawes, Wilton G., "Weatherman in Khaki." *Grand River Valley Review,* Vol. 5, No. 2, pp. 22-28.

Lane, Winthrop D. "Prohibition: What Elimination of the Liquor Traffic Means to Grand Rapids." *Survey,* November 6, 1920, pp. 189-204.

"Letters of Lucius Lyon." *Michigan Pioneer and Historical Collection,* Vol. 27, 1897, pp. 412-604.

Lynes, Russell, "The Treatment in Grand Rapids." *Harpers,* January 1962.

"A Michigan Civil War Soldier Writes Home." *Grand River Times,* Vol. II, No. 2, November, 1980, pp. 4-5.

Tebbel, John, "Most Maligned Town in the U.S." *Holiday,* Vol. 97, No. 104, February 1952, pp. 97, 104-6.

Tower, Prudence, "The Journey of Ionia's First Settlers." *Michigan Pioneer and Historical Collections,* Vol. 28, 1900, p. 145.

Wallace, Dave, "Chairmen Recollections Become Festival Classics." *Accent Grand Rapids,* Vol. 8, No. 4, May 1979, pp. 14-15.

"A Winter in the South." *Harper's New Monthly Magazine,* September 1857, pp. 433-51.

Index

Index page entries marked with an "i" indicate illustrations.